This original book examines the way in which the Romantic period's culture of posterity inaugurates a tradition of writing which demands that the poet should write for an audience of the future: the true poet, a figure of neglected genius, can only be properly appreciated after death. Andrew Bennett argues that this involves a radical shift in the conceptualisation of the poet and poetic reception, with wide-ranging implications for the poetry and poetics of the Romantic period. He surveys the contexts for this transformation of the relationship between poet and audience, engaging with issues such as the commercialisation of poetry, the gendering of the canon, and the construction of poetic identity. Bennett goes on to discuss the strangely compelling effects which this new reception theory produces in the work of Wordsworth, Coleridge, Keats, Shelley and Byron, who have come to embody, for posterity, the figure of the Romantic poet.

Andrew Bennett is Reader in English Literature at the University of Bristol. His previous books include *Keats, Narrative and Audience: The Posthumous Life of Writing* (1994), and with Nicholas Royle *Elizabeth Bowen and the Dissolution of the Novel: Still Lives* (1995) and *An Introduction to Literature, Criticism and Theory: Key Critical Concepts* (1995; second edition 1999).

CAMBRIDGE STUDIES IN ROMANTICISM 35

ROMANTIC POETS
AND THE
CULTURE OF POSTERITY

This series aims to foster the best new work in one of the most challenging fields within English literary studies. From the early 1780s to the early 1830s a formidable array of talented men and women took to literary composition, not just in poetry, which some of them famously transformed, but in many modes of writing. The expansion of publishing created new opportunities for writers, and the political stakes of what they wrote were raised again by what Wordsworth called those 'great national events' that were 'almost daily taking place': the French Revolution, the Napoleonic and American wars, urbanisation, industrialisation, religious revival, an expanded empire abroad and the reform movement at home. This was an enormous ambition, even when it pretended otherwise. The relations between science, philosophy, religion and literature were reworked in texts such as *Frankenstein* and *Biographia Literaria*; gender relations in *A Vindication of the Rights of Woman* and *Don Juan*; journalism by Cobbett and Hazlitt; poetic form, content and style by the Lake School and the Cockney School. Outside Shakespeare studies, probably no body of writing has produced such a wealth of response or done so much to shape the responses of modern criticism. This indeed is the period that saw the emergence of those notions of 'literature' and of literary history, especially national literary history, on which modern scholarship in English has been founded.

The categories produced by Romanticism have also been challenged by recent historicist arguments. The task of the series is to engage both with a challenging corpus of Romantic writings and with the changing field of criticism they have helped to shape. As with other literary series published by Cambridge, this one will represent the work of both younger and more established scholars, on either side of the Atlantic and elsewhere.

For a complete list of titles published see end of book

ROMANTIC POETS
AND THE
CULTURE OF POSTERITY

ANDREW BENNETT

CAMBRIDGE
UNIVERSITY PRESS

PUBLISHED BY THE PRESS SYNDICATE OF THE UNIVERSITY OF CAMBRIDGE
The Pitt Building, Trumpington Street, Cambridge, United Kingdom

CAMBRIDGE UNIVERSITY PRESS
The Edinburgh Building, Cambridge CB2 2RU, UK   http://www.cup.cam.ac.uk
40 West 20th Street, New York, NY 10011-4211, USA   http://www.cup.org
10 Stamford Road, Oakleigh, Melbourne 3166, Australia

© Andrew Bennett 1999

First published 1999

Printed in the United Kingdom at the University Press, Cambridge

Typeset in Monotype Baskerville 11/12½ in QuarkXPress™   [SE]

A catalogue record for this book is available from the British Library

Library of Congress cataloguing in publication data
Bennett, Andrew, 1960–
Romantic poets and the culture of posterity / Andrew Bennett.
p.   cm. – (Cambridge studies in Romanticism: 35)
Includes bibliographical references and index.
ISBN 0 521 64144 6 (hardback)
1. English poetry – 19th century – History and criticism – Theory, etc.
2. Romanticism – Great Britain. 3. Reader response criticism.
4. Authors and readers. I. Title. II. Series.
PR590.B34   1999
821'.709145 – dc21   99–55152 CIP

ISBN 0 521 64144 6 hardback

For Anna

Contents

Acknowledgements

In the last chapter of this book, chapter 8, I spend some time contemplating the complex ramifications of debt repayment, paying honour, and the rendering of a gift. In the context of having written that chapter, it should come as no surprise to me to find that the acknowledgements pages of a book turn out to be some of the hardest to write. In full knowledge of such difficulties, I would nevertheless like to thank a number of people. Michael Bradshaw, Nicholas Roe and the two readers for Cambridge University Press read an earlier draft of the book when I thought that it was more or less finished, and showed me that it wasn't: I am grateful to them for their detailed comments and for helping me to make sense of this book and, I hope, to make it make sense. Lucy Newlyn, whose work on the anxiety of reception in Romantic poetry and poetics is in many ways close to my own, generously allowed me to read some of her as yet unpublished research and has provided a sympathetic and challenging audience for parts of my book. Stephen Cheeke, Josie Dixon, John Lyon, Andrew Nicholson, Nicholas Royle, Timothy Webb, and the Cambridge Studies in Romanticism series editors made significant contributions to the final shape of the book by reading and commenting on my ideas as they developed. All of these people have given generously of their time and energy, and this would have been a lesser book without their responses, without their challenges to me to rethink and refine my ideas, and without their interest in my work. During the years that I have been writing this book I have taught English at the Universities of Tampere, Aalborg and Bristol, and I would like to acknowledge the way that the heads of department in all three institutions – Ralf Norrman, Ernst Ullrich-Pinkert and Timothy Webb – supported my research during this time. Undergraduate and postgraduate students, particularly at the University of Bristol, have responded, often quizzically, often energetically, to my attempts to develop some of these ideas in seminars. On a more personal level, I would also like to acknowledge the way that, over the years, friends and family have supported me and shown interest in work which is often very far from their own personal and professional concerns, and I would particularly like to thank my mother, Ann Bennett, who has given me crucial practical support, including somewhere to stay on my frequent visits to Cambridge University Library. I have presented parts of this book as papers at seminars and conferences in Aalborg, Aarhus, Bangor, Bristol, Chichester, Debrecen, Durham, Loughborough, New York, Stirling, Swansea, Tampere and Tartu, and I am grateful to the organisers of these occasions, and to their audiences, for the chance to try out my ideas and for the stimulus to write, think and rethink. My greatest debt is to my wife, Anna Hämäläinen-Bennett, who has lived with this book through from its inception to its afterlife as printed text and to whom the book is dedicated.

Parts of this book have already appeared elsewhere and are republished here by permission of the editors of the respective publications. Parts of chapters 1 and 2 were published as 'Coleridge on Reputation', in *La Questione Romantica* 5 (1999); a short section of chapter 4 appeared as 'Speaking with the Dead: New Historicism in Theory', in David Robertson (ed.), *English Studies and History* (Tampere English Studies, 1994); a slightly shorter version of chapter 6 appeared as 'Keats's Prescience, His Renown', in *Romanticism* 2:1 (1996); an earlier version of chapter 7 was published as 'Shelley in Posterity', in Betty T. Bennett and Stuart Curran (eds.), *Shelley: Poet and Legislator of the World* (Baltimore, MD: Johns Hopkins University Press, 1996); some paragraphs from chapter 1 appeared as part of an essay entitled 'On Posterity' in *The Yale Journal of Criticism* 12:1 (1999). I am grateful to the editors of these volumes for permission to use this material.

Abbreviations

OED   *Oxford English Dictionary*, prepared by J.A. Simpson and E.S.C. Weiner (Oxford: Clarendon Press, 1989).

PBSL   *The Letters of Percy Bysshe Shelley*, ed. Frederick L. Jones, 2 vols. (Oxford: Clarendon, 1964).

PFL   *Penguin Freud Library*, 15 vols., ed. James Strachey *et al.* (Harmondsworth: Penguin, 1973–1985).

Prose   *The Prose Works of William Wordsworth*, ed. W.J.B. Owen and Jane Worthington Smyser, 3 vols. (Oxford: Clarendon Press, 1974).

SCH   *Shelley: The Critical Heritage*, ed. James E. Barcus (London: Routledge and Kegan Paul, 1975).

SCW   *The Complete Works of Percy Bysshe Shelley*, ed. Roger Ingpen and Walter E. Peck, new edn., 10 vols. (New York: Gordian Press, 1965).

SPP   *Shelley's Poetry and Prose*, ed. Donald H. Reiman and Sharon B. Powers (New York: Norton, 1977).

Supplement   *The Letters of William and Dorothy Wordsworth: A Supplement of New Letters*, ed. Alan G. Hill (Oxford: Clarendon, 1993).

Talker   *Coleridge the Talker: A Series of Contemporary Descriptions and Comments*, eds. Richard W. Armour and Raymond F. Howes (Ithaca, NY: Cornell University Press, 1940).

TT   Samuel Taylor Coleridge, *Table Talk*, 2 vols., ed. Carl Woodring (London: Routledge, 1990).

White   Newman Ivey White, *Shelley*, 2 vols. (New York: Alfred A. Knopf, 1940).

Works   *The Complete Works of William Hazlitt*, 21 vols., ed. P.P. Howe (London: Dent, 1930–34).

Journals

CI   *Critical Inquiry*

ELH   *English Literary History*

JEGP   *Journal of English and Germanic Philology*

KSJ   *Keats–Shelley Journal*

MLQ   *Modern Language Quarterly*

MP   *Modern Philology*

SEL   *Studies in English Literature, 1500–1900*

SiR   *Studies in Romanticism*

Introduction

> For the future is the time in which we may not be, and yet we must
> imagine we will have been.
>
> (Gillian Rose, *Mourning Becomes the Law*)

I cannot imagine being dead: therefore I don't believe that I will ever die.
Since reason, hearsay and everything that I see and hear present irref-
utable evidence that it is the ultimate destiny of all living beings to cease
to exist, I must construct a story of survival which will compensate for
the fact that I will finally and without question die and which will negotiate the disparity between the impossibility of imagining my own death
on the one hand and its inevitable occurrence on the other. It is for this
reason that I resort to one or more of a number of strategies for survival. If I am able to produce children I can be genetically encoded into
my offspring; if I am loved I will have a temporary afterlife in the memories of those who survive me; if I am a politician or military leader, programmed into the future of my nation will be an ineradicable trace of
my existence, I will survive as history; if I believe in God, then I can
imagine for myself an afterlife of the soul; given sufficient cash, cryogen-
ics will enable my body to be preserved after my death for future restoration; any attainment of fame or infamy, even that which brings me to
public notice for a mere fifteen minutes, can provide me with a sense that
I have made an indelible mark on the world; if I write books, then the
paper, this paper, will preserve that part of myself which I identify in
writing: inscribed in text, now, I will survive in a bookish afterlife.

During the eighteenth century, the textual afterlife becomes increasingly important as an impulse for the production of poetry and increasingly prominent in the theory of literature. Writers, artists and other
manufacturers of cultural artefacts have a perennial fascination with the
immortality effect, the ability of a poem, novel, statue, painting, photograph, symphony to survive beyond the death of the artist. But during

the eighteenth century this quality begins to be figured as a determining force in cultural production. The poet (who, in this story of literary production, is gendered as, primarily, male) no longer writes simply for money, contemporary reputation, status, or pleasure. Instead he writes so that his identity, transformed and transliterated, disseminated in the endless act of reading, will survive. It is with Romanticism that this impulse is most clearly and most thoroughly theorised and practised. Indeed, Romanticism itself might be described in terms of a certain value accorded the theory and practice of writing for posterity.

A number of interlocking factors to be explored from different perspectives in the course of this book provide the context and structure for the Romantic culture of posterity. In the first place, the question of the role and identity of the author becomes increasingly important in literary and aesthetic thinking during the eighteenth century. By the early nineteenth century, authorial identity has become crucial to the shape of the more advanced modern poetry. Indeed, poetry begins to be understood as not only recording the life of the poet but actually constructing that life: poetry appears to *produce* the writer's identity. But, as the Keatsian phrase 'negative capability' and Hazlitt's idea of the 'disinterested' nature of action both suggest, Romantic writing also tends to inscribe the dissolution of personal identity into its ideal of the writer. In this sense, the poet is taken out of 'himself' in writing. Writing is seen to both construct and evacuate the subjectivity of the author: authorial identity is both produced and dispersed in a 'crisis of subjectivity' which conditions the Romantic and post-Romantic act of composition.[1] It is in this way that the poet is able to conceive of himself as living on in his work and as being inscribed in that work as what Nietzsche calls the 'monogram' of the genius's 'most essential being'.[2] The author in the text is both present and absent, self-identical and anonymous. Posterity validates the poet, but does so in the future perfect tense ('we must imagine we will have been' – it is in this grammatical glitch that Romantic posterity intersects with the postmodern) whereby it is constituted as a proleptic reversion.

It is my suggestion that the particular predicament of early nineteenth-century poetry publication not only allowed for but, for certain writers and for a certain culture of writing, demanded deferred reception. Once the conditions of publication and the market for books have given poetry audiences a certain anonymity, and once the democratisation of the readership has allowed a certain degradation and, by association, a *feminisation* of reading to become credible as a narrative of reception, then poets begin to figure reception in terms of an ideal audience – masculine, generalised and anonymous – deferred to an unspecified future. Romanticism develops a theory of writing and reception which stresses the importance of the poet's originating subjectivity, and of the work of art as an expression of self uncontaminated by market forces, undiluted by appeals to the corrupt prejudices and desires of (bourgeois, contaminating, fallible, feminine, temporal, mortal) readers. This Romantic theory of artistic autonomy requires a new theory of audience. The autonomy of the work of art allows no direct appeal to readers: the act of writing poetry becomes a self-governing and self-expressive practice. The poet is a nightingale singing, as Shelley puts it, to please himself: poetry is overheard while 'eloquence' is heard, according to John Stuart Mill.[3] Nevertheless, the Romantic theory of posterity still requires that the work finally be judged and discriminated from other, lesser work. Indeed, with the invention of the modern concept of the (English, literary) canon in the mid-eighteenth century, the possibility of such discriminations becomes crucial to reading and to the new discipline of literary criticism. In order to discriminate the poet from the scribbler or hack, the poem from common, everyday verse, Romantic theories of poetry produce an absolute and non-negotiable opposition between writing which is original, new, revolutionary, writing which breaks with the past and appeals to the future, and writing which is conventional, derivative, a copy or simulation of earlier work, writing which has an immediate appeal and an in-built redundancy. The sign of the great poem, then, is originality. Originality, in turn, generates deferred reception since the original poem is defined as one which cannot (immediately) be read. The original poem is both new and before its time. Indeed, it is before its time precisely *because* it is new. The fallible, shallow, fashion-conscious, morally vicious contemporary audience cannot be trusted to make judgements of aesthetic value. Since what Coleridge calls the 'absolute Genius' (*BL* 1.31) is, by definition, set apart from the mass of people and by virtue of this difference conceived as 'original', it is not possible for him to be fully understood until the future, preferably until after his death. Only after he has created the taste by which he may be judged will he be appreciated. And since the original and autonomous poem is *only* one which has been produced by the genius, the guarantee of true poetry inheres, finally, in the identity of the poet himself, his signature leaving its indelible trace throughout the work. We can only know that we are reading a 'great' poem because of the signature of the genius, that ineffable but theoretically unmistakable identification of the work by and with the poet himself, an identity which will live on in the future, will, indeed, come to life in posterity.

The effect of originality is, then, that the poem and therefore the poet, inscribed in language, will survive, and our highest praise for any poem, still, is to say that it will last, that it will live on, in the future, beyond the particular contingent circumstances of its author's life and beyond its contemporary reception. It is the project of writers of genius to write for the future: 'In the inward assurance of permanent fame' declares Coleridge, writers of genius 'seem to have been either indifferent or resigned, with regard to immediate reputation' (*BL* 1.33). The case is put most strongly and most clearly by Hazlitt at the beginning of his lecture 'On the Living Poets' (1818):

Those minds, then, which are the most entitled to expect it, can best put up with the postponement of their claims to lasting fame. They can afford to wait. They are not afraid that truth and nature will ever wear out; will lose their gloss with novelty, or their effect with fashion. If their works have the seeds of immortality in them, they will live; if they have not, they care little about them as theirs. They do not complain of the start which others have got of them in the race of everlasting renown, or of the impossibility of attaining the honours which time alone can give, during the term of their natural lives. They know that no applause, however loud and violent, can anticipate or over-rule the judgment of posterity; that the opinion of no one individual, nor of any one generation, can have the weight, the authority (to say nothing of the force of sympathy and prejudice), which must belong to that of successive generations. (*Works* v.145)

For the Romantics, as this suggests, posterity is not so much what comes after poetry as its necessary *prerequisite* – the judgement of future generations becomes the necessary condition of the act of writing itself. While the poetry of the Renaissance may be said to be obsessed with the question of immortality and while Enlightenment poetics figure the test of time as the necessary arbiter of poetic value, Romanticism reinvents posterity as the very condition of the possibility of poetry itself: to be neglected in one's lifetime, and *not to care*, is the necessary (though not of course sufficient) condition of genius.

As will become clear, however, this model of the Romantic culture of posterity is never less than a site of conflict and subversion, never amounting to a stable and coherent foundation for poetic production. Inherently and necessarily paradoxical, the appeal to posterity continues to constitute one of Western culture's most cherished claims to artistic significance while, at the same time, continuing to constitute a repeatedly challenged and ironised topos. So it is that while on the one hand I shall argue that the appeal to a posthumous reception is central to the project of Romantic poetics, on the other hand I shall attempt to trace the ways in which that claim is ironised and subverted. If the Romantic culture of posterity is what Leo Bersani calls a 'culture of redemption',[4] it is one which effects its own dissolution or deconstruction. And it is my suggestion that it is in the collapse of this theory in its working through, in multiple, conflicted ways, of an impossible figuration of audience, that we may look to understand the survival of those poets who so forcefully argue for a deferral of reception. My final claim, then, is that what has helped the Romantic culture of posterity to endure is precisely the articulation of the idea of posthumous recognition and the disturbances and dislocations it produces in poetry written under its auspices.

In part I of this book I present an account of the configuration of posterity in Romantic poetics, the importance and significance of this figure, and the distinction between the Romantic culture of posterity and other forms of poetic immortality. In chapter 1, I attempt to clarify my sense of this 'culture' by briefly contrasting it with Renaissance concerns with immortality on the one hand and by tracing its development from eighteenth-century neoclassical arguments concerning aesthetic evaluation and the 'test of time' on the other. In chapter 2, I seek to develop this analysis by elaborating in more detail the discourse of posterity in the work of such writers as Hazlitt, Isaac D'Israeli, William Henry Ireland, Coleridge and Wordsworth in the late eighteenth and early nineteenth centuries. As I seek to show, even in its most canonical moment, however, this cultural production of a necessary deferral of judgement is compromised by the resurgence of complexity and paradox. In chapter 3, I attempt to trace the alignments of the Romantic culture of posterity with a masculine poetics. I discuss ways in which poetry written by women during the period is coded as feminine in part by virtue of its resistance to or ironisation of the Romantic culture of posterity and by its celebration of the ephemeral. Women writers of the period responded to this culture by the construction of feminine poetic identity as distanced from its imperatives.

In addition to this gendering of the appeal to posterity, I suggest that within the poetry and poetics of the five canonical male poets studied in part II there are troubling discontinuities and displacements.[5] This accounts for the concentrations and displacements of my five author-centred chapters: while I attempt to account for central, indeed foundational, aspects of these poets' work, I refrain from simply rehearsing their various engagements with the topic of posterity. In each case, I attempt to trace a specific and, I believe, exemplary aspect of the after-life in the work of the poet at the expense of what would be a more gen-eralised but perhaps more repetitive, even monolithic account of how posterity is framed by each writer. My intention in these chapters has been to move away from the *fact* of the centrality of posterity for Romanticism towards an examination of the *consequences* of that fact for a reading of these poets' work – consequences which are complicated by the curious tautology of the fact that we are talking, in posterity, about the figures of posterity in their poetry. In each case, the culture of pos-terity finds its own particular forms and modes pertaining to what might be seen as an individual poetic career. And yet, in each case, these forms are traversed by a crisis in representation determined not least by the impossible demands of a cultural imperative of prescience and endless deferral. My suggestion is that the complexities and stubborn difficulties which constitute these poets' articulations of the culture of posterity are themselves sites of desire and fascination for future readers. Above all, my readings seek to convey some of that fascination by tracing the strange effects of posterity theory in these writers' work.

In chapter 4, I argue that Wordsworth's sense of posterity is above all a family affair. While Wordsworth is one of the central theorists of Romantic posterity, he is also intimately concerned with an alternative figuration of the trope: for Wordsworth, posterity, in its ideal form, also involves more conventional intergenerational survival. I seek to explore ways in which Wordsworth's sense of familial reproduction complicates his fascination with literary survival, and the way in which, finally, it pro-duces a certain 'trembling' in and of that project. In the case of Coleridge (chapter 5), I have focused on the key element in the poet's reputation during the latter half of his life. I trace his concern with con-versation, with that which cannot be maintained or retained in writing, and specifically with the phonetics, the *noise*, of talk. Hazlitt argues that Coleridge bartered posthumous recognition for the more immediate but necessarily ephemeral gratifications of direct conversational response, and in this chapter I try to see what happens when we take this judge-ment at face value. To this end, I examine the tensions involved in poetry which celebrates the momentary noise of talk within the terms of an overarching poetics of survival. It is with the second generation of Romantic poets, however, that we might hope to discern a more fully developed, more central and centred articulation of the culture of pos-terity. And yet here again there are particular divergencies and inflections to be registered. While we cannot ignore Keats's well-known proclamations about his desire to be 'among the English Poets' after his death, his true significance in the culture of posterity involves his self-production and subsequent reception as corpus and corpse, as a fetishised figure of neglect and posthumous life: after Chatterton, it is Keats's body, his *corpus*, that is to say, which most fully plays out the myth of the neglected poet recognised after his death, and in discussing Keats (chapter 6) I seek to suggest that the retrospective celebration of his poetic *prescience* in this regard is a necessary and indeed constitutive aspect of his afterlife. In the case of Shelley (chapter 7), I explore ways in which the poet's engagement with a future life, with life after death, is bound up with his convulsive or hysterical reaction to or vision of ghosts: for Shelley, living on involves a haunting of the future inextricable from the uncanny and from a theory of ghosts. Shelley's cult of posterity, that is to say, is also a ghost: his faith in the efficacy of a poetic afterlife cannot be disengaged from a belief in and fear of the spectral. In chapter 8, I suggest that Byron deconstructs the Romantic culture of posterity both by appealing to this construction of the 'self' of the poet and by ironising it in himself and others: for Byron, posterity both offers and withholds the redemption to which the poet appeals. I suggest that there is in Byron a crucial disturbance of representation which may be elaborated around a certain conception of rendering – a problematic of the gift and of future reception but one defined by or subject to a mimetic instability, a troubling of the relation of the literal to the figurative.

This book is particularly concerned with poets and poetry. The predicament of the early nineteenth-century novelist, dramatist or essayist requires a very different kind of analysis from that which is proposed here. Poetry, figured within the culture of literary, 'high' Romanticism as the primary vehicle for artistic survival, involves a particular kind of engagement with its audience, both actual and imagined, and I have attempted to trace certain configurations of this engagement in what follows. While a concern with posterity is certainly not limited to that part of written culture that we call poetry, I want to suggest that it is in poetry that this project is most clearly promulgated and sustained. To this end, much of this book engages in detailed readings of a limited number of poems. On the one hand, I focus on some of the most well-known, most canonical poems of the Romantic period – Wordsworth's 'Tintern Abbey' and Book Five of *The Prelude*, Coleridge's 'Conversation Poems' and 'The Ancient Mariner', Keats's Odes, Shelley's 'Ode to the West Wind', Byron's *Don Juan*. On the other hand, I have spent what might look like an inordinate amount of time considering somewhat more marginal poems, or at least poems which have been more resistant to the critical machine in the posthumous lives of their authors – Wordsworth's 'Surprised by Joy', Keats's 'This Mortal Body of a Thousand Days', Byron's 'Churchill's Grave', as well as a series of poems by poets such as Helen Maria Williams, Felicia Hemans, Letitia Landon, who have only recently begun to receive sustained critical attention. Part of the impulse behind such a strategy is the desire not only to present new readings of canonical poems but also to refocus attention on poems which otherwise might look marginal to the concerns of Romantic poetry and poetics. This book, then, is also about Romanticism's production of its own oppositional discourse. If, as I am suggesting, permanence or survival are crucial to that discourse, one of the ways in which poets engage with those topoi is through a consideration of the ephemeral. 'Surprised by Joy', 'This Mortal Body of a Thousand Days' and 'Churchill's Grave' all, in their different ways, celebrate or commemorate the momentary, the ephemeral – a moment of 'joy' and its dissolution into the equally momentary 'pang' in Wordsworth's poem; the ephemeral physicality, the impermanent somatic *presence* of the poet's impermanent body in Keats's poem; a moment of impossible reciprocation, an enactment of the impossible payment or gift of remembrance in Byron's. This counter-discourse of the Romantic culture of poetry – articulated in the texts of the major, canonical poets and, rather differently, in the poetics of the 'feminine' which I explore in chapter 3 – has a crucial place in my argument, since it is in the space of internal conflict produced by the culture of posterity that we, posterity, find our proper place.

PART I

CHAPTER I

Writing for the future

It is a lamentable case that no Author's fame gets warm till his body gets cold.

(J.H. Reynolds to John Dovaston)

For something which cannot be known nor spoken of nor represented, death is the subject of an enormous amount of talk. Death has its own literary, artistic and musical forms – the elegy, dirge, threnody, monody and epitaph, the death march and the requiem, the death mask, the photograph; its own psychic states – mourning and melancholia, intro-jection and internalisation; its own celebration – funeral, wake, memo-rial service; its own clichés – *ars longer, vita brevis, memento mori*, 'you only live once', 'life's too short . . .'; its own euphemisms – some of them listed by Coleridge in a translation of the German 'Sterben': 'to die, decease, depart, depart this life, starve, breathe your last, expire, give up the ghost, kick up your heels, tip off, tip over the Perch' (*CN* I. 350); its own social rituals – the burial service, letters of condolence, visits, mourning customs; its own wardrobe – shroud, armband, black tie, widow's weeds; its own furniture and architecture – the urn, casket, coffin, the tomb, monument, grave and cenotaph; its own places – the hospital, hospice, funeral garden, cemetery, graveyard, crypt; its own crafts – the wreath, tombstone, funerary sculpture; its own legal forms – inquest, death certificate, post mortem or autopsy; its own experts – the coroner, pathologist, thanatologist, theosophist, medium, poet, undertaker, embalmer, priest, theologian.[1] Death has its own literary canon: Jeremy Taylor's *Holy Dying* (1651), Sir Thomas Browne's *Hydriotaphia* (1658), John Donne's *Biathanatos* (c.1609), Edward Young's *Night Thoughts* (1742–45), William Wordsworth's three *Essays on Epitaphs* (1809–10), Thomas Lovell Beddoes's *Death's Jest Book* (1825–28), Tennyson's *In Memoriam* (1850), Hardy's poems of 1912–13, Joyce's 'The Dead' (1914), the 'Hades' episode from *Ulysses* (1922) and *Finnegans Wake* (1939), and more or less

everything that Samuel Beckett ever wrote. And death has its philosophical texts, a canon where the proliferation of recent studies – Ernest
Becker's *The Denial of Death* (1973), Antony Flew's *The Logic of Mortality*
(1987), Derrida's *The Gift of Death* (1992) and *Aporias* (1993), Gillian Rose's
Mourning Becomes the Law (1996) – shouldn't blind us to earlier works such
as Freud's *Beyond the Pleasure Principle* (1920), nor indeed to a tradition that
goes back at least as far as Plato's *Phaedo* (c.385 BC). Finally, death has its
own texts of literary and cultural criticism, including, most recently,
Garrett Stewart's *Death Sentences* (1984), Michael Wheeler's *Death and the
Future Life in Victorian Literature and Theology* (1990), Elisabeth Bronfen's
Over Her Dead Body: Death, Femininity and the Aesthetic (1992), Michael
Millgate's *Testamentary Acts* (1992), Christopher Ricks's *Beckett's Dying
Words* (1992), Jahan Ramazani's *The Poetry of Mourning* (1994), Esther
Schor's *Bearing the Dead* (1994), Jonathan Dollimore's *Death, Desire and Loss
in Western Culture* (1998). The present book is intended as a contribution
to this cacophony of voices talking, incessantly, about death. But it is
also, as are many of these voices, about the other side of death, about
forms of the afterlife – specifically that which I term 'living on', the
textual life after death.

   This book concerns just one aspect of the discourse of death, then:
secular life-after-death. With the word 'secular' I seek to delimit my book
to a particular tradition, one which is unable to find consolation or
redemption in the thought of a non-human, non-physical, non-earthly
future; and I seek to bring to the fore Leo Braudy's suggestion that in
secular society 'fame and the approval of posterity replace belief in an
afterlife'.[2] The word 'secular' comes from the Latin *saeculum*, meaning
'generation, age, the world'. On the one hand, the word denotes that
which pertains to the world (*OED* adjective 3a: 'Of or belonging to the
present or visible world as distinguished from the eternal or spiritual
world'), while on the other hand it denotes that which will last 'an age'
or a very long time (adjective 6: 'Living or lasting for an age or ages'). I
attempt to investigate this double sense of the secular: that which is concerned both with this world, now, for a lifetime, and that which is concerned with this world in the future, for lives after life. Robert Southey
brings out the duplicity of the secular in one of his characteristically up-
beat comments: 'if I cannot be a great man in the way of the world this
generation – why I will be a very great one after my own in the next, &
all that are to come in secula seculorum'.[3] In this sense, the present book
is concerned with remains, with what is left on our leaving, what is left
of us when we leave. It concerns the proleptic future-anterior sense that

we will have left something, that, in Wallace Stevens's words, 'with our bones / We left much more, left what still is / The look of things, left what we felt // At what we saw'.[4] This stilled perception, this leaving, always spoken in the future, from the future, of the past, involves a dissolution or disturbance of the semantic force of both 'leave' and 'remain', their antithetical awkwardness. In particular, this book is about that particular form of leaving or remains that might be called 'literature after life', a specific mode of writing, or a specific recognition in writing of the nature of writing in general. Literature after life, or what I have elsewhere termed the 'posthumous life of writing', is writing which, in various ways, inscribes itself as a manual practice occurring, necessarily, in a time after its own, in after years, after the death of the writer.[5] And this thanatological event of inscription concerns such questions as (auto-)biography, or more precisely, 'autobiothanatographical writing'[6] as well as questions of posterity or living on.

Living on, life-after-death, posthumous life as a form of textual continuation of personal identity is not, of course, restricted to art or literature. Indeed, according to certain thinkers in the secular tradition, the projection of one's self, one's work or one's life into a future beyond death is, in fact, the very definition of the human. In his *Ethics* (1926), for example, Nicolai Hartmann comments on 'The great gift of foresight and pre-determination (teleology), which is peculiar to man' and argues that 'It inheres in the nature of all effort that looks to an objective value, to go on beyond the life and enterprise of the individual, into a future which he no longer can enjoy. It is not only the fate but is also the pride of a creative mind and is inseparable from his task, that his work survives him, and therefore passes from him to others, in whose life he has no part'.[7] The difficulty or paradox contained within this argument – one which, I shall suggest, amounts to a founding problematic of Romantic discourse – involves the question of personal identity. Recent work in what might be called the 'ethics of the future' and, in particular, in that field of analytical philosophy concerned with environmental ethics, is illuminating in this regard. Ernest Partridge, for example, argues that 'a concern for future others' is part of the fundamental nature of being human as such, so that someone without such a concern is both lacking in (human) moral sense, and 'seriously impoverishing his life'. The need is, according to Partridge, part of a more general feature of humanity that he calls 'self transcendence', the 'basic need' to 'seek to further, the well-being, preservation, and endurance of communities, locations, causes, artifacts, institutions, ideals and so on, that are outside

themselves'.[8] 'Self transcendence' as a primary motive for caring for as
well as caring about the future, however, seems to presuppose an
unproblematic dissolution of the self, of self-interest and of personal
identity in relation to a posthumous life. Against this, Avner de-Shalit
argues that in fact personal identity 'extends into the future, including
those times subsequent to one's death'.[9] De-Shalit redefines the 'unity of
the self' in terms of a certain 'continuity' constituted by 'relations
between my future selves and my present self, in that the future represents the implementation of present (or past) intentions'. In this case, de-
Shalit continues, 'there is no reason why, when the body stops
functioning, further future events should not count as implementations
of present intentions'. In other words, 'part of one's personal identity
during one's life is the expectation of the fate of one's acts and ideas after
one's death'.[10] This discussion in environmental ethics, then, suggests an
idea of posterity as a mode which encompasses both self-perpetuation
and self-annulment. In some ways such arguments echo those of a nineteenth-century writer such as William Hazlitt who, in his early philosophical work *An Essay on the Principles of Human Action* (1805), declares
that 'It is only from the interest excited in him by future objects that man
becomes a moral agent', but at the same time tries to argue for man's
natural disinterestedness by suggesting that this future self is fundamentally different from the past or present self. Indeed, in a somewhat puz-
zling manoeuvre, Hazlitt argues that the future self is structurally similar
to the selves of others: 'The imagination, by means of which alone I can
anticipate future objects, or be interested in them, must carry me out of
myself into the feelings of others by one and the same process by which
I am thrown forward as it were into my future being' (*Works* 1.1–2). What
Hazlitt adds to the discussion of Partridge, de-Shalit and other twentieth-century thinkers, is a sense of the dissolution of subjectivity inherent in this futuring of the self, the paradox, implicit in any attempt to
retain the self after the dissolution of death, that any such survival can
only be predicated on the loss of self.

Zygmunt Bauman explores the cultural importance of a futuring of
personal identity to a time beyond death in *Mortality, Immortality and Other
Life Strategies* (1992). Bauman argues that the fact of human mortality
itself *produces* culture, that culture in general is a response to the possibility, or necessity, of dying. Culture, in this respect, fends off death, denies
it: 'Since the discovery of death (and the state of having discovered death
is the defining, and distinctive, feature of humanity) human societies
have kept designing elaborate subterfuges, hoping that they would be

allowed to forget about the scandal'.[11] Culture is a direct result of the knowledge of death, a kind of distraction from that knowledge. Without death, or without knowledge of death, there would be no culture. Bauman appeals to Schopenhauer's dictum that all religious and philosophical systems are 'primarily an antidote to the certainty of death which reflecting reason produces from its own resources'.[12] Culture, then, as an antidote to death, as a redemptive form of amnesia: 'There would probably be no culture were humans unaware of their mortality', comments Bauman, 'culture is an elaborate counter-mnemotechnic device to forget what they are aware of. Culture would be useless if not for the devouring need of forgetting; there would be no transcending were there nothing to be transcended'.[13] It no doubt supports Bauman's argument that, employing a rather different kind of vocabulary, Cicero presented much the same case as long ago as the first century AD in his defence of the poet Archias in *Pro Archia Poeta* (AD 62): 'If the soul were haunted by no presage of futurity', urges Cicero, 'if the scope of her imaginings were bounded by the limits set to human existence, surely never then would she break herself by bitter toil, rack herself by sleepless solicitude, or struggle so often for very life itself'. 'But', he continues, 'deep in every noble heart dwells a power which . . . bids us see to it that the remembrance of our names should not pass away with life, but should endure coeval with all the ages of the future'.[14] A similar point is made by Francis Bacon in *The Advancement of Learning* (1605): 'Let us conclude with the dignity and excellency of knowledge and learning in that whereunto man's nature doth most aspire; which is immortality or continuance; for to this tendeth generation, and raising of houses and families; to this tend buildings, foundations, and monuments; to this tendeth the desire of memory, fame, and celebration; and in effect, the strength of all other human desires'.[15] And in the early twentieth century the argument is produced in a relatively neglected work by the psychoanalyst Otto Rank, *Art and Artist* (1932), where this generalised human impulse becomes a specialised function of the aesthetic, of Art. Rank figures the urge towards immortality as the primary impulse of certain kinds of creativity: it is the 'individual *urge to eternalization* of the personality, which motivates artistic production', he declares.[16] Indeed, for Rank, this 'urge' is '*inherent in the art-form itself*, in fact its essence', and 'the impulse to create productively is explicable only by the conception of immortality' (pp. 11, 47). The 'redeeming power of art' inheres in its ability to give 'concrete existence' to the idea of the soul (p. 13). For the 'modern' artist, the work is an attempt to escape the transience of experience: 'the creative impulse' arises from the artist's 'tendency to immortalize himself' and, as such, is an escape from 'transient experience' which 'eats up his ego'. The artist gives 'shape' to experience and thereby turns 'ephemeral life into personal immortality' (pp. 38, 39). According to Rank, then, the artist has an ambivalent relationship with his own work – one which explains, for example, 'writer's block' – since the 'totality-tendency' of artistic creation involves the artist's 'sacrifices' of himself for his work. To 'eternalize' oneself in the work of art is also, paradoxically, to risk death, annihilation: 'Not only . . . has the completed work of art the value of an eternity symbol, but the particular creation process, if it involves an exhaustive output, is, by the same token, a symbol of death, so that the artist is both driven on by the impulse to eternalization and checked by the fear of death' (p. 386).

In this book I attempt to historicise the idea of poetic survival by showing how, during the Romantic period, those effects of amnesia, distortion or catachresis that we call culture themselves begin to articulate the possibility of death as the precondition for certain forms of writing known as 'literature'. I suggest that literature after life – in particular in the form of poetry – is formulated and articulated most intensively at a particular historical moment – the end of the eighteenth and the beginning of the nineteenth century. If Cicero, Bauman and Schopenhauer are right in saying that the recognition of death ultimately determines all culture, that culture is a distorting reflection on the certainty of our own death, an amnesic response to death, then the concern with immortality that we find in Romantic and post-Romantic poetry will not, in any decisive sense, be new or original. What *is* new, however, is the specific formulation and articulation of this desire in Romantic writing. To put it simply, if neoclassicism may be said to involve the invention of the (English, literary) canon as a category of dead writers, Romanticism involves the imaginative insertion of the *living* writer into that canonical cadre: for Romanticism, as defined in this book, the function of writing is to achieve – in the sublime and impossible moment of inscription – immortality, posthumous life, life after death. The distinctiveness of this formulation for Romantic writing, I will suggest, is evinced simply by the sheer weight of concentration on the topic in critical writing of the period, its centrality in theoretical accounts of poetry. But it is also possible to discern four necessary conditions in the formulation of Romantic posterity which allow us to conceive of its particular character and its distance from earlier articulations of the desire for immortality:

(1) Romantic posterity involves the text-based survival of the self that writes;
(2) contemporary neglect is the necessary but not sufficient condition for posthumous survival;
(3) living on, survival in posterity, amounts to an adequate compensation for, or redemptive supplement of, life itself;
(4) posterity is constitutive, in the sense that it not only redeems or functions as a substitute for the poet's life but is finally the condition of the possibility of the identity of the poet.

Earlier expressions of the desire for immortality often include a number of these features,[17] and all four features are occasionally to be found in earlier writing, while, on the other hand, each of these features are contested from within Romanticism itself. In the Romantic period, however, a consensus develops regarding the nature of poetry centred around textual survival, contemporary neglect, and the redemptive possibilities of a posthumous life.

Since the early nineteenth century, then, poetics has been dominated by a concern with posthumous reception. The concern is both commonplace and international. 'To whom does the poet speak?', asks Osip Mandelstam in an essay from 1913, and answers by quoting a poem by Evgeny Abramovich Baratynsky: 'So will I find a reader in posterity'.[18] 'Poetry as a whole', Mandelstam remarks, 'is always directed at a more or less distant, unknown addressee, in whose existence the poet may not doubt without doubting himself'.[19] Similarly, Robinson Jeffers declares that 'great poetry is pointed at the future' and that the poet 'intends to be understood a thousand years from now . . . let him not be distracted by the present; his business is with the future'.[20] Known and unknown, present and absent, the poet's addressee, his or her reader, is both crucial to the modern poet and vitally displaced to an uncertain future. The Romantic culture of posterity, in this sense, is determined by what Antoine Compagnon has called a 'pathos of the future'.[21] The kind of audience figured by Mandelstam, Jeffers and others is first fully theorised in the early nineteenth century: from now on the audience is displaced to an unknown future. This, to put it simply (and, for the Romantics, anachronistically), is the ideology of the *avant-garde*.[22]

It is my argument, then, that when we talk about 'Romanticism' we are talking, not least, about a certain kind of belief in life after death. One way of meeting the challenge of death – the challenge to one's sense of identity and meaning – is to write for an endlessly deferred reception. Writing is, as such, a redemptive act. The present book is concerned with the remarkable predominance of a theory of writing which involves the possibility that a future reception of poetry will atone not only for the poet's sense of neglect, but for his or her life itself. We are concerned with what Leo Bersani has called 'the culture of redemption'.[23] Bersani and Ulysse Dutoit use this phrase to indicate and indict art of the late nineteenth and the twentieth centuries which 'serve[s] the complacency of a culture that expects art to reinforce its moral and epistemological authority'.[24] As Bersani comments, a 'genealogy of the culture of redemption' would involve a study of 'the relation of modern ideas of art as redemptive to earlier notions of art as preserving otherwise perishable experience'.[25] My concern is with those forms of secular redemption produced by the idea that the poet and his or her poetry or experience might be preserved in writing.

Romantic poetic theory, then, figures poetry as enabling redemptive commemoration. The poet lives on by reading and by intertextual inscription in future texts. Just as she or he resuscitates the work of dead poets by allusion, reference, imitation, plagiarism, pastiche, parody, repetition or 'misreading', so his or her work will be inscribed in the work of future writers. Thus Wordsworth can declare in 'Michael' that his poem is for 'youthful Poets' who will constitute his 'second self when I am gone' (lines 38–9).[26] In this sense, the Romantic theory of posterity involves what Harold Bloom calls the 'anxiety of influence' and what W. Jackson Bate calls the 'burden of the past':[27] in as much as we accept such accounts of influence, the Romantic culture of posterity would involve a refining and an intensification of such desires and such anxieties. In this respect, my book might be seen as a complement to such work on the writer's relation to the past – a relation which is certainly enriched by his or her relation with the future. When Keats says that life for Milton would be death to him (*LJK* II.212), such a statement might be re-read, in the context of the Romantic culture of posterity, as indicating as much a *desire* as an anxiety of influence, the desire for the poetry of Milton to 'live' in his own work, for his writing to take on the properties of such a precursor – the desire, that is, for death. More generally, though, this culture figures the poet living on in the minds or thoughts of readers, literally inhabiting the minds of others, not as a memory of the dead in the survivor, but as the poet's own thoughts, his or her words reinscribed in the readerly mind, rethought. Hazlitt makes the point in an evocative sentence from *Spirit of the Age* (1825), which draws on Ben Jonson's sense of Shakespeare as a 'monument without a tomb': 'The poet's cemetery is the human mind, in which he sows the seeds of never-ending thought – his monument is to be found in his works' (*Works* XI.78).

In this sense, individual identity is transferred or metamorphosed into language, becomes language, which is then dispersed or disseminated in the minds of others. Paradoxically, this thought leads to the possibility that the poet's individual identity *while alive* is more a matter of writing, of language, than of living: Keats figures the poet as a 'camelion' and argues that the poet is the most 'unpoetical' of creatures since he has no identity (*LJK* 1.387); Wordsworth writes his life into poetry, composes himself, in *The Prelude*, as a prelude to writing his great but never written epic *The Recluse*; Shelley figures the effect of poetry as a kind of haunting power and proceeds to ghost-write his own life, to ghost himself, in poems like *Alastor*, *Adonais* and *The Triumph of Life*; Byron makes of his life an image or series of images for public consumption.[28] Life itself is constituted as autobiography – what we might call autoscription – in its widest sense. Autoscription does not need to be 'about' the poet's life in the way that an autobiography is, because the life of the poet is inscribed in poetry, the life in the writing. At the end of his essay 'On the Feeling of Immortality in Youth' (1827), Hazlitt poignantly describes those dead who must rely on an ever-dwindling stock of survivors' memories (*Works* XVII.189–99). By contrast, the Romantic and post-Romantic poet is able, forever, to live on, autoscriptively, inhabiting the minds of others. Rather than autobiographical in any conventional sense, however, this autoscriptive afterlife is, finally, anonymous, impersonal. The notorious Romantic emphasis on the self is a fiction of autoscription, a fiction of personhood constructed for public consumption, for life after death. If, as Harold Bloom has proposed, English Romantic Poetry amounts in some respects to footnotes to Milton, Romantic poetics may be said to amount to a belated transformation of Milton's argument in *Areopagitica*, that 'books . . . contain a potency of life in them to be as active as that soul whose progeny they are', that they 'preserve as in a vial the purest efficacy and extraction of that living intellect that bred them', and that 'a good book is the precious life blood of a master spirit, imbalm'd and treasur'd up on purpose to a life beyond life'.[29] It was for the Romantics to adopt this suggestive figuration of the effect of books and to transform the very institution of literature under its rubric – to *invent* literature, we might say – such that literature becomes a paradoxical strategy of self-preservation and, at the same time, self-dissolution – the very being of the poet inscribed in text, inscribed *as* text, in a life beyond life.

In recent years, critics and historians have explored a general shift in the relationship between poets and their readers and audiences in the late eighteenth and early nineteenth centuries. A number of factors provide the context for a rethinking of the nature of poetry audiences at this time: technological developments in the print industry allowed for a remarkable expansion in the market for books while the spread in literacy resulting from widening opportunities for education produced a thirst for cheap and widely disseminated printed texts. More generally, historians have recognised that the commodification of social and cultural production during the eighteenth century amounts to what Neil McKendrick has called a 'consumer revolution'.[30] Controversies concerning literary property centring on debates over copyright law also indicate crucial changes in author–publisher and author–public relations.[31] As a response to these forces and to changing conditions of patronage and an increasing professionalisation and commercialisation of writing, the role of the poet may be understood to have been transformed.[32] The revolutionary conditions of poetic production at the beginning of the nineteenth century were most ably exploited by Byron and his publisher, who managed to dispose of 10,000 copies of *The Corsair* on the day of publication on 1 February 1814, and more than a million copies of *Don Juan* overall.[33] As Jerome Christensen argues in his study of the extended media-event which was 'Byronism', 'The Wordsworthian aspiration to create the taste by which one is to be appreciated had become the practical effect of the publishing machine'.[34] But what Christensen refers to as the period's 'tremendous elasticity of demand' for poetry,[35] also results, by contrast, in disappointing sales for poets such as Shelley, who estimated the total readership for *Prometheus Unbound* to be only five or six, and Wordsworth who, at least until about 1820 and arguably throughout his life, failed to reach a wide audience.[36] The case of Keats is exemplary. His 1817 volume was a failure to the extent that his publishers declared that 'We regret that [Keats] ever requested us to publish his book'.[37] *Endymion* (1818) was remaindered and in February 1821 Taylor and Hessey, his second publishing firm, reported having lost £110 on it.[38] Despite the fact that 160 copies of Keats's 1820 volume were bought by subscription prior to publication (so that, as Richard Woodhouse can comment wryly, 'the bard's works begin to get in request'), his publishers also report that it made a loss of £100,[39] and Taylor commented to John Clare in August 1820 that 'We have had some trouble to get through 500 copies of [Keats's] work', while still in March 1822, he tells Clare that 'Of Keats's poems there have never yet been 500 sold'.[40] Even in 1835 Taylor writes to Clare that he 'should like to print a complete Edition of Keats's Poems' but that 'the world cares nothing for him – I fear that even 250 copies would not sell'.[41] For such poets, developments in readership, print-technology and the commodification of culture result in what was seen as the disintegration of a coherent and sympathetic audience. The ramifications of this disintegration during the eighteenth and early nineteenth centuries are such that Bertrand Bronson can comment that it is 'one of the most far-reaching influences of modern times in our Western civilization' – by contrast with an earlier age in which the 'reading public of Milton, Cowley, Waller, Dryden, Prior – and even, to a degree . . . of Pope himself – was probably roughly commensurate with their social world as a whole'.[42] In the 1802 Preface to the *Lyrical Ballads*, Wordsworth asks of the poet 'To whom does he address himself?' (*Prose* 1.138), a question to which he gives no proper answer. This is the predicament of what Lyotard calls 'modernity', a situation in which the writer 'no longer knows for whom he writes'.[43] The biographies, letters, poems, essays and other records of Wordsworth, Coleridge, Keats, Shelley and, of course, Byron suggest ways in which they all attempted to cash in on the vast opportunities offered by the market for poetry: indeed, the democratisation of poetry reading becomes a pivotal concern in their poetics. At the same time, however, what Freud would call the 'reaction formation' to their neglect in an appeal to a future reception, and the possibility that a true understanding of these poets' work would only occur after their death – once the taste has been created by which they might be appreciated – becomes an increasingly important strategy in Romantic poetry and poetics. These are the contexts within which the cult and culture of Romantic posterity, and its theory of the contemporary neglect and posthumous recognition of the poet, are generated.

The culture of posterity is not only a crucial dimension in the production and reception of Romantic poetry, then; it is also a central concern in Romantic literary theory. In the most well-known texts of English Romantic poetics, the traditional distinction is repeatedly emphasised between two different kinds of poetic reception: an immediate and popular applause on the one hand and an initial rejection of the artwork followed by more lasting and more worthwhile appreciation on the other.[44] William Hazlitt begins his lecture 'On the Living Poets', for example, by establishing the distinction between fame and popularity, whereby fame is 'the recompense not of the living, but of the dead' (*Works* v. 143): by his account, the writings of genius can only be recognised as such after life. Such a distinction is both an echo of, and is echoed by, many similar pronouncements. As we shall see in chapter 2, Coleridge insists on the distinction between eternal 'fame' and contemporary 'reputation'; in his letters, Keats talks about being 'among the

English Poets' after his death and comments on the fact that England produces many great writers *because* it unfailingly neglects them during their lifetime (*LJK* 1.394, 115); Shelley formulates a theory of the poet as 'unacknowledged legislator' and argues in his *Defence of Poetry* that 'no living poet ever arrived at the fulness of his fame' (*SPP* 486); J.H. Reynolds comments that 'fame and popularity are as different as night and day';[45] and in his *Specimens of the Later English Poets* (1807) Southey comments that 'good' poets write 'for posterity' and that fame 'is of slow growth' and 'like the Hebrew language' has 'no present tense', while popularity 'has no future one'.[46] Such formulations of contemporary neglect followed by posthumous recognition can be found in countless less well-known works such as Isaac D'Israeli's *The Literary Character* (1818), William Henry Ireland's *Neglected Genius: A Poem* (1812), T.N. Talfourd's *An Attempt to Estimate the Poetical Talent of the Present Age* (1815), Arthur Hallam's 1831 review of Tennyson's poems, Richard Henry Horne's *Exposition of the False Medium and Barriers Excluding Men of Genius from the Public* (1833), as well as in common responses to such figures as Otway, Chatterton, Burns, Henry Kirke White, and others – writers who come to be respected during the period just in so much as they are figured as having been unjustly neglected during their lifetime, 'mute inglorious Miltons', as that crucial central eighteenth-century celebration of neglect, Gray's 'Elegy', puts it. It is no coincidence that Byron opens his attack on contemporary poetry and poetics in *Don Juan* with a 'Dedication' which homes in on what he sees as poets' self-serving claims on future recognition: 'He that reserves his laurels for posterity / (Who does not often claim the bright reversion?) / Has generally no great crop to spare it, he / Being only injured by his own assertion' (*CW* v. 5–6).[47] The most concentrated and influential account of the inescapable obscurity of the living genius is perhaps that of Wordsworth in his 1815 'Essay, Supplementary to the Preface', where, in order to explain his own disappointing reception over the previous twenty years, he presents a brief reception history of English Poetry showing that neglect during their lifetime has always been the fate of poets of genius. Every original writer, Wordsworth famously declares, 'has had the task of *creating* the taste by which he is to be enjoyed' (*Prose* III.80).[48]

    The technological and cultural transformations of the book trade at the beginning of the nineteenth century, then, may be understood to provide the context for the reinvention of posterity as the crucial determinant in Romantic conceptions of audience. But this is not to deny that the appeal to posterity is a conventional poetic topos, since there is evidence to suggest that the tradition of Western poetry has always been bound up with a certain survivalism. In his 'Epilogue' to *Metamorphoses*, for example, Ovid declares that 'not the wrath of Jove, nor fire nor sword / Nor the devouring ages can destroy' his work; and that after his death he will 'be borne, / The finer part of me, above the stars, / Immortal, and my name shall never die'; and in the *Amores* he declares 'so I, / When the last flame devouring me has gone, / Shall still survive and all that's best live on'.[49] Similarly, Horace famously asserts poetic immortality in the last of his odes – '*non omnis moriar*'[50] – and Heraclitus tells us that 'The best choose one thing in exchange for all, everflowing fame among mortals'.[51] 'Writing so as not to die', comments Foucault, glossing Blanchot, 'is a task undoubtedly as old as the word'.[52] In *The Western Canon*, Harold Bloom makes clear the connection between canonicity and textual immortality: 'A poem, novel, or play acquires all of humanity's disorders, including the fear of mortality, which in the art of literature is transmuted into the quest to be canonical, to join communal or societal memory'.[53] Such a fiction of future response receives extensive elaboration in the Renaissance: as Raymond Himelick comments, 'the literary fame convention was in the Elizabethan air'.[54] While the Romantic figure of posterity owes much to these traditions, and while such historical developments are necessarily mobile and their limits often transgressed, at the same time it is possible to discern a cultural shift by the beginning of the nineteenth century. One aspect of this shift in emphasis involves the way that the fiction or figure of immortality for the hero or the subject of the poem is at some point transferred to or infects the celebration – indeed the celebrator – itself. Harold Bloom points to the mid-eighteenth century, in particular to the odes of William Collins, as inaugurating in English a secular (literary) canon and, in consequence, a revolutionary theory of posterity.[55] In other words, despite its obsessive focus on the immortality of both the young man and his own writing, it is possible to conceive of such texts as Shakespeare's sonnets as producing a significantly different sense of posterity from that of writers in the Romantic period for whom the literary convention that the subject of the verse will survive develops into the convention that the subject who writes will. But I want to suggest that the refiguration of posterity at the end of the eighteenth century is more general than this and concerns the very idea of Literature itself – its social function, its compositional impulse and its institutional status. While Socrates and Cicero produce arguments for the importance of certain kinds of personal survival, and while writers from Horace to Shakespeare elaborate the trope

of literary survival in their poems, the Romantic period put a crucial
spin on the idea of textual immortality by linking it fundamentally to the
very structure of writing, of literary composition, itself. The theory of
poetic production in the Romantic period evolves into a theory of posthumous survival.

   In order to suggest the specificity of Romantic posterity it is worth
spending a little time contemplating the nature of the Renaissance
concern with immortality in poetry. Robert Herrick wittily sums up the
Renaissance sense of posterity in his laconic six-line 'Poetry Perpetuates
the Poet' (1648):

> Here I my selfe might likewise die,
> And utterly forgotten lye,
> But that eternall Poetrie
> Repullulation gives me here
> Unto the thirtieth thousand yeere,
> When all now dead shall re-appeare.[56]

What the poet is given is a 'repullulation', a kind of eternal re-budding,
something less than a life, perhaps, but more than death. Not only does
the poet welcome such a fate with a certain lack of enthusiasm, but
writing as an Anglican priest within the tradition of Christian theology,
he also suggests that the 'immortality' of poetry will eventually be superseded by resurrection.[57] Another, rather more extended seventeenth-
century consideration of posterity appears in William Davenant's
Gondibert (1650). In his 'Author's Preface', Davenant asks 'why I have
taken so much paines to become an Author', and answers the question
by declaring that 'Men are cheefly provok'd to the toyle of compiling
Bookes, by love of Fame, and often by officiousnesse of Conscience'.[58]
Aligning himself with those who write for fame, Davenant then defines
fame: 'Fame being (when belonging to the Living) that which is more
gravely call'd, a steddy and necessary reputation', while 'Tis of the Dead
a musicall glory, in which God, the author of excellent goodnesse,
vouchsafes to take a continuall share'.[59] In addition to this double importance of fame, Davenant also argues for its moral effect on future generations, as at least as significant as its redemptive function for the living:
'Fame is to our Sonnes a solid Inheritance, and not unusefull to remote
Posterity; and to our Reason, tis the first, though but a little taste of
Eternity'.[60] For Davenant, then, contemporary fame and posthumous
reputation go hand in hand: one is the consequence of the other. While
it is not necessary to be dead to achieve proper recognition, posthumous
fame is a subdivision of a religious afterlife. In *Gondibert* itself, Davenant

opens canto three, book three with an apostrophe to the reader 'who dost live, when I have long been dead' and imagines, rather than glory to himself, the morally beneficial effects of his 'Story':

> Thus when by knowing me, thou know'st to whom
> Love owes his Eies, who has too long been blinde;
> Then in the Temple leave my Bodies Tomb,
> To seeke this Book, the Mon'ment of my Mind. (Stanza 11)

While there is a self-aggrandising sense of the monumentalisation of the writer here, it is also self-abnegating ('leave my Bodies Tomb') and clearly subordinated to the ethical effects of the poet's work. Davenant is expressing what may be the universal desire to survive, but his survival is conventionally conceived as a memorialisation of the 'Mon'ment' of his 'mind', his thoughts and ideas, in a future in which *he* is absent. And the significance of any such survival inheres in what that mind can do for a future age, rather than what that future age can do for the mind. Similarly, in a 'Postscript to the Reader', written in prison awaiting trial for treason and possible execution, Davenant justifies his poem written 'in an unseasonable time' by arguing that 'he who writes an *Heroick Poem*, leaves an Estate entayl'd; and he gives a greater Gift to Posterity, then to the Present Age':[61] again, the value of writing is as a 'gift' that is given to future generations as much as the 'honour' that it imposes on the writer. Davenant's insistence on the significance of posterity, then, is also an insistence both on the continuity of contemporary and future response and on the radical absence of the poet in this future.

Another, somewhat earlier, instance of an explicit engagement with posterity is Samuel Daniel's *Musophilus* (1599). In this poem, Philocosmos quizzes Musophilus on his attempt to 'attain that idle smoake of Praise' by writing at a time when 'this busie world cannot attend / Th'untimely Musicke of neglected layes' (lines 9–11). Replying that if his 'unseasonable Song' comes 'out of time, that fault is of the Time' (lines 21–2), Musophilus begins his defence by pointing to the posthumous life of writing:

> And give our labours yet this poore delight,
> That when our daies doe end, they are not done:
> And though we die, we shall not perish quite,
> But live two lives, where others have but one. (lines 39–42)

In many ways, such a declaration would seem to prefigure the Romantic culture of posterity. And yet even here, such concerns can be discriminated from those of the early nineteenth century. It is clear to

Musophilus that his 'Arte' can 'never stand my life in steede' (line 17) and, as Raymond Himelick comments, Daniel's sense of immortality involves the desire to 'salvage something out of mutability and transience, not to disregard the world they are part of'.[62] Such an interest in poetic immortality is similarly important in, for example, the poetry of John Donne – which, as Robert Watson has recently shown, 'makes extensive and ingenious use of . . . the idea that the author will survive through his writings'[63] – and in Milton's declaration in 'Lycidas' that 'Fame is the spur' and that 'Fame is no plant that grows on mortal soil' (lines 70, 78). But such examples are bound up with a religious conception of the afterlife which would necessarily rebuke secular concerns with fame, reputation and earthly survival. Milton's 'Lycidas' is exemplary in this respect. Its most famous lines present an influential expression of the Renaissance sense of posthumous fame:

> Fame is the spur that the clear spirit doth raise
> (That last infirmity of noble mind)
> To scorn delights, and live laborious days;
> But the fair guerdon when we hope to find,
> And think to burst out into sudden blaze,
> Comes the blind Fury with th'abhorred shears,
> And slits the thin-spun life. But not the praise,
> Phoebus replied, and touched my trembling ears;
> Fame is no plant that grows on mortal soil,
> Nor in the glistering foil
> Set off to the world, nor in broad rumour lies,
> But lives and spreads aloft by those pure eyes,
> And perfect witness of all-judging Jove;
> As he pronounces lastly on each deed,
> Of so much fame in heaven expect thy meed.[64]

With the 'guerdon' of fame, the 'sudden blaze' of public acceptance, comes death, the 'abhorred shears' which 'slits the thin-spun life': the poet cannot hope to achieve true fame except in the grave. But this crucial prefiguration of the Romantic culture of posterity is also bound up with a religious conception of the afterlife – articulated in references to the paganism of the 'all-judging Jove' and the Christian mythology of 'heaven'. While the residual religiosity of a Wordsworth or Coleridge and, rather differently, a Shelley or Keats, might lead us to expect that Romanticism is often similarly bound up with a metaphysical afterlife of the soul, the Romantic culture of posterity that I explore in the present book is, on the whole, quite separate from any such belief-system. Moreover, Milton's seminal expression of the 'last infirmity of noble mind' fails to figure this afterlife as constitutive of the compositional act: composition for Milton does not, as I am suggesting it does for the Romantics, allow for the writer's production of authorial identity through his engagement with a future audience. The limitations of the seventeenth-century engagement with posterity are clearly expressed in a provocative formulation of textual immortality in Bacon's *The Advancement of Learning*: 'The images of men's wits and knowledges remains in books', he comments, 'exempted from the wrong of time and capable of perpetual renovation. Neither are they fitly to be called images, because they generate still, and cast their seeds in the minds of others, provoking and causing infinite actions and opinions in succeeding ages'.[65] While they are more than images, these remains of authors are less than what will be expected from writers in the nineteenth century.

Milton's celebrated – and, in the Romantic period, often quoted – declaration that he writes for a 'fit audience . . . though few'[66] offers another perspective on such matters. The claim is not, as it would be 150 years later, accompanied by arguments for the necessary contemporary neglect of the poet nor for the deferral of reception. In fact, it is nineteenth-century (mis)readings of Milton's declaration which romanticise the poet as neglected: Isaac D'Israeli, for example, elaborating the Biblical adage concerning the prophet's neglect in his own country, asserts in *Quarrels of Authors* (1814), that 'while in his own day, Foreigners, who usually anticipate posterity, enquired after MILTON, it is known how utterly disregarded he was'.[67] Milton's sense of the limitations of his own audience, however, may be conceived rather differently: his claim may be understood to be *celebrating* the exclusivity of his audience, an audience made up of what J.W. Saunders calls the 'intellectual *élites* of Europe'.[68] Interestingly, as John Lyon argues in an essay on the test of time in the Renaissance, elegies written in commemoration of Donne imply that the poet's *non*-survival is a 'condition of his greatness': Donne, a poet who had 'no concern for literary posterity' and whose contemporaries 'expressly denied such a possibility' is, Lyon suggests, 'misrepresented by our persistence in thinking in such terms'.[69] Such misrepresentations, I suggest, and more generally the imposition of the culture of posterity back onto the seventeenth century, are a function, not least, of the Romantic rewriting of literary history. It is from the Romantics that we learn to value as a mark of our own modernity our appreciation of poets from earlier times for what those earlier times cannot appreciate.

Perhaps the only writer from this period to come close to a later, Romantic sense of posterity is Ben Jonson, obsessed as he is both by the vicissitudes of his own reception and by the possibility of the immortality bestowed by poetry. Ian Donaldson comments that Jonson 'placed great faith in the judgement of posterity', and that 'however spurned or neglected his works might be in his own age, he never ceased to believe that their true value would be recognised in the years to come'.[70] (One of the ironies of this desire, Donaldson suggests, is that while posterity eternalised and universalised Shakespeare, a century or two after his death Jonson was seen as transitory, ephemeral – a poet of his age but *not* for all time.) But as Donaldson and other critics argue, Jonson's relation with his audience was highly idiosyncratic and unrepresentative of the early seventeenth century: what is remarkable about Jonson, as it is *not* remarkable in the same way in the Romantic poets, is his antagonism towards contemporary degraded audiences and his faith in the vindication of posterity.[71] Jonson's appeal to posterity was highly individual and notable precisely for its apparent perversity: it was anything but a part of a general and generalised theorising of the nature of poetry and its relation to audiences.

Shakespeare's sonnets constitute, amongst other things, exemplary Renaissance expressions of the importance of posterity – indeed, they constitute what must be the most sustained meditation on immortality and survival to reach us from the early modern period[72] – but in this respect they can nevertheless be distinguished quite clearly from the culture of Romantic posterity. The central concern of the first 126 of the sonnets is the possibility of the young man's survival: as is conventional in Renaissance and classical epideictic poetry, this survival is made possible by the recording of the young man in language.[73] When Shakespeare claims that 'Not marble nor the gilded monuments / Of princes shall outlive this pow'rful rhyme' in sonnet 55, the statement is preliminary to the claim that the young man – rather than the poet – will live on in the verse.[74] Indeed, the sonnet sequence begins with seventeen poems urging the young man to reproduce in order to preserve his beauty. In other words, while recognising that a substantial proportion of Shakespeare's sonnets contemplate immortality, we should also remember that the major fiction which the sonnets promulgate concerns the survival of the subject recorded by the verse rather than the subject who records. The sonnets work through and work around the convention that the survival of the poet's writing is subservient to the survival of the young man. I suggest that just as they misread Milton as neglected, the Romantics misread Shakespeare's sonnets as appeals to posterity over the heads of a neglectful contemporary audience. Coleridge, for example, maintains that the sonnets implicitly articulate Shakespeare's 'confidence of his own equality with those whom he deem'd most worthy of his praise' (*BL* 1.35, citing sonnets 81 and 86). The 'implicit' nature of this claim, however, makes the point more or less unfalsifiable, and Coleridge certainly offers no evidence to support his claim. In fact, the idea of the survival of the subject of the verse – rather than the subject who writes – is a conventional *topos* in both classical and Renaissance writing, and Jonathan Swift's exposure of the convention as patently self-serving in his 'Thoughts on Various Subjects' (1711) ('Whatever the Poets pretend, it is plain they give Immortality to none but themselves: It is *Homer* and *Virgil* we reverence and admire, not *Achilles* or *Æneas*'[75]), does not detract from its importance before the late eighteenth century.

The proposition that a writer can only be properly judged in the future is by no means original for the early nineteenth century, indeed it is central to Enlightenment poetics, and develops out of discussions of the 'test of time' which go back at least as far as Horace.[76] In the fourteenth century, Petrarch explored the significance of the test of time, arguing that 'The writings or deeds of anyone who is still alive are hardly ever pleasing; death lays the foundations for the praises of men'. The reason for this, according to Petrarch, is simple: jealousy. 'With the body dies envy, just as it lives with the body', he declares, and he tells his reader that if he or she should want his or her work to be praised 'Then you must die', for then 'you cease being an obstacle to yourself'.[77] Three hundred years later, Samuel Johnson's 'Preface to the *Plays of William Shakespeare*' (1765) opens with a similar discussion. Johnson begins with a consideration of the assertion that 'what has been longest known has been most considered, and what is most considered is best understood'. Shakespeare, Johnson asserts, 'has long outlived his century, the term commonly fixed as the test of literary merit'.[78] Having outlived 'personal allusions, local customs, or temporary opinions', the 'effects of favour and competition', his 'friendships and his enmities', 'opinion' and 'faction', Shakespeare's work can now be read 'without any other reason than the desire of pleasure . . . unassisted by interest or passion'.[79] It is this ability to survive into a time when disinterested reading has become possible which guarantees the excellence of Shakespeare's work. But it is also, for Johnson, this delay which makes such a judgement possible.

For Johnson, as for other critics, posthumous survival involves the abstraction of the artwork from the warping perspective of the poet's contemporaries. Johnson returns to this point in a passage from *Rasselas* (1759), which even more strongly prefigures Romantic and particularly Shelleyan accounts of posterity: the poet, Imlac declares, 'must divest himself of the prejudices of his age or country' in order to 'rise to general and transcendental truths' and, for this reason, he must 'content himself with the slow progress of his name; contemn the applause of his own time, and commit his claims to the justice of posterity. He must write as the interpreter of nature, and the legislator of mankind, and consider himself as presiding over the thoughts and manners of future generations'.[80] Writing only two years before this, David Hume also argues for endurance as the guarantor of genius in 'On the Standard of Taste' (1757): 'a real genius, the longer his works endure . . . the more sincere is the admiration which he meets with'.[81] Thirty years later in *The Lounger* for 1786, Henry Mackenzie begins an essay on Burns by arguing that the 'divinity of genius' is 'not easily acknowledged in the present time' due to envy and jealousy, but also due to a 'familiarity' which is 'not very consistent with the lofty ideas' which we desire to form of the genius. But Mackenzie then goes on to make a crucial point which marks a subtle but decisive shift into the dominant Romantic conception of posterity when he remarks that 'our posterity may find names which they will dignify, though we neglected, and pay to their memory those honors which their contemporaries had denied them'.[82] Building on the idea that the judgement of posterity is the final arbiter of poetic worth, posterity as the fit judge of the value of poetry, Mackenzie articulates what will become the crucial Romantic sense that the living poet is, necessarily, *always* neglected.

Posterity is a site of debate and conflict in eighteenth-century poetics since, on the one hand, it was understood to provide the necessary distance between author and the assessment of his or her work while, on the other hand, it was seen to provide a refuge from criticism for weaker poets. Thus Johnson begins his 'Preface' to Shakespeare by analysing the motive for an appeal to posterity in those who 'being forced by disappointment upon consolatory expedients, are willing to hope from posterity what the present age refuses, and flatter themselves that the regard which is yet denied by envy, will be at last bestowed by time'.[83] Similarly, in his satirical appeal to posterity in *A Tale of a Tub* (1704), 'Epistle Dedicatory, to His Royal Highness Prince Posterity', Jonathan Swift makes ironical play with such an appeal. The work of Edward Young displays the ambivalence of eighteenth-century figurations of posterity very clearly. Young ends his *Conjectures on Original Composition* (1759) by arguing, through allusion to Horace, that his work is, in effect, a posthumous monument to Addison's *Cato*:

If powers were not wanting, a monument more durable than those of marble, should proudly rise in this ambitious page, to the new, and far nobler *Addison*, than that which you, and the public have so long, and so much admired . . . heads, indeed, are crowned on earth; but hearts only are crowned in heaven: A truth which, in such an *age of authors* should not be forgotten.[84]

Although Young frames the notion of posthumous reward and acceptance in specifically Christian terms, the impulse towards what I have called the textual afterlife is clear. Writing in the 1720s, however, Young appeared to be far more sceptical about the value of posthumous recognition. In *The Love of Fame* (1727–28), Young echoes Swift and anticipates Godwin and the early Coleridge when he satirises the claims of posterity:

> But ah! not *inspiration* can obtain
> That Fame, which poets languish for in vain.
> How mad their aim? who thirst for glory, strive
> To grasp, what no man can possess *alive.*
> Fame's a *reversion* in which men take place
> (O late reversion!) at their own decease.
> This truth sagacious *Lintot* knows so well,
> He *starves* his authors, that their works may *sell.*[85]

As late as 1797 in his essay 'Of Posthumous Fame', William Godwin makes a scathing attack on the idea of posterity, and suggests that, eternally divided in its opinion of the achievement of any particular poet, it cannot provide a final arbiter of artistic value. He also follows Johnson in arguing that the idea of posterity is little more than a consolation for neglected authors: 'It is common however for persons, overwhelmed with this sort of disappointment, to console themselves with an appeal to posterity, and to observe that future generations, when the venom of party is subsided, when their friendships and animosities are forgotten, when misrepresentation shall no longer disfigure their actions, will not fail to do them justice'.[86] Despite his scepticism towards the value of posthumous renown as a redemptive consolation, however, Godwin does finally admit to a sense of the value of such a desire: 'After all however, reputation for talents is not the ultimate object which a generous mind would desire. I am not contented to be admired as something strange and out of the common road; if I desire any thing of posthumous honour, it is that I may be regarded with affection and esteem by ages yet unborn'.[87] In his essay, Godwin discusses one of the central problems in Romanticism's theory of posterity, the way in which it seeks to provide a lasting identity for that which will have been dissolved or which will no longer be present, and in an early undergraduate Latin exercise written in 1792, Coleridge rehearses just such an argument against the desire for posthumous fame. 'The Desire of Posthumous Fame is Unworthy a Wise Man' borrows extensively from Cicero's *Tusculan Disputations* to argue that 'of all the errors in which men are steeped the desire for Fame has most misled them'.[88] Coleridge argues that the desire for posthumous fame is universal: 'to bear an immortal name, ever to fly through the mouths of men, and in some part to survive death – to whom do these things not offer some allurement?' But he mocks such a desire, asking 'what use would it be to you?':

For if I wholly die, and consciousness is lost with life, what have I to do with glory? But if there is life after death, and if I am to be carried with one leap, as it were, to the heavens, I shall scorn and despise it. Nay, more, call to mind the inconstancy of fame, how many once celebrated whose very names have not survived today; how many, too, of those who celebrated them have been taken from our midst.

'Fame', Coleridge declares, 'seems to me, while we live a vapour, after death Oblivion'.[89]

What has been called Pope's 'seemingly unquenchable thirst for admiration'[90] might suggest a crucial eighteenth-century figure in any discussion of the development of the Romantic theory of posterity. But Pope's ironic comments on fame include a radical scepticism towards posthumous renown. In *An Essay on Man*, for example, fame is figured as 'a fancy'd life in others' breath, / A thing beyond us, ev'n before our death' (epistle 4, lines 237–8), while in *The Temple of Fame*, Pope exclaims 'How vain that second Life in others' Breath, / Th'Estate which Wits inherit after Death' (lines 505–6).[91] Indeed, as Donald Fraser points out, Pope's theory of satire is based on a privileging of the contemporary effects of poetry over its possible influence on posterity: in a letter from Pope and Bolingbroke to Swift of 1732, Pope declares that 'if we three were together but for three years, some good might be done upon this Age; or at least some punishment made effectual, toward the Example of posterity'.[92] While it is clear that Pope often expressed what Fraser refers to as his 'usual hope of speaking to posterity' and his 'hope that he would be personally remembered in future generations',[93] such statements of the desire for posthumous fame are habitually framed as a subset of his more general concern with reputation.[94] Posterity, in other words, is simply another, in some ways more privileged, aspect of reputation. Pope's satirical scepticism does not allow him to accept unquestioningly the redemptive force of posterity: since Pope's poetics tend towards an *ethics* of satire rather than an *aesthetics* of the sublime, his theory of posterity can only be part of a more general theory of reputation and fame.

One of the most fully developed discussions of posterity in the eighteenth century emerges in France out of an exchange of letters between Denis Diderot and his friend the sculptor Étienne-Maurice Falconet, written between December 1765 and April 1767.[95] Again, what is most evident in this discussion is the controversial, *debatable* nature of the culture of posterity. Beginning as a conversational disagreement over the value of posterity and developing into an extended series of letters, this exchange polarises the major eighteenth-century arguments over posthumous fame. Falconet argues that posterity is a 'lottery', an *ignis fatuus* ('un feu follet'), a 'chimera',[96] that the judgement of posterity is both fallible and often demonstrably absurd, and that his own reward for his sculpture comes in pleasing himself, his friends and the critics. Diderot opposes these points by arguing both for the soundness of critical judgement in posterity and by claiming that, in fact, posterity is valuable because the praise of future generations can be enjoyed in the present. It is not posterity 'on behalf of the dead' that concerns Diderot: rather he is 'interested in its praise, legitimately presumed and guaranteed unanimously by contemporaries, as a present pleasure for the living'. In the first of these letters, Diderot admits that 'it is all a nonsense', that the appeal to posterity is a delusion. 'But', Diderot goes on, 'confine happiness to the meagre allotment called reality and tell me what it is worth'.[97] Diderot formulates this appeal of posterity in a memorable metaphor of half-heard music:

Since it is sweet to hear, at night, a distant concert of flutes, whose scattered sounds my imagination, helped by my discerning ear, succeeds in assembling into a connected melody – one that charms all the more because, in good part, it is my own creation – I must conclude that a concert near at hand would be well worth hearing. But will you believe me, my friend, when I say it is not this nearby concert which enthralls me but the other one? The sphere in which we are admired, the length of time in which we live and hear ourselves praised, the number of those who give us our well-deserved eulogy in person, all that is too little for our ambitious soul. We do not feel ourselves sufficiently rewarded, perhaps, by the genuflections of an existing world; we want to see people yet unborn upon their knees, beside those already kneeling. Only so limitless a crowd of worshippers can satisfy a mind whose impulsions are always towards the infinite.[98]

By analogy with the idea that half-heard melodies are sweeter than those fully heard, Diderot argues that the imagined praise of a future audience is more gratifying than contemporary recognition. But Diderot also makes the point that the value of posterity consists in the way that it can be enjoyed by the living: 'Eulogy in the hand, paid for in hard cash, is what we get from our contemporaries; presumed eulogy, eulogy on a credit basis, is the kind we hear from a distance and is that of posterity'. In this way the materialist philosopher is able to avoid the charge that he gives credibility to a metaphysical belief in the afterlife: 'That immortal voice will, no doubt, fall silent for you when you cease to exist; but you hear it at present, and it is immortal in spite of you, and it will go on its way, crying "Falconet, Falconet!"'.[99] You do not need to live for ever or to go on existing after your own death to appreciate the admiration of posterity. It is the *idea* rather than the experience of the future which is important.

But Diderot also argues, more radically, and in what Falconet sees as a perverse example of intellectual sophistry, for the inevitability, the ines- capability of the impulse towards posterity. Even arguments *against* pos- terity, Diderot claims, will be read by posterity and, as such, may be understood to respect that future – posterity, in this sense, is inescapable: 'It is posterity that is the destination of all that is written so eloquently against her. The frightful work of injury addressed to her is a great mark of respect given to her'.[100] Diderot's sense of the importance of poste- rity is also expressed in his entry for 'Immortality' in the *Encyclopaedia*, which begins by describing its own *raison d'être* as its capacity for inform- ing future generations. Diderot defines literary 'immortality' in terms which are echoed repeatedly in the Romantic period when he empha- sises sacrifice as central to artistic endeavour: immortality is 'that kind of life that we acquire in the memory of men . . . We hear in ourselves the eulogy which they [our fellow men] will make of us some day, and we sacrifice ourselves. We sacrifice our lives; we really cease to exist in order to live in their memory. If immortality considered from this aspect is a chimera, it is the chimera of great souls'.[101]

One of the touchstones in what I am trying to suggest is a pervasive if sometimes obscure debate over the meaning and value of posterity in the eighteenth and the early nineteenth centuries is the figure of

Shakespeare. In particular, discussions of Shakespeare often focus on the question of whether a genius is aware of or concerned with his own reputation. In the 'First Epistle of the Second Book of Horace Imitated', for example, Pope declares that Shakespeare 'For gain, not glory, winged his roving flight, / And grew immortal in his own despite', just as Ben Jonson 'as little seemed to heed / The life to come, in every poet's creed' (lines 71–4).[102] It is this tradition that Hazlitt builds on in his essay 'On Posthumous Fame, Whether Shakespeare Was Influenced By It'. Hazlitt makes it a central quality of Shakespeare's genius that he is unaware of the possibility of a poetic afterlife: there is 'scarcely the slightest trace', Hazlitt argues, 'of any such feeling' as the desire for poetic immortality in Shakespeare's writing, and 'this indifference may be accounted for from the very circumstance, that he was almost entirely a man of genius' (*Works* IV.23). For Hazlitt, Shakespeare's insouciance with regard to immortality is bound up with what Keats calls his 'Negative Capability' (*LJK* I.193), his 'revel[ing] in the world of observation and fancy' and the fact that he 'seemed scarcely to have an individual existence of his own' such that he had little desire 'to embody that personal identity in idle reputation after death, of which he was so little tenacious while living' (*Works* IV.23). In 'Whether Genius is Conscious of its Powers?', published in *The Plain Speaker* in 1826, Hazlitt claims not only that a poet or artist *cannot* know whether he or she will survive in posterity, but that the genius, by definition, is not concerned with this question: 'The definition of genius is that it acts unconsciously; and those who have produced immortal works, have done so without knowing how or why' (*Works* XII.118). Geniuses such as Correggio and Rembrandt, Hazlitt claims, wouldn't have produced their works if they had been thinking of immortality (pp. 119–20). This idea, anyway, is absurd: a name ' "fast-anchored in the deep abyss of time" ', Hazlitt asserts, 'is like a star twinkling in the firmament, cold, silent, distant, but eternal and sublime; and our transmitting one to posterity is as if we should contemplate our translation to the skies' (p. 125). In this sense, Hazlitt points to a further source of paradox in Romantic posterity. The undoubted concern with posterity in the period, with living on or surviving in a textual afterlife, is balanced by an anxiety concerning the appropriateness of such a concern: the narcissistic concern to survive in the future might itself be the cause of one's inevitable neglect in that future.

The subtle but decisive shift from the neoclassical to the Romantic versions of posterity becomes evident once we compare these comments by Hazlitt to remarks by Pope and Johnson on Shakespeare. Both Pope and Johnson argue in terms very similar to those of Hazlitt, but both also suggest that Shakespeare's lack of interest in the future of his work was not so much a result of his genius as of his contemporary popularity. In his 'Preface to Shakespeare' (1725), for example, Pope declares that Shakespeare:

. . . writ to the people, and writ at first without patronage from the better sort, and therefore without aims of pleasing them; without assistance or advice from the learned, as without the advantage of education or acquaintance among them . . . in a word, without any views of reputation and of what poets are pleased to call immortality – some or all of which have encouraged the vanity, or animated the ambition, of other writers.[103]

The fact that Shakespeare 'writ to the people' means that he didn't write for reputation and posterity, and it is this insouciance which saves him from vanity. The point is put even more clearly in Johnson's comments in his 'Preface to Shakespeare':

It does not appear, that *Shakespeare* thought his works worthy of posterity, that he levied any ideal tribute upon future times, or had any further prospect, than of present popularity and present profit. When his plays had been acted, his hope was at an end; he solicited no addition of honour from the reader . . . So careless was this great poet of future fame, that . . . he made no collection of his works . . . [104]

In both cases, the critics argue that Shakespeare is concerned to please a contemporary public. It is this desire, rather than Hazlitt's sense of Shakespeare's unconscious genius, that is the reason for the poet's neglect of posterity. And it is significant that, for both Pope and Johnson, Shakespeare's popularity is implicitly linked to the idea of his 'immortality'.[105] Both are writing in the tradition of Ben Jonson's elegy for Shakespeare which announces that Shakespeare is both the 'Soul of the age!' and 'not of an age, but for all time!'.[106] In the Romanticism of Hazlitt and others, the Pope/Johnson logic of posterity is developed such that popularity itself becomes suspect in the writer of genius: for such writers, contemporary neglect is necessary for the genius. In this respect, the transition from Pope and Johnson to Wordsworth and Hazlitt is significant: while Pope and Johnson appear to suggest that Shakespeare survives by virtue of his contemporary popularity, the Romantics will argue that popularity and future recognition are the incompatible poles of artistic production. Coleridge is unequivocal on this point in the *Biographia Literaria* when he argues of the 'men of the greatest genius' that 'In the inward assurance of permanent fame, they

seem to have been either indifferent or resigned, with regard to immediate reputation' (*BL* 1.33). Posterity in Romantic theory becomes, finally,
a function of the poet's contemporary obscurity, and popularity an indication of the depth to which a writer has descended.

The poetics of the Romantic period, then, develop a series of concerns in seventeenth- and eighteenth-century poetics regarding the
nature of the poetic genius, of literary and aesthetic judgement, and of
poetry audiences and posterity. Posterity is redefined to include contemporary neglect as a precondition for posthumous recognition and
becomes inscribed in Romantic writing as the necessary possibility of
that writing itself. The Romantic appeal to posterity becomes increasingly central as a justification for artistic production itself, and this
justification folds back into the act of writing, to the extent that the function of writing is itself bound up with reception in posterity. Thus it is
that Wordsworth ends a number of poems by assuring himself and his
readers that his writing will be justified in its remains: 'Tintern Abbey'
ends by looking forward to a time, in 'after years', when this poem will
remain in the 'mansion' of Dorothy's memory; *The Prelude* (1805) ends
with the hope that it and the work of Coleridge, Wordsworth's
addressee, will 'speak / A lasting inspiration' (book 13, lines 442–3); and
the 'River Duddon' sonnet sequence ends with a sonnet entitled 'After-
Thought', which presents, as the possibility of a time after thought, an
afterthought that it is 'Enough, if something from our hands have power
/ To live, and act, and serve the future hour' as 'tow'rd the silent tomb
we go' (lines 10–12).[107] In the next chapter I look in more detail at the
social and cultural conditions of such declarations and at the transformations in poetic theory which made such assertions central to the
project of Romanticism.

CHAPTER 2

The Romantic culture of posterity

> One of the great reasons that the english have produced the finest
> writers in the world; is, that the English world has ill-treated them
> during their lives and foster'd them after their deaths.
>
> (Keats to Sarah Jeffrey)

Historians of literature and literary criticism have described a series of
overlapping and complementary shifts in the conception, deployment
and institutions of the literary during the later eighteenth and early nineteenth centuries and have outlined certain changes in ideas about
authorship, genius, the canon, originality, artistic integrity and the
autonomy of the poetic work. Or to put the point more strongly, critics
have argued that authorship, genius, the canon and so on are produced
as the foundations of aesthetic value, and indeed, that the institutional-
isation of the aesthetic as an autonomous realm and as a value in and of
itself is inaugurated during the Romantic period. Such transformations
in poetic theory have been linked to the emergent conditions of publication at the end of the eighteenth century. These include technical
developments in the printing and dissemination of books and other
materials, changes in the copyright laws, the spread of literacy and the
growth of a middle-class reading public, as well as factors such as the
gendering of poetry audiences, the professionalisation of the writer and
a decline in patronage, the increasing commercialisation of poetry,
novels and other cultural artefacts, and the emergent discourses, as dis-
crete disciplines, of economics, philosophy, literary criticism and aesthetics. Late-eighteenth and early nineteenth century cultural and
technological forces are understood to have resulted in an ideological
shift in the counter-discourse of the theory and practice of 'literature'
towards a non-instrumentalist, non-utilitarian aesthetics of the autonomous artwork or poem.[1]

Raymond Williams gives a succinct account of the 'invention' of Art in his chapter on 'The Romantic Artist' in *Culture and Society* (1958). 'At a time when the artist is being described as just one more producer of a commodity for the market', comments Williams in what he admits is a 'simplification' of the historical predicament, 'he is describing himself as a specially endowed person'.[2] Indeed, as Williams comments, it is in the late eighteenth century that 'the principles on which the new society was being organized' – principles of industrialisation and industry, of utilitarianism and the development of the mass-market for books – 'were actively hostile to the necessary principles of art'. The new 'necessary principles' of art included those of original genius, autonomy, ineffectuality and authorial isolation. Such principles constituted a reaction against a new commercialisation and commodification of art by which the artist was isolated and distanced from the conditions of the production and consumption of the work. 'What was laid down as a defensive reaction', comments Williams, 'became in the course of the [nineteenth] century a most important positive principle'.[3] The principle of art as separate from society, Williams suggests, both enables a radical critique of that society and, by virtue of its self-positioning as society's abjected other, disables that critique through a self-representation of art as increasingly irrelevant and powerless. In this way, Williams explains the transcendentalisation of the artist, and his book accounts for the politics of posterity – the way in which, isolated from society and directed towards an ideal future, the artist mounts a critique of commercial, bourgeois, industrialised society, while at the same time developing an increasingly quietist ideology of social redundancy and political irrelevance. Posterity, from the perspective of the producer, at least, is the ideal mechanism for extracting 'art' or 'literature' from its enabling conditions of production, from commerce. In this chapter, I begin by briefly surveying alterations in conceptions of writing and publishing that sanctioned such theories of the aesthetic, focusing on the developing discourses of copyright and authorship. In this context I then go on to discuss the varying configurations of the Romantic culture of posterity in the work of, especially, Wordsworth, Coleridge, Isaac D'Israeli, W.H. Ireland, and William Hazlitt.

Arguably the most significant and widely recognised development in aesthetics of the eighteenth century involves the invention of the modern concept of authorship, the 'birth' of the author. Recent studies have aligned this 'invention' with debates surrounding the copyright law, and have scrutinised those debates and the subsequent legislative changes in order to trace developments in the understanding of the author.[4] Thus, Mark Rose argues that 'the representation of originality as a central value in cultural production developed . . . in precisely the same period as the notion of the author's property right'.[5] With the copyright law of 1710, the author started to become central to the institutional separation of the category of 'literature': Rose comments that 'What was novel about the statute was that it constituted the author as well as the bookseller as a person with legal standing'.[6] The mid-eighteenth century case of *Tonson v Collins* locked the newly established legal entity of the author into place with the literary work: 'To assert one is to imply the other', comments Rose, 'and together, like the twin suns of a binary star locked in orbit, they define the center of the modern literary system'.[7] Commenting on the copyright act of 1814 (which extended the period of copyright to the longer of twenty-eight years or the lifetime of the author), John Feather places the crucial change rather later when he argues that this 'put the author at the very centre of the whole arrangement'.[8] While Rose and Feather disagree over the interpretation of details, both note the significance of the fact that between 1710 and 1814 changes in copyright law involved a shift away from booksellers' claims to perpetual copyright in the early eighteenth century to authors' claims on the same right one hundred years later.[9]

A key element in the modern conception of 'literature', then, is the commodification of authorship: the author is now a legally enforced and enforceable entity, and his or her literary output, his or her *works*, are embedded within the capitalist economic system. And yet, paradoxically, this commodification of the author in the mid- to late eighteenth century also defines the terms in which the counter-discourse of autonomy, genius and posterity emerges. The figure of the Poet develops as a reaction against its constitution as part of the exchange system of capitalism. The vexed relationship between authorship and capitalism is encapsulated in an ongoing debate over the extent to which authors should be the owners of their own work. In his 'Enquiry into the Copyright Act' published in the *Quarterly Review* for 1819, for example, Robert Southey quotes a notorious passage from a pamphlet by Lord Camden first published in the context of the debate over the Bookseller's Bill of 1774: Camden argues that any financial reward degrades and corrupts the author. Bacon, Newton, Milton and Locke, he argues, felt it 'unworthy' to 'traffic with a dirty Bookseller': when Milton accepted £5 for *Paradise Lost*, he 'knew that the real price of his work was immortality, and that posterity would pay it' (Southey's comment is scathing: 'Is it possible that this declamation should impose upon any man?').[10] According to Camden's aristocratic view, 'trafficking' with booksellers is beneath the dignity of the poet. The argument amounts, of course, to a booksellers' charter, but exaggerated and polarised as it is, it clearly exposes one discursive limit of the debate. Authors do not seek financial reward since they are interested in what Keats calls 'posterity's award' ('To My Brother George'). And while such an argument served the purposes of booksellers very well, it can also be seen in, for example, the early, aristocratic rejection by Byron of financial reimbursement for the trade of writing, or in Keats's ambivalence towards publishing, appealing to a wide audience and making money from poetry.[11] When Southey quotes this passage his purpose is to turn the argument around, to argue that the true poet's heirs should be financially rewarded since the poet himself is unlikely to gain anything like full recompense for his work during his lifetime: for Southey, as for Wordsworth, it is precisely the financial reward of the future, what Wordsworth calls his 'posthumous remuneration', that is the author's inheritance.[12] Since the author cannot be recompensed during his lifetime – or if he can be, then since he will be in 'thraldom' to the 'degenerate taste' and 'slavish principles' of the 'living generation'[13] – he should be able to pass on the copyright to his heirs. And such writers argued that if posterity is to make any sense, it must ultimately mean the right of the author over his work in perpetuity. Thus Wordsworth, in a letter of 1819 to J. Forbes Mitchell, asks 'why the laws should interfere to take away from those pecuniary emoluments which are the natural Inheritance of the posterity of Authors'.[14]

Wordsworth's position on copyright reform is influenced by his sense that the 'originality' of his own poetry leads to a delay between publication and a full or proper reception: as he argues in the 'Essay, Supplementary to the Preface' of 1815, works of genius must create the taste by which they will be understood and accepted. In this essay (his most extended exposition of his theory of posthumous recognition, one designed to account for his first 'collected works'), Wordsworth goes to great and inaccurate lengths to show, against much historical evidence, that no canonical English poet has ever been properly recognised in his lifetime. More than twenty years later, writing in order to attempt to effect a change in the copyright law in 1839, Wordsworth argues that poets such as himself, 'have engaged and persevered in literary labour, less with the expectation of producing immediate or speedy effect, than with a view to interest and benefit society, though remotely, yet permanently'.[15] It is in this sense that I am suggesting that the early nineteenth century saw a *reinvention* of posterity – posterity as the *necessary* time of reception. As Martha Woodmansee argues, the very conception of the author as unique and special is a 'by-product of the Romantic notion that significant writers break altogether with tradition to create something utterly new, unique – in a word, "original" ': 'We owe our modern idea of an author to the radical reconceptualization of writing which came to fruition' in Wordsworth's 'Essay, Supplementary'.[16] The originality of the art-object resulting from the profundity of genius and the isolation and autonomy of the author, leads to a necessary delay in reception. Although the first proposal for posthumous rights in parliament was as late as 1837,[17] in fact, as Wordsworth's comments suggest, and as the following passage from Southey's essay of 1819 makes clear, the appeal was bound up with earlier nineteenth-century arguments for the rights of authors: 'The decision which time pronounces upon the reputations of authors, and upon the permanent rank which they are to hold, is unerring and final. Restore to them that perpetuity in the copyright of their works, of which the law has deprived them, and the reward of literary labour will ultimately be in just proportion to its deserts'.[18]

With the institution of authorship, however, its role, profession or social and legal identity was split: authorship is divided at its origins.[19] As Roger Chartier comments: 'in the latter half of the eighteenth century a somewhat paradoxical connection was made between a desired professionalization of literary activity (which should provide remuneration in order for writers to live from their writings) and the authors' representation of themselves in an ideology of literature founded on the radical autonomy of the work of art and the disinterestedness of the creative act'.[20] The literary movement that we call Romanticism may be said to be defined, in certain respects, at least, in terms of its need to separate one form of authorship from another: the poet from the scribbler, the inspired, prophetic figure of the genius on the one hand, from the mercenary, professional craftsman – what Wordsworth calls the 'useful drudge' skilled in mechanical invention – on the other (*MY* 1.266). As Terry Eagleton comments, in what he calls a 'notable historical irony', the ideas of the genius and the autonomy of the work of art are created 'just when the artist is becoming debased to a petty commodity producer': the Romantic ideology of the Poet or Author may be understood as a 'spiritual compensation for this degradation'.[21]

The newly defined author, then, is at the still point of the turning world that is 'literature'. As Howard Erskine-Hill and Richard McCabe comment, the function of the Romantic poet 'was to make visible in his works the source of his own poetic talent, the medium would become the message, the text be the man'.[22] According to Mark Rose, the attempt to establish the significance of certain forms of writing, leads to a chain of deferrals intended to ground writing in the identity of the author-as-genius, thereby guaranteeing the significance of the work:

The distinctive property was said to reside in the particularity of the text . . . and this was underwritten by the notion of originality, which was in turn guaranteed by the concept of personality. The sign of personality was the distinctiveness of the human face, but this was only the material trace of the genius of the immaterial self, and this when examined dissolved completely into contingency and flux. The attempt to anchor the notion of literary property in personality suggests the need to find a transcendent signifier, a category beyond the economic and to warrant and ground the circulation of literary commodities.[23]

The personality of the author – as Vates, Seer, Poet, Genius[24] – that is to say, guarantees the value of the work, guarantees its *property* as a literary work, as owned, valued, bought and sold on the one hand, and as beyond economic value, transcending the material conditions of its production on the other. Paradoxically, the work's *value* in economic terms cannot be disengaged from its rejection of such value, since its economic value is linked to its aesthetic worth, which is in turn underwritten by its supposed escape from the circulation of economic exchange. A work takes on aesthetic value in the new economics of cultural exchange just to the extent that it is figured and read as transcending economics. This, as John Guillory comments, 'is the dynamic of the work of art', one which, therefore, is still in operation.[25] And this transcendence is most powerfully evoked by means of a particular figuration of authorship as 'original' and therefore as isolated, autonomous and separate from society: as, ultimately, necessarily *neglected*.

The modern institution of authorship, then, if we accept the arguments of Rose, Woodmansee, Feather and others that it is intimately linked to the discourse of property and developments in copyright law of the eighteenth and nineteenth centuries, is also inextricably connected to the question of audience since, as is self-evident, the audience constitutes the market for books, producing or withholding value for the *property* of the literary work. Indeed, the very project of Romanticism itself may be conceived in terms of a response to what Lucy Newlyn terms an 'anxiety of reception' and what I have elsewhere called an 'anxiety of audience'.[26] As I have suggested, on the one hand poets realised the radical potential of a mass readership and, in the cases of such poets as Byron, Scott, Hemans and Landon, were able to cash in by selling, at best, tens of thousands of copies of their poems. On the other hand, such a mass audience was equally able to provoke a sense of dislocation, alienation and disillusionment in poets who never managed to sell more than a few hundred, or at most a few thousand, copies of their poems. By the 1810s, Wordsworth and Coleridge had begun a reversal of what for them had previously been a democratisation of reading – attacking what Coleridge calls 'promiscuous' readers (*BL* II.142), and attempting to argue, as Coleridge did, that the poet wrote for a category of superior, quasi-professional readers, the intelligentsia or 'clerisy', or as Wordsworth did, that the poet wrote for an audience of the future.[27] The degradation of the contemporary reading public is epitomised for Coleridge by the 'devotees of the circulating libraries' whose 'beggarly daydreaming', rather than reading, requires nothing but 'laziness and a little mawkish sensibility': this is not so much reading, Coleridge continues in a footnote to the *Biographia Literaria* (1817), as the 'indulgence of sloth, and hatred of vacancy' (*BL* 1.48). The fear of the democratisation of reading is made clear when Coleridge develops a paranoid caricature of the reading public: 'all men being supposed able to read, and all readers able to judge, the multitudinous PUBLIC, shaped into personal unity by the magic of abstraction, sits nominal despot on the throne of criticism' (*BL* 1.59). Similarly, in *The Statesman's Manual* (1816), Coleridge refers to a 'promiscuous audience' whom he spurns in favour of a clerisy, and complains of the 'misgrowth of our luxuriant activity', and of a 'READING PUBLIC – as strange a phrase, methinks, as ever forced a splenetic smile on the staid countenance of Meditation': 'It would require the intrepid accuracy of a Colquhoun to venture at the precise number of that vast company'.[28] Literature, in the face of this dispersal, dilution and degradation of audience, will constitute what Arthur Hallam calls a 'redemptive power'.[29] As David Riede puts it, literature becomes the 'expression of the unified selfhood in its perfect health', a 'therapeutic discourse' and as such 'an alternative to all other discourses, which reflect or express the fragmentation of reality'. Literature, finally, becomes a 'compensation for the suffering and fragmentation imposed by capitalist society'.[30] And the mechanism of such compensation is, for the Romantic poet, the fiction of posterity, the idea of his own posthumous recuperation and canonical survival as text.

A brief account of Wordsworth's engagement with questions of reputation, publication, book sales and posterity from the evidence of his surviving letters will put into focus the kind of issues which are raised by the predicament of the writer in the early nineteenth century. The career of Wordsworth is exemplary both because it extends from his first publication in the 1790s until his death and the publication of *The Prelude* in 1850, and because it is in his prose that the theory of posterity as a reaction to contemporary neglect is first fully formulated. Writing on William's poems in August 1815, Dorothy Wordsworth declares that 'I now perceive clearly that till my dear Brother is laid in his grave his writings will not produce any profit . . . I am sure it will be very long before they have an extensive sale – nay it will not be while he is alive to know it. God be thanked he has no *mortification* on this head . . . His writings will live – will comfort the afflicted and animate the happy to purer happiness when we and our little cares are all forgotten' (*MY* II.247). This lack of 'mortification' becomes, in a comment by Elizabeth Fenwick from 1839, its complement, the poet's certainty of his own 'greatness': 'Nothing appears more remarkable to me in him than the constant and firm persuasion of his own *greatness*, which maintained itself through neglect and ridicule and contempt, and when in devoting himself to that culture which he conceived best adapted to it he encountered a life of poverty and obscurity, and must have incurred the censure of his friends, as leading a life of idleness originating in self-conceit and vanity'.[31] Wordsworth's sense of his own greatness is truly remarkable. As Dorothy Wordsworth and Elizabeth Fenwick suggest, for many years Wordsworth managed to maintain, against all odds – against the evidence of reviews, of sales-figures, even apparently against the opinion of his friends – that his poetry would survive, that his writing would 'live'.[32] He had, as Henry Crabb Robinson comments, 'the expectation of posthumous renown'.[33]

The letters, however, suggest a rather more complex, nuanced story of Wordsworth's sense of posterity and reputation. In December 1839, for example, long into what Harold Bloom refers to as 'the longest dying of a major poetic genius in history', his 'dreadful poetic dotage' from 1807 to 1850,[34] Wordsworth writes a letter to the youthful American Henry Reed: 'I am standing on the brink of that vast ocean I must sail so soon', he remarks, 'I must speedily lose sight of the shore and I could not once have conceived how little I am now troubled by the thought of how long or short a time they who remain upon that shore may have sight of me' (*LY* III.751). This lack of concern for being remembered is then explicitly linked to his lack of interest in 'any literary monument that I may be enabled to leave behind' (*LY* III.752). In making these statements on the insignificance of posterity, Wordsworth contrasts his disinterestedness with Reed's youthful concern with the poet's fame, immortal and immortal. 'It is well however', Wordsworth concludes, 'that men think otherwise in the earlier part of their lives' (*LY* III.752). Wordsworth is making a point similar to that of Hazlitt in his essay 'On the Feeling of Immortality in Youth': in both cases, the desire for 'immortality' is defined as a youthful delusion and one which decreases over time. Nevertheless, the letter makes clear Wordsworth's sense of the importance of such a desire as an impulse towards creation and for the production of 'literary monuments'.[35]

As such a letter might lead us to expect, Wordsworth was concerned throughout his life with questions of the publication, sales and reputation of his poetry.[36] From an early stage in his career, he developed a sense of the inevitable time-lag between publication and proper appreciation, ascribing the delay to the 'originality' of his writing. In June 1801, for example, he comments that 'the reputation of L[yrical] B[allads] is spreading every day, though slowly, as might be expected from a work so original' (*EY* 337). Almost a year earlier, in September 1800, Dorothy had made a similar point on the collection in a letter when she remarked that 'we' had never had 'much doubt of its finally making its way' but that 'poems so different from what in general become popular immediately after publication were not likely to be admired all at once' (*EY* 298).[37] Such comments come after *An Evening Walk* and *Descriptive Sketches* of 1793 had been, Wordsworth considers, 'treated with unmerited contempt by some of the periodical publications', while 'others have spoken in higher terms than they deserve' (*EY* 120), and in the context of Wordsworth's sense that sales of *Lyrical Ballads* had been damaged by 'The Ancient Mariner' (*EY* 264) and by Cottle's sale of the second issue of the first edition to J. and A. Arch rather than to Johnson (*EY* 262–3). Such circumstances – inaccurate reviews, the inclusion of Coleridge's work and incompetent booksellers – were prominent in Wordsworth's sense of the reasons for disappointing sales of *Lyrical Ballads*. As these comments might suggest, during the early years of his career Wordsworth's primary impulse for publishing would appear to be financial: 'My aversion from publication increases every day' he remarks in July 1799, 'so much so, that no motives whatever, nothing but pecuniary necessity, will, I think, ever prevail upon me to commit myself to the press again'.[38] 'He has no pleasure in publishing', remarks Dorothy of William in May 1808, 'he even detests it – and if it were not that he is *not* over wealthy, he would leave all his works to be published after his Death' (*MY* 1.236). 'There is little need to advise me against publishing', Wordsworth remarks to James Tobin in March 1798, 'it is a thing which I dread as much as death itself . . . privacy and quiet are my delight' (*EY* 211).[39]

The slow sale of his books – whether imaginary or real – concerned Wordsworth throughout his life, even after he had become a well-known and even eminent poet in the 1830s and 1840s, and at least until 1820 the sales figures were indeed very modest. 'The two last volumes scarcely sell at all', remarks Dorothy in May 1809 (*MY* 1.326), while writing in December 1822, she comments that her brother's poems 'hang on hand – never selling' (*LY* 1.178). De Quincey sums up Wordsworth's career by saying that 'up to 1820, the name of Wordsworth was trampled under foot; from 1820 to 1830, it was militant; from 1830 to 1835, it has been triumphant'.[40] As a result, the detailing of book-sales is a recurrent topic in Wordsworth's letters. Writing to Alaric Watts in October 1825, for example, Wordsworth reports his negotiations with Longmans for a new edition of his poems: 'Mr Longman acknowledges that there is no doubt of a thousand copies being ultimately sold, but he says that the last edition of five hundred copies took five years to go off. This is not quite accurate. The *Poems* and *Excursion* were both ready for publication in the autumn of 1820, and, if I am not grossly mistaken, they cleared the expense of printing in less than a year; and in June, 1824, there were none of the *Excursion* on hand, and only twenty-five copies of the *Miscellaneous Poems* remaining' (*LY* 1.390–1; compare pp. 443–4, 450). By the 1820s, Wordsworth had begun to discern a disparity in his reputation and his sales: since early in the 1820s, his name had become well known and his reputation as a poet secure.[41] But still sales were poor: of the 2,000 copies of the 1832 edition of his poems, he complains to John Kenyon in September 1833, less than '400 had been sold last June; a fact which, contrasted with the state of my poetical reputation, is wholly inexplicable, notwithstanding the depressed state of the book-market in England'.[42]

Increasingly the question of pecuniary return for publishing poetry is a source of discomfort and irritation to Wordsworth: 'for considerably more than half my life', Wordsworth complains to Edward Moxon in October 1834, 'I have been from time to time a Publisher, tho' mostly in a small way – and the Sum of my gains has not probably done much more than equal ½ the wages of a day-labourer in that time' (*LY* 11.745). And in November he comments to Henry Crabb Robinson that the delay in the publication of his latest volume is lucky, since 'neither

Othello, Mackbeth nor the Paradise Lost, if now first produced, would
be attended to' (*LY* II.748). Nevertheless, in April 1835, Wordsworth felt
confident enough to declare that despite 'bad criticism', 'in case of my
Writings . . . their sale for the last 35 years has shown that notwithstanding every endeavour to impede their circulation they have been in constant and regular, though not in great demand' (*LY* III.45). Similarly,
writing to his family from London in June 1836 on an anonymous 'stray
or love note' that he had recently received and which he thinks may be
a hoax, he comments that 'The Ladies appear to be my chief admirers,
and whatever the creatures may think of me I appear in the absence and
default of others perhaps to be grown into popularity' (*LY* III.241), and
in another letter of a few days later, 'My admirers are greatly increased
among the female sex' (p. 247).[43]

'What do you think of an edition of 20,000 of my Poems being struck
off at Boston', Wordsworth asks Henry Crabb Robinson in January 1837,
'An Author in the English language is becoming a great Power for good
or evil – if he writes with spirit' (*LY* III.355). Nevertheless, writing in 1841,
Wordsworth returns to his sense of the 'wretched state of the Book
Trade': 'Moxon tells me that only 250 Copies of my last thousand have
been sold . . . This is poor encouragement to print the Vol: I have been
about making ready' (*LY* IV.261; see also pp. 289–90). Similarly, as late as
November 1842, Wordsworth can declare not only that 'Publication was
ever to me most irksome; so that if I had been rich, I question whether
I should ever have published at all' and that his latest volume has 'called
out a good deal of sorry criticism, as in truth happens to all my publications in succession and will do so long as anything of mine comes forth'
(*LY* IV.390), and in June 1844 he still fears that 'it will be long before' his
latest volume is 'off' (*LY* IV.556). In October 1846 Wordsworth contrasts
public interest in poetry with interest in railways: 'I have little hope that
the Edition of my own Poems which I am preparing will bring me satisfaction by its Sale. The world is in general little disposed to Poetry; and
at this time in particular nothing but Railways engages public attention'
(*Supplement*, p. 251). Despite the gradual increase in sales and reputation
after about 1820, then, Wordsworth continued to perceive his poetry as
neglected and misunderstood. It is in this context that he gradually
developed and refined his sense that a proper understanding of his work
would only be available in a future beyond his own life.

It is during the early years of the nineteenth century, after the relatively slow sales of the *Lyrical Ballads* and after what Wordsworth saw as
its disappointing, not to say unjust, critical reception, and briefly before

and just after the publication of his 1807 volume, that his sense of the potential critical and financial remuneration from his poetry starts to become more doubtful. At this time, Wordsworth seems to have moved away from a belief in the unfortunate contingencies of publishing as a factor in the disappointing sales towards a firm sense of his own inevitable contemporary neglect as a function of his originality. Writing to Walter Scott in November 1806, for example, Wordsworth comments that he is planning to publish his 1807 *Poems* 'with great reluctance' and remarks on 'how indifferent I am to its present reception', but that he has hopes that 'it will one day or other be thought well of by the Public'.[44] Wordsworth's anxiety is even more pronounced a few months later, in a letter to Lady Beaumont of May 1807 on his recently published volumes:

It is impossible that any expectations can be lower than mine concerning the immediate effect of this little work upon what is called the Public. I do not here take into consideration the envy and malevolence, and all the bad passions which always stand in the way of a work of any merit from a living Poet; but merely think of the pure absolute honest ignorance, in which all worldlings of any rank and situation must be enveloped, with respect to the thoughts, feelings, and images, on which the life of my Poems depends. (*MY* 1.145)

But Wordsworth then goes on, in rhetorical mode, to state, explicitly and unequivocally, for perhaps the first time, his trust in the afterlife of writing:

Trouble not yourself upon their present reception; of what moment is that compared with what I trust is their destiny, to console the afflicted, to add sunshine to daylight by making the happy happier, to teach the young and gracious of every age, to see, to think and feel, and therefore to become more actively and securely virtuous; this is their office, which I trust they will faithfully perform long after we (that is, all that is mortal of us) are mouldered in our graves. (*MY* 1.146)[45]

The letter builds, finally, to an assertion borrowed from Coleridge which will be repeated and made famous eight years later in the 'Essay, Supplementary': 'never forget', he tells Lady Beaumont, 'what I believe was observed to you by Coleridge, that every great and original writer, in proportion as he is great or original, must himself create the taste by which he is to be relished; he must teach the art by which he is to be seen' (*MY* 1.150).[46] 'No poem of mine will ever be popular', Wordsworth remarks to Sir George Beaumont in 1808, but this is of little consequence: 'let the Poet first consult his own heart as I have done and leave the rest to posterity; to, I hope, an improving posterity' (*MY* 1.194, 195).

Developing alongside his sense of contemporary popular and critical neglect, then, are comments in the letters which mark out the future, in particular the posthumous future, as the site of Wordsworth's proper appreciation. Writing to Thomas Poole in April 1814, for example, Wordsworth quotes Milton when he declares his hope that *The Excursion* is a poem that 'future times will "not willingly let die"' (*MY* II.146).[47] Similarly, in March 1816 he declares that he writes 'chiefly for Posterity' (*MY* II.292). On 15 April of the same year Wordsworth implicitly contrasts his own immortality with the ephemerality of his contemporaries when he complains that he is '*Mobbed*' in Sir Egerton Brydges's poem *Restituta* 'with the "chief of the present day", most of whom Posterity will know just as much about, as we do about the Restituta of your worthy Friend' (*MY* II.300–1). 'Posterity will settle all accounts justly', he declares in 1835, so that 'works which deserve to last will last; and if undeserving this fate, the sooner they perish the better' (*LY* III.25).[48] The importance of posthumous fame for the Wordsworth Circle might be indicated by the pains that Dorothy takes in March 1815 to transcribe into two letters to friends an extract from a letter from John Edwards in which Edwards quotes a letter to him from James Montgomery. Montgomery claims that *The Excursion* 'sets Mr W. beyond controversy above all the living and almost all the dead of his fraternity' (*MY* II.213; see also p. 222), and that just by virtue of his friendship with the poet, Edwards has 'got a passport to posterity signed by Wordsworth' (*MY* II.222).

The relationship of the early nineteenth-century writer to the technologies and economics of publication on the one hand and to poetic immortality on the other, may be succinctly characterised by a brief account of the work of Isaac D'Israeli. Although relatively obscure now, a series of books by the father of the future prime minister and novelist Benjamin Disraeli which catalogued the tribulations of authorship sold well in the early decades of the nineteenth century. Indeed, in 1818 Byron declared to John Murray (D'Israeli's as well as Byron's publisher) that he had read D'Israeli's works 'over and over and over repeatedly' and that 'I don't know a living man's books I take up so often, or lay down more reluctantly, as *Israeli's*'.[49] Starting life as *An Essay on the Manners and Genius of the Literary Character* in 1795, D'Israeli's *The Literary Character, Illustrated by the History of Men of Genius, Drawn from their own Feelings and Confessions* was enlarged in a second edition of 1818 (published by Murray), and had gone into a fifth edition by 1827. Rather less successful but still important in the early nineteenth-century mapping of the 'literary character' was D'Israeli's *Calamities of Authors* of 1812, and the frequently republished and re-edited *Curiosities of Literature* (first edn, 1808). D'Israeli's work is useful because of the unique way that it combines poetics and literary history with its anecdotal discussion of the material, social and economic conditions of the writer in the late eighteenth and early nineteenth centuries. Moreover, the popularity and wide dissemination of D'Israeli's books make them not only valuable as a source of information concerning the representation of the writer in the early nineteenth century, but also an important element in the contemporary establishment of the 'character' of the author: his books both analyse and construct the role of the writer within a context of the professionalisation and the contemporary vicissitudes of the writing life. In particular, D'Israeli repeatedly expresses both fascination and despair at the predicament of the neglected genius. Responding to, and helping to shape, a range of contemporary developments in the figure of authorship, then, D'Israeli's work constitutes both a scattered and unsystematic social history of the author and, as might be suggested by the fact of Byron's fascination with his work, a *model* of authorship.

In the earlier reincarnation of *The Literary Character* as *An Essay on the Manners and Genius of the Literary Character*, D'Israeli elaborates his position by situating authorship within a history of the technology of the book. He observes that an increase in literary production has led to a qualitative deterioration in writing. According to D'Israeli, prior to the invention of printing, authorship was an extremely rare occupation. Now, however, he claims, there is 'a universal diffusion of books' such that, with the 'incessant industry' of the eighteenth century, volumes have multiplied and prices have fallen. Calculating the number of books in circulation and imagining the number that the nineteenth century will 'infallibly produce', D'Israeli loses himself 'among billions, trillions, and quartillions' until, overwhelmed by the idea of this 'future universal deluge', he has to 'stop at infinity'.[50] Books are now 'accessible to the lowest artisans', and as a result, 'the Literary Character has gradually fallen into disrepute'.[51] In *Calamities of Authors*, D'Israeli also accounts for this increased production by reference to the expansion of the readership. But unlike writers such as Coleridge, who see in such an expansion of the reading public a degeneration of critical reception, D'Israeli is concerned with the effect of this dissemination on authors. He suggests that far from being economically advantageous to writers this popularisation of reading was, in fact, detrimental: 'When we became a reading people, books were to be suited to popular tastes, and then that trade was opened that leads to the Work-house'.[52] In this context, D'Israeli engages with contemporary critiques of copyright law, arguing that the present law dispossessed authors of their rights over their own work on publication.[53] D'Israeli repeatedly laments the financial predicament of authors which leads either to the debtors' jail or to exploitative piece-work. (Dryden is one of his favourite examples, by virtue of the fact that he contracted to 'supply the bookseller with 10,000 verses at sixpence a line'.[54]) One of the major claims of D'Israeli's work is that genuine authors were neglected in the past and that such neglect should be avoided in the future. His work is essentially moralistic and even propagandistic: it is intended, above all, to alert the contemporary public to the neglect of contemporary authors.[55]

The recurring theme of D'Israeli's work, especially of the various editions of *The Literary Character*, then, is the sense of dislocation between the contemporary *neglect* of genius by contrast with the interest which people show in the genius of the past. For D'Israeli, as for others, this is a particular characteristic of the contemporary era. The preface to *An Essay* makes the point very clearly:

The Literary Character has, in the present day, singularly degenerated in the public mind. The finest compositions appear without exciting any alarm of admiration, they are read, approved, and succeeded by others; nor is the presence of the Author considered, as formerly, as conferring honours on his companions; we pass our evenings sometimes with poets and historians, whom it is probable will be admired by posterity, with hardly any other sensation than we feel from inferior associates.[56]

It is this circumstance of neglect that is at the heart of D'Israeli's investigation and the apparently illogical and unreasonable condition of contemporary authorship is resolved by the notion of posthumous fame:

To this enthusiasm, and to this alone, can we attribute the self-immolation of men of genius. Mighty and laborious works have been pursued, as a forlorn hope, at the certain destruction of the fortune of the individual . . . Martyrs of literature and art, they behold in their solitude that halo of immortality over their studious heads, which is a reality to the visionary of glory.[57]

In an early poem, *A Defence of Poetry* (1790), D'Israeli established a major theme of his later prose works when, apostrophising 'ingenuous youth', he declares that they should 'court posterity'. The passage will be echoed by Shelley in his *Defence of Poetry* thirty years later, when he compares the poet to the nightingale 'who sits in darkness and sings to cheer its own solitude with sweet sounds', an 'unseen musician' (*SPP* 486):

DARE! AND BE VIRTUOUS THEN: be bold, yet sage
AND COURT POSTERITY, and leave THIS AGE.
Like the sweet Lark, that quits it's [*sic*] nest to sing,
Till WARBLING FAR responsive echoes ring;
UNSEEN the chauntress all her song assumes,
And shakes, in conscious pride, her rapturous plumes.
So must the BARD (confirm'd by many a tale)
But feel Posterity his labours hail;
'Tis what CAMOENS confest, what MILTON knew;
So close allied the LAUREL to the YEW.   (lines 222–31)

By the early nineteenth century, then, the figure of the neglected genius had become firmly established as a major, if contested element of poetics and aesthetics. Texts such as Edward Young's *Conjectures on Original Composition*, Diderot and Falconet's letters, William Godwin's essay 'On Posthumous Fame', Gray's 'Elegy Written in a Country Churchyard', the pictorial, poetic and prose responses to the death of Chatterton, William Henry Ireland's *Neglected Genius. A Poem*, D'Israeli's *Calamities of Authors* and *The Literary Character*, Wordsworth's 'Essay, Supplementary to the Preface', Shelley's prose, the letters of Coleridge and Keats, Byron's *Don Juan*, and William Hazlitt's lectures and essays all provide explicit and unequivocal affirmations of the importance of the topos of contemporary neglect and posthumous fame – even if, as in the case of Godwin's essay, this affirmation takes the position that the 'consolation' of posterity is, in fact, a 'gross imposition'.[58] As Leo Braudy comments in *The Frenzy of Fame*, 'in the late eighteenth and early nineteenth century an increasingly fame-choked world was beginning to reach out for solace and value to anonymity and neglect as emblems of true worth . . . The concept of neglected genius', Braudy asserts, is 'the era's special turn on the old Horatian paean to posterity'.[59]

One of the most sustained and itself neglected articulations of this particular 'spirit of the age' is a remarkable volume of poetry entitled *Neglected Genius* published in 1812 by the poet and forger William Henry Ireland. The volume included a series of pastiches of neglected (and not-so-neglected) geniuses. At the age of 17, in 1794, Ireland had begun to produce a series of forged literary manuscripts and other supporting documents which included two lost Shakespeare plays, *Henry II* and *Vortigen*. Ireland's work, then, reproduces the figure of youth, forgery and neglect already established by Chatterton. Unlike Chatterton, however, Ireland has been almost entirely forgotten, except as the subject of the Shakespearean editor Edmond Malone's five-hundred page *Inquiry into the Authenticity of Certain Papers* (1795), and through a review of *Neglected Genius* by Byron published in the *Monthly Review* of 1813 – a review in which Byron comments caustically that if Ireland's imitations of the neglected poets 'resemble the originals, the consequent starvation of "many British poets" is a doom which is calculated to excite pity rather than surprize'.[60] Despite – or perhaps because of – its neglect and obscurity, Ireland's volume is exemplary in its statement of the importance of neglect. The prose preface enquires into 'the probable cause of this worldly contempt evinced towards those who, after death, are held up as its greatest ornaments'.[61] The answer involves the necessary and intrinsic difference of genius from others: 'The mind of a genius differs so widely from that of human nature taken in the aggregate, that a close assimilation between them is rendered impossible' (p. xix). And Ireland generalises the case of the neglect of genius to affirm that 'It is with great truth affirmed, that real talent is almost uniformly accompanied with diffidence' (p. xx). Similarly, this generalisation of the neglect of genius occurs in a poem entitled 'Delineation of the Fate of a Modern Poet': 'While glowing genius in seclusion sighs, / And, nipp'd by penury, with sorrow dies' (p. 107). The poets that Ireland includes in his volume are a heterogeneous collection of the more or less remembered: Spenser, Milton, Samuel Butler, Thomas Otway, Dryden, Nathan Tate, Edmund Waller, George Lillo, James Hammond, James Thomson, Oliver Goldsmith, Richard Savage and, especially, Chatterton. Reflecting and reproducing contemporary concerns with the relationship between genius and neglect, Ireland's volume is indicative of the discourse of posterity in the early nineteenth century. It asserts as an explanation for contemporary neglect, the *difference* of genius and, as such, suggests the *necessity* of contemporary neglect for the poet of genius; it emphasises the importance of the relationship between genius and early death, the idea that the genius must suffer for art – ultimately, must die for art; and, finally, it argues for the validity of the judgement of posterity, posthumous judgement as the final and accurate arbiter of genius.

But evidence of the crucial place of the figure of contemporary neglect and posthumous fame in Romantic poetics is also to be found in its sheer pervasiveness as an explanatory schema. In a dramatic review from *The Champion* for 1817, for example, John Hamilton Reynolds describes the myth of neglected genius when he makes the by now conventional point that true fame and contemporary popularity are mutually exclusive: 'Poets that enjoy great applause during their sojourn with us, ere they go away, like flowers that have gladdened our eyes and perfumed the air we breathed, – are seldom the great possessors of true fame'. Reynolds goes on to argue that the 'intoxication' of popularity is indeed detrimental to poetry:

The favour of the world is a dangerous compliment to human intellect, when lavished on living exertion, for it generally leads its object from the great pursuit. The poet that hears the voice of the world ringing in his ears, is too apt to turn to that voice, and to become a truant to poesy, his immortal mistress! He tunes his song to temporary tastes, and is intoxicated with a fair, momentary, and fleeting reputation . . . It is in solitude – in trouble – in a patient poverty – that we generally find those works are produced which 'are for all time'. Great intellects are naturally above those of their surrounding kind, and are led on to exertion by their own intensity; – they delight in high works, and finding their own age unfit to enjoy them, are content to trust them to posterity.[62]

Similarly, it is argued forcefully in an anonymous letter 'On the Neglect of Genius' published in *The Imperial Magazine* in 1821 that 'the greater part of those whose writings are now read with avidity, passed their days in obscurity and contempt; whilst, after their journey through this "vale of tears" is over, they are hailed too late by the epithets of "divine", and "immortal" '.[63] In a reply to this letter, published in the next number of the magazine, even more exaggerated claims are made: 'Could we by any possible means take a retrospective glance at the genius of every man who had lived within the last century, we should find that few, very few indeed, have met with the encouragement they deserved or expected'.[64] Arthur Hallam's important 1831 review of Tennyson's *Poems, Chiefly Lyrical* begins with an extensive argument for the importance of posthumous fame for certain kinds of poet. Poets of the 'new school' found it appropriate to concur with Wordsworth, and to 'appeal from the immediate judgment of lettered or unlettered contemporaries to the decision of a more equitable posterity'.[65] By contrast with poets such as Shakespeare and Milton, whose 'poetic impulse went along with the general impulse of the nation', modern, post-enlightenment poets constitute a 'reaction against' that national 'impulse': it is for this reason, Hallam asserts, that 'modern poetry in proportion to its depth and truth is likely to have little authority over public opinion'. Thus Tennyson's poems are introduced as *inevitably* unpopular as a direct result of their alignment with a Keatsian and Shelleyan poetics: 'true to the theory we have stated, we believe his participation in their characteristic excellencies is sufficient to secure him a share of their unpopularity'.[66]

By the mid-nineteenth century, such assumptions concerning the contemporary neglect and posthumous recognition of the poet, were simply taken for granted. In his essay on Oliver Goldsmith, for example, De Quincey connects popular writing with transience, and 'self-degradation' (*DQW* v.206) and, writing about Wordsworth in 1845, he comments that 'Not . . . in the "Excursion" must we look for that reversionary influence which awaits Wordsworth with posterity' (*DQW* v.259). Five years before the poet's death, De Quincey is looking forward to Wordsworth's posthumous life for his true reputation to be declared. 'Whatever is too original will be hated at the first', declares De Quincey, and taking up the theme of Wordsworth's 'Essay, Supplementary', he argues that such writing 'must slowly mould a public for itself; and the resistance of the early thoughtless judgments must be overcome by a counter resistance to itself, in a better audience slowly mustering against the first' (*DQW* v.267–8). Similarly, writing in 1849, John Ruskin shows posterity to be fully integrated as a principle of art when he declares that 'Every human action gains in honour, in grace, in all true magnificence, by its regard to things that are to come'.[67] As Orestes Brownson declares in an article on 'Shelley's Poetical Works' in the *Boston Quarterly Review* (October 1841), 'It is the fate of most great men to be unknown or unadmired by their own age and country' (*SCH* 394).[68]

While all the canonical Romantic poets contemplated, wrote about and appealed to their own survival in posterity in letters, notebooks, essays, poems and conversations, it may be useful briefly to consider Coleridge's distinctive contribution to the Romantic culture of posterity as expressed in his development of the idea of the separation of 'fame' on the one hand from 'reputation' on the other.[69] Coleridge's discussion of this distinction over a number of years clearly illustrates the conceptual difficulties that arise in any attempt to theorise about the Romantic culture of posterity. His first major exploration of the two categories appears in a letter written in the Spring of 1808 and it is then elaborated in two letters written in 1810 and 1811 respectively.[70] In a letter dated 4 April 1808, Coleridge responds to Matilda Betham's linking of his name with 'fame':

The only word in [your letter], which a little surprized me, was that of '*fame*'. I assure myself, that your thinking and affectionate mind will long ago have made a distinction between fame and reputation; between that awful thing, which is a fit object of pursuit for the good, and the pursuit of which is an absolute Duty of the great; that which lives & is a fellow-laborer of nature under God, producing even in the minds of Worldlings a *sort* of docility, which proclaims, as it were, *silence* in the cant of noisy human passions – & the reward of which

without superstition we may well conceive to be the consciousness in a future
state of each Being, in whose mind & heart the Works of the truly Famous have
awakened the impulses & schemes of after excellence . . . But putting Fame out
of the Question, I should have been a little surprized even at the word 'reputation' – having only published a small volume, twelve years ago, which as my
bookseller well knows, had no circulation – & in honest truth did not deserve
any, tho' perhaps as much as many that have attained it . . . I *should* have been
surprized even at any *publicity* of my name, if I were less aware of that sad sad
stain of the present very *anti-gallican* but woefully *gallicizing* Age, the rage for personality – of talking & thinking ever and ever about A. and B. and L. – names,
names, always names!   (*CL* III.83–4)[71]

Coleridge ends the passage by suggesting that his name has become
known by virtue of his association with Southey and Wordsworth and
not on account of his own poetry. In this letter, then, Coleridge elaborates a distinction between fame and reputation as well as distinguishing between reputation and publicity. Although he suggests that Betham
will 'long ago' have made the first distinction, the letter gives a sense of
Coleridge's spontaneous production of the three categories as he writes.
For this reason, perhaps, 'reputation' remains undefined as the clauses
which are introduced by 'between that awful thing . . . ' are left grammatically unresolved by the expected balancing clauses on reputation.
We might speculate, however, that Coleridge wants to ascribe a residual
value to 'reputation', a value to a certain kind of contemporary renown,
which he can then distinguish from the woeful 'rage for personality'
which is denoted by the term 'publicity'.[72] By contrast, Coleridge's analysis of fame is very detailed. Fame is curiously anthropomorphised and,
at the same time, theologised, by being figured as both alive and linked
to the absolute arbiter of ethics, to ontology and, apparently, to aesthetics as 'a fellow-laborer of nature under God'. Seen as something
towards which the 'great' must strive as a 'Duty', and capable of silencing even 'Worldlings', fame is given a quasi-theological status as an
absolute and transcendent virtue, underwritten by God. It is fame itself
towards which human striving is directed, a transcendent force which is
ultimately a function of death and posthumous existence since it
involves 'the consciousness in a future state of each Being' and is a
product of 'the impulses and schemes of after excellence'. But the ambiguities embedded within the syntax of these phrases indicate the
difficulties which Coleridge encounters in framing the precise location
and operation of fame: his analysis remains unclear as to whether or not
fame affects the living, whether the genius can become 'conscious' of it

(in the present), and how the precise temporality of this 'excellence' might work.

The distinction between fame and reputation appears a number of times during the next few years[73] until, in January 1810, Coleridge writes a second, more detailed account of reputation. In a letter to Lady Beaumont concerned with the failure of *The Friend* to gain an audience sufficient to make the journal financially viable (people consider it 'dull, paradoxical, abstruse, dry, obscure, & heaven knows what else!', he complains), Coleridge declares that he receives 'a deeper delight from the knowledge that I have half a dozen readers, like your Sister, than I should have from as large a promiscuous sale, as Avarice could crave or Vanity dream of' (*CL* III.276, 277). He goes on to explain that as a young man his desire for 'sympathy' – rather than his vanity – led him to desire the '*outward proofs*' of his literary power. Now, however, things are different:

At present, I am more inclined to shun than seek *Reputation*, for its own sake, and exclusive of it's [*sic*] contingent consequences in the increase of my utility – using the word, Reputation, in it's [*sic*] etymological sense, as the opinions of those who *re-suppose* the *suppositions* of others. Quod Hic *putavit*, ille *reputat*: re-echoes an echo. FAME (from the Greek φημί = the Latin, fari) is indeed a worthy object of pursuit for all men, and to seek it is even a solemn Duty for men endowed with more than ordinary powers of mind: first, as multiplying the ways and chances by which a useful work comes into the hands of such as are prepared to avail themselves of it; secondly, as securing for such a work that submissiveness of Heart, that *docility*, without which nothing really good can be really acquired; and lastly, because the *individuality* of the Author, with all the associations connected with his name & history, adds greatly both to the pleasure & the effect of a work. Who does not read Othello with greater delight from the knowledge, that it was written by the Author of Hamlet, &c &c – that it is SHAKESPERE's! Besides (a more subtle but not unimportant reason) Individuality is essential to the exercise of our moral *freedom*: and if the latter be a most sacred duty, it must likewise be our duty to secure for it it's [*sic*] best and most natural *sphere* of action. FAME is truly the synonyme of *Fatum* (quod optimi homines *fati* sunt) – the fate-like Sentence of the good & wise in a succession of generations, who inevitably decide the ultimate character of Works & actions, from the *permanence* of clear insight, and the *fidelity* of disinterested Love compared with the craving after Novelty, and with those malignant Passions which are under an equal necessity of changing & varying their Objects. (*CL* III.277–8)[74]

Coleridge emphasises the repetitive nature of 'reputation' (from *re-* and Latin *putare*, 'to reckon, consider') its doubling of what he sees as already an 'echo' or representation of the original, a reckoning.[75] He is then able to argue that embedded within the etymology of 'reputation' is a disabling repetition doubly displaced from the thing in itself or from truth – a representation of a representation or an echo of an echo. His etymological analysis leads Coleridge to a sense of reputation as a displaced supplement, a degraded 'echo' which has no necessary connection with the object itself. By intruding the etymologically irrelevant notion of echo into his analysis, Coleridge is able to give a further sense of displacement, and his notion of reputation seems to involve hearsay, the gossiping 'publicity' mentioned in the earlier letter. 'Fame', by contrast, and by means of a somewhat more credible etymological analysis, comes to be a 'fate-like Sentence' by means of its root in what is said – *fārī* – which it shares with 'fate'. As the *OED* comments ('fate', substantive), the primary sense of Latin *fārī* is 'a sentence or doom of the gods (= Greek θέσφατον)'. Since fame is also the product of repetition, however – since it is the result of the repeated judgement of a 'succession of generations' – it becomes clear that the important distinction to be made by means of Coleridge's discussion of etymology is not so much the act of repetition in itself as that which distinguishes an originary and true judgement, one which coincides with the object of contemplation, from one which is mediated, displaced or deferred. It is for this reason that fateful fame is pronounced by the 'good & wise', that fame is to be judged and re-judged by those who themselves have the attributes of that fame, those who are 'fated' in a certain way. In this sense, Coleridge is able to suggest that each aesthetic act of sentencing, each 'sentence of the gods', is itself originary. It is a circular argument, which suggests that the act of critical judgement is in some sense tautologous in that the judges themselves must share the qualities of the judged (in both cases 'permanence' and the quality of disinterestedness are fundamental.) The fatal judgement of the good and wise is, finally, a paradox: speaking (for) fame, theirs is at once an expression of individuality and the denial of individuality, both unique and universal, singular and iterative.

In a related complication of definition, Coleridge's account addresses the question of whether fame is historically contingent or universal. Since it is *fated*, the predetermined sentence of transcendent beings, constant over time, eternal, fame is not subject to change or historical circumstance. But since it must be repeatedly declared 'in a succession of generations', it is, by definition, historical, subject to time and generational contingency. The problem comes down to the status of those that judge and their judgement in a paradox which is never far away in the Romantic culture of posterity. In as much as the judgement of true aesthetic value is the same in all ages, unvarying and unchangeable, it transcends temporality and the contingency of historical circumstance. In effect, such judgements are not 'acts' at all but a permanent state of affairs. But in as much as the 'proof' of posterity can only be the repetition of such judgements in successive generations, those judgements are temporal, historical and contingent: individual *acts* of judgement. Embedded within the Coleridgean account of 'fame', then, is the irresolvable paradox of the Romantic culture of posterity, inherited from the neoclassical theory of the 'test of time'. If time is to validate the category of genius it can only do so by repeated acts of judgement by successive mortals, fallible and human as they are. It is the *collective* judgement over time which guarantees the eternal and universal work of art, the work which transcends both its own time and the temporality of historical reception, but that very permanence and atemporality can only be guaranteed in and through time. In attempting to elude historical contingency, the Romantic culture of posterity can only embrace it.

Coleridge's third and final substantial consideration of the relationship between fame and reputation comes in a letter to Edward Jenner of September 1811.[76] In this letter, Coleridge recalls phrases and arguments from the two earlier letters in order to develop his most coherent and carefully worked-through statement of the distinction. In particular, Coleridge develops his account of the temporality of fame:

O dear sir! how must every good and warm-hearted man detest the habit of mouth panegyric and the fashion of smooth falsehood, were it only for this, – that it throws a damp on the honestest feelings of our nature when we speak or write to or of those whom we do indeed revere and love, and know that it is our *duty* to do so; those concerning whom we feel as if they had lived centuries before our time in the certainty that centuries after us all good and wise men will so feel. This, this, dear sir, is true FAME as contradistinguished from the trifle, reputation; the latter explains itself, quod iste *putabat*, hic *putat*, one man's echo of another man's fancy or supposition. The former is in truth φήμη, i.e. ὃ φάσιν οἱ καλοκἀγαθοί, through all ages, the united suffrage of the Church of Philosophy, the fatum or verdict unappealable. So only can we live and act exempt from the tyranny of time: and thus live still, and still act upon us, Hippocrates, Plato, Milton. And hence, too, while reputation in any other sense than as moral character is a bubble, fame is a *worthy* object for the best men, and an awful duty to those, whom Providence has gifted with the power to acquire it. For it is, in truth, no other than benevolence extended beyond the grave, active virtue no longer cooped in between the cradle and the coffin. (*CL* vi.1026)

By translating '*putat*' as 'echo', Coleridge once again emphasises his sense of reputation's distance from truth, and by asserting that fame is 'the fatum or verdict unappealable' and as 'exempt' from the 'tyranny of time', he once again stresses the universal, ahistorical and *essential* nature of fame. But the passage again raises difficulties in its attempt to quarantine the one from the other, since it is also concerned to argue for the importance of contemporary recognition of genius. Coleridge's assertion that such people can be imagined as if they lived in the past, by phantasmal projection of this reputation into the future, suggests that contemporary judgements aspire to the grammar of the future perfect tense, to the assertion of what will have been.[77] But by allowing 'the habit of mouth panegyric and the fashion of smooth falsehood' as constitutive of the contemporary recognition of men of genius, Coleridge threatens to undermine the whole edifice of his carefully wrought distinction. The hygienic separation of our treatment of men of fame from those of reputation collapses as it becomes clear that it is our duty to praise men of genius in the present.

The figure of fame and the possibility of living on permeates Hazlitt's work. While the critical and theoretical contributions to the emerging and evolving culture of posterity by Coleridge, Wordsworth and others are important, Hazlitt is the single most determined and most comprehensive theorist of posterity from the period: as Leo Braudy comments, 'It would not be too far wrong to call [Hazlitt] the first great fame theorist of the modern age'.[78] Like Coleridge, Hazlitt distinguishes between two kinds of fame – the transient and permanent: in 'On the Living Poets' from his *Lectures on the English Poets* (1818), he opposes 'fame', which he associates with immortality, to 'popularity', which is temporary or ephemeral. But he goes further, to argue in the opening sentences of the essay that death is a necessary precondition of fame:

Genius is the heir of fame; but the hard condition on which the bright reversion must be earned is the loss of life. Fame is the recompense not of the living, but of the dead. The temple of fame stands upon the grave . . . Fame itself is immortal, but it is not begot till the breath of genius is extinguished. For fame is . . . the spirit of a man, surviving himself in the minds and thoughts of other men, undying and imperishable. (*Works* v.143–4)

'Death cancels everything but truth', Hazlitt declares in his essay on Byron in *The Spirit of the Age* (1825): it is 'a sort of natural canonization' which 'installs the poet in his immortality' by distinguishing 'the irritable, the personal, the gross' from 'the finer and more ethereal parts' (*Works* xi.78). Hazlitt even makes the ability to *wait* for posterity the mark of genius itself (by contrast with the man who is 'eager to forestall his own immortality, and mortgage it for a newspaper puff' (*Works* v.144).

The genius, Hazlitt argues, is both ignorant of his audience, and, finally, ignorant of himself, self-effacing. Indeed, the requirements of genius are constituted by a double bind of the desire to be 'great' in others' estimation and to be nothing in one's own: 'he who would be great in the eyes of others, must first learn to be nothing in his own' (*Works* v.145). In 'On Different Sorts of Fame', Hazlitt again distinguishes between a 'fleeting reputation' and 'our only certain appeal', posterity, where the latter is 'disinterested', 'abstracted', and 'ideal' (*Works* IV.94). For Hazlitt, however, it is the condition of the contemporary age to be more concerned with immediate applause than with waiting for future acclaim: 'The spirit of universal criticism has superseded the anticipation of posthumous fame, and instead of waiting for the award of distant ages, the poet or prose-writer receives his final doom from the next number of the *Edinburgh* or *Quarterly Review*' (*Works* IV.95). In Hazlitt's cultural theory, posterity turns into a stick with which to beat his contemporaries: love of the judgement of posterity, it seems, is a thing of the past.

The Spirit of the Age is a key text in the development of the Romantic theory of posterity, since in its influential establishment of the 'spirit' of the early nineteenth century through an account of its representative men, it repeatedly returns to the public status of those figures, as if the spirit of the age is defined in terms of public recognition and reputation.[79] The opening sentence of the book quotes the biblical adage that, as Hazlitt has it, 'A prophet has most honour out of his own country' (*Works* XI.5) to introduce Jeremy Bentham as a thinker who has 'legislated for future times' (*ibid.*). Hazlitt remarks that Bentham has been heard to say that he would like to be able to see the effect of his writings 'six or eight centuries' in the future,[80] but declares that the philosopher's name 'will hardly live so long' since he has not 'given any new or decided impulse to the human mind' (*Works* XI.7). The opening to the second essay also circles around the figure of posterity in its consideration of William Godwin. Hazlitt argues that although Godwin was 'in the very zenith of a sultry and unwholesome popularity' twenty-five years ago, now 'he has sunk below the horizon, and enjoys the serene twilight of a doubtful immortality' (*Works* XI.16). This, for Hazlitt, is the exemplary condition of reputation in the early nineteenth century: 'The Spirit of the Age', he decares, 'was never more fully shown than in its treatment of this writer'. Godwin has achieved 'a sort of posthumous fame' while still alive, since his later work is ignored and neglected while his earlier works, in particular *Political Justice* and *Caleb Williams*, continue to be read and to exert influence. Still living, Godwin is 'thought of now like any eminent writer a hundred-and-fifty years ago, or just as he will be a hundred-and-fifty years hence' (*ibid.*).

Each of the accounts which follow includes a consideration of the contemporary reputation of the writer inflected towards a consideration of their probable posthumous fame. Coleridge is considered by Hazlitt to have exchanged permanent recognition as a writer for the more immediate response of audience for his talk, 'he lays down his poem to make sure of an auditor, and mortgages the admiration of posterity for the stare of an idler' (p. 30); Edward Irving is announced as having an 'unprecedented' popularity as a preacher but is 'not "one of the fixed"' (p. 38); Horne Tooke 'has left behind him to posterity' his *The Diversions of Purley*, whose etymologies 'will stand the test' (p. 54); Scott is 'undoubtedly the most popular writer of the age' and his novels have 'secured the admiration of the public (with the probable reversion of immortality)' (p. 68) but have unfortunately been sacrificed to party politics and to Scott's 'littleness, pique, resentment, bigotry, and intolerance' (*ibid.*). Along with Scott, Byron is one of 'the greatest geniuses of the age' (p. 69); he is a writer whose 'contempt of his contemporaries makes him turn back to the lustrous past, or project himself forward to the dim future' (p. 74), he is 'always quarrelling with the world about his *modicum* of applause', 'equally averse to notice or neglect, enraged at censure and scorning praise' (p. 76), but at least Hazlitt allows that he has in addition to 'a seat in the House of Lords, a niche in the Temple of Fame' (p. 77). The essay on Wordsworth begins, once again, with an appraisal of the poet's likely posthumous reputation: although he finds it 'a toil to climb in this way the steep of Fame' (p. 86), Wordsworth is 'the most original poet now living', who, despite ridicule, has 'probably realized Milton's wish, – "and fit audience found, though few"' (p. 91). But in his layered and finely nuanced assessment, Hazlitt also suggests that Wordsworth has 'thought too much of contemporary critics and criticism; and less than he ought of the award of posterity' (p. 95). A similar ambivalence marks the essay on Malthus, who, while undoubtedly popular now, 'will in all probability go down to posterity with more or less of renown or obloquy' (pp. 103–4). Finally, in his comments on Campbell, Hazlitt ends with an ironising flourish on the trope of posterity. He is a poet who, having produced two poetic 'gifts to a world', is able to 'linger out the rest of his life in a dream of immortality' (p. 160):

Happy is it for those few and fortunate worshippers of the Muse . . . who already enjoy in their life-time a foretaste of their future fame, who see their names accompanying them, like a cloud of glory, from youth to age . . . and who know that they have built a shrine for the thoughts and feelings that were most dear to them, in the minds and memories of other men, till the language which they lisped in childhood is forgotten, or the human heart shall beat no more! (p. 161).

The Spirit of the Age, then, is a text which judges that spirit, the spirit of the early nineteenth century, in terms of its effect on a future age. Hazlitt's poetics in these essays are intimately bound up with a thinking of the culture of posterity. This influential summing-up of an age is conditioned by its sense of the future reputations of its subjects – indeed, those reputations may be said to be the primary topic of *The Spirit of the Age*.[81] And yet, throughout the book, Hazlitt's cultural theory of posthumous response is traversed by ambivalence and a destabilising ironisation of the trope. As he remarks in 'On Posthumous Fame, – Whether Shakespeare Was Influenced By a Love of It', 'to be the idol of posterity, when we are no more, [is] hardly a full compensation for being the object of the glance and scorn of fools while we are living': such 'universal fame' is 'a vague phantom of blind enthusiasm' (*Works* IV.24). While Hazlitt may be taken as the spokesman for the poetics of a generation, then, he also distances himself from one of that generation's shibboleths, the consolatory or redemptive function of posterity. Indeed, Hazlitt's ambivalence concerning the problem of posterity might be read as, in part, a response to the popularisation of posterity theory in the easy rhymes and cheap sentimentality of a prosodically awkward poem like Southey's most anthologised piece, 'My Days Among the Dead are Past' (1818). The last stanza of Southey's poem provides a summary of the degraded sense of posterity which Hazlitt may be said to be resisting and complicating:

> My hopes are with the Dead, anon
> My place with them will be,
> And I with them shall travel on
> Through all Futurity;
> Yet leaving here a name, I trust,
> That will not perish in the dust.[82]

CHAPTER 3

Engendering posterity

Touch not the harp to win the wreath:
Its tone is fame, its echo death!
The wreath may like the laurel grow,
Yet turn to cypress on the brow!

(Elizabeth Barrett, 'To a Poet's Child', 1833)

In 1979, Sandra Gilbert and Susan Gubar began their influential account of the nineteenth-century tradition of women's writing, *The Madwoman in the Attic*, by arguing that in the Western patriarchal tradition the author is equated with the father – a 'progenitor, a procreator, an aesthetic patriarch whose pen is an instrument of generative power like his penis'. For Gilbert and Gubar, the pen is like the penis in its ability not only to 'generate life' for the poet but also to 'create a posterity to which he lays claim'.[1] Gilbert and Gubar's striking formulation of the literary pen(is) has been elaborated, rather differently, by Marlon Ross in *The Contours of Masculine Desire* (1989). Ross comments on the male Romantic poet's ambivalence towards sexual reproduction and his desire for an alternative 'transcendence' achieved through *literary* reproduction: he can live on in his work rather than in his offspring. Ross argues that, by contrast, 'Feminine influence' is 'based on the necessity of shared space (the womb), on the necessary limits of beginning (birth) and ending (death) in time and space, on the need to share knowledge without a hierarchy of rewards (the training and nurturing of children without remuneration)'.[2] What Ross terms the 'myth of masculine self-possession' is, he suggests, linked to changes in 'socioeconomic status for the poet' and in 'his relationship to his audience and his society'.[3] By contrast, what Anne Mellor calls 'feminine Romanticism' is less concerned with phallic mastery, the sublime and individualistic assertion of identity, or the possibility of personal survival: for Mellor, 'feminine Romanticism' is 'based on a subjectivity constructed in relation to other subjectivities' and involves a self that is 'fluid, absorptive, responsive, with permeable ego boundaries'.[4] As Susan Wolfson puts it in her discussion of the identity of Dorothy Wordsworth: ' "I" enters her prose only as a voice of encouragement and assurance, in solidarity with a most generously construed "you" '.[5] The Romantic culture of posterity as an assertion or construction of (posthumous) identity is, according to such reasoning, a specifically masculine phenomenon.

In this chapter, I seek to explore the implications of such claims, in particular by thinking about ways in which the 'female' or 'feminine' discourses of the Romantic period are constructed as counter-discourses to the culture of posterity. According to such reasoning, the particular logic of Romantic posterity that I am attempting to trace in this book – the contemporary neglect and posthumous fame of the poet performatively figured in writing such that an author's posterity is both anticipated in and produced by his writing – would be understood to be characteristic of and fundamental to the careers and self-representations of certain male writers, but dissonant or transgressive in the careers of female writers of the period. An examination of women's poetry in the period should then disclose certain alternative trajectories to Romantic posterity. A preliminary list of such alternatives includes the following permutations: contemporary fame and posthumous neglect; contemporary *and* posthumous neglect; the poet's concern with contemporary fame but unconcern towards her posthumous reputation; the poet's 'domestic' neglect of fame both present and future; the poet's active *rejection* of fame both contemporary *and* posthumous and her expression of a desire for oblivion; the poet's articulation of a 'domestic' and necessarily temporary afterlife as an effect of personalised mourning; and finally the poet's expression of a desire for posthumous renown which is at odds with an actual posterity which 'remembers' her only as neglected. I want to suggest that women writers of the period did indeed adopt and theorise about a number of these alternative positions as counter-discourses to the hegemony of (male) poetics and as self-defensive strategies of self-effacement. But rather than *simply* a female resistance to the male ideology of posterity, I also want to suggest that this counter-discourse infects and affects the dominant mode. Masculinity, that is to say, is always already determined by its other, the other it attempts to exclude, by a resistant 'femininity', by the ephemeral, the 'domestic', the familial.[6]

The causes of the gendering of the Romantic culture of posterity are complex, but Anne Mellor's influential – if somewhat simplified and, in its valorisation of the feminine, idealistic – account might give us some sense of the issues involved in the gendering of the so-called 'Romantic ideology'. Mellor argues that women writers of the period had little interest in those concerns which are typically taken to signify this ideological formation – they are, she suggests, little concerned with 'the capacities of the creative imagination, with the limitations of language, with the possibility of transcendence or "unity of being", with the development of an autonomous self, with political (as opposed to social) revolution, with the role of the creative writer as political leader or religious savior'. By contrast, Mellor argues, women writers were concerned with community and with respect for difference, basing their 'moral systems' on an 'ethic of care' (in Carol Gilligan's formulation) which valorises both family and community as well as 'their attendant practical responsibilities'. Finally, women writers 'grounded their notion of community on a cooperative rather than possessive interaction with a Nature troped as a female friend or sister, and promoted a politics of gradual rather than violent social change, a social change that extends the values of domesticity into the public realm'.[7] Mellor's binary model of gender difference in Romantic poetics, then, contrasts the abstract with the material, the sublime with the beautiful, identity with community, self-assertion with cooperation. The Romantic culture of posterity – in its fascination with transcendence and the nature of personal identity, with competition and the heroic – is, according to this model, masculine and patriarchal.

While Mellor's summary is, as she admits, 'introductory and necessarily crude', it might nevertheless suggest the extent to which women's writing can be understood to constitute a counter-discourse to the Romantic culture of posterity. This is perhaps most clear in the ideological construction of audiences: crudely put, audiences can be conceived in terms of the abstraction and anonymity of 'masculine' desire on the one hand and the personification and domestication of 'feminine' desire on the other. 'Domesticity', that stereotypically 'feminine' arena, includes, in this sense, the reception of a poet's work.[8] The argument that Romanticism may be defined in terms of a certain 'anxiety of reception' or 'anxiety of audience' is, according to this thinking, itself determined by a prior opposition of masculinity to femininity, whereby masculine identity is threatened by the illicit incursions of readers by contrast with a certain configuration of femininity which is reinforced by the scene of readerly interaction: as Sonia Hofkosh argues, 'the male writer . . . dreads, as he desires, being read by others – a reading that rewrites him and thus compromises his powers of self-creation'.[9] In this respect, the Romantic culture of posterity involves a specifically male resistance to readers, to being read.

This is not to deny that women's writing of the period is concerned with questions of fame and posterity, with audience and reputation. In her Preface to *Sappho and Phaon* (1796), for example, Mary Robinson, 'the English Sappho', makes a forceful case for the connection between genius and neglect: 'there has not been, during a long series of years, the smallest mark of public distinction bestowed on literary talents. Many individuals, whose works are held in the highest estimation, now that their ashes sleep in the sepulchre, were, when living, suffered to languish, and even to perish, in obscure poverty: as if it were the peculiar fate of genius, to be neglected while existing, and only honoured when the consciousness of inspiration is vanished for ever'.[10] And yet, as the Preface continues it becomes clear that the neglected geniuses to whom Robinson alludes are, primarily, men. This is made clear in her conclusion, where she includes women specifically as a *supplement* to the male poets she has been discussing: 'I cannot conclude these opinions without paying tribute to the talents of my illustrious country-women; who, unpatronized by courts, and unprotected by the powerful, persevere in the paths of literature, and ennoble themselves by the unperishable lustre of MENTAL PRE-EMINENCE!' [11] A similar gendering of genius and neglect is apparent in Isabella Lickbarrow's poem 'On the Difficulty of Attaining Poetical Excellence' (1814), which figures the 'few who bear the poet's name' and who 'Shall share the lasting wreath of fame', who 'live in the historic page, / Beyond the limits of an age' as exclusively male: 'Still to complete the poet's name, / To give *him* never-ending fame: / And to immortalize *his* song . . . '[12]

In fact, however, such unquestioning expressions of the Romantic culture of posterity, gendered or not, are relatively rare in women's writing. More commonly, women writers express a deep scepticism towards the redemption supposedly offered by literary posterity. If, as we have seen, Romantic posterity presupposes a sense of the redemption of a textual afterlife, there is evidence to suggest that such a compensatory schema is less easily acceptable to women writers, or less easily accommodated within the poetics of the feminine. An alternative tradition involves a concerted privileging of the moment, of the momentary, of ephemeral and transient experience. Anna Laetitia Barbauld, for example, famously reverses the ideal or transcendent function of poetry in 'Washing Day' (1797), where classical inspiration is transformed into a domestic muse. In so doing she identifies the discourse of ephemerality with that of women:

> The Muses are turned gossips; they have lost
> The buskined step, and clear high-sounding phrase,
> Language of gods. Come, then, domestic Muse,
> In slip-shod measure loosely prattling on
> Of farm or orchard, pleasant curds and cream,
> Or drowning flies, or shoe lost in the mire
> By little whimpering boy, with rueful face;
> Come, Muse, and sing the dreaded *Washing-Day*.[13]

The loose prattling of the lines involves not only the slip-shod metre or measure of the blank-verse form, but also the loose listing of incident and object, the bathetic belittling and the literalising force of the poetic topos with its incidental and unmotivated enumeration. Responding to Pope's 'slip-shod sibyls', Barbauld maps out a site and a style for women's poetry, one which articulates the 'domestic' sphere and one which is articulated in 'domestic' discourse, in the gender-coded language of gossip. 'The poetic genres chosen by Romantic women poets thus function to create and sustain community', comments Anne Mellor.[14] But such sustenance of community, and its topos of the ordinary, the everyday, has, according to Stuart Curran, been effaced by the Romantic ideology: 'Quotidian values . . . have been largely submerged from our comprehension of Romanticism, with its continual urge for visionary flight'.[15] As such, this concern with the domestic challenges the importance and influence of, as well as the need for, the redemptive force of the future.[16] Thus Barbauld's poem ends after eighty-odd lines, with a metaphor for its own insignificance in the soap-bubbles of washing day:

> Earth, air, and sky, and ocean, hath its bubbles,
> And verse is one of them – this most of all.

The assertion of the ephemerality of women's poetry is, in fact, repeated endlessly by, especially, women poets of this and the next generation. It is almost as if the popularity and influence of women's poetry needs to be defended by a reassurance of its ephemerality.[17] Since inclusion in the canon involves, by general agreement, the quality of permanently pleasing readers, assertions of and interest in the ephemeral may be read as coded expressions of women writers' self-exclusion from that canon. One way to mark such an exclusion is to focus on and valorise the ephemeral. Canonical poems of epiphany such as Keats's 'Ode on a

Grecian Urn' attempt to express the moment as eternally poised, as evermore about to be, while canonical memory-poems such as Wordsworth's 'Tintern Abbey' attempt to reconstruct or memorialise the lost moment of youthful forgetfulness. These texts contrast with the work of Barbauld and poems by women such as Sydney Owenson – whose 'Joy' (1807) argues against Edward Young's assertion that 'Joy's a fix'd state – a tenure, not a start' by listing the ephemera of emotion, the 'bright, tho' transient *heaven* of despair', '*Delight's* wild throb', and joy, 'transient' and 'fleeting' in its 'poignant pleasure' – or Mary Russell Mitford – whose 'Song' (1811) elaborates the opening declaration that 'The fairest things, are those which live, / And vanish ere their name we give'.[18] Such poems articulate and celebrate the momentary, the ephemeral, for its own sake, precisely for its transience. If the Romantic culture of posterity emphasises the importance of the poet's *transcendence* of his own time – to the extent, finally, of defining poetry by this concern – the fascination with the quotidian and ephemeral and its association with a feminine poetics would figure the idea of a woman poet as a contradiction in terms, or, as Marlon Ross puts it, a non sequitur.[19]

This gender-coding of transience is, in fact, addressed by contemporary literary criticism and theory. In his Lecture 'On the Living Poets', for example, Hazlitt codes the transient as female and the permanent as male or as ungendered.[20] As we have seen, Hazlitt opens his lecture with an extended exploration of the theme of posterity. He then provides a summary of the 'living poets' in this context. Having briefly mentioned the ephemeral women poets Barbauld, Hannah More and Joanna Baillie, he turns to Samuel Rogers, whom he describes as 'a very lady-like poet' (*Works* v.148). In enumerating Rogers's qualities as a writer, Hazlitt is therefore also describing the qualities, as he sees it, of the female writer. Indeed, in the following passage, the vocabulary insistently enforces the sense of Rogers's almost physiological *femininity* and links it to his 'feebleness' as a writer:

He is an elegant, but feeble writer. He wraps up obvious thoughts in a glittering cover of fine words; is full of enigmas with no meaning to them; is studiously inverted, and scrupulously far-fetched; and his verses are poetry, chiefly because no particular line, or syllable of them reads like prose . . . [his poetry is] a tortuous, tottering, wriggling, fidgetty translation of every thing from the vulgar tongue, into all the tantalizing, teasing, tripping, lisping *mimminee-pimminee* of the highest brilliancy and fashion of poetical diction . . . The whole is refined, and frittered away into an appearance of the most evanescent brilliancy and tremulous imbecility' (*Works* v.148).[21]

The feminine character of Rogers's poetry, then, is a product of its triviality and ephemerality, its vulgarity and 'brilliancy', its improbable,
enigmatic and 'inverted' nature, and its embodiment of instability.
Campbell, Hazlitt's next poet, suffers from similar effects of timidity and
triviality: he writes, Hazlitt assures us, 'according to established eti-
quette' and 'offers the muse no violence', he is too circumspect, thinking too much of what critics will say. Being 'careful of his own
reputation' he is 'economical of the pleasures of his readers' (pp.
149–50). Once again, Hazlitt associates such characteristics with femininity and, in particular, with sexual danger and social scandal: 'The
poet, as well as the woman, that deliberates, is undone' (p. 149). Thomas
Moore is also characterised by ephemerality and femininity: 'He wants
intensity, strength, and grandeur. His mind does not brood over the
great and permanent' (p. 151). Since 'intensity, strength and grandeur'
have already been coded as male in Hazlitt's lecture – and in the culture
of the early nineteenth century more generally – Hazlitt is clearly
opposing ephemerality to permanence along gender lines.[22] Similarly,
he characterises Moore's poetry by a series of adjectives which suggest
effeminacy, impermanence and insincerity: 'detached, desultory, and
physical'; 'gorgeous colours' which 'brighten and fade like the
rainbow's'; a 'sweetness' which 'evaporates'; a 'gay laughing style' concerned only with 'immediate pleasures'; a 'sentimental romantic vein';
an 'affectation' and 'sickliness of pretension'; 'flowery tenderness',
'mawkish sensibility', 'prettinesses', 'glittering hardness'. Such poetry is,
finally, 'effeminate and voluptuous' (pp. 151–2). In this context, Hazlitt's
description of Moore's poetry as 'heedless, gay, and prodigal of his poetical wealth' (p. 151) might involve an implicit comparison with a woman
careless of her sexuality. Even Scott, according to Hazlitt 'to the great
poet, what an excellent mimic is to a great actor', is, like Rogers and
Moore, 'effeminate' (p. 155) and, predictably by now, Hazlitt declares
that his poetry will not survive: 'There is no determinate impression left
on the mind by reading his poetry. It has no results' (p. 155). Only Byron,
the greatest of the minor living poets, is coded as male. The adjectives
used to describe him are stereotypically 'masculine' throughout: 'vigour'
and 'force', 'depth of passion', 'force and impetuosity', 'violent and
sullen, fierce and gloomy', and so on (p. 153).[23] But in spite of this masculinity, Hazlitt refrains from arguing for Byron's permanent place in
the canon. Indeed, rather than simply opposing male permanence to
female ephemerality, Hazlitt's lecture concludes in a *disgendering* of the
canon. The lecture ends in what must be one of the most extraordinary,

eloquent and acute contemporary accounts of Wordsworth and
Coleridge together with a brief account of Southey. Placing the 'Lake
Poets' in the context of the French Revolution, Hazlitt makes it clear
that Wordsworth and Coleridge are the nearest that the present age
comes to poets of genius. In so doing, and by contrast with each of the
earlier accounts, Hazlitt censors his prose of the rhetoric of gender.
While all the other poets have been characterised by their masculinity
or emasculation, Wordsworth and Coleridge are described in terms
which escape any specific gender alignment. For Hazlitt, in other words,
the genius is the poet who is not a woman (since qualities of femininity
in poetry are necessarily ephemeral) and, at the same time, beyond
gender.[24]

But as we have seen, it is not only male writers who define female poets
or the feminine in poetry in terms of its impermanence. An important
aspect of the resistance of women poets to the Romantic culture of posterity is their resistance to the prospect of fame. Writers such as Anna
Barbauld, Joanna Baillie, Mary Robinson, Helen Maria Williams,
Letitia Landon and Felicia Hemans are all wary of such a consequence
of writing and publishing. While the (male) Romantics often express a
distinctly ambivalent sense of the value of fame and reputation, an
ambivalence which nevertheless allows for the possibility of, especially,
posthumous fame, it is a convention of feminine poetics of the period
that fame is unsought and unwelcome: 'The thirst of Fame my bosom
robbed of rest' declares Hannah More in an early poem, 'The Search
After Happiness' (1773), 'And envious Spleen became its constant
guest'.[25] More positively, Matilda Betham, author of the *Biographical
Dictionary of the Celebrated Women of Every Age and Country* (1804), declares,
in a poem not published until the twentieth century, 'We wish not the
mechanic arts to scan' (1798), that 'The flame burns strongest that is most
concealed', and that '*We* have the substance *they* [men] keep the name'.[26]
A somewhat more complex sense of the value of fame, and of the relationship between fame and reading/writing poetry, is expresssed in
Helen Maria Williams's 'An Address to Poetry' (1790). Williams's poem
opens with a stanza which details the speaker's objections to ambition,
and a second which seeks to express an alternative poetics:

> While envious crowds the summit view,
> Where danger with ambition strays;
> Or far, with anxious step, pursue
> Pale avarice, through his winding ways;
> The selfish passions in their train,

Whose force the social ties unbind,
   And chill the love of human kind,
And make fond Nature's best emotions vain;

   Oh Poesy! Oh nymph most dear,
To whom I early gave my heart,
   Whose voice is sweetest to my ear
Of aught in nature or in art;
   Thou, who canst all my breast control,
Come, and thy harp of various cadence bring,
   And long with melting music swell the string
That suits the present temper of my soul.[27]

While the first stanza presents the speaker's reasons for rejecting 'ambition' – including, in particular, its 'unbinding' of 'social ties', and its
'selfish passions' which 'chill the love of human kind' – the second suggests that poetry is in fact antithetical to such ambition. Poetry, for
Williams, appears to constitute a resistance to, rather than an expression
of, ambition. But this somewhat paradoxical position is clarified as the
poem continues, and it becomes clear that this paean to poetry concerns
reading poetry rather than *writing* it. The speaker meditates on the effect
of reading Shakespeare, Milton, Homer, Thomson, Pope, Macpherson,
Gray, of nursery-rhymes, ballads and so on: in other words, Williams's
poem on poetry paradoxically figures the poet as a reader rather than a
writer. The poet is innoculated against ambition by reading and by an
effacement of the woman as poet in the face of tradition. The poem ges-
tures towards its own self-dissolution in an ending which considers the
relation between poetry, fame and the eternity of art, but which distances the present poet from such matters:

   Can fame on painting's aid rely,
Or lean on sculpture's trophyed bust?
   The faithless colours bloom to die,
The crumbling pillar mocks its trust;
   But thou, oh muse, immortal maid!
Canst paint the godlike deeds that praise inspire,
   Or worth that lives but in the mind's desire,
In tints that only shall with Nature fade!

   Oh tell me, partial nymph! What rite,
What incense sweet, what homage true,
   Draws from thy fount of purest light
The flame it lends a chosen few?
   Alas! These lips can never frame
The mystic vow that moves thy breast;

> Yet by thy joys my life is blest,
> And my fond soul shall consecrate thy name.[28]

The poet paradoxically and explicitly excludes herself from poetry, from the speech-event by which she herself will be 'consecrated'. Williams, or the alter ego which speaks the 'I' of this poem, inserts herself into the exclusively male tradition of poetry only as a reader, excluding herself as writer. Thus while poetry itself is figured as female, as 'nymph most dear' and 'partial nymph', the poets in the canon are exclusively male.

Similar reservations concerning the female writer's identification with the role of poet are expressed in Anna Maria Porter's 'Address to Poesy' (1797). Once again, the poem opens with an apostrophic appeal to poetry figured as female:

> Hail, heavenly maid! thou source of thousand joys!
> Say, can a humble suppliant's untaught voice
> Be heard by thee, where throned in vernal bowers
> Of living laurel, near Pierian fount,
> O'er the immortal chords that strain thy lyre,
> Thy fingers sweep, and a whole world resounds
> To the vibrations of thy tuneful song?[29]

The poem opens by contrasting the assured eternity of poetry and its universal influence with the doubtful qualifications of the speaker, her 'untaught voice'. The speaker's request, her 'Ambitious wish', is that she can make poems 'resembling thine', which is to say resembling those of Orpheus and of Petrarch. But the poem enacts its own rejection by 'poesy' as 'away she turns her frowning face, / And scatters to the wind my useless prayers'. The speaker is not one of the 'happy few', is excluded from the realm of an anthropomorphised Fame and from the imaginary labyrinth of 'Young Love'. The poem is typical, then, of a certain mode of women's writing of the 1790s in which the poet preserves her femininity by turning away from the role of poet and from the possibility of fame. And such a decanonisation of women poets is perhaps not surprising given the contemporary marginalisation of women writers. The multi-volume collections of British poets which built on Samuel Johnson's collection and Thomas Warton's literary history from the 1770s and 1780s, for example, featured exclusively male poets. As Roger Lonsdale points out, no women poets were included in the anthologies of either Robert Anderson (1792–95) or Alexander Chalmers (1810), and even Alexander Dyce's 1825 collection *Specimens of the British Poetesses* managed to trivialise the poetry of women, by asserting that 'the grander inspirations of the Muse have not been often breathed into the softer frame'.[30]

It is the second generation of women poets of the Romantic period, those who came to prominence in the 1820s and 1830s, and in particular Felicia Hemans, Maria Jane Jewsbury and Letitia Landon, who articulate most vividly a certain convention of female irony or resistance towards the possibility of posterity as a redemptive supplement to life. Hemans, one of the most famous women writers of the nineteenth century, repeatedly returned to the subject of fame and repeatedly contrasted it with the consolation of domesticity. Her epigraph to 'Joan of Arc, In Rheims' from *Records of Woman* (1828), puts her case concisely:

> Thou hast a charmed cup, O Fame!
>   A draught that mantles high,
> And seems to lift this earth-born frame
>   Above mortality:
> Away: to me – a woman – bring
> Sweet waters from affection's spring.[31]

The illusion of fame's recompense is not available to the woman poet, for whom 'affection' is the true source of comfort. As Letitia Landon commented in an article published just after Hemans's death, 'On the Character of Mrs. Hemans's Writing', 'Fame, which the Greeks idealized so nobly, is but the fulfilment of that desire for sympathy which can never be brought home to the individual':[32] fame, that is to say, its desire and its fulfillment, is constituted in and by lack. And Landon's article ends on a similar note, identifying that lack specifically with gender: 'Ah! Fame to a woman is indeed but a royal mourning in purple for happiness'.[33]

Hemans's 'Properzia Rossi', also from *Records of Woman*, involves a complex engagement with the Romantic culture of posterity but deploys against it its more general other, the suicide note. In its obsession with the young Werther and Chatterton, amongst others, Romanticism and, in particular, the Romantic culture of posterity, develops a complex relationship with suicide and suicide notes. Whereas Romantic posterity asserts the future recognition of the poet by an impersonal and abstract audience, and asserts the possibility of the poet living on in the minds of readers after his death, the suicide note has a more immediate, more personalised and particularised – more 'domestic' – vision of its posthumous effect. The suicide note – and, in particular, the lover's suicide note – is intended to produce a particular effect in a specified person or group

of people.[34] And while the Romantic culture of posterity might include
a premonition of the survivors' regret for their neglect of the genius as
an incidental aspect of its effect, for the suicide or the author of the
suicide note the production of regret for the neglect, rejection or ill-
treatment of the suicide, is often central to the act of inscription. Indeed,
it could be said that the note itself is often simply an articulation or expli-
cation of the act of suicide and, as such, strictly unnecessary since the
act itself would ideally constitute the most eloquent expression of the
text's 'message' to posterity. In other words, it might be said that just as
a note declaring the intention to commit suicide might act as a substitute for the act of suicide itself, suicide may be said to substitute or supplement the suicide-note – an acting out or bodily inscription of the
declaration of intent. Apart from Chatterton's note, the nearest that the
canonical (male) Romantic poets come to writing suicide notes may be
Keats's 'This living hand' (c.1819) – a text which doesn't require the act
of suicide in order to have effect.[35] Indeed, Keats's poem might be
thought of as a deconstruction of the suicide note since it both performatively puts into play the death of the writer ('see, here it is . . . '), and
denies the death on which such an effect is based ('This living hand, now
warm and capable / Of earnest grasping, *would* . . . ') – or, more concisely, the poem both asserts and denies the writer's death in the phrase
'see, here it is'. At the same time, and since the poem does not declare
the suicide of the poet, 'This living hand' allows for a more generalised
reading of itself as a text which engages with the 'suicidal' nature of
every act of inscription. Torn from every context, the poem-fragment
evokes the decontextualised or 'fragmentary' possibilities of writing in
general. The poem can be read both ways, and in ways that conventional
suicide notes resist by their constitutive embedding within specific personal and historical contexts. In this respect, Keats's poem articulates
more generally the condition of the Romantic culture of posterity and,
in turn, Romanticism's construction of literature itself as both embedded within a certain cultural discourse or formation, and as escaping or
evading that context. The suicide note, by this definition, is outside the
discourse of literature: in this case, it might be argued that women poets'
fascination with the poetry of suicide notes constitutes a resistance to the
Romantic construction of 'literature' as such.

    Hemans's poem is a monologue or 'monodrama' in which Properzia
Rossi, a 'celebrated female sculptor of Bologna' speaks of her last work,
a bas-relief of Ariadne. Ariadne, the very figure of the forsaken lover,
represents the sculptress herself – 'thou shalt wear / Thy form, my lin-

eaments . . . Thou art the mould / Wherein I pour the fervent thoughts, th' untold, / The self-consuming'.[36] Rossi's interest in making this figure of Ariadne, then, is in its ability to speak to her indifferent lover, after her death, in the hope that the image will 'pierce' his 'bosom'. But while she recognises that her image of Ariadne will be famous, it is for her a 'worthless fame' since 'in *his* bosom [it] wins not for my name / Th' abiding place it asked!' (p. 52). Indeed, as the ending to the poem makes clear, for the speaker the sole value of fame inheres in the possibility that it will allow her to be remembered by her lover:

> Yet I leave my name –
> As a deep thrill may linger on the lyre
> When its full chords are hush'd – awhile to live,
> And one day haply in thy heart revive
> Sad thoughts of me: – I leave it, with a sound,
> A spell o'er memory, mournfully profound,
> I leave it, on my country's air to dwell, –
> Say proudly yet – *"Twas hers who loves me well!'* (p. 54)

Living on is figured as itself transient ('awhile to live'), particularised (it is the neglectful lover who will remember), and an effect of mourning rather than art. Indeed, the poem is exemplary in its transformation of *Romantic* posterity into *romantic* or erotic posterity, in its deflection of the concern for a textual afterlife onto a concern for the affections and 'living' memory. It both appeals to and distances itself from the ideology of Romantic posterity. The poem is complicated, however, by two prefatory texts: a prose explanation of Rossi's identity which frames the poem in historical terms, and an epigraphic verse of eleven lines, apparently written by Hemans herself, which has an ambiguous relation to the main body of the poem. Apparently spoken by the same character, and apparently summarising the themes of the poem, the epigraph is also distanced both typographically and narratively from that poem:

> – Tell me no more, no more
> Of my soul's lofty gifts! Are they not vain
> To quench its haunting thirst for happiness?
> Have I not loved, and striven, and fail'd to bind
> One true heart unto me, whereon my own
> Might find a resting-place, a home for all
> Its burden of affections? I depart,
> Unknown, tho' Fame goes with me; I must leave
> The earth unknown. Yet it may be that death
> Shall give my name a power to win such tears
> As would have made life precious. (p. 49)

The lines are exemplary in their resistance to the significance and compensatory effects of fame on life.[37] At the same time, they express a deep
ambivalence towards the very condition of the reputation of the speaker
herself: 'I depart / Unknown, tho' Fame goes with me; I must leave /
The earth unknown'. The speaker appears to want it both ways, wants
to be both known and unknown. For while the force of 'leave / The
earth unknown' involves the world not knowing about the death itself, it
can also be read as indicating that the speaker is more generally
unknown, despite her fame. Similarly, 'tho' Fame goes with me' can be
read in terms of the ending of fame in death, or as a declaration of posthumous fame, depending on our sense of 'goes'. The lines, that is to say,
appear to question the very basis of what it means to be 'known', radically disturbing the faith of the Romantic culture of posterity in the
redemptive effects of reputation. If these lines cannot be disentangled
from or purged of their contradictions and ambiguities, it is precisely
such difficulties in thinking the future which are significant. While the
final three lines refer to the common trope of the suicide note and
Romantic posterity – the crucial possibility that the death of the writer
will, in itself, produce an effect on the survivors – such consequences are
specifically domesticated as personal responses to a death.[38] Just as
Letitia Landon's pathetic late poem 'Night at Sea' (1839) repeatedly asks
'My friends, my absent friends! / Do you think of me, as I think of you?',
demanding a personalised, reciprocal and contemporary remembrance,
so the suicide note demands only a temporary, and personalised memorialisation.[39] It is at this point that Hemans most clearly departs from the
Romantic culture of posterity: the tears that the speaker's death may
bring '*would have* made life precious', whereas for this 'culture' it is such
a *possibility* that gives value to life. Posthumous recognition does not need
to actually be experienced by the writer for that writer to gain the compensatory benefits of such recognition.

In 'The Image in Lava' (1828), Hemans once again domesticates posterity and opposes feminine and specifically maternal love to monumentalisation. In a footnote, Hemans explains that the title refers to the
impression of the bodies of a woman and a baby found in an archeolog-
ical site at Herculaneum. Hemans meditates on the way that the image
has outlived empires:

> Temple and tower have moulder'd
> Empires from earth have pass'd, –
> And woman's heart hath left a trace
> Those glories to outlast!

The poem amounts to little more than a repeated declaration of the survival of this 'trace' of love far beyond the end of empire, monument and renown:

> Oh! I could pass all relics
>   Left by the pomps of old
> To gaze on this rude monument,
>   Cast in affection's mould.

> Love, human love! What art thou?
>   Thy print upon the dust
> Outlives the cities of renown
>   Wherein the mighty trust! [40]

This specifically gendered figuration of posterity, posterity as a function of (female, maternal) love rather than a physical and public monument, opposes an emotion only contingently, accidentally preserved to those artifacts specifically designed to last. The ability to remain, in this case, has nothing to do with intent or purpose, nor with power, fame, wealth or influence. As such, the poem constitutes a remarkable contrast with or complement to Shelley's 'Ozymandias', with its satirical commentary on the expression of male power as self-monumentalisation.

In 'The Last Song of Sappho' (1831), Hemans returns to the question of fame in the context of suicide, and again expresses scepticism towards its compensatory value.[41] The poem is prefaced by an epigraph borrowed from Byron's 'Prophecy of Dante' which declares that 'Poesy' creates 'an external life beyond our fate' but figures the poet as a tortured Prometheus – the 'pleasure given' with the gift of poetry 'repaid with pain'. Hemans's poem, taking its cue from this sense of the poet's torment, concentrates on the desolate isolation of the poet who has 'sought / In vain one echoing sigh, / One answer to consuming thought / In human breasts', and whose heart has 'poured on desert sands its wealth away'. While articulations of poetic isolation may be entirely conventional in the Romantic culture of posterity, what the speaker resists is the sense that such neglect will be compensated for by the knowledge of 'posterity's award': rather than imagining posthumous recognition, the speaker yearns, insistently, for precisely the opposite, for an ever greater degree of anonymity, obscurity, and isolation in death and after death:

> Give to that crown, that burning crown,
>   Place in thy darkest hold!
> Bury my anguish, my renown,
> With hidden wrecks, lost gems, and wasted gold!

Thou sea-bird, on the billow's crest,
Thou hast thy love, thy home!
They wait thee in the quiet nest –
And I – unsought, unwatched for – I too come![42]

The particularity of this figuration of posterity – what we might call its feminisation – is its expression of the desire for obscurity and anonymity, its paradoxical articulation of a desire not to be articulated, and its identification of 'anguish' with 'renown'. It is as if Hemans is constructing a suicide note not to be read, a suicide note which resists reading. What is being imagined here, what is being expressed in the discourse of sentimentalism, is an assertion of self-effacement, but one which gains its prominence, its renown or name, from desire for oblivion. (This, indeed, is the oxymoronic heart of the discourse of sensibility: the *public* assertion of self-*effacement*, a dissolution of the ego in sympathetic identification.) Hemans is expressing the feminisation of the Romantic culture of posterity: the desire to survive as identity-less, effaced, invisible, forgotten, obliterated, anonymous – in other words, a desire for survival which amounts to non-survival. The figure for this survival – survival as non-survival – is, most commonly, annihilation, disappearance, burial or drowning, obscurity topoi evident in such poems as Frances Burney's 'To [Charles Burney]' (1778), Mary Robinson's 'Ode: To the Snow-Drop' (1797), Jane Taylor's 'The Violet' and 'The Poppy' (both 1804), Mary Tighe's *Psyche* (1805),[43] Isabella Lickbarrow's 'To an Opening Rose' (1814) and Dorothy Wordsworth's 'Floating Island' (written 1820s; published 1840). In all of these poems, the poet fantasises her own obscurity after death in the burial, drowning, obliteration or dissemination of the body, allowing only for an impermanent trace of remains. As Susan Wolfson remarks of Dorothy Wordsworth's poems, and in particular of 'Floating Island', their 'potency' has to do with 'their release from the burdens of self-reference that oppress the speakers of William [Wordsworth]'s poems; though "lost" to her, they abide to "remain" as potential elements of "other ground"'.[44] Whereas the Romantic culture of posterity involves both dissemination and self-constitution in a posthumous life, for Dorothy and for other women poets, the end of life – its goal and its conclusion – is, simply, the dissemination of an anonymous and finally obliterated self. Nowhere is such a desire more nakedly and more evocatively expressed than in an often quoted letter by Mary Shelley of April 1829 in response to Edward Trelawny's proposal to publish a life of Percy Shelley:

There is nothing I shrink from more fearfully than publicity . . . Could you write my husband's life, without naming me it were something – but even then I should be terrified at the rouzing the slumbering voice of the public – each critique, each mention of your work, might drag me forward . . . now that I am alone in the world, [I] have but the desire to wrap night and the obscurity of insignificance around me. This is weakness – but I cannot help it – to be in print – the subject of *men*'s observations – of the bitter hard world's commentaries, to be attacked or defended! – this ill becomes one who knows how little she possesses worthy to attract attention – and whose chief merit – if it be one – is a love of that privacy, which no woman can emerge from without regret . . . I only seek to be forgotten.[45]

Mary Shelley's vulnerability seeks the shelter of anonymity and obscurity: there is danger in '*men*'s observation', and she fears the prospect that, like lions, the public will rise 'after slumber / In unvanquishable number' (*SPP* 310): Percy's prospect of a liberatory social uprising in 'The Mask of Anarchy' becomes Mary Shelley's terror at 'rouzing the slumbering voice of the public'. What Mary Shelley's letter demonstrates most forcefully is the connection between the desire not to be publicly attacked in the press and the desire to be forgotten. It is ironic, perhaps, but no less pertinent, that Hemans's appeals to, and expressions of desire for, obscurity are from a woman who, as Norma Clarke points out, rivalled Byron 'in popularity in her own time and throughout the nineteenth century' and who 'arguably formed the poetic taste of the Victorian period'.[46]

It is in the poetry of Letitia Landon that the feminine counter-discourse of the Romantic culture of posterity is most fully explored. In her well-known elegy 'Felicia Hemans', Landon recognises what she sees as Hemans's impulse to write 'immortal verse', but she also questions its redemptive power: 'Was not this purchased all too dearly? – never / Can fame atone for all that fame hath cost'. Indeed, as the poem goes on to argue, it is the very condition of both women and poets to suffer: 'The fable of Prometheus and the vulture / Reveals the poet's and the woman's heart'. It is unclear here whether poets and women are mutually exclusive categories, but what *is* clear is that fame is unable to atone for a world where it is the condition of both women and poets to be 'Unkindly . . . judged – unkindly treated – / By careless tongue and by ungenerous words'. Hemans's death is figured in this poem as an end to such torments: the poem comes to *bury* the poetess, not to celebrate her posthumous life:

> Fame's troubled hour has cleared, and now replying,
>   A thousand hearts their music ask of thine.
> Sleep with a light, the lovely and undying
>   Around thy grave – a grave which is a shrine.[47]

These, the final lines of the poem, suggest no possibility of posthumous life – it is the light which is 'undying', and what remains is the grave – and give no sense of the compensatory effects of such a life. Rather, for the female poet, death is redemptive only in its finality, in its end. By contrast, in her poem celebrating Wordsworth's poetic powers, 'On Wordsworth's Cottage, Near Grasmere Lake' (1839), Landon expresses no doubts about the male poet's monumentalisation. Ironically, perhaps, even before his death, Landon makes Wordsworth a monument in lines which echo Ben Jonson's description of the dead Shakespeare as 'a monument without a tomb':

> Eternal as the hills thy name,
>   Eternal as thy strain;
> So long as ministers of fame
>   Shall love and hope remain.
> The crowded city in its streets,
>   The valley, in its green retreats,
>   Alike thy words retain.
> What need hast thou of sculptured stone?
> Thy temple is thy name alone.[48]

While Landon cannot conceive of a redemptive textual afterlife for Hemans, even after the poet's death, her poem on Wordsworth imagines his death in order to engage precisely in such a remembrance.

In her 'Song' from *The Golden Violet* (1827) Landon meditates on her own obscurity in death:

> My heart is like the failing hearth
>   Now by my side,
> One by one its bursts of flame
>   Have burnt and died
> There are none to watch the sinking blaze,
>   And none to care,
> Or if it kindle into strength,
>   Or waste in air.
> My fate is as yon faded wreath
>   Of summer flowers;
> They've spent their store of fragrant health
>   On sunny hours,
> Which reck'd them not, which heeded not

When they were dead;
Other flowers, unwarn'd by them
  Will spring instead.
And my own heart is as the lute
  I am now waking;
Wound to too fine and high a pitch
  They both are breaking.
And of their song what memory
  Will stay behind?
An echo, like a passing thought,
  Upon the wind.
Silence, forgetfulness, and rust,
  Lute, are for thee:
And such my lot; neglect, the grave,
  These are for me.[49]

The naked pathos of the poem, its almost Hardyesque limpidity of despair, its verbal attrition and desolation, produce a sentimentalism unparalleled in canonical Romantic poetry, but it is one which works against the poem's own sense of neglect since it urges a response which will *not* forget.[50] Just as the suicide note articulates the negation of self in a gesture of inscription which ensures at least a temporary survival of that self, this poem exploits an emotional force inherent but rarely deployed in Romantic posterity for the production of responsive affect – in particular, of guilt. While our paradigm of the canonical Romantic 'suicide' poem, Keats's 'This living hand', appears to focus on the hauntedness of the survivor's conscience, it can also be read in more general terms as a meditation on the constitutive possession of readers by poems. Keats's poem is explicitly and performatively redemptive, articulating the implicit possibility of the Romantic culture of posterity, of the resuscitation, the literal posthumous life of the writer on being read. The desolation of Landon's 'Song' at the thought of oblivion might suggest that it too articulates a version of the redemptive culture of posterity – that it presupposes a sense of posterity as potentially (but not in this case) compensatory. If neglect and oblivion are to be lamented, that is to say, then renown and posthumous recognition would appear to be valued. And yet, in Landon's poem it is precisely the posthumous *neglect* of the poet that gives that poet value; it is precisely because she will be forgotten that she can experience, and produce, the pathos that she so clearly seeks and to which her readers can respond in sympathetic identification. Once again – here in the discourse of sentimentalism – there is a resistance to the redemptive value of posterity, and an

identification of the proper end of women's writing as posthumous
obscurity.

In 'Lines of Life' (1829), Landon also writes of the redeeming function of fame and posterity in a poem which seems to come close to a conventional (male) Romantic figuration of posthumous recognition. The
poem begins by describing the spiritual, emotional, ethical and social
deadening and dishonesty of life. After twelve stanzas, it begins to meditate on an alternative life:

> Surely I was not born for this!
>   I feel a loftier mood
> Of generous impulse, high resolve,
>   Steal o'er my solitude.

The speaker gazes at the stars and wishes for a similar existence, hoping
'To benefit my kind' and feeling 'as if immortal power / Were given to
my mind'. The final stanzas meditate on posthumous fame, the future
and the self:

> I think on that eternal fame,
>   The sun of earthly gloom,
> Which makes the gloriousness of death,
>   The future of the tomb –
>
> That earthly future, the faint sign
>   Of a more heavenly one;
> – A step, a word, a voice, a look, –
>   Alas! My dream is done.
>
> And earth, and earth's debasing stain,
>   Again is on my soul;
> And I am but a nameless part
>   Of a most worthless whole.
>
> Why write I this? because my heart
>   Towards the future springs,
> That future where it loves to soar
>   On more than eagle wings.
>
> The present, it is but a speck
>   In that eternal time,
> In which my lost hopes find a home,
>   My spirit knows its clime.
>
> Oh! not myself, – for what am I? –
>   The worthless and the weak,
> Whose every thought of self should raise
>   A blush to burn my cheek.

But song has touch'd my lips with fire,
And made my heart a shrine;
For what, although alloy'd, debased,
   Is in itself divine.

I am myself but a vile link
   Amid life's weary chain;
But I have spoken hallow'd words,
   Oh do not say in vain!

My first, my last, my only wish,
   Say will my charmed chords
Wake to the morning light of fame,
   And breathe again my words?

Will the young maiden, when her tears
   Alone in moonlight shine –
Tears for the absent and the loved –
   Murmur some song of mine?

Will the pale youth by his dim lamp,
   Himself a dying flame,
From many an antique scroll beside,
   Choose that which bears my name?

Let music make less terrible
   The silence of the dead;
I care not, so my spirit last
   Long after life has fled.[51]

There is, perhaps, from the Romantic period, no more powerfully direct statement of the value of posterity as a redemptive supplement to life: as Glennis Stephenson comments, the poem 'ends with a powerful affirmation of the consolations inherent in fame'.[52] And yet, while identifying with the Romantic culture of posterity and its valorisation of posthumous recognition, the poem diverges from such an ideology in two ways. In the first place, the poem *particularises* its own posthumous effect by figuring a scene of romance and loss within which Landon's poetry might be sought as a compensation. In particularising and thus sentimentalising the reading scene in this way, Landon departs from the figure of Romantic posterity for which such a scene constitutes precisely the kind of trivialisation that it seeks to transcend.[53] In the second place, the last four stanzas express a *hope* that the poetry will survive and be remembered as 'My first, my last my only wish', but they express no certainty. In other words, the compensatory effects of posterity are hypothetical and contingent. This contingency in effect counteracts the value

of posthumous recognition, as the fragility of such an imagined future
makes clear: '– A step, a word, a voice, a look, - / Alas! My dream is
done'. The poet is subject to 'the earth's debasing stain', is 'but a name-
less part' of the world, is 'worthless and weak', and the redemptive sense
of posthumous fame can only temporarily resist such thoughts. While
the poem idealises posterity, then, at the same time it resists the compensatory effect of posthumous fame and privileges effects of the ephemeral.

An even more explicit expression of the redemption afforded by the
culture of posterity is found in an earlier poem by a poet whose work is
now almost entirely forgotten, Isabella Lickbarrow. In her poem on the
by now conventional topic of the fate of Chatterton, 'Stanzas, Supposed
to be Written at the Grave of Chatterton' (1814), the speaker imagines
various honours given to the poet's tomb but then, in the last three
stanzas, turns to question the value of such honours:

> But ah! Can all this vain parade,
> This useless show of honour paid
> Departed talents, soothe his shade,
>   For former woes?
>
> For the deep anguish of his heart,
> Pierc'd by affliction's keenest dart,
> Which, with intolerable smart,
>   To madness rose;
>
> And, in an hour of dark despair,
> Made him the unknown future dare,
> In hope to find oblivion there,
>   And calm repose.[54]

Lickbarrow's ambivalence concerning posterity is evident in the blur-
rings of the final stanzas, which frame the suicide as seeking 'oblivion'
in death while, at the same time hoping that the 'honour paid' to his
talents after his death might 'soothe his shade'.

Perhaps the most carefully ironised examination of the value of posterity in women's writing of the period appears in the work of Maria
Jane Jewsbury. Jewsbury's resistance to the Romantic culture of posterity is evident in her *Phantasmagoria; Or, Sketches of Life and Letters* (1825), an
often flippant and satirical collection of parodies and pastiches – poems,
essays, fictional reviews and biographies, critical and aesthetic essays,
travel-writing, and so on. Jewsbury herself calls her work an 'amphibi-
ous production', and classifies it as belonging to the 'shred and patch
school of writing'.[55] Volume I opens with an essay entitled 'The Age of

Books' which takes up the common theme that everyone is now writing and publishing and goes on to argue that the 'overweening estimate' that contemporaries have of themselves is precisely the factor that will 'prevent our productions being of a nature to endure the strict test of time'. 'Our writers are . . . full of themselves', Jewsbury continues, 'and their writings are a tissue of localities'. Contemporary poetry is concerned with 'flitting fancies and evanescent interests' but ignores the 'silent depths of human nature'. She contrasts such concerns with the concerns of those whose work will endure, whose 'minds wandered forth amongst holy and imperishable things' (1.8). Dedicated to William Wordsworth, then, *Phantasmagoria* opens with a Wordsworthian critique of contemporary writing and an assertion of a focus on the *permanent* in writing which endures. And yet, at the same time, the book expresses a sharply critical perspective on the Romantic culture of posterity. In 'The Young Author', for example, Jewsbury presents a satirical account of a fictional poet, quoting extensively from his pocket-book and ironising his arrogant certainty that he is a neglected genius. Jewsbury wittily undermines the figure of the neglected genius by decoding the self-aggrandising discourse of self-pity. The youth's sense of injustice at having been born at the wrong time, for example, is undercut by his sense that recognition is a competitive affair: 'Mem: – Miserable thing for genius to be born either after or before the age capable of appreciating it, as the chances of distinction diminish in exact proportion to the numbers who have already acquired, and the numbers who are now seeking to acquire it . . .' (1.193). Once again, Chatterton figures as the model for the young man's vanity and Jewsbury pointedly suggests the pointless hubris of his desire for immortal fame:

I will write, though none may read; I will print, though none may purchase; and if the world's neglect canker my young spirit, and studious days and sleepless nights, 'sickly my brow with the pale cast of thought', till, like 'Chatterton, the marvelous boy', I sink into an early and untimely grave! – how small the sacrifice: How glorious the reward! when the world for which I toiled becomes sensible of its injustice! And the marble monument and laurelled bust – (1.197)

The dramatic aposiopesis of the ending to the note suggests, against its hyperbolic rhetoric, that the rewards of genius are, in fact, unimaginable and, as such, a worthless fiction. By writing a pastiche of the private thoughts of the poet who believes himself to be a neglected genius, Jewsbury exposes the egotism and vainly boastful spirit of such a posture. *Phantasmagoria*, then, perceptively expresses the way in which, by the mid-1820s, the culture of posterity had become a hackneyed and clichéd pose, an antisocial and deluded response to an unsatisfactory life. And it is no coincidence that each of the geniuses that the book ventriloquises, whether neglected justly or unjustly, are men. This scepticism towards and gendering of the Romantic culture of posterity is even more explicit in Jewsbury's next book, *The History of an Enthusiast* (1830), in which she suggests its redemptive power for men and its irrelevance for women:

A *man* may erect himself from such a state of despondency; throwing all his energies into some great work, something that shall beget for him 'perpetual benediction'; he may live for, and with posterity. But a woman's mind – what is it? – a woman – what can she do? – her head is, after all, only another heart; she reveals her feelings through the medium of her imagination; she tells her dreams and dies. *Her* wreath is not of laurels but of roses, and withers ere it has been worn an hour![56]

'What is fame to woman', the heroine Julia declares in a letter, 'but a dazzling degradation'.[57]

'Romantic poeticizing', argues Marlon Ross, 'is not just what women cannot do because they are not expected to; it is also what some men do in order to reconfirm their capacity to influence the world in ways socio-historically determined as masculine'.[58] If 'Romantic poeticizing' can be identified with the function of the Romantic culture of posterity, we might say, developing this idea, that the statement 'I will live beyond this life' is, within the discourse of the Romantic ideology, another way of saying 'I am a (male) poet'. In this respect, the counter-discourse of the ironisation of the Romantic culture of posterity which we find in the works of women writers of the period may account for the fact that such writers have largely been excluded from the canon.[59] It may be that the conventional and conventionally 'feminine' expression of the desire for oblivion amounts to a self-fulfilling prophecy, since the desire for oblivion is precisely excluded in the discourse of canonical Romantic literature: if, as I am suggesting, the Romantic canon is largely constituted by an engagement with the figure of contemporary neglect and posthumous fame, the easiest way out of the canon is to value posthumous oblivion, to neglect posterity. Another way to think of this is in terms of Marlon Ross's striking reversal of our common-sense notion that canons come before ideologies, or in other words in terms of the way that the Romantic ideology – including the Romantic ideology of posterity – is itself responsible for our notion of who is in and who is out of the canon: 'romantic ideology began to dominate the literary establishment *before* the romantic canon, as we know it, was established', comments Ross, 'and, in fact, it was the rise to power of romantic ideology that eventually enabled the consolidation of one of the most closely guarded canons of literature, the small group of male poets who have come to represent the apex of a whole literary tradition'.[60] It may just be that Romanticism inaugurates a certain logic of canonisation whereby comparative neglect and future recognition are themselves the entry requirements for the canon. In this sense, the question of the exclusion of women from the Romantic canon would be a function not so much of a value of their writing (women poets of the Romantic period are excluded from the canon because their poems are qualitatively inferior) but of a certain expression of desire (women are excluded because one of the conditions for inclusion is the expression or performance of the desire to remain and a rejection of the ephemeral).

Recent accounts of Romantic women's poetry have urged a rereading of such work with a view to a reorganisation of the canon. Anne Mellor, for example, argues that 'Women poets' choice of genres . . . exists in contestation both with the eighteenth-century ordering of the arts and the masculinist poetics this hierarchy reflects', and that we 'need to learn once again how to read these alternative poetic genres in a way that acknowledges their cultural power, their creation of a *popular* culture that perhaps more than other literary productions defined British literary Romanticism to itself'.[61] And yet such an appeal to an originary, prelapsarian reading might itself prompt a rethinking of both Romanticism and the discourse of literature itself. Thus Ross ends his study of the 'Rise of Women's Poetry' in the Romantic period with a call to 're-examine romanticism itself' and even to 'reconstruct our critical vocabulary and the theoretical bases on which that vocabulary has been grounded'.[62] But we might go further: if the discourse of literature is constituted in opposition to the ephemeral, then such a rereading would amount to a deconstruction of that discourse.[63] We might need to rethink what amounts to a fetishisation of remains, a fixation on permanence and posterity. For some, of course, this would involve a destruction of literary value since, in the Johnsonian or Humean as well as in the Romantic tradition, value is tied to the ability of poems to endure. Literary posterity, in the sense of the quality of permanence ascribed to certain poems is, in these traditions, the ground on which assertions of aesthetic value can be made. But the assumption that the literary value of certain texts is guaranteed by their longevity may be understood to involve a refusal to engage with the question of evaluation. Not only does it elide the question of why certain texts might be valued above others and of the way in which 'permanence' is not so much permanent as historically and culturally specific, but it also fails to question whether longevity is the necessary arbiter of poetic worth. The appeal to posterity as the judge of value, in other words, amounts to a failure to make value judgements. This point is made forcefully by Barbara Herrnstein Smith. Summarising the position of 'American critical theory' with regard to value, Smith suggests that the association of value with endurance overlooks the importance of its other in literary texts: 'Beguiled by the humanist's fantasy of transcendence, endurance, and universality, it has been unable to acknowledge the most fundamental character of literary value, which is its mutability and diversity'. Smith continues: 'at the same time, magnetized by the goals and ideology of a naïve scientism, distracted by the arid concerns of philosophic axiology, obsessed by a misplaced quest for "objectivity" and confined in its very conception of literary studies by the narrow intellectual traditions and professional allegiances of the literary academy, it has foreclosed from its own domain the possibility of investigating the dynamics of that mutability and understanding the nature of that diversity'.[64] A rethinking of literary endurance might, in its turn and as Smith recognises, amount to a reconsideration of the institution of literary criticism, which itself feeds off the cultural value accorded to works which 'last': how would such an institution justify its object of study and, therefore, its own practices, once the quality of permanent value were questioned?[65]

At the very least, a disengagement from fetishised remains might allow us to think more seriously about the kinds of ambivalence expressed in Paul de Man's declaration in 'Shelley Disfigured' that 'what we have done with the dead Shelley, and with all the other bodies that appear in romantic literature . . . is simply to bury them, to bury them in their own texts made into epitaphs and monumental graves',[66] or, rather differently, about the revulsion expressed by Mary Wollstonecraft (in her letters from Scandinavia) in her reaction to bodily preservation on seeing a tomb full of embalmed bodies in a Norwegian church:

Life, what art thou? Where goes this breath? this *I*, so much alive? . . . What will break the enchantment of animation? – For worlds, I would not see a form I loved – embalmed in my heart – thus sacrilegiously handled! – Pugh! My stomach turns. – Is this all the distinction of the rich in the grave? – They had better quietly allow the scythe of equality to mow them down with the common mass, than struggle to become a monument of the instability of human greatness.[67]

Better a bodily remembrance, an embalming in the heart, of the heart, than this socially constituted monumentalisation of the corpse. And it is not by chance that the letters from Scandinavia were written during a visit which took place between two attempts at suicide. Rather than the redemptive possibilities of an immortal posthumous life, textual or otherwise, what is desired, and what is linked to the very constitution of the self in this passage, is obliteration. Self, identity, this I, so much alive, may be constituted, may come into being as 'self', only on condition of taking seriously the end, the oblivion, without recompense, without salvation or redemption, that is death.[68] A renewed poetics of women's poetry of the early nineteenth century would not simply revise the canon, but revise canonicity itself and its relation to the Romantic culture of posterity. And as I seek to show in the second part of this book, the oppositional discourses which are so important in women's engagements with posterity haunt the very texts which so forcefully and pervasively justify its values. What writers such as Hemans and Landon allow us, finally, is a new reading of Wordsworth, Coleridge, Keats, Shelley, Byron, an understanding of the complex negotiations which take place in their work between permanence and the ephemeral, identity and its dissolution, monumentalisation and life.

PART II

CHAPTER 4

Wordsworth's survival

> The image of a world emptied of others, a world that testifies to my
> ultimate triumph as a survivor, is unbearable . . . Is not survival,
> therefore, a self-destructive and self-defeating impulse? Is not it the
> case that it can fulfil itself only in its defeat?
>
> (Zygmunt Bauman, *Mortality, Immortality and Other Life Strategies*)

Wordsworth's poetry presents us with one of the most disturbing paradoxes of survival and an engagement with its ultimate failure: the
fantasy of survival is, finally, bound up with the possibility of non-survival. To the extent that one's survival is predicated on the survival of
others, one's survival of them is 'self-destructive', 'self-defeating'.
Wordsworth's sense of posterity, I want to suggest, is, like the survival
poetics of a Hemans or Landon, intimately involved in the scene of the
family. While Wordsworth's major poetry and poetics are centrally concerned with the anonymous and generalising futuring of audience that
I am suggesting is characteristic of the (male) Romantic culture of posterity, his work is also determined, and in some ways compromised, by
his investments in personal, familial survival. Wordsworth's survival
poetry, then, brings out the complex disturbances predicated on the idea
of personal continuation in Romantic poetics. To survive, for
Wordsworth, means, fundamentally, to live on in the lives of others. The
possibility that those others, the others in whom Wordsworth survives,
will die therefore produces a crisis in writing, a scandal of representation. The representation of others' deaths is a site of anxiety which I
shall call Wordsworth's trembling, for while such representations allow
for survival – the survival of both reader and poet beyond the life of the
represented subject – they also articulate that which prevents survival,
the death of the other who will guarantee the survival of the poet. In this
chapter, I attempt to establish the importance of the figure of permanence in Wordsworth's writing before going on to explore the paradox

of such survival – the paradox that by surviving, by living on beyond the death of others, one risks not surviving, since the bearers of one's name, one's memory, are not able to carry that name and memory into the future. While the present book is concerned with textual survival as a Romantic preoccupation, I want to explore, alongside this, the importance and impossibility for Wordsworth of a variation or what might amount to a metonymic substitution for 'literary' survival, the continuation of life in one's heirs.[1] For Wordsworth, such survival is necessarily bound up with writing, with representation, so that writing about one's survival through others is also, itself, part of the possibility of such survival. And I want to suggest that this produces a vital complex of trembling in Wordsworth's writing. What Wordsworth's poetry expresses more clearly than that of other Romantic poets is the *fear* of survival. But Wordsworth's sense of the personal, domestic and familial dimensions of survival lead to very different results from those that we have discussed in the work of Hemans or Landon. For Wordsworth, the fear of survival involves the fear of being forgotten not because one's name remains obscure, but simply because there is no one left to continue that name.

Wordsworth's poetry is pervaded by a sense of and a desire for forms of the permanent, of perpetuity: as Susan Eilenberg comments, 'Durability was what mattered to Wordsworth'.[2] A fascination with such survival is embedded in much of Wordsworth's poetry and prose and, as he famously declares, goes back as far as his childhood: 'Nothing was more difficult for me in childhood than to admit the notion of death as a state applicable to my own being'.[3] The 'Intimations of Immortality' relies on the Platonic convention that our intimations of a future immortality are, in fact, *memories* of a previous pre-natal existence:[4] life is the continuation of pre-natal existence, and the logic of pre-natal existence (there must have been something rather than nothing before our birth) is transferred to the possibility of an afterlife (there must therefore be something rather than nothing after our death). The fundamental project for Wordsworth's writing may be said to be the articulation and practice of such survival, the expression of his conventional desire that he 'might leave / Some monument behind me which pure hearts / Should reverence'.[5] As Laurence Goldstein comments, 'The perpetuation of life by oral and written records remains an obsessive concern of Wordsworth's mature work'.[6] Writing, for Wordsworth, involves a sense of the past – the inscription of memory or experience – and an assertion of that which will remain in the future. The 1805 *Prelude*, for example, explicitly expresses this double logic of remains when it refers to itself as an attempt to 'enshrine the spirit of the past / For future restoration' (XI.341–2). Writing, for Wordsworth, notwithstanding his sense of poetry as the 'spontaneous overflow of powerful feelings', is the representation of the past in the future.

The Prelude ends with an explanation of its own impulse: Wordsworth and Coleridge, 'joint labourers' (XIII.439) in the 'redemptive' work of instruction will leave, we are told, a 'lasting inspiration' (XIII.443). These poets will instruct their readers:

> how the mind of man becomes
> A thousand times more beautiful than the earth
> On which he dwells, above this frame of things
> (Which, 'mid all revolutions in the hopes
> And fears of men, doth still remain unchanged)
> In beauty exalted, as it is itself
> Of substance and of fabric more divine. (XIII.446–52)

In admitting the 'substance and fabric' of the mind even while transcendentalising it, Wordsworth opens the way, at the end of the poem on the growth of the poet's mind, for a singular materiality of mind, the remains of consciousness as not only real but corporeal. The ending to *The Prelude* clearly establishes the mind as Wordsworth's topos, his place, locus or site – the 'haunt, and main region of my song' as he puts it in the Prospectus to *The Recluse*,[7] or the 'mansion' which remains in and as the mind of Dorothy in 'Tintern Abbey'. But the permanence of 'this Frame of things' which 'doth remain unchanged' suggests a dissolution of the conventional opposition between the mind or soul or spirit as 'exalted' and 'divine', as permanent or eternal on the one hand, and the body, 'frame' or 'earth' as temporary or transient on the other. Remaining, for Wordsworth, involves a shifting of the grounds of the opposition of transience to permanence, mind to body, the infinitely divisible moment of the present to the temporal difference – the delay – of the future. In this sense, the Wordsworthian culture of posterity is markedly *material*, unthinkable outside a certain materiality of that culture.

It is not surprising, therefore, that the problem of remains as a central concern in Wordsworth's poetry is nowhere more evident than in his almost obsessive dwelling on the nature of dwellings. Dwellings provide a crucial figure of place in Wordsworth's poetry. Indeed, many of Wordsworth's poems have as their focus the dwelling-place: the cottage, house, mansion, hovel or hut. Similarly, many of his narratives concern attempts to return home, or the loss of home, as well as conflicts over homes, property and boundaries. 'The Ruined Cottage', for example, narrates the ruin and loss of a home, 'The Discharged Soldier' an attempt to return home, 'Goody Blake and Harry Gill' a dispute over the boundaries of a home, 'Anecdote for Fathers' a discussion of which home is more desirable, 'We are Seven' a misunderstanding over what constitutes a home, 'Strange Fits of Passion' a journey to a home, 'Home at Grasmere' a eulogy of (a) home, 'Michael' the tragedy of leaving home, *The Prelude* a journey away from home which continually circles around and returns home. And Wordsworth's poetry is everywhere concerned with place or locus, with the home, ground, spot, grave, plot, as well as with *placed* language, poetry inscribed on a rock, bench, tree and so on. Indeed, for Wordsworth, poetry itself is constituted as a kind of home: *The Prelude* is described as like a home when Wordsworth speaks of 'building up a work that should endure' (XIII.278), so that figures of building such as reparation and restoration – as in the title to book XI, 'Imagination, How Impaired and Restored' – function as important tropes of Wordsworthian poetic making.

Such figures of dwelling may be read as sites of survival, expressing the desire to remain as a placing of that desire within a familial and familiar locus. Related to the home in complex ways, however, are two supplements of the home or dwelling-place, both of which may be read as the remains of home: the ruin, and the tomb or grave. If Wordsworth's figuration of dwelling-places are expressions of the possibility of personal survival, it is in the tomb, the dwelling of the dead, that remaining – in the form of literal remains – is finally to be encountered. And, like the tombstone, grave or funerary monument, the ruin itself articulates a form of survival: rather than a dwelling which contains or encloses the remains of the dead, the ruin is itself a kind of dead house, the carcass or corpse of a home, that which remains of the home after its ruin. And in Wordsworth's poetry and poetics this concern for the site of the dead is often in turn displaced to the literary or scriptive form of the grave, monument or ruin – the epitaph. In the epitaph, Wordsworth's concern with survival and remaining, with homes or dwelling-places, with ground or place, encounters its apotheosis, is expressed in and as language.

In his 'An Essay on Epitaphs', Samuel Johnson comments that epitaphs are 'probably, of the same age with the art of writing'.[8] It is no coincidence that the epitaph is as ancient as human records since what remains of primitive societies is, by definition, that which those societies attempted to preserve – most often, memorials to their dead. Memorials to the dead, including epitaphs, function as both monuments recording those who have died and, as such, performative acts of memorialisation, acts of immortalisation. What has remained of earlier civilisations is, unsurprisingly, the expression of the desire to remain. While funerary rites and practices are variable – historically, culturally and socially specific – they are always composed of a double gesture: such traditions both cancel or annihilate in burial or cremation and memorialise in the *mark* of the inhumation, the sign which records and so saves the body from oblivion. The desire for immortality and the desire to live on would appear to be timeless, immortal, monumental human conceptions and desires.[9] The epitaph is a monument to this logic of the afterlife, even as the epitaph itself constitutes a certain afterlife, allowing the subject to live on, to remain after his or her death. The fact that inscriptions and monuments to the dead, together with theories of the afterlife, are in evidence from the earliest periods of civilisation suggests that monuments, inscriptions, graves, tombs and so on – all the paraphernalia of memorialisation – performatively inscribe the immortality that they proclaim: the memorialisation of the dead is precisely a kind of life which survives the death of the subject. The subject lives on in his own death-work. But epitaphs, tombstones and other funerary monuments have another significance: remembering the dead allows a future for the living.[10] By commemorating the dead we guarantee a future for ourselves in the minds of others, we remind ourselves – and others – that we too will not be forgotten. In this sense, epitaphs and funerary monuments constitute memorialisation for us, now.

The epitaph, then, is the sign not only of death but, more importantly, of immortality, of memorialisation and remaining, and of the denial, by the living, of their own annihilation. As John Hodgson remarks, both Wordsworth's inscriptions and his epitaphs represent 'one more small way of staving off the second death of oblivion'.[11] It is not insignificant, in this context, that Wordsworth's major critical work is a series of three essays on the epitaph, that books 6 and 7 of *The Excursion* may be read as a series of epitaphs, that, as Frances Ferguson comments, *The Prelude* 'virtually constitutes a series of epitaphs spoken upon former selves', and that Wordsworth himself wrote numerous epitaphic inscriptions.[12] Such writings suggest the extent of Wordsworth's engagement with questions of survival and posthumous existence. In his first essay on epitaphs, Wordsworth begins by establishing that the epitaph, the assertion of the dead subject's continued existence in the lives of the living, involves a

supplementary afterlife, the possibility of immortality and that 'without
the consciousness of a principle of immortality in the human soul, Man
could never have had awakened in him the desire to live in the remembrance of his fellows' (*Prose* II.50). For Wordsworth, this desire is peculiarly human; indeed it is the defining characteristic of the human. A
dog or a horse, Wordsworth suggests, 'is incapable of anticipating the
sorrow with which his surrounding associates shall bemoan his death, or
pine for his loss; he cannot preconceive this regret, he can form no
thought of it; and therefore cannot possibly have a desire to leave such
regret or remembrance behind him' (*Prose* II.50). The desire to survive
one's own death depends upon one's ability to imagine the loss of self
proleptically, or the ability to make one's own death present to oneself,
to live, indeed, posthumously. For Wordsworth, there is no time before
which a child believes in his or her own immortality, no time before
which he or she has an 'intimation or assurance . . . that some part of
our nature is imperishable' (*Prose* II.50). But he also distinguishes between
this feeling of immortality in youth and the desire to be remembered.
The 'wish to be remembered by our friends or kindred after death, or
even in absence', Wordsworth declares, develops with '*social* feelings',
and the 'sense of immortality' is 'if not a co-existent and twin birth with
Reason . . . among the earliest of her offspring', to the extent that
'affection' is said to be 'inconceivable' without this sense (II.50, 51). The
desire for a posthumous life, then, may be considered as an analogue for
the Lacanian sense of identity as constituted by and as the entry into language. While Lacan argues that both our relationships with others
(Wordsworth's 'affection'), and our so-called 'rational' faculty, are constituted by language itself, for Wordsworth they are constituted by the
desire to be remembered by others. To be human – to have both reason
and identity – is to sense that one will survive after death in the minds
and hearts of those people by whom one is known and through whom
one comes to know oneself.

The epitaph, then, is central to Wordsworth's poetics of survival. But it
is, as his 'Essays on Epitaphs' suggests, necessarily bound up with familial or personal remembrance. The relation between the epitaphic and
the familial is played out in complex ways in a central passage from the
poem that one critic has called 'the most comprehensive "epitaph" in
our language', *The Prelude*.[13] Book v of *The Prelude*, the generalising, theoretical and polemical book on books, on reading and on education, is
famously opened by a vision of apocalypse, of the end of the world and

the end of survival. The passage is Wordsworth's most uncanny, most powerful and perhaps most disturbing discussion of the relationship between literary survival on the one hand and familial survival on the other. In an extraordinary turn on the argument for the relationship between familial and personal survival (written some years before the 'Essays on Epitaphs'), Wordsworth appears to weigh up the virtue of saving books as against saving his family. But if, as John Hodgson comments, 'the loved thing Wordsworth fears to lose is not another being, but his own intellectual identity and power',[14] I also want to suggest that Wordsworth's fantasy of survival as non-survival which opens book v of *The Prelude* acknowledges that those forms of 'inscription' which make survival possible at once threaten the identity on which any such survival is founded.[15] Even within his curious and curiously powerful discussion of literary as opposed to familial survival, Wordsworth appears to be suggesting a personal inscription of self into other selves. The paradox of survival for Wordsworth in this passage is that, in order to remain one must inscribe one's identity into the memory of others, memorialise oneself, but that such memorialisation may threaten that identity since it risks dissolving the ineradicable difference of self and other. But writing as a strategy of survival is equally tenuous, since it both constitutes identity through the sense of permanence that inscription affords and threatens identity by exposing it to the materiality and therefore the *im*permanence of the written word.

The induction to book five of *The Prelude*, then, constitutes Wordsworth's most considered critique of the redemptive comforts of posterity. 'Even in the steadiest mood of reason', the poet declares, there is sadness in the thought of the achievements of 'man', the thought of those human 'Things worthy of unconquerable life' which, however, we know 'must perish': 'Tremblings of the heart / It gives, to think that the immortal being / No more shall need such garments' (v.1, 19, 21–3). The heart trembles, it seems, at the thought that in his immortal state, after life, man will have no need of those 'Things worthy of unconquerable life' that he has created – the idea that such things are disposable, 'garments'. A trembling of the heart might involve a sense of dread and a disturbance or dissolution of self, of the 'heart', in such intimations of a future without, outside of or beyond the identity produced by the works of man.[16] Books appear to act as a temporary substitute or supplement for mortality, for the fact of death. The second half of the sentence, however, reverses the fantasy by figuring man as mortal and the unspecified 'Things' as lost:

> . . . and yet man,
> As long as he shall be the child of earth,
> Might almost 'weep to have' what he may lose –
> Nor be himself extinguished, but survive
> Abject, depressed, forlorn, disconsolate. (v.23–7)

The thought of living on without the marks or traces of permanence which artworks constitute is disconsolating and 'man' is figured as in a state of proleptic mourning for what may be lost. The thought of survival, just as much as the thought of non-survival, trembles the heart.

This trembling is followed by a further fantasy of apocalypse, in which what Wordsworth calls, in a letter to Southey of February 1805, 'this perishable planet' (*EY* 543), is imagined as destroyed. Although a 'living presence' is conceived as 'still subsist[ing]' beyond this destruction, the 'consecrated work of bard and sage' has only a temporary and fragile existence. It is precisely because of its materiality – that which *appears* to guarantee its permanence – that the literary work will be destroyed.

> Oh, why hath not the mind
> Some element to stamp her image on
> In nature somewhat nearer to her own?
> Why, gifted with such powers to send abroad
> Her spirit, must it lodge in shrines so frail? (v.44–8)

Commenting on book v of *The Prelude*, Mary Jacobus has remarked that 'For a poet, particularly, the question becomes: will I be saved if I write? Will my writings survive?'[17] And yet, in these lines Wordsworth appears to be making precisely the opposite case – that man's 'spirit' cannot but survive, given the intimations of immortality constituted by the 'soul divine' in which we 'participate' (v.16). The pathos of the passage involves a tragic sense of survival, the sense that while man survives, in spirit, his works, the temporal material traces of his 'sojourn on this planet' will, by virtue of this very materiality, be eradicated. But Jacobus is right, of course, for what becomes clear in this passage is the sense that intimations of human immortality can never be other than, precisely, intimations. Belief in the conventional human afterlife as a separate, other-worldly, transcendental existence can never, finally, compensate for the literal, physical, felt existence – 'we feel – we cannot chuse but feel' – of life (v.20). It is only in such material manifestations of the human 'spirit' as books – physical, tangible and therefore necessarily *impermanent* – that we can find compensation for human mortality, and a redemptive supplement to life. But it is precisely the qualities of human materiality and impermanence, qualities that allow books to compensate for mortality, which, by the same token, mark their afterlife as 'fragile', perishable.[18] 'Tremblings of the heart', indeed: for what Wordsworth expresses is his sense that the sole resource of mortality is, necessarily, temporal, transient. Identity itself might tremble at such recognition. Wordsworth's fantasy of survival, then, is the fantasy of non-survival: to survive is not to survive. For Wordsworth, survival necessitates the transfer of human qualities into that which is both permanent and material. But the material, the *literal*, that which pertains to this planet is necessarily and by its very nature, impermanent, transitory. By the same token, that which is both immaterial and, at least in our apprehension, fleeting and ephemeral – the 'spirit' – is our only recourse to permanence.

It is this paradox of mortality and immortality, materiality and immateriality, which is addressed in the dream of the Arab passage which follows this induction. The semi-Quixote, in the face of imminent apocalypse, seeks to bury two books '(The knowledge that endures)', of geometry and poetry. Wordsworth – husband, father, lover – declares that in the same circumstances, in the face of imminent apocalypse, and despite the apparent madness of such an act, he too would save books:

> Enow there are on earth to take in charge
> Their wives, their children, and their virgin loves,
> Or whatsoever else the heart holds dear –
> Enow to think of these – yea, will I say,
> In sober contemplation of the approach
> Of such great overthrow, made manifest
> By certain evidence, that I methinks
> Could share that maniac's anxiousness, could go
> Upon like errand. Oftentimes at least
> Me hath such deep entrancement half-possessed
> When I have held a volume in my hand –
> Poor earthly casket of immortal verse –
> Shakespeare or Milton, labourers divine. (v.153–65)

The survival of wives and children is pitted against the fragile and ephemeral existence of books, and the fragile materiality of these books against the 'immortal' nature of their contents. Curiously, it is the tactile physicality of books, and the physicality of reading, the half-possession of the trance of reading, which has brought about this fantasy: the very transience and physical immediacy of the act of reading brings on a 'maniac's anxiousness' to preserve, to maintain the un-preservable, the 'poor earthly casket of immortal verse'. The uncanny, disturbing vision of the opening 165 lines of book v, then, constitutes Wordsworth's most profound contemplation of the possibilities of survival, a vision which involves the perception of the inhumanity – the resistance to material-ity, to life, to other people, to the 'earthly' – of this desire to 'save' 'immortal' verse. Wordsworth cannot square such desires with his humanity, with his humanism, with the familial nature of his own sense of identity. For, as these lines suggest, the desire for textual immortality involves a rejection, a dissolution or denigration of the human and familial, of the human and the family – including posterity in its genetic or reproductive sense – as the source and main region of all value.

Paul D. Sheats has commented that 'Tintern Abbey' concerns the 'dis-tinction between transience and permanence, between what has changed and what remains'.[19] 'Tintern Abbey' is, amongst other things, a poem of remains, a poem which remains and which desires remains, expresses a desire to remain. The poem opens with what Harold Bloom describes as the repressed desire, the 'ultimate, divinating desire to live forever'.[20] 'Tintern Abbey' is, then, about the desire to remain, but a desire radically displaced to the past (the desire to remain as one once was) or to the future (the desire to remain when one will have left). Thus, as critics have noted, the poem is concerned with repetition, a concern signalled repeatedly in the opening lines of the poem, not only by the subtitle 'On *Re*visiting the Banks of the Wye . . . ' (italics added) but, emphatically, through the repetition of 'again' in the opening to the poem: 'and again I hear' (line 2), 'Once again / Do I behold' (lines 4–5), 'I again repose / Here' (lines 9–10), 'Once again I see' (line 14). Repetition, then, as a form of linguistic remaining, a substitute or sup-plement of remains, a tautology of remains – the remains of remains. Repetition – in particular, the self-reflexive repetition of the word which denotes repetition, 'again' – constitutes survival's most forceful expres-sion in 'Tintern Abbey'. In this poem, the possibility of living on depends on the possibility of repeating what has gone before, of speak-ing it, writing it, 'again'. On the one hand, Wordsworth's presence, his 'I' speaking in the present, constitutes a repetition of a past self. On the other hand, he imagines a future in which Dorothy will repeat his pres-ence, remain him.

But the crucial expression of remains comes with a turn of apos-trophe towards the end of the poem. The speaker of 'Tintern Abbey' makes an unexpected and unaccountable turn, at line 115, to a directly addressed person hypostasised as present and listening – a turn from an addressee to an interlocutor, 'thou my dearest Friend, / My dear, dear Friend . . . My dear dear Sister' (lines 115–21). Addressing Dorothy in the final paragraph of the poem, William constructs her future mind – her memory – as a mansion (from Latin *manere*, meaning 'remain, stay'), a place for remains, a place which, by its very nature, remains:

> . . . and, in after years,
> When these wild ecstasies shall be matured
> Into a sober pleasure; when thy mind
> Shall be a mansion for all lovely forms,
> Thy memory be as a dwelling place
> For all sweet sounds and harmonies . . . (lines 138–43)

The force of 'Tintern Abbey' is to suggest that Dorothy provides a doubling of memorialisation for William: not only will *she* remain, remembering him in the future, but this thinking, now, of a future remembrance constitutes a kind of proleptic remembering of the poet as present, now, as he speaks. And yet this fact of remembrance curiously denotes the poet's absence, now.[21] (And we might think of the Abbey itself, devastated by time, as a mansion of remains, itself, differently, absent from the poem despite – or because of – its titular presence.) William is writing in memory of himself. But he is also writing in memory of Dorothy, in the sense that his writing constitutes a kind of proleptic memorialisation of what will have been. Wordsworth allows us to 'remember' the remembering of Dorothy. Just as Dorothy is represented as remembering Wordsworth in the future, the poem represents the act of remembrance, repeats it and thus memorialises it.[22] If Dorothy is figured as remaining in the future, she is also *figured*, repeated, represented or, in a word, memorialised.

The final paragraph of the poem seeks to present Dorothy as a repetition of Wordsworth's earlier self, a kind of copy or supplement, or, in some sense, his remains:[23] Dorothy is Wordsworth's remains to the extent that he is able to 'catch / The language of my former heart' in her voice and 'read / My former pleasures' in her eyes (lines 116–18). Reading Dorothy as a kind of text, then, William can read his own remains. William, in this sense, figures his own death: after the sense of community with which William turns to Dorothy at the beginning of the final verse-paragraph, it becomes clear that she is envisaged as being alone. 'Therefore', says William, 'let the moon / Shine on thee in thy solitary walk' (lines 135–6). William, then, writes his own death:

> oh! then,
> If solitude, or fear, or pain, or grief,
> Should be thy portion, with what healing thoughts
> Of tender joy wilt thou remember me,
> And these my exhortations! Nor, perchance,
> If I should be where I no more can hear
> Thy voice, nor catch from thy wild eyes these gleams
> Of past existence . . .   (lines 142–9)

A future in which solitude, fear, pain and grief are Dorothy's 'portion' would be a future in which William himself would be radically absent, dead. Similarly, a future in which the poet can no longer hear Dorothy's voice or see her eyes is a future after his death.[24] But in writing of the future beyond his own death, William makes it clear that he will remain in memory in such a future. The force of 'Tintern Abbey', then, is to allow the poet to be remembered, and to allow him to be remembered in the future, now, by himself. The poem presents a scene of proleptic commemoration and aligns remembering the person ('me') with a memory of his words ('these my exhortations'). Wordsworth's poetry, in other words, can be conceived in terms of a performative memorialisation, a performance of memory, the paradoxical achievement in the present of a future remembrance. And yet, as with writing in *The Prelude* book v, the permanence achieved, the imaginary resolution of the conflict between inscription and family, is illusory since the gap between poet and survivor, William and Dorothy, has collapsed: William does the remembering for Dorothy, he remembers himself.

Isobel Armstrong comments on 'Tintern Abbey' that 'it is strange to find "unremembered" in a poem about memory'.[25] In another poem, 'Surprized by Joy', unremembering, forgetting, is that which fissures the possibility of remains, of remaining in memory. While Hazlitt discusses the importance of being remembered and forgotten by those one leaves behind at the end of 'On the Feeling of Immortality in Youth' (*Works* XVII.189–99), a more specific mode of remembrance involves the way in which sexual reproduction is itself a form of survival. In this respect, annihilation would involve the possibility of not being remembered by one's children or, more generally, not being survived by them. The point is put movingly by a contemporary of Wordsworth in an anonymous article in the *London Magazine* for 1821, signed 'A Father', who writes that 'Children are the best living possession and posthumous existence' since they allow the parent to survive death: 'the living transcripts of his face and figure are still moving upon the earth; his name survives, embodied in another self; his blood is still flowing through human veins, and may continue its crimson current till the great wheel shall stand still. What posthumous memorial so vital as this?'.[26] There is, in fact, a venerable tradition according to which being remembered, and ultimately immortality itself, is contingent upon one's children, upon the possibility of living on in the lives of one's heirs. The argument that sexual reproduction involves personal reproduction is outlined both in Plato's *Symposium* and in the *Laws*. In the *Symposium*, Socrates argues through the speech of Diotima that the aim of love is permanence and that such permanence can only be achieved through the self-reproduction of procreation: 'Love's purpose is physical and mental procreation in an attractive medium'.[27] Procreation, Diotima argues, 'is as close as a mortal can get to being immortal and undying': 'Given our agreement that the aim of love is the *permanent* possession of goodness for oneself, it necessarily follows that we desire immortality along with goodness, and consequently the aim of love has to be immortality as well'.[28] In this Ancient Greek version of the 'selfish gene' theory, Diotima argues that, like animals, humans do everything they can to live for ever, but that the 'sole resource' for such immortality 'is the ability of reproduction constantly to replace the past generation with a new one'.[29] Eros, in Nicolai Hartmann's epigrammatic summary, 'is participation in immortality'.[30] The Athenian offers a similar analysis in the *Laws* when he declares that child-bearing is how 'by nature's ordinance' a man 'shares in immortality, a thing for which nature has implanted a keen desire': humankind is made immortal 'by leaving behind it children's children and continuing ever one and the same'.[31] As David Heyd explains, in his discussion of the Platonic argument for the ethics of reproduction, 'producing children is a typical expression of self-transcendence, as it is far-reaching in time, indefinitely extending parts of our existence and identity in future people'.[32] Like Schopenhauer, Otto Rank and Zygmunt Bauman in the nineteenth and twentieth centuries, both the Athenian and Diotima suggest that 'the prospect of undying virtue and fame . . . [is] what motivates people to do anything' – including writing poetry – but such impulses, for Diotima, can only finally be achieved through sexual reproduction.[33] Wordsworth's most explicit reference to this tradition comes in his comments to Elizabeth Fenwick on his 'Vernal Ode': 'Composed to place in view the immortality of succession where immortality is denied, as far as we know, to the individual creature.'[34]

But what happens when this order of death is reversed? Wordsworth himself remarks on such a possibility in the third of his 'Essays on Epitaphs' (written by 28 February 1810), when he comments that the death of the child before the parent 'run[s] counter to the course of nature, which has made it matter of expectation and congratulation that Parents should die before their Children': for a mother to survive her children, he goes on, would be a 'bitter desolation, where the order of things is disturbed and inverted' (*Prose* II.87–8). What would be worse than dying, more preposterous, monstrous, precocious and perverse, would be survival – surviving the loved one, the one who will remember, or the one who will repeat oneself, reproduce oneself, the one who will be, in Derrida's words 'the last to preserve what I wanted to pass on'.[35] In *The Post Card*, Derrida repeatedly returns to the death of Freud's daughter Sophie at the age of 26 in 1920, and elaborates such a calamity, such a monstrous event:

> Freud said that the most monstrous thing is to see one's own children die, this is the thing of his that I have best understood . . . To survive one's own, to survive one's children, to bury one's heirs, nothing worse, is there? . . . The precocious death, and therefore the mutism of the legatee who can do nothing about it: this is one of the possibilities of that which dictates and causes to write . . . All speculation . . . implies the terrifying possibility of this *usteron proteron* of the generations.[36]

This reversal of the womb, this strange, un-natural temporal and generational disordering of the order of death is what most threatens remains, survival and, for Diotima, the Athenian, Socrates, Plato, Wordsworth, Freud and Derrida, marks the monstrous or, more properly, the preposterous possibility of the child's death.[37]

Such a preposterous, unthinkable reversal of survival logic, reverse remains, also haunts Wordsworth's later poetry, poetry written after the death of his daughter Catharine in June 1812 at the age of three and of his son Thomas in December of the same year at the age of six.[38] Stephen Gill comments that 'The more penetrating impact of these shocks continued to register deeply, for the rest of [Wordsworth's] life.'[39] Gill quotes Aubrey de Vere's description of Wordsworth, more than forty years later, recounting the details of Catharine's and Thomas's illnesses 'with an exactness and impetuosity of troubled excitement, such as might have been expected if the bereavement had taken place but a few weeks before'.[40] As Mary Moorman comments, the death of Thomas in particular was a 'well-nigh unbearable blow' to Wordsworth.[41]

Wordsworth's reactions to these deaths in the days and weeks following them are recorded in letters and poems, and allow us a privileged insight into the Wordsworthian logic of the culture of posterity and its working through of the familial relation. The news of the death of Catharine on 4 June reached Wordsworth in Bocking, Essex a week later on 11 June. The news makes him turn to face another way, as he records in a letter to his friend Catherine Clarkson: 'I arrived here on Monday Evening and purposed on Saturday to take the Coach for Bury; but it is now my duty to turn my face another way. Tomorrow morning I take coach for London and in the evening shall proceed by the mail for Ludlow; hoping still to be at Radnor in time to break the Melancholy News to my dear, I might say, *our* dear Mary' (*MY* 11.24). Writing to Catherine Clarkson again exactly a week later, Wordsworth has turned his attention to the mourning of his wife, realising that her attention cannot be turned from the preposterous death: 'I had hopes to prevail upon Mary to take a little Excursion in this neighbourhood that might beguile her heaviness, but I am now inclined to give this up . . . I fear no benefit will be derived from any attempts to turn her attention to other objects' (*MY* 11.26). By contrast with Mary's unbeguiled sorrow, William's mourning seems almost half-hearted.[42] In his self-analysis of his own reaction to this death he recognises that sadness or sorrow is only half the story: what affects him most, he suggests, in a postscript to the first letter to the surviving Catherine, is uncertainty: 'I write with a full heart; with some sorrow, but most oppressed by an awful sense of the uncertainty and instability of all human things' (*MY* 11.25).

Six months later, on 1 December, Thomas Wordsworth died. Wordsworth's reaction, recorded in a letter to Southey the following day, was again one of uncertainty, of shock, of surprise, as well as a kind of affirmation, a kind of joy. But inexpressible pain is suggested by the apostrophic call for his friend's sympathy which ends the letter:

For myself dear Southey I dare not say in what state of mind I am; I loved the Boy with the utmost love of which my soul is capable, and he is taken from me – yet in the agony of my spirit in surrendering such a treasure I feel a thousand times richer than if I had never possessed it. God comfort and save you and all our friends and us all from a repetition of such trials – O Southey feel for me! (*MY* 11.51)

The reference to repetition acknowledges the fact that Wordsworth's other children were, at the time, also sick and in mortal danger.[43] But it might also be read as a reference to the fact that this death is a repetition of Catharine's in June: as Wordsworth makes clear in a letter to Lord Lonsdale of two weeks later, what is so shocking in Thomas's death is that it is, in some sense, a repetition of Catharine's: 'The suddenness of this blow has overwhelmed me, following so close upon another as sudden which deprived me of a Daughter last mid-summer' (*MY* II.52). Curiously, though, this death is, these deaths are, not unadulterated loss: Wordsworth feels 'a thousand times richer' and expresses this richness as itself part of mourning, part of loss. The loss, that is, cannot be separated from what has been gained, by the 'treasure' of the child's existence. Wordsworth ends another letter, addressed to Elizabeth Monkhouse and dated 6 December, by asserting the consolations of mourning: 'our bitter sorrow will in time become sweet and kindly, and never such, at no moment such, as we should wish to part with'.[44] Wordsworth looks forward to a future in which sorrow itself, the final sweet remainder of this death, these deaths, will be all that will remain, never to be forgotten, to be parted with, 'never such, at no moment such'.[45] 'These perfections', Dorothy comments on Catharine's 'surpassing sweetness of temper' in a rhetorical *hysteron proteron* soon after her death, 'are an inheritance that remain with us' (*MY* II.45)

We know that at some point between 4 June 1812 and the middle of October 1814, Wordsworth composed 'Surprized by Joy'. Elizabeth Fenwick's note recording Wordsworth's comments on the poem is unequivocal as to its subject: 'This was in fact suggested by my daughter Catherine [*sic*] long after her death'.[46] The note makes it clear that the poem is about the daughter and not about the son. Nevertheless, focusing on the phrase 'long after', critics have tended to date the poem as having been written during 1813 or even 1814 – after the death of Thomas. If this is the case, then the poem and the note may be understood to elide the doubling of death in 1812, the fact that not one but two children died in that year. In itself, this may be of little significance: there is no reason why Wordsworth should not remember Catharine and her death in isolation from that of Thomas. But Wordsworth's letters written after Thomas's death produce at least one verbal echo in the poem: 'my heart's best treasure' of the poem might be read as a compacted version of 'the utmost love of which my soul is capable . . . such a treasure' in the letter to Southey on Thomas's death.[47] Such an echo could signify one of two things: either the poem was written before Thomas's death, in which case the letter, rather than just responding spontaneously to that death also produces a thought already thought, an intertextual allusion to the poem; or the poem was written after the boy's death, which allows for the possibility that it may be as much about Thomas as about Catharine, since then the poem may be understood to be quoting from a letter articulating Wordsworth's second experience of loss, the repetition of mourning. While neither possibility is likely to be confirmed in a documentary or empirical sense at this late stage, for the purposes of this reading I propose to follow other critics by assuming that 'long after' means at least six months later, so that rather than a prophetic sense of the repetition of death and mourning, 'Surprized by Joy', in its singularity, marks an uncanny reduction of two to one – two deaths making one poem, one memory, one forgetting and one mourning. My choice of chronology will be understood to be somewhat arbitrary: another reading of the poem, a kind of shadow-reading, unarticulated in the present chapter, must haunt what I have to say about the text. This shadow-reading would understand the poem to have been written within six months of the death of Catharine, in reaction to a single loss. In this reading, Wordworth's sense that the poem was written 'long after' Catharine's death would appeal to the psychic lengthening of minutes into hours, days, weeks, in the aftershock of loss.[48] In my reading, however, the poem is about forgetting and remembering, but it also *enacts* a certain forgetting and an uncertain remembering by collapsing the death of two children into one. In particular, this forgetting constitutes the anonymity of the one who is mourned: neither the age nor the gender of the dead addressee of the poem is recorded so that in blurring or effacing the identity of the dead child, the poem can work for more than one death.[49] The striking anomaly of this poem on the death of a loved one, then, is that it is only in a note dictated some twenty years later, that the identity of the child is revealed.

As we have seen from his letters in response to the deaths of Catharine and Thomas, while Wordsworth is able to 'turn' in response to the death of Catharine – a defensive troping of mourning which Mary is unable to achieve – it is the repetition of this death which produces a fixation, a refusal to turn, and indeed a hope for the absence of such a (re)turn. These thematics of turning and troping, of mourning, remembering and forgetting, are played out in the strange turns of 'Surprized by Joy':

> Surprized by joy – impatient as the Wind
> I turn to share the transport – Oh! with whom
> But thee, deep buried in the silent Tomb,
> That spot which no vicissitude can find?
> Love, faithful love recalled thee to my mind –
> But how could I forget thee? Through what power,
> Even for the least division of an hour,
> Have I been so beguiled as to be blind

To my most grievous loss? – That thought's return
Was the worst pang that sorrow ever bore,
Save one, one only, when I stood forlorn,
Knowing my heart's best treasure was no more;
That neither present time, nor years unborn
Could to my sight that heavenly face restore[50]

The poem narrates the speaker's forgetting of his grief, his surprise at an unprecedented and unlooked-for experience of joy, his turn towards his daughter and then his remembering that this turn is not possible because the child is dead, followed by his sense of remorse on thinking that he has forgotten that death, and his recollection of the original moment of mourning and the unrepeatable event of her death. Taken out of himself, then, the speaker is transported as, he remembers, his daughter has been. The poem involves a narrative of turning – playing on what, in *The Prelude*, Wordsworth defines as poetic language itself, 'the turnings intricate of verse' (v.627). The speaker turns at the turn of the line ending – is transported – and turns to face his daughter who is not there. In discovering or remembering that his daughter is absent, dead, he produces the apostrophic 'turn' of prosopopoeia: 'Oh! with whom / But Thee'. This turn of address constitutes a figurative or rhetorical 'turn', or 'trope' (from Greek *tropos*, 'turn') which is itself constituted by a rhetorical turn of address ('apostrophe' is, of course, a 'turn' of the speaker to an inanimate or absent or dead object, a turn which, as prosopopoeia, 'gives a face' to that addressee). The poem turns on this paradoxical trope: the poet *cannot* address the person whom he *does* address. And the impossibility of this trope, this turn, suggests the impossibility of all turns in this poem. Indeed, it is the governing fiction of the poem that the turn of address, the trope of prosopopoeia, is not figurative, not a trope: in this poem, despite the silence of the tomb, Wordsworth both turns and is unable to turn to Catharine. Wordsworth speaks with the dead who do not speak with him.

But what do we mean by the word 'turn'? What does it mean to turn? And what would it mean to 'turn' to a dead person. The turning and changing senses of the word 'turn' are suggested by a selection of the flood of definitions given in the *OED* in its description of the verb 'turn': to rotate or revolve, whirl, spin, to change or reverse position, to change or reverse course, to deviate, to cause or command to go, to change, alter, transmute, transform, to disturb or overthrow the mental balance, to make mad or crazy, distract, dement, infatuate. Passion, movement, transformation, metamorphosis, desire, madness – a trembling of the

heart or mind – presence, but presence fissured by a movement of revolution or transformation are all involved in this turn of language, this
trope. Life, motion, mutability, then, are characteristic of the turn and
of turning. And it is precisely such turning and the ability to turn that is
absent for the dead: the dead, after the final turn of mortality, are 'deep
buried in the silent tomb, / That spot which no vicissitude can find'. The
grave is the place where mutability, the vicissitudes of life, the troubling
fact of mortality's irreducible changeableness or mutation, its turns, are
absent. (The point is emphasised, rather than contradicted, by the way
that the dead girl becomes part of the turning – or 'rolling' – 'earth' in
'A slumber did my spirit seal'.) In this respect, it is the experience of
turning that the dead child cannot share. The child is immune to turns,
changes, vicissitudes, life: the changes – of time, of place, of physical
experience, but especially of mood or emotion – which the speaker goes
through are those which the child can no longer experience. If death is
a place in which there are no 'vicissitudes', then life is constituted by the
turns of mutability. Similarly, to the extent that the child is dead, she
cannot be turned to, cannot be 'recalled'. Indeed, while the speaker
recalls the child in the sense of remembering, and re-calls the child in
the sense of addressing her or calling to her (again), it is precisely this
recalling which figures her absence or figures her as absent. Perhaps this
is why we must be reminded that the child – the child unnamed, uncalled
in this sense, too – is recalled 'to my mind': what would it mean to 'recall'
the dead but not 'to my mind'? Finally, the turn introduces a splitting or
doubling, a necessary absence within 'life', presence, motion. That
which constitutes 'life' – the turn – also constitutes its other, death, in the
absence produced by turning.

The problem of the remembered return is most clearly evident in the
turn of line 9: 'That thought's return / Was the worst pang that sorrow
ever bore'. The question raised by this turn is whether it is the return of
the thought of the child's death which pains, or the thought that this
return is a return, and that, as such, what pains is the previous *absence*
(the forgetting) of the pain of remembrance. The lines raise the question
of the status of 'that thought': what is the thought that is returned or that
returns? Characteristically, for Wordworth, it is thought itself, the
difficulty involved in the act of thinking and in thinking about thinking,
which captures our thoughts. But lines 9–10 also suggest the paradox
that, in recalling the pang of loss – the originary moment of mourning
within which the speaker may properly be said to mourn, without the
vicissitudes of time intervening and turning loss to a forgetting – in

recalling this moment, and in substituting for the original sensation of loss the pang of remembering having lost that sensation (as *the only possible substitute* for the experience of that loss), we find that in order to remember the pang of loss we must precisely forget that loss.[51] In order to return to the originary moment of loss we must forget and then remember that we have forgotten. If this is the case, however, and if we can only return to the originary moment of loss through this remembrance of a forgetting, then it would seem that we must repeatedly, incessantly forget and then return to this moment. The sensation of remembering that one has forgotten is a 'pang', the kind of pain which is *constituted* by its impermanence – 'a sudden transitory fit' (*OED*). In order properly to mourn his loved one, the speaker must repeatedly experience such a pang, repeatedly, endlessly forgetting the child and then remembering his forgetting in an oscillating movement of loss and return which figures in Freud's account of the game of Fort/Da (*PFL* XI.283–7). To remember is to forget: forgetting is that which *restores* the intensity of the original loss.[52] The poem ends, however, with a final turn in the memory of mourning. To remember that someone is dead is to remember that that person can no longer be remembered, restored or returned and that that person can no longer be addressed, cannot be turned to: the speaker reminds himself, and us, 'That neither present time, nor years unborn / Could to my sight that heavenly face restore'.[53]

But the fundamental ambivalence of gender and identity in this poem complicates matters further, for while the reading which we have just outlined may be said to be an analysis of strategies of mourning in general, Wordsworth's poem is split, doubled, by the way in which it makes single a death which is in fact two. What we might see as the repression or the *duplicity* of this poem involves a forgetting of the multiplicity of death, its plurality. In a tragic game of numbers which somehow echoes the title of 'We are Seven', and the first line of the only poem that Wordsworth ever wrote about Thomas, the epitaph 'Six months, to six years added', the poet 'forgets' that two of his children have died. Deep buried in the silence of this poem, then, is another form of forgetting of deaths which is irretrievable, never remembered, uncalled for and not recalled. While the strategies of mourning for Wordsworth remind us that forgetting is remembering, the preposterous event of the death of one's children, one's heirs, may lead to the possibility that forgetting, *pace* Freud, really is forgetting. The narration of this poem, then, which rests on the possibility of reversing forgetting, of turning, and of re-living the event of death, is reversed – or re-versed –

with regard to the monstrous possibility of one's children dying before oneself. For if the possibility of the second *hysteron proteron* is allowed in the poem, this would open up the possibility that not just one but *all* of one's children may die before oneself[54] – in which case what will be forgotten is not these deaths but the very life of the poet himself. 'I seem to possess all my children in trembling', Wordsworth remarks in a letter to Catherine Clarkson in December 1814 (MY II.183). Inscribed within this poem, then, but not remembered, is the death of Thomas and the recognition of the preposterous possibility of not being remembered, not being repeated or reproduced in one's children. Far from constituting a cynical expression of the 'Wordsworthian or egotistical sublime', such apparently 'narcissistic' desires, we should remember, are an effect of love, the very definition and expression of love, just as, however, narcissism itself, not least in Freudian terms, is the foundation for the very possibility of love.[55] What the poem approaches but cannot touch, calls for but does not recall, turns to but cannot face, faces but cannot speak, is the fantasy of survival – like the Last Man fantasy so common in the Romantic period – in which one's survival means one's non-survival.[56] Survival, in the preposterous logic of posterity, must be feared and forgotten, since it would necessitate one's disappearance from the face of the earth.[57] Tremblings of the heart: what Wordsworth forgets in 'Surprized by Joy' and then forgets to forget, as he must, is his own mortality. The unbearable loss of Wordsworth's children also involves the unthinkable possibility of the poet's non-survival, a possibility both remarked upon and forgotten in an act of inscription – the writing of a poem which must, itself, supplement familial or personal survival in other lives. For Wordsworth, then, the Romantic culture of posterity is both crucial to his poetry and poetics and a site of disturbance and vexation, of trembling, permanently in conflict with that other survival, living on in his children.

CHAPTER 5

Coleridge's conversation

Vox audita perit, littera scripta manet.

Coleridge talks too much. This, in short, is the considered opinion of William Hazlitt. 'If Mr. Coleridge had not been the most impressive talker of his age, he would probably have been the finest writer', he comments in *The Spirit of the Age* (*Works* xi.30). Talking and writing are in opposition and in competition: you cannot talk and write at the same time. The difference for Coleridge is that by contrast with the deferral of response which structures writing, talk is immediate: Coleridge 'lays down his pen to make sure of an auditor, and mortgages the admiration of posterity for the stare of an idler' (*Works* xi.30). It is Coleridge's desire for immediate recognition, then, that leads to the compulsion of his talk, and it is this compulsion which will prevent him from being remembered in posterity. While writing remains, that is to say, talk falls only momentarily on the ear.[1]

Since his achievement of the last few years of the eighteenth century and the early years of the nineteenth century, Hazlitt goes on to argue, Coleridge has been living on borrowed time, his existence has been a kind of afterlife of the voice: 'All that he has done of moment, he had done twenty years ago: since then, he may be said to have lived on the sound of his own voice' (*Works* xi.30). For Hazlitt, the tragedy of Coleridge's genius is that his writing is 'inferior to his conversation'. The problem with talk, though, is its transience, its vaporous dissolution in air. Coleridge wastes himself on the momentary effect of sound-waves: 'Mr Coleridge, by dissipating his [intellect], and dallying with every subject by turns, has done little or nothing to justify to the world or to posterity, the high opinion which all who have ever heard him converse, or known him intimately, with one accord entertain of him' (*Works* xi.36).

In the same year as Hazlitt's critique, Coleridge wrote despairingly in a letter that 'the thought of writing for posterity alone and of benefiting my contemporaries by kindling and inseminating the minds of a few Individuals, as I have hitherto done in the *Nos non nobis* way of Conversation would be pleasurable to me': 'I have not a single sparkle of the Love of literary Reputation for it's [*sic*] own sake', he continues (*CL* v.510). We have seen how important posterity was for Coleridge, *pace* Hazlitt, in our discussion of his concern with the distinction between fame and reputation in chapter 2. The concern is also apparent in poems such as 'To William Wordsworth', in which Coleridge's friend is figured as being amongst the 'choir / Of ever-enduring men', those that 'Are permanent': with them, Wordsworth is destined to win 'gradual fame / Among the archives of mankind' (lines 49–57).[2] But Hazlitt allows us to define a crucial and, for Coleridge, inescapable series of tensions, between speaking and writing, prose and poetry, immediate response and posthumous renown.[3] Hazlitt's critique allows us to read Coleridge's talk – representations of Coleridge talking, and Coleridge's representations of talk – in terms of the question of the Romantic culture of posterity. If Coleridge exchanges the possibility of posthumous textual life, of writing 'for the PERMANENT' (*CL* III.352), for the immediate gratification of talk, then that talk becomes of crucial importance for thinking about Coleridge in terms of this 'culture'. If Hazlitt is right, Coleridge's notorious facility for and delight in his own talk is itself in conflict with his desire for posthumous recognition.[4] In this chapter, I begin by examining Coleridge's reputation as a talker. One of the paradoxes of Coleridge's reputation is that he survives, at least in the nineteenth century and still today to some extent as a conversationalist. So I also want to explore ways in which the ephemerality of speech might survive in displaced ways and, perhaps, allow for a certain permanence of voice. But I am also interested in ways in which such a phantom or quasi-survival in talk, of talk, may be said to be programmed into Coleridge's canonical poetry, ways in which his poetry works against itself to privilege the very *noise* (that which cannot survive in writing) of a poetic voice. The bulk of this chapter, then, concerns what I call Coleridge's 'sonocentric' poetry, talk as the aporia of poetry, its noise. Taking Hazlitt seriously, I seek to examine ways in which Coleridge's concern with the immediacy of speech, even in the poetry, works in tension with the Romantic culture of posterity.

Coleridge's talk, what de Quincey calls 'his splendid art of conversation' (*DQW* xi.102), was (in)famous: remembering the Coleridge of the 1820s,

De Quincey recalls 'What a tumult of anxiety prevailed to "hear Mr Coleridge", or even to talk with a man who *had* heard him' (*ibid.*). 'It is impossible for man to talk better' opines John Payne Collier in 1811, and writing in 1847, Noah Porter declares Coleridge to be 'the greatest talker of his day' (*TT* II.328).[5] His spoken words, according to Anton Langerhanns, 'resound endlessly in the ears of the hearer: they descend into the soul like lightning bolts and illuminate it as if with the flames of revelation' (*TT* II.437). Thomas Carlyle is more wary: 'he distinguished himself to all that ever heard him as at least the most surprising talker extant in this world, – and to some small minority, by no means to all, as the most excellent' (*TT* II.408). 'Zounds! I was never so bethumped with words', complains John Morritt, losing an argument against the weight of Coleridge's talk in April 1828 (*TT* I.558).

'He talks as a bird sings', comments Wordsworth, 'as if he could not help it' (*MY* II.664). The particular characteristic and, indeed, the peril of Coleridge's talk was its continuity, the sheer extent of its uninterrupted and uninterruptible flow. 'He would talk from morn to dewy eve, nor cease till far midnight', Charles Lamb remembers, 'yet who would ever interrupt him, – who would obstruct that continuous flow of converse . . . ?' (*Talker*, p. 280). John Sterling records in 1827 having been in Coleridge's company for three hours '& of that time he certainly spoke during two hours & three quarters'; and he goes on to comment that Coleridge could have spoken 'just as well' for the next forty-eight hours (*TT* II.401). In 1832, Coleridge's estranged wife Sara, on meeting the poet again, notes that 'His power of continuing talking seems unabated, for he talked incessantly for full 5 hours' (*Talker*, p. 163). There was, De Quincey remarked to James Hogg, 'always one difficulty, and sometimes two': 'It was sometimes a great difficulty to get him to begin to talk; it was always so to get him to stop' (*TT* I.563). 'Unless he could have all the talk', De Quincey comments in an essay on 'Conversation', he 'would have none' (*DQW* XIII.170).[6] 'I have heard Coleridge talk, with eager musical energy, two stricken hours', declares Thomas Carlyle, 'and communicate no meaning whatsoever' (*TT* II.409). This sense of the senselessness of Coleridge's talk is often remarked: Samuel Rogers, for example, also remembers listening to Coleridge for two hours, during which time Wordsworth listened 'with profound attention, every now and then nodding his head as if in assent. On quitting his lodgings, I said to Wordsworth, "Well, for my own part, I could not make head or tail of Coleridge's oration: pray, did you understand it?" "Not one syllable of it", was Wordsworth's reply' (*Talker*, p. 336).

As with Lamb's description of Coleridge's 'continuous flow of converse', the metaphor most commonly used to evoke his talk is of a river. Wordsworth, for example, remembers Coleridge's talk as 'a majestic river, the sound or sight of whose course you caught at intervals, which was sometimes concealed by forests, sometimes lost in sand, then came flashing out broad and distinct, then again took a turn which your eye could not follow, yet you knew and felt that it was the same river' (*TT* I.xli). Similarly, Thomas Grattan remarks that Coleridge 'seemed to breathe in words' and that his talk was 'a broad, deep stream, carrying gently along all that it met with on its course' by contrast with a 'whirlpool that drags into its vortex, and engulfs what it seizes on' (*Talker*, p. 226–7), and Charles Cowden Clarke compares him to 'a cataract filling and rushing over my penny-phial capacity' (*Talker*, p. 133).[7] Writing in 1851, Thomas Carlyle also used irriguous metaphors, less flatteringly, to convey his sense of Coleridge's conversational digressions: 'it was talk not flowing anywhither like a river, but spreading everywhither in inextricable currents and regurgitations like a lake or sea . . . most times, you felt logically lost; swamped near to drowning in this tide of ingenious vocables, spreading out boundless as if to submerge the world' (*TT* II.409). But an alternative, even less flattering metaphor, is that of a machine out of control: Carlyle used this figure when he described Coleridge in the flow of talk as 'a steam-engine of hundred horses power – with boiler burst' (*TT* I.lix), and Charles Cowden Clarke also used the metaphor: 'and so he went on like a steam-engine – I keeping the engine oiled with my looks of pleasure, while he supplied the fuel' (*Talker*, p. 133). Similarly, James Fennimore Cooper compared Coleridge to a 'barrel to which every other man's tongue acted as a spigot, for no sooner did the latter move, than it set his own contents in a flow' (*TT* I.553).

This sense of conversational isolation, of conversation which is monologue, is often referred to by contemporary witnesses: Coleridge's monoglossial flow of talk was less a *colloquium*, in De Quincey's distinction, than '*alloquium*' (*DQW* XIII.170). Similarly, Coleridge himself, in a letter to Thomas Allsop, speaks of 'our former Thursday Evening *Conver-* or to mint a more appropriate term, *One*versazioni' (*CL* VI.790). Mme de Stael's famous definition was that Coleridge was 'a master of monologue, mais qu'il ne savait pas le dialogue' (*TT* I.xlv).[8] Once he starts, indeed, there is a sense in which he cannot stop 'I am glad you came in to punctuate my discourse', he says to a newly arrived guest, 'which I fear has gone on for an hour without any stops at all' (*TT* I.392). In fact, though, others record that Coleridge was rarely stopped by interruptions, and would continue talking after the briefest of interludes. Indeed, according to De Quincey, Coleridge '*could* not talk unless he were uninterrupted' (*DQW* XIII.171). 'Such a mode of systematic trespass upon the conversational rights of a whole party', complains De Quincey, 'is fatal to every purpose of social intercourse' (*DQW* XIII.170). There is, indeed, a sense almost of desperation in Coleridge's talk, a sense that he *cannot* stop, whether he wants to or not, until his body gives up.[9] Coleridge would 'hold forth', John Herman Merivale remembers, 'mazed and half entranced, forgetting time, place, and company, in his eagerness to unburden himself of the strange contents of his imagination, until his physical powers were exhausted, and his hearers dismissed at last through the ivory gate of his philosophical limbo' (*CCH* II.31–2). What Carl Woodring terms Coleridge's 'compulsiveness' in talking (*TT* I.xlvi) is exemplified by Carlyle's sense that the burst boiler of Coleridge talking is out of control: 'his mind seems totally beyond his own controul; he speaks incessantly, not thinking or imagining or remembering, but combining all these processes into one; as a rich and lazy housewife might mingle her soup and fish and beef and custard into one unspeakable mass and present it trueheartedly to her astonished guests' (*TT* I.lix). Bryan Waller Procter also suggests the compulsive nature of Coleridge's talk when he notes that 'Coleridge was prodigal of his words, which in fact he could with difficulty suppress' (*Talker*, p. 318). Similarly, Thomas Dibdin, in his *Reminiscences of a Literary Life* (1836) records the way in which talking removes Coleridge from himself: 'he would sometimes seem, during the more fervid moments of discourse, to be abstracted from all and every thing around and about him, and to be basking in the sunny warmth of his own radiant imagination' (*TT* II.320). Coleridge, according to Julian Charles Young (who heard him talk in 1828), 'conscious of his transcendent powers, rioted in a license of tongue which no man could tame' (*TT* II.419). Even the government spy is said to have reported that 'There is not much harm in Coleridge; for he is a whirl-brain, that talks whatever comes uppermost'.[10] The peril of Coleridge's talk, then, is in the way that it appears to be out of control, literally to take over the body of the speaker. His talk is compulsive, his body a machine for talk, his mind 'totally beyond his own control'. This sense of the engine-like automaton of Coleridge's talk is most evocatively suggested by Harriet Martineau in her *Autobiography* (1877) when she compares it to the first computer ('Babbage's machine'). Martineau says that she is 'glad to have seen his weird face, and heard his dreamy voice' since it has clarified her idea concerning possession and prophecy, of 'involuntary speech from involuntary brain action': 'I believe the philosophy and moralising of Coleridge to be much like the action of Babbage's machine; and his utterances to be about equal in wonder to the numerical results given out by the mechanician's instrument' (*Talker*, p. 298).

The effect of Coleridge's talk is also, in a particular sense, perilous for his auditors who, in Hazlitt's description, become a 'Circean herd' (*Works* VIII.203).[11] The effect of his talk is reported as electric, mesmeric, hypnotic: John Taylor Coleridge records that 'He astonishes you, he electrifies you almost as he goes on, but you cannot remember the train afterward' (*TT* I.li). A similar effect of seduction and later disillusionment is recorded in a review of the first edition of *Table Talk* by John Merivale: 'all were held alike by an inexplicable fascination of voice and manner, which seemed, while the display continued, to influence them as if they were in the presence of actual inspiration; although upon reflection they might not unfrequently conclude, that they had been deceived into imagining a transcendental meaning, where the speaker was in fact carried out of the sphere of meaning altogether by the force and rapidity of his own conceptions' (*CCH* II.31). The dangerous seduction of Coleridge's rhetoric in his lectures was such that, according to John Heraud, 'one was fearful, if resigned too often to the enchantment, of surrendering the independence of one's modes of thought, and of submitting to his without will or power of extrication': according to Heraud, in order to maintain their 'intellectual freedom', many resorted to reading his work and foregoing 'the living commentary of his personal discourse' (*Talker*, p. 258). In the Preface to the first edition of *Table Talk* (1836), H.N. Coleridge remarks that upon his listener, 'there would steal an influence, and an impression, and a sympathy; there would be a gradual attempering of his body and spirit, till his total being vibrated with one pulse alone, and thought became merged in contemplation' (*TT* II.10). Writing in 1862, Thomas Colley Grattan, who heard Coleridge talk in 1828, recollects his 'voluptuous and indolent strain of talk, flowing in a quiet tone of cadenced eloquence . . . somewhat drowsy . . . But there was something too dreamy, too vapoury to rouse one to the close examination of what he said' (*Talker*, p. 228–9).[12] Similarly, Thomas Dibdin remembers Coleridge's auditors as 'rapt in wonder and delight', and his sense that Coleridge himself was secretly convinced that 'his auditors seemed to be entranced with his powers of discourse' (*TT* II.319, 320). As these comments would suggest, a major part of the effect of Coleridge's talk was the sound of his voice: 'its sound alone', declares

Hazlitt, in his lecture 'On the Living Poets', 'was the music of thought' (*Works* v.167). Both Coleridge and Wordsworth, according to Hazlitt, recite and talk with a certain 'chaunt . . . which acts as a spell upon the hearer . . . disarming judgment' (Works xvii.118). This might be compared to the effect that Coleridge records in a notebook: 'I have often heard a long sentence & without its being repeated found that I had understood it yet for some sounds I have been so ear-poniarded with the physical sound, that it was like seeing a fist that had just struck fire from your Eye' (*CN* 2812). And it is the 'physical sound', the noise, of Coleridge's voice to which witnesses repeatedly return. Procter for example, comments that 'When he spoke his words were thick and slow, and when he read poetry his utterance was altogether a chant' (*Talker*, p. 318); and H.N. Coleridge, in a review of Coleridge's *Poetical Works*, comments on 'the slow and continuous enunciation, and the everlasting music of his tones' (*Talker*, p. 143).[13] In John Payne Collier's account, Coleridge's lecturing voice is both peculiar and mesmeric: 'All he says is without effort, but not unfrequently with a sort of musical hum, and a catching of his breath at the end, and sometimes in the middle, of a sentence, enough to make a slight pause, but not so much as to interrupt the flow of his language' (*TT* ii.336). John Sterling remarks that Coleridge has 'the most expressive voice in the world' (*TT* ii.402). In his preface to *Table Talk*, H.N. Coleridge comments on the mesmeric rhythms of Coleridge's talk: 'How many a time and oft have I felt his abstrusest thoughts steal rhythmically on my soul, when chanted forth by him!' (*TT* ii.11). One of the most detailed accounts of Coleridge's voice is from an article in *Blackwood's*, September 1840 by John Wilson: 'His voice was a very peculiar one; it was soft, not strong; sweet, and yet with a strange huskiness, amounting almost to harshness, in its notes like the voice of a river when half crusted over with ice. He had a burr, too, and a lisp, which completed the contradictory elements which mingled in it. Yet, on the whole, it produced a melodious effect . . . ' (*Talker*, p. 372–3).[14]

Finally, it is often not only Coleridge's speech and voice which attracts attention but his indefinably grey eyes, what Merivale calls his 'mysterious grey eye' (*CCH* ii.30) and what H.N. Coleridge refers to as the poet's 'quick yet steady and penetrating greenish grey eye' (TT i.lxxxii).[15] Similarly, Elizabeth Grant remembers Coleridge from an occasion when, as a young girl, she met the poet: 'That poor, mad poet, Coleridge, who never held his tongue stood pouring out a deluge of words meaning nothing, with eyes on fire, and his silver hair streaming down to his waist' (*Talker*, p. 91). Thomas Hood remarked that 'Like his own bright-eyed marinere, he had a spell in his voice that would not let you go' (*Talker*, p. 265). In even more melodramatic terms, John Sterling accounts for Coleridge's powers of 'conversation – or rather his monologue' in terms of his 'glittering eye', and compares him with the Ancient Mariner: 'It is painful to observe in Coleridge that with all the kindliness & glorious far-seeing intelligence of his eye – there is a glare in it – a half light unearthly half morbid. It is the glittering eye of the Ancient Mariner. His cheek too shows a flush of over-excitement – the red of a storm-cloud at sunset. When he dies – another, & one of the greatest, of their race, will rejoin the few "immortals" – the ill-understood – & ill-requited – who have ever walked the earth' (*TT* II.401).[16]

Coleridge's talk, then, that dangerous, unstoppable noise of allo-quium or *one*versazioni, comes to define the poet for many of his acquaintances. It is talk which Coleridge himself cannot stop, talk which endangers both speaker and his auditors. And it is talk which both ensures and endangers Coleridge's survival in posterity. While Coleridge is remembered, above all, for his talk, talk can only survive in effigy, through the partial medium of writing (lacking voice, gesture, tone, accent), a medium which almost entirely eradicates its specificity, its grain, its *noise*. As we have seen, the voice of Coleridge often appears to be more noise than sense; its 'physical sound' seems to have had a mes-meric or hypnotic effect, a dehumanising quality which transfers the 'auto-motive' function of Coleridge's talk – talk which is out of control, compulsive – onto the consciousness of its hearers. It is, in particular, I would like to suggest, the uncanny, perilous effect of the sound of voice – noise, what David Appelbaum calls the 'vocalness of voice'[17] – that may be said to be crucial to effects of talk in Coleridge or by Coleridge. And it is this grain of the voice, this noise, which Coleridge's most well-known poems call on and call for. For Coleridge, writing acts as an inad-equate substitute, a degraded supplement for the noise of talk.

In a lecture given on 10 March 1818, Coleridge argues that human com-munication consists, primarily, of sound: 'Man communicates by artic-ulation of Sounds, and paramountly by the memory in the Ear'. He then states that nature communicates 'by the impression of Surfaces and Bounds on the Eye' and that writing involves a kind of translation from sound to vision: 'The primary Art is *Writing*, primary if we regard the purpose, abstracted from the different modes of realizing it . . . picture Language – Hieroglyphics – and finally, Alphabetic / These all alike consist in the *translation* as it were, of Man into Nature – the use of the visible in place of the Audible.'[18] Writing, for Coleridge, is a displaced representation of noise, a translation to the visual from the aural. As a number of critics have argued, the paradigmatic communicative situation for Romantic poetics is that of speech, of dialogue: 'Generally speaking', Michael Macovski comments, 'the Romantics' recurrent concern with conversational encounters, colloquial diction, and the "spontaneous" immediacy of the impassioned imagination reveals a desire to inscribe the language of orality into their printed discourse . . . Their prefaces, essays, and other commentary on language betray a pained mistrust of the written word, an attempt to reach beyond the dead letter of the static text, to locate poetry within the interactive orality of vocative forms.'[19] It is with Coleridge, I suggest, that the conflict between the immediacy and ephemerality of talk on the one hand and the potential permanence of writing and its abstraction from human interaction on the other is most acute.[20] It has not gone unremarked that most of Coleridge's best-known poems are centred on the trope of talk, figuring poetry as a mode of speech.[21] The speaker in 'Kubla Khan', for example, imagines a poet with the dangerous power of what might be called inspired noise. At the end of the poem the speaker remembers a damsel with a dulcimer and claims that:

> Could I revive within me
> Her symphony and song,
> To such a deep delight 'twould win me,
> That with music loud and long,
> I would build that dome in air . . .

The speaker imagines a sound – the 'symphony and song' – which, translated into poetry, aural words, would constitute the pleasure dome that he has tried and failed to describe. Speech as noise would not simply represent the pleasure dome – as written language, poetry attempts to do – but would *be* that dome. The perils of such an achievement are suggested by the dangerous poet with 'flashing eyes and floating hair' who must be controlled by social ritual. The dangers of and the desire to control speech also determine the plot of 'Christabel': Geraldine puts a spell on Christabel so that she cannot tell anyone what she has experienced: 'In the touch of this bosom there worketh a spell, / Which is lord of thy utterance' (lines 267–8). And while Geraldine has the power to silence Christabel, her own voice is itself repeatedly described as both orally and aurally challenged. The poem emphasises her loss of voice: 'her voice was faint and sweet' (line 72), 'I scarce can speak for weariness' (line 74), ' "I cannot speak for weariness" ' (line 142), 'soon with altered voice, said she' (line 204), 'And why with hollow voice cries she' (line 210), 'And with low voice and doleful look' (line 265). Geraldine's control of voice, of other voices, is only matched by the loss of her own. Finally, Geraldine is the daughter of Lord Roland de Vaux of Triermaine, a name which allows for an aural disturbance of naming in the potential for mishearing, or mis-saying, 'Vaux' – as 'vox ' or 'voice'. A witch, Geraldine is also embodied voice, voice personified.

Tim Fulford has argued that 'speech, with its possibility of intimate unity between speaker and listener, was the condition to which Coleridge's actions and writings aspired'.[22] I want to suggest, however, that this 'possibility', inherent in speech (with its promise of intimacy, of presence, with its indication of redemptive community) is precisely what Coleridge's poetry disturbs. Most, if not all, of Coleridge's major poems are concerned with the irreducible difference or absence on which speech relies, the sense that speech enacts a form of remaining or survival which is only more evident in writing. His poems explore ways in which speech is structured by absence and deferral. Critics have noted, for example, the way that the interlocutors in the so-called 'conversation poems' tend to seem strangely absent: Sara Coleridge is 'pensive', the baby is *en fans*, without speech and without language,[23] Charles Lamb is literally absent, as are Sara Hutchinson, the Lady, Wordsworth, William and Edmund, the various interlocutors in the 'Dejection' ode in its different manifestations.[24] 'This Lime-Tree Bower my Prison' is exemplary in this respect. The poem is premised on the absence of the auditor and therefore on the impossibility of the act of communication by which conversation is defined. The poem is inspired by the impossibility of talk – by the fact that Charles Lamb is not present – it is, in fact, *about* the absence of the interlocutor, and yet it repeatedly reinforces and re-emphasises the fiction of interlocutorial presence, a presence first marked, for example, by the apostrophic 'but thou, methinks, most glad, / My gentle-hearted Charles!' (lines 27–8). Without Lamb's absence, that is to say, there could be no such poem – talk would have taken its place – so that as a 'conversation', the poem only functions on the basis that it cannot be a conversation. This conversation poem produces an aporia of poetic talk: it appeals to the condition of the auditor's presence, a condition on which the poem would not have been written, since it has no other topic than his absence.[25]

But another sense in which the very possibility of communication is disturbed in Coleridge's verse concerns the ways in which his talk – by which I wish to appeal to his poetic talk in the 'conversation poems', as much as his talk more conventionally conceived – engages with its own materiality, its 'physical sound'. Speech, for Coleridge, the poet who was for Wordsworth 'quite an epicure in sound',[26] is constantly invaded or controlled or directed by its other, by noise. Noise is a curiously neglected aspect of poetry and poetics, almost always overlooked for the regularity and sense-making of such effects as rhythm, rhyme, assonance, alliteration, onomatopoeia. Such effects tend to be regarded as enhancing or supplementing sense, so that, in the critical tradition, noise is assimilated to meaning. And yet noise, the sound-effect of poetry, the effect of sound displaced, distanced from sense, is central to Coleridge's poetics.[27] Again and again, Coleridge's poems articulate the inarticulable, the remains of voice, that which does *not* remain in writing, talk's ephemera, its noise. If the ideal of a Coleridgean poetics is, as Fulford suggests, conversation, I want to suggest that elements of voice which cannot be recorded in writing also concern Coleridge as poet. It is not – or not only – a question of Coleridge's attempt to record his voice in poetry that makes Coleridgean poetry a contradiction in terms but the way in which that voice is constituted by the materiality of sound, sound abstracted from sense, the grain and graze of the voice. It is the inarticulacy of the articulate and the articulacy of the inarticulate which dominate Coleridge's poetry, which direct his poetics. It is, in Hazlitt's terms, the 'dramatic' or *performative* in poetry that concerns Coleridge, poetry as act, speech act, most evidently and most irreducibly apparent in the inarticulate cacophonies of voice, its grazing, its timbre, accent, pitch, its unmeaning meaning.[28] To adopt Derrida's declaration in *Of Grammatology*, Coleridge's poetics record the impossibility of phonetic writing.[29] This may help us towards a thinking of Coleridge's poetic career, his repeated declaration of the end of poetic composition: for Coleridge, poetry can never be, only talk about, gesture towards, the condition of sound, of noise, of voice.[30]

All of the 'conversation poems' are pervasively concerned with sounds and silences, but 'The Eolian Harp' and 'Frost at Midnight' are particularly telling in this respect. 'The Eolian Harp' is structured by the metaphor of poetry as noise, the inorganic, mechanical, arbitrary and senseless noise of wind over harp-strings, the 'witchery of sound' (line 20). This witchery is stranger than it might at first appear: we – or Sara – are asked to listen to the world, a world –

> . . . so hush'd!
> The stilly murmur of the distant sea
> Tells us of silence.   (lines 10–12)

Coleridge appears to be indicating a space between silence and noise – silence which yet murmurs, and sound which 'Tells us of silence': neither silence nor noise, the murmur is both at once in a passage which disturbs the oppositional logic of the two.[31] But the passage also links both silence and noise to effects of meaning by suggesting that the murmur can 'Tell us' something, and by suggesting that that something is 'silence'. On the other hand, effects of meaning are simultaneously compromised in the phrase 'stilly murmur' not only by the way that the murmuring of 'murmur' enacts its own sound, sounds it, but also by the way in which 'stilly' seems to be undecidably both adjective and adverb – a grammatical disturbance of meaning within a phrase which records an aural evocation of meaningfulness. Stillness returns, in fact, at the end of the 'one Life' passage added in 1817: 'it should have been impossible', the poet declares, 'Not to love all things in a world so filled; / Where the breeze warbles, and the mute still air / Is Music slumbering on her instrument' (lines 30–3). Once again, the lines both refer to and approach the condition of babble, of noise or 'warble', by suggesting that sound and silence coexist: 'While the breeze warbles, *and* the mute still air . . . '. The ambiguous nature of 'and' allows us to imagine a breeze which is both warbling and mute at the same time. Nonsense-noise, noise as the elimination of sense, is also embedded within the turn at the end of the poem where the poet describes the 'serious eye' of Sara delivering a 'mild reproof' to these 'shapings of the unregenerate mind' (lines 49, 55). The poet's words, his secular thoughts, are 'Bubbles that glitter as they rise and break / On vain Philosophy's aye-babbling spring' (lines 56–7). The poem ends, in other words, with a rejection of itself, of its own babbling, and with a silencing of such philosophical babble in a pledging of the poet to his wife and his God, to silence. Poetry, that is to say, in the form of such a philosophico-poetic effusion, is babble, a form of talk beyond talk, a 'continuous murmuring sound like a brook' (*Chambers*), incessant, idle, senseless, confused. The poetry of noise, then, poetry *as* noise, is the condition towards which this poem moves, talk which babbles, murmurs, a witchery of sound, warbling, mute, still.

'Frost at Midnight' develops the Coleridgean poetics of noise but also adds a counternoise by giving priority to the other of noise, to silence. The opening to the poem describes the noises that fracture the 'strange / And extreme silentness' of the night (lines 9–10). But rather than the cacophonous cry of the 'owlet' – which 'Came loud – and hark, again! loud as before' (line 3) – what 'disturbs / And vexes meditation' (lines 8–9) is not noise but its other, the uncanny sounding of silence, 'Inaudible as dreams' (line 13). In this poem, the effect of sound is to produce a series of disconcerting dislocations in sound, a series of absences or vacancies in auditory phenomena. If the condition to which 'The Eolian Harp' aspires is that of the noise – the noise of voice – the condition to which 'Frost at Midnight' aspires is that of the vacancies embedded within vocal and other articulation, to silence. The second verse-paragraph develops this celebration of the silence of noise by exploring the silence of memorised sound. In a doubling of memory – a memory of memory – Coleridge describes how the 'stranger' on his fire reminds him of his schooldays, when another 'stranger' appeared to be both 'presageful' and remindful of an earlier time in his 'sweet birth-place'. He remembers remembering the sound of the bells of 'the old church-tower' on the 'hot Fair-day', as the poor man's only 'music' which rang:

> So sweetly, that they stirred and haunted me
> With a wild pleasure, falling on mine ear
> Most like articulate sounds of things to come! (lines 31–3)

The dislocated temporal movements of memory and presage, their uncanny and aurally undecidable nature, suggest a power beyond that of noise, a power of 'articulation'.[32] Noise, here, in the form of a kind of music, is articulate, distinctive, discriminatory, meaningful. And yet the noise to which Coleridge appeals is precisely one which is *not* present, a noise of memory – indeed, the memory of a memory – a noise defined by its silence, its not sounding. In fact, even in its originary plenitude, this campanological articulation is deferred, a haunting which tells of things to come, the sound 'falling on mine ear / Most like . . . ': the sound is not itself but *like* a sense of the future, like a proleptic haunting.

The third verse-paragraph opens with the noise of the 'Babe's' 'gentle breathings', a sound which takes the place of thought itself: the baby's 'breathings',

> . . . heard in this deep calm,
> Fill up the interspersèd vacancies
> And momentary pauses of the thought! (lines 45–7)

Sound acts as a substitute for thought, filling its place as if a sound was the same substance as a thought.[33] It's a strange thought, although entirely – almost fanatically – phonocentric. Except that it might be thought to amount to a deconstruction of phonocentrism, since what takes the place of thought is not the effect of speaking-to-oneself which Derrida sees as characterising consciousness within the metaphysics of presence, but rather a noise.[34] For a sound – and in particular, an undifferentiated, unarticulated sound – to be a thought suggests the possibility that thought itself aspires to the condition of noise. In order to distinguish this from the vocal and therefore implicitly human and meaningful sense of 'phonocentrism', I propose to use the sonically awkward term 'sonocentrism': Coleridge, that is to say, goes beyond phonocentrism to sonocentrism.

In the course of a discussion of Milton's *Paradise Lost*, Christopher Ricks declares that it is 'the relationship of sound to sense which most enables a poet's words to be at once fully an experience and fully an understanding', and such a sense of sound is certainly borne out by the 'articulate sounds' of Coleridge's poem (line 33), its 'sounds intelligible' (line 59).[35] And yet there is a contrapuntal sense of sound here, sounds as nonsense, sounds even beyond noise to silence:

> . . . whether the eave-drops fall
> Heard only in the trances of the blast,
> Or if the secret ministry of frost
> Shall hang them up in silent icicles,
> Quietly shining to the quiet Moon. (lines 70–4)

One of the remarkable things about this ending is the way in which it seems to articulate a metaphysics which would be defined by the possibility of hearing what is, more or less, inaudible (another aspect of sonocentrism). On the one hand, Coleridge wants to offer the thought of the minimal sound of the drops of water (one normally overwhelmed by the noise of the 'blast'). On the other hand he wants (us) to attend to the quiet of their not falling at all since they are ice. The tautological effect of the final line only reinforces this fixation on noise and its other. Sounds signify, in the end, at the end, in their very cacophony, their silent unmeaningness. In this sonocentric poem, sounds articulate the other of meaning, of language, of speech: silence, or noise. But it is articulate silence, inarticulate noise, which produces poetry just out of its resistance to meaning, out of the dissonance of meaning, its absence. And it is precisely this audible material, this aural materiality, which is lost, not articulated, in poetry on the page. The phenomenology of silence which structures 'Frost at Midnight' may be said to be the self-undoing condition of noise in poetry: noise, silence – neither can be recorded in poetry and yet both are, paradoxically, what makes poems poems. Articulate silence, then: nonsense, noise.

The trouble with voice, with the noises that voices make and their dangerous potential to exert power over others, as well as their troubling loss, is powerfully elaborated in 'The Rime of the Ancient Mariner', a poem which is centred on questions of voicing, of hypnotic suggestion and of the dangerous gulf between speech and writing.[36] One consequence of retitling and, in particular, respelling 'The Rime of the Ancyent Marinere' in the second edition of the *Lyrical Ballads* 'The Ancient Mariner. A Poet's Reverie', for example, is to effect a distinct but subtle shift in the relationship between speech and writing, between the phonemic and graphemic resources of language. The alteration discriminates between the poet's voice and his hand, between talk and script. Thus the archaic spelling of 'Ancyent Marinere' produces a question of voicing and a questioning of voice – how should we pronounce this writing? How archaise our voice(s)? This effect is repeated and developed as the poem progresses in its earlier 1798 version, not only in the repetitions of the words 'Ancyent' and 'Marinere', but in various other spellings such as 'sate' (line 21), 'Minstralsy' (line 40), 'Emerauld' (line 52) and so on. Given the emphatically oral figuration of the poet in Wordsworth's idea of a 'Man speaking to men' in the 1800 Preface and, more generally, in the context of the Romantic valorisation of the speaking voice, Coleridge's respelling of his poem's title in the second edition can be seen as, in part, a response to a theory of the vocalisation of poetry, of poetry as a spontaneous articulation, poetry as incarnated speech.[37] The interplay of the multiple versions of Coleridge's text might then be read in terms of the space between speech and writing. By contrast with the modernisation and (arguably) the oralisation of the second edition, for example, the addition of the editorial gloss to the 1817 version printed in *Sibylline Leaves* dislodges any direct and unmediated vocalisation of the poem. In terms of a recitation of 'The Rime of the Ancient Mariner', this supplementary gloss would necessitate two voices or a double voicing – an impossible cacophony. As with Coleridge's sonocentric conversation poems, speech, voices, sounds, noises – and, by contrast, silence, the written, muteness and the unspeakable – may be said to structure and deconstruct Coleridge's most famous poem.[38]

    First published in the *Lyrical Ballads* and in many ways the most traditional of those ballads, the most concerned to reproduce the aural and oral effects of the traditional ballad form (a self-consciously traditional or archaic diction, metrical regularity, the use of rhymes, alliteration and assonance, repetition, the stanza form, etc.), the poem's representation of the rejection of the Mariner's hand by the wedding guest ('Hold off! unhand me, grey-beard loon!' cries the guest in line 11 of the revised version) may also be read as an elaboration of the implicit rejection of writing by the adoption of the ballad form itself. The poem emphasises bodily images of interlocutorial presence – not only the eye ('He holds him with his glittering eye', line 13, immediately follows this rejection), but also the ear: 'The Wedding-Guest sat on a stone: / He cannot choose but hear' (lines 17–18; repeated line 38). The poem can be read as a drama of bodily displacement from eye and hand to ear. By the end of the poem we have found that what the wedding-guest hears is no ordinary sound, no ordinary speech: the Ancient Mariner possesses and is possessed by 'strange power of speech' (line 587). But the desired orality of the poem is belied by the Mariner's hand, his skinny grasp, his hold. The eye and the hand necessary for writing are, as we have noted, most specifically designated by the marginal gloss which requires a moving eye to read it and a moving hand to write it. The gloss cannot be voiced at the same time as the poem: to do so, supposing one had two voices, or two people to voice, would be to create a cacophony of noises, an incoherent jargoning of sound. What Coleridge adds in 1817, a gloss, an extra tongue, disturbs the possibility of voice, or voicing.[39]

The poem concentrates sound in excess of other sensory features, such as sight or touch. And sounds produce a sense of the uncanny:

> The ice was here, the ice was there,
> The ice was all around:
> It cracked and growled, and roared and howled,
> Like noises in a swound!   (lines 59–62)[40]

How can we say this? How might we give voice to 'noises in a swound'? Prompted by the reviewer in the *British Critic*, who declares that the phrase is 'nonsensical' (*CCH* 1.58), we might remark that it is not entirely clear how we should pronounce – or read – the word 'swound'. Our reading of this word depends, not least, on its sounding, the way we make it sound. The articulation of the word – whether silent or aloud – will affect our reading not only of this line but of the poem more generally. The *OED* and the rhyme with 'around' both direct us to articulate the word to rhyme with 'sound'. But its modern sense of 'swoon', the fact that, as the *OED* informs us, 'swound' is a 'later form of *swoune*, SWOON, with excrescent *d*', and that the same book gives an example of 'swound' rhyming

with 'wound' from 1856, may give us pause.[41] The voicing of 'swound',
then, might involve its phonetic materialisation as 'swoon'. 'Swoon', that
is to say, going against the grain of the word's proper (but to the 'modern'
reader potentially baffling) enunciation, is a necessary and inescapable
reading of the word. Swooning, of course, is a major bodily figure in this
poem. What is involved in noises in a swoon or swound? The word
'swound' recurs in part 5 of 'The Ancient Mariner', when the Mariner
swoons and hears voices: the ship lurches with a 'sudden bound' which
'flung the blood into my head' so that the Mariner 'fell down in a swound'
(lines 390–92). Before he recovers from the swound, the Mariner 'heard,
and in my soul discerned / Two voices in the air' (lines 396–7). This is, in
Shelley's phrase, a 'visioned swound' (*The Revolt of Islam*, canto 9, stanza
11). These voices which, like noises more generally, inhabit a liminal space
between the inside and the outside of the subject's head, never become
more than voices, are never embodied. Rather, the voices are 'Two voices
in the air': that is, the voices are pure sound, unencumbered by the physical attributes of the vocal apparatus which produces voicing, voices
without voice. The voices perform a dialogue based on the formula of
question and answer of which, however, the answers only provide further
riddles. The answers are given by the 'second voice', a 'softer voice, / As
soft as honey-dew' (lines 406–7). The voice of poetry, this voice has not
only fed, like the poet in 'Kubla Khan', on 'honeydew', but is the vocal
equivalent of such classical inspiration. This is what inspiration, unencumbered by the distortions and contortions of human language would
sound like: pure air. The unresponsiveness of this voice's responses, then,
serves only to re-echo the dysfunctional in language, the irrelevance, in
this context, of response. Indeed, the first voice itself seems concerned
with the quality of the sound rather than the quality of the answers provided by the second voice: 'But tell me, tell me! speak again, / Thy soft
response renewing' pleads the first voice (lines 410–11).

In this poem, as in 'The Eolian Harp', even light signifies in terms of
sound, or the absence of sound.[42] The moonlight, for example, is
'steeped in silentness' (line 478), and the bay is 'white with silent light'
(line 480). At this point of sensory conflation, the Mariner 'sees' a
'seraph-man', a 'man all light' (line 490), standing 'On every corse' (line
491), 'Each one a lovely light' (line 495). The silence of these light-men
produces a sense of sound:

> No voice did they impart –
> No voice; but oh! the silence sank
> Like music on my heart (lines 497–99)

This light-music leads to the approach of the Hermit, an approach signalled by the sound – the Mariner *hears* the Hermit and the pilot
approach, *hears* the Hermit's voice ('How loudly his sweet voice he
rears!', line 516) – and to the most uncanny, most appalling, apocalyptic
sound of the poem as the Hermit's boat approaches the ship. At this
point an eerie, uncanny sound of tremendous, indeed apocalyptic,
power is described, a sound which stuns its hearer:[43]

> The boat came close beneath the ship,
> And straight a sound was heard.
>
> Under the water it rumbled on,
> Still louder and more dread:
> It reached the ship, it split the bay;
> The ship went down like lead.
>
> Stunned by that loud and dreadful sound,
> Which sky and ocean smote,
> Like one that hath been seven days drowned
> My body lay afloat;
> But swift as dreams, myself I found
> Within the Pilot's boat.   (lines 544–55)

It is this apocalyptic noise, this unexplained noise of the sea, which
'saves' the Mariner as he is swept off the haunted ship and into the
Pilot's boat. The word 'stunned' is itself specifically keyed to noise by
its sense of being dazed or bewildered by a noise or din (*OED*) and, as
our earlier discussion of 'swound' has suggested, by the phonological
complex of sound–swound–swoon. When the word 'stunned' is
repeated at the crucial position of the poem's end, it only reinforces
the strange collation of noise with paraconsciousness: in the last stanza
the wedding guest leaves 'like one that hath been stunned, / And is of
sense forlorn' (lines 622–3). Just as the Mariner is stunned by the brute
noise of the undefinable sound, so the wedding guest is stunned by
what he hears, by the sound of the Mariner's tale.[44] This disturbing
and uncanny repetition, and its association with the curious 'swound'
is highly suggestive: the poem is made of sound, is sound in silence, the
poem on the page is an effect of light, a visual embodiment of non-
vocalised sounds, instructions for making noises. As such, the poem is
also, potentially, itself pure sound – pure air – the awful possibility of
vocal noise. For, indeed, the echo of the inanimate and originless
sound which sinks the Mariner's ship is a form of speech, a form of
telling:

> Upon the whirl, where sank the ship,
> The boat spun round and round;
> And all was still, save that the hill
> Was telling of the sound (lines 556–9)

While the hill is telling of the sound (and the repeated rhymes and half-rhymes of 'sound', internal and at line endings, between lines 545 and 559 – 'sound', 'louder', 'loud', 'sound', 'drowned', 'found', 'round and round', 'sound' – make the *sound* of 'sound' unmistakable), the Mariner himself attempts to speak and is answered by another sound – the inarticulate sound of the terrified Pilot: 'I moved my lips – the Pilot shrieked / And fell down in a fit' (lines 560–1). Noises, vocal or otherwise, are perilous in this poem.

The plot of the 'The Rime of the Ancient Mariner' can itself be summarised – in terms of its causes and effects – with reference to the question of (the noise of) speech. In the first place, a sailor kills an albatross and is punished both by a lack of water and by a loss of voice. Thus, one of the effects of the punishment is to deny speech: the punishment of drought is directly and explicitly related to a loss of voice (lines 135–9). Although the Mariner temporarily regains his voice at lines 160–1 when he drinks his own blood, his redemption comes later when, on seeing a group of water-snakes ('no tongue / Their beauty might declare'), he is able to bless them, and begins his rehabilitation (lines 282–91). From a recognition and declaration of the absolute and universal inexpressibility of the water-snakes' beauty, the Mariner is able to bless spontaneously, so that in speaking the beauty of the snakes he frees himself to speak.[45] (The aporia of aphasia, embedded within an alternative 'talking cure': in order to begin to speak one must have begun to speak – speech cures the loss of speech.) Between this redemptive speech-act and the end of the poem there are a number of vocal sound-effects – the strange speech or singing of the dead crew, the disembodied voices of 'First Voice' and 'Second Voice', the 'sweet voice' of the Hermit and his fear of the Mariner's voice (line 560), and so on. But the most notable effect of voice in the poem is perhaps the Mariner's eternal impulse to talk: the Mariner is 'forced to begin [his] tale' and has 'strange power of speech'. The redemption of the Mariner is a redemption achieved only on condition of an inescapable and haunting voicing. Speech, then, its loss and regain, its power, strangeness and threat, may be read as the motive force of the poem's plot: if speech is redemptive, both its loss and its necessity can also function as punishments. Speech faces both ways and cannot be disengaged from an uncanny, inescapable and inexplicable ethics. A strangely distorting ethics of speech which will, finally, present us with a question of the ethics of reading: reading as a sounding of written texts. Reading as sound or swound.

One of the most haunting and certainly one of the most powerful and difficult sections of the poem with respect to speech concerns the speech of the dead crew:

> For when it dawned – they dropped their arms,
> And clustered round the mast;
> Sweet sounds rose slowly through their mouths,
> And from their bodies passed.
>
> Around, around, flew each sweet sound,
> Then darted to the Sun;
> Slowly the sounds came back again,
> Now mixed, now one by one.
>
> Sometimes a-dropping from the sky
> I heard the sky-lark sing;
> Sometimes all little birds that are,
> How they seemed to fill the sea and air
> With their sweet jargoning!
>
> And now 'twas like all instruments,
> Now like a lonely flute;
> And now it is an angel's song,
> That makes the heavens be mute.
>
> It ceased; yet still the sails made on
> A pleasant noise till noon,
> A noise like of a hidden brook
> In the leafy month of June,
> That to the sleeping woods all night
> Singeth a quiet tune.   (lines 350–72)

The action of speaking or, more probably, of singing, has been translated into a physiological description of the emissions of sounds: 'Sweet sounds rose slowly through their mouths, / And from their bodies passed'. The two marginal glosses which Coleridge added to these lines in 1817 are also significant in this respect: 'The bodies of the ship's crew are inspired and the ship moves on; But not by the souls of the men, nor by demons of earth or middle air, but by a blessed troop of angelic spirits, sent down by the invocation of the guardian saint'. This inspiration occurs by means of an invocation, a word which carries with it the sound and etymology of a vocalisation: the spirits are invoked, are called to and themselves call. What they call, or sing, however, is an inexpressible music, sounds which cannot be presented in words, which can only be suggested by a multiplying chain of metaphors – sounds flying to the sun, sky-larks singing, instruments, an angel's song, together with the echo or resonance or remainder of this sound in the sails of the ship, a noise which itself must be compared to a series of other objects. This sound is always other to itself or to its representation. The othering of this sound is most clearly apparent as the noises clash with words, with language, in 'jargoning'. 'Jargoning' at once recalls the archaic sense of the 'twittering' or 'chattering' of birds, and, at the same time, encompasses the modern meaning of scholarly or professional overuse – even to obfuscation and meaninglessness – of a technical vocabulary, jargon. But the word traverses this dichotomy of noise and speech: 'jargoning' signifies 'unintelligible or meaningless talk or writing; nonsense . . . a cipher, or other system of characters or signs having an arbitrary meaning . . . barbarous, rude or debased language' (*OED*, 'jargon', substantive 3, 4, 5).[46] The word transgresses the boundary of sense and nonsense and it also inhabits an undecidable space between speech and writing, of spoken and written sounds. At the heart of this poem, then, in its climactic representation of the unpresentable, its sublime invocation of sound, of vocalised music, is the nonsense of language, the nonsense of spoken and written signs, jargoning: noise.

How does a dream sound? This is the kind of question which we can imagine Coleridge himself asking even if there is no record of his doing so.[47] The relation of dreaming to noise is never far away in Coleridge. In 'Frost at Midnight' dreams constitute a standard of the inaudible – 'Sea, hill, and wood, / With all the numberless goings-on of life, / Inaudible as dreams' (lines 11–13). Similarly, 'Kubla Khan', that sleep-poem, dreamt of from within what the Preface declares to be 'a profound sleep, at least of the external senses', provides ambiguous evidence concerning the possibility of aural sensation in dreams: on the one hand there are references to a woman 'wailing', to the 'tumult' of the river and the sound of 'ancestral voices', the sounds of a 'mingled measure' and the damsel's song, while on the other hand, sounds are figured – like the whole vision according to the preface – as unremembered and unrememberable, as unrevivable.[48]

A notable entry in Coleridge's notebook explores the possibility of sound in sleep, reminding us of the way that the auditory can cross over into sleep, penetrating the dream-world from the outer world of the sleeper's environment:[49]

Dosing, dreamt of Hartley as at his Christening – how as he was asked who redeemed him, & was to say, God the Son / he went on, humming and hawing, in one hum & haw, like a boy who knows a thing & will not make the effort to recollect it – so as to irritate me greatly. Awakening <gradually I was able compleatly [*sic*] to detect, that> it was the Ticking of my Watch which lay in the Pen Place in my Desk on the round Table close by my Ear, & which in the diseased State of my Nerves had *fretted* on my Ears – I caught the fact while Hartley's Face & moving Lips were yet before my Eyes, & his Hum and Ha, & the Ticking of the Watch were each the other, as often happens in the passing off of Sleep – that curious modification of Ideas by each other, which is the Element of *Bulls*. – I arose instantly, & wrote it down – it is now 10 minutes past 5. (*CN* 1620)

'In dreams, to be sure, we hear nothing, but we see', remarks Freud.[50] And yet sounds, as in the dream recorded by Coleridge in 1803, are what connect the dream-state with waking or, to put it differently, are what transgress the border between the two.[51] In this respect, noise would be the scandal of a dream or swound, the transgressive, illicit or unacceptable other of dreams. This may allow us to move towards a conclusion concerning dreams, noise, talk and poetry in Coleridge. In a notebook entry from May 1804, Coleridge comments that poetry is 'a rationalized dream' (*CN* 2086), and in a marginal comment on Southey's *Life of Byron* he refers to writing as 'manual somnambulism'.[52] Similarly, while 'The Ancient Mariner' was at one point subtitled 'A Poet's Reverie', in 'Kubla Khan' the dream *is* the poem which can never be written. By this logic, if noise is the other of dreams, that which dreams must exclude or deny, that which transgresses and *ends* dreaming, then the function of noise in poetry may also be understood to be a disruption or disturbance. In this respect, noise, sound, the very stuff of poems, constitutes both the material of poetry and the site of its disruption, scandal or negation. Technological, commercial and educational developments in printing during the Romantic period made the oral transmission, the translation from 'mouth to mouth', poetry as sound-effect, increasingly and as never before redundant. Coleridge's symbolic resistance to this aspect of modernity would involve his holding back from publication such poems as 'Christabel' and 'Kubla Khan', allowing them to get around in manuscript and by word of mouth, noisily, for several years. But for Coleridge, I suggest, this technological transition from sound to silence comes to look more and more like the necessary condition for poetry itself rather than just the arbitrary and contingent effect of the historical conditions of the production of books. For Coleridge, silence – an auditory effect which resounds throughout the represented noises of the so-called 'conversation poems' – is poetry in its ideal state: poems, inaudible as dreams. And it is noise, the transgressive, perilous, fleshy, seductive, uncontrollably oral *stuff* of poetry, its 'physical sound', which constitutes its perilous and fatally defining other. But in its sounding, poetry for Coleridge – his own poetry, anyway – is ineluctably sonocentric, determined in its materiality by the sound-effects of voice, by noise. The paradox of Coleridge's sonocentric disorder, his poetics, is that in order to survive, to live on after the momentary phenomenalisation in sound, poetry must be written, stabilised in writing, dematerialised, silenced. But Coleridge can't stop talking. Like the Ancient Mariner, his noise, which cannot be represented in writing, is his power.[53] Coleridge's consummate poetic achievement is the other of poetry, that which cannot survive, that which we cannot but cannot not read: the *noise* that poems make.

CHAPTER 6

Keats's prescience

'I am literally worn to death, which seems my only recourse.'
(Keats to Fanny Brawne)

'Had there been no such thing as literature, Keats would have dwindled into a cipher'.
(De Quincey, 'John Keats')

We read Keats too quickly. I am not referring to the possibility of per-forming the kind of langorous, indolent reading that a certain Keatsian discourse appears to demand or to the way in which, you might say, there is never enough time for Keats. Nor am I making an unlikely claim about critical attention to the complexities and ambiguities of a poem such as 'Ode on a Grecian Urn'. In saying that we read Keats too quickly, I am referring to the way in which we hurry through our reading of what Derrida calls that 'little, insignificant piece of the whole corpus', the name.[1] While the name of every author is no doubt transformed by met-onymic substitution into his or her writing, I want to suggest that reading John Keats provokes particularly difficult and unavoidable, if unanswer-able questions. Keats – his name and renown, his body, writing and life – is multiply inscribed in whatever it is that we think we are doing when we read 'Ode to a Nightingale', for example, or 'Isabella', or 'Hyperion'. This chapter concerns the renaming of Keats, his renown.[2]

In the early reviews and commentary on Keats and his poetry, the poet's name was, literally, a site of disturbance and conflict. In the first place, there is Leigh Hunt's moniker 'Junkets', suggested by its phonetic congruence with John Keats but also, no doubt, by its sense of 'a dish consisting of curds sweetened and flavoured, served with a layer of scalded cream' (*OED*). More aggressive mis-nominations include repeated references to 'Mr K'[3] and his name repeatedly misspelt as 'Keates';[4] John Croker appears to disbelieve in his name: 'Mr Keats, (if that be his real name, for we almost doubt that any man in his senses would put his real name to such a rhapsody,)' (*KCH* 111); in *Blackwood's* he is 'Pestleman Jack';[5] John Gibson Lockhart refers to 'Mr John', 'Johnny Keats', and 'Johnny';[6] Byron variously refers to Keats as 'Johnny Keats', 'Johnny Keates', 'Mr John Ketch', and 'Jack Keats or Ketch, or whatever his names are' (*KCH* 129, 130); and writing in 1854, James Russell Lowell comments that 'You cannot make a good adjective out of Keats, – the more the pity, – and to say a thing is *Keatsy* is to condemn it' (*KCH* 359).[7] Nowadays, by contrast, the renowned John Keats is always properly named, twentieth-century criticism having become immune to the instability of the poet's name. In fact, the name has undergone a transformation such that, as with other canonical poets, it is ubiquitously used to denote a body of work. Two recent books on Keats exemplify this change: on the first page of *The Sculpted Word*, Grant Scott claims that we 'often feel, in Keats, that we are wandering through a museum . . . ',[8] and many of the contributors to Nicholas Roe's collection of essays *Keats and History* use a similar short-hand: 'a diversity of critical and theoretical approaches to Keats'; 'subsequent readers of Keats . . . our understanding of Keats today'; 'I wish to avoid this way of reading Keats . . . the reading of Keats'; 'by applying the historical method to Keats . . . Keats is one instance of . . . the Romantic ideology'; 'other applications of literary history in Keats'; and, slightly differently, 'The Keats of *To Autumn*'.[9]

This chapter concerns the question of the name, and what it denotes: what are we reading when we 'read Keats'? 'We always pretend to know what a corpus is all about', Derrida remarks.[10] In order to rethink the corpus of Keats, this chapter will culminate in a reading of his sonnet written at the birth-place of Robert Burns in the summer of 1818 – especially its first line, 'This mortal body of a thousand days'. I want to suggest that this line – with its scandalous deixis, with its unequivocal assertion of the presence, here and now, of the body that writes, the body that speaks, of, in short, 'Keats' – that this line has been both central to and largely obliterated in the critical tradition: this line, and the poem as a whole, suppressed by Keats himself, is what we might term the repressed of Keats criticism. What little commentary there is on the line turns on whether it should be read 'literally' or 'figuratively' – in other words, on the question of what Keats can possibly mean by 'This'. The alternative readings are polarised in two biographies. While Aileen Ward argues that the line represents Keats 'staring at the prospect of his own death, less than three years ahead', Robert Gittings claims that it is 'a purely rhetorical opening line'.[11] Furthermore, the question of the relationship between life and the literal is overdetermined in recent criticism on Keats's life as allegory, and by Keats's famous letter in which he argues that 'A Man's life of any worth is a continual allegory' and that 'Lord Byron cuts a figure – but he is not figurative' – a letter in which Keats baldly states that 'above all . . . they are very shallow people who take every thing literal'.[12] It is within this space of biography and criticism, of rhetorical and somatic figuration, of the literal and the figurative, of writing lives and writing death, of prospective and retroactive reading, of Keatsian prescience and the scandal of deictic and nominal reference that this chapter will attempt to read, all too quickly, 'John Keats'. 'John Keats', I want to suggest, is determined by a certain prescience of posthumous renown. It is in this figure that the Romantic culture of posterity might be said to find its proper referent. Supremely aware of the kinds of shifts in the relationship between poet and audience encountered by Wordsworth and Coleridge and theorised by Isaac D'Israeli, Hazlitt and others, the figure of 'John Keats' is produced within and produces this new poetic dispensation. The present chapter attempts to think through the relationship between the reception of Keats and his prescient prefiguration of that reception.

We might start with Keats's first life. What is Richard Monckton Milnes's *Life, Letters, and Literary Remains, of John Keats* (1848)? Both biography and collected works, this inaugural Keats book presents both the body of Keats – his life – and his corpus – his letters and literary remains. In a gesture from which criticism has never fully recovered, the book conflates, undecidably, the life with the writing. The first sentence of the narrative of Keats's life reads as follows: 'To the Poet, if to any man, it may justly be conceded to be estimated by what he has written rather than by what he has done, and to be judged by the productions of his genius rather than by the circumstances of his outward life.'[13] The life of Keats, then, in the first, unequivocal sentence of this first life is conceived as supplementary to the writing. But by the end of the paragraph, this proposition has curiously shifted its ground so that instead of the life being obliterated by the poetry, the writing becomes an *expression* of, and therefore in turn supplementary to, the poet's life. By contrast with that of historians, novelists and philosophers, Milnes argues, the writing of poets constitutes a direct transcription of an authentic and confessional voice:

the Poet, if his utterances be deep and true, can hardly hide himself even beneath the epic or dramatic veil, and often makes of the rough public ear a confessional into which to pour the richest treasures and holiest secrets of his soul. His Life is in his writings, and his Poems are his works indeed.[14]

To the extent that we take Milnes's biography as an authoritative and prescriptive nineteenth-century framing of the life, letters and literary remains of John Keats, the inaugural biography as a decisive factor in the inscription of Keats into the poetic canon, then these comments are crucial to any understanding of what I shall call, after Sidney Colvin, Keats's 'after-fame'.[15] The specificity of poetry, its singularity and marked difference from other discursive regimes, is constituted in Milnes's analysis by its elimination of the mediating and distorting elements of form or generic convention – in short, the 'epic or dramatic veil' – and by its direct articulation, representation or what we might term, after Milnes, 'confession', of the poet's self. The 'full speech' implied by Milnes's extravagant metaphor of confession is achieved by means of its *biographical* revelation: 'His Life is in his writings'. As Keats himself ambiguously comments in a letter to J.H. Reynolds, with regard to Robert Burns, 'We can see horribly clear in the works of such a man his whole life, as if we were God's spies' (*LJK* 1.325).

The opening – indeed the very title – of Milnes's *Life, Letters and Literary Remains of John Keats* is, however, traversed by death as an inescapable determinant of life. 'These pages', comments Milnes in the second paragraph, 'concern one whose whole story may be summed up in the composition of three small volumes of verse, some earnest friendships, one passion, and a premature death'.[16] It is this death, its fact and its structural anachronism, its prolepsis, which defines and regulates this and any biography of John Keats. Indeed, as Milnes's next, most extraordinary sentence suggests, it is in dying that the character of Keats – his personality, self or soul – is expressed or represented. Keats's death and his life in posterity determines, for Milnes, our 'impression' of Keats. Milnes's sense of Keats's after*life*, his living on, is expressed both in his assertion that Keats 'walk[s] among posterity', and in a hallucinatory grammatical presence produced by the uncanny suspension of Milnes's present participles:

As men die, so they walk among posterity; and our impression of Keats can only be that of a noble nature perseveringly testing its own powers, of a manly heart bravely surmounting its first hard experience, and of an imagination ready to inundate the world, yet learning to flow within regulated channels and abating its violence without lessening its strength.[17]

Milnes canonises a certain oppositional rhetoric of power and masculinity against the feminising and attenuating representation of the early reviewers which has marked criticism and biography of Keats up to the present day.[18] At the same time, Milnes defines Keatsian nature in terms of the containment of revolution – a violence and inundation regulated within the context and rhetoric of 'channels' and 'strength'. But, most importantly perhaps, Milnes institutes a rhetoric of posthumous *life* for Keats, his 'walking among posterity', which saturates later criticism and biography of the poet. It is this effect of living on, of surviving – what we might call Keats's after-effect, or after-affect – which may be said to characterise the corpus known as 'Keats'.

In the next paragraph, Milnes develops this rhetoric of posterity when he argues, by a conventional comparison of Keats with Chatterton, that early death acts as an enobling substitute, an empowering supplement to a 'fulfilled poetical existence'. It is precisely because Keats died young that he is a poet, Milnes proposes: 'The interest indeed of the Poems of Keats has already had much of a personal character: and his early end, like that of Chatterton, (of whom he ever speaks with a sort of prescient sympathy) has, in some degree, stood him in stead of a fulfilled poetical existence.' To say that Keats's early death has 'stood him in stead of a fulfilled poetical existence' involves the recognition that such an end works as a redemptive supplement, an alternative to life. Keats, who could have been living when this was written, could have been (although it is the premise of the present chapter that this is unthinkable) in his early fifties, has another life, the life of a *poet*, through his death. But Milnes goes further than this, in parenthesis, to suggest that Keats articulates the fact of his own death in terms of what Milnes calls a 'prescient sympathy' with Chatterton. Keats is sympathetic to Chatterton, we are led to conclude, because he knows that he too will die neglected and young.[19] This rhetorical figure – the coincidence of Keats's constitutive poetic act of dying with a certain prescience of that death – is a fundamental concatenation in the reception of Keats in the nineteenth and twentieth centuries, in his after-fame. Our understanding of Keats as a poet, I am suggesting, is determined, in multiple and complex ways, by Milnes's insistence on the relationship between his early death and a certain prescience. Crucial to the figuration of Keats as Poet is an early death which is presciently inscribed within the poet's life and work – an early death which he *knows about*.[20] Milnes elaborates Keats's prescient sympathy with Chatterton a few pages later when he introduces Keats's poem 'Oh Chatterton! how very sad thy fate' and suggests (via an allusion to Wordsworth's 'Resolution and Independence') that Keats's poem involves a proleptic intertextual reference to the end of Shelley's *Adonais* – that Keats's poem includes a reference to another poet's yet-to-be-written elegy on his own death:

The strange tragedy of the fate of Chatterton 'the marvellous Boy, the sleepless soul that perished in its pride', so disgraceful to the age in which it occurred and so awful a warning to all others of the cruel evils, which the mere apathy and ignorance of the world can inflict on genius, is a frequent subject of allusion and interest in Keats's letters and poems, and some lines of the following invocation bear a mournful anticipatory analogy to the close of the beautiful elegy which Shelley hung over another early grave.[21]

Both the tenor of Keats's poem on Chatterton (the sense that the earlier poet lives on in a transcendental afterlife) and the vehicle of the sidereal metaphor (Keats's figuration of Chatterton as 'among the stars' and that 'to the rolling spheres' he 'sweetly singest') echo, in prescient sympathy, Milnes suggests, the sense of Shelley's Adonais as 'like a star' which, in the last line of his elegy, 'Beacons from the abode where the Eternal are' (*SPP* 406). In this respect, Milnes's biography frames Keats in terms of an aesthetics of prescience, in terms of the poet's proleptic articulation of his own death. The afterlife of Keats's reputation, that is to say, is regulated by a sense that it has been prophetically inscribed within the poet's life and writing. In this respect, Keats's relationship with Chatterton is fundamental, since it provides the critic and biographer with a way of talking about this recognition by means of the figure of identification. Critics can talk about Keats's prescience – what Susan Wolfson has recently termed his 'weirdly prophetic intuition'[22] – without talking nonsense.

Keats did not, of course, invent the role of neglected genius and his early death. Rather, he was responding to a by now clearly defined figuration of the young genius, a characterisation most clearly and most pathetically rendered in the life and reputation of Thomas Chatterton. While critics have long recognised the influence of Chatterton's poetry on Keats,[23] what has been rather less well documented is the significance for Keats of the *corpus* of Chatterton, his written and writing body, the reputation or renown of the poet's imaginative construction, his figure. It is the image of Chatterton, in particular his youth, genius and neglect at death, which was crucial to the Romantic figuration of the poet – for Keats most of all – once the debate concerning the authenticity of his poems had evolved, in the last twenty years of the eighteenth century, into a concern with the image of neglected genius.[24] In this sense, it is possible to discern a pervasive response in the poetry of Keats not so much to the poetry of the earlier poet, but to the myth of Chatterton, such that his poetry may be said to be intertextually saturated – in a finally undecidable manner – by representations of that myth.[25]

One example of the early nineteenth-century construction of the Chattertonian figure is 'A Monody on Chatterton' by Thomas Dermody (1775–1803) posthumously published in *The Harp of Erin* (1807). The poem presents Chatterton in diction and imagery which will become crucial to the Keatsian project a decade later:

> Had he but gain'd his manhood's mighty prime,
> Bright as the sun, and as the sun sublime;
> His soaring soul had borne the awful wand
> Of magic power, and o'er the fairy land
> Of Fancy, shed a new poetic race,
> Lending creation to his favour'd place.
> But ah! the dying sounds decay,
> Ah! they fade away,
> Melting, melting, melting,
> Melting from the ear of day . . . [26]

While any 'echoes' of Dermody's work would be pure conjecture (there is no evidence to suggest that Keats read this little-known poet's work), it is nevertheless possible to conceive of verbal resonances in Keats's poetry as responding to a pervading construction of Chattertonian authorship, writing and response (such resonances would include the 'magic power' of Dermody and the 'magic hand of chance' in Keats's fantasy of early death, the sonnet 'When I have fears that I may cease to be'; Dermody's 'fairy land / Of Fancy' and the 'faery lands forlorn' and cheating 'fancy' of the 'Ode to a Nightingale'; the fading of Dermody's lines and not only the fading of the Nightingale ode but also that of 'To Autumn', as well as the multiple repetitions of 'Ode on a Grecian Urn'[27]). Dermody's poem is just one early nineteenth-century example of the poetic figuration of the corpus of Chatterton. More important, perhaps – not least because it is known to have been read and studied by Keats[28] – is the standard life and works of Chatterton edited by Robert Southey and Joseph Cottle with a reprinted biography by George Gregory, *The Works of Thomas Chatterton* (1803). The life itself frames Chatterton in terms of the desire for fame and the myth of neglect. In the first place, Gregory argues that Chatterton had 'one ruling passion', a 'desire of literary fame' and that 'this passion intruded itself on every occasion, and absorbed his whole attention'.[29] Second, Gregory includes in his biography a series of poems and extracts from poems on Chatterton and on his death which offer a number of pertinent resonances in the poetry of Keats. Thus, while Robert Gittings argues that Keats's 'Isabella' echoes Chatterton's 'Mie love ys dedde, / Gon to hys deathe-bedde, / Al under the wyllowe tree' from *Aella*,[30] Gregory quotes from the much neglected poet laureate Henry Pye's poem 'Progress of Refinement', which figures the response of the muse to Chatterton's death in terms which may also be compared to Isabella's tearful fixation on the basil plant:

> Yet as with streaming eye the sorrowing muse,
> Pale CHATTERTON's untimely urn bedews;
> Her accents shall arraign the partial care,
> That shielded not her son from cold despair. (p. lxxxvi)[31]

Similarly, Keats's 'Bright Star' sonnet may have echoes of Mrs Cowley's 'O Chatterton! For thee the pensive song I raise', which ends with the phrase which opens and titles Keats's sonnet: 'Bright Star of Genius! – torn from life and fame, / My tears, my verse, shall consecrate thy name!' (p. lxxxviii). In a note to Scott's 'And Bristol! Why thy scenes explore', Gregory draws attention to lines from a poem by William Mason which may be heard, in addition to *The Faerie Queen*, in Keats's exhortations to Shelley to 'curb your magnanimity and be more of an artist, and "load every rift" of your subject with ore' (*LJK* II.323): Scott speaks of the bard 'whose boasted ancient store / Rose recent from his own exhaustless mine', with reference to which Gregory draws attention to Mason's 'Elegy to a young Nobleman': 'See from the depths of his exhaustless mine / His glittering stores the tuneful spendthrift throws' (p. lxxxviii). Another parallel might be discerned between the poet's struggle as he approaches Moneta in Keats's 'The Fall of Hyperion', I.121–36 and William Hayley's description of the death of Chatterton in 'Essay on Epic Poetry':

> Near a vile bed, too crazy to sustain
> Misfortune's wasted limbs, convuls'd with pain,
> On the bare floor, with heaven-directed eyes,
> The hapless Youth in speechless horror lies
> The pois'nous phial, by distraction drain'd,
> Rolls from his hand, in wild contortion strain'd:
> Pale with life-wasting pangs, it's [*sic*] dire effect,
> And stung to madness by the world's neglect . . . (p. xci)

Finally, Coleridge's 'Monody on the Death of Chatterton', also included by Gregory, seems to resonate with, not least, Keats's poem on the relationship between death and art, 'Ode to a Nightingale': 'Is this the land', asks Coleridge, 'where Genius ne'er in vain / Pour'd forth his lofty strain?' (p. xcii): 'Now more than ever seems it rich to die, / to cease upon the midnight with no pain, / While thou art pouring forth thy soul abroad / In such an ecstasy' cries Keats. And Coleridge's poem details the physical dissolution of Chatterton ('corse of livid hue', 'haggard eye' and 'wasted form' (pp. xcii–xcciii)) which become Keats's youth growing 'pale, and spectre thin', just as Chatterton's death through poison evoked in Coleridge's poem is transformed into Keats's imagined hemlock in the second line of his poem. And, in addition to the Keatsian image of 'Fancy' in Coleridge's poem ('elfin form of gorgeous wing'), the sixth stanza opens with a dying fall which resonates in both 'Ode to a Nightingale' and 'To Autumn': 'Ah! Where are fled the charms of vernal Grace, / And Joy's wild gleams, high-flashing o'er thy face?' (p. xciii).

The corpus of Chatterton, then, that fetishised body of the self-poisoned poet and the fetishised image of the poet's corpus, his work, is transformed into the very stuff of Keats's canonical writing. It is not necessary to align Keats's poetry with the specific intertextual resources of either Chatterton's poetry, as critics have done, or with the Chatterton myth, as I have tried to do – nor to appeal to the various direct references in both Keats's poetry and letters[32] – to perceive Keats acting out, in his life and writing, a Chattertonian figuration of writing and the writer. The figure of the neglected young poet, in particular the sick, poisoned or dead poet, is overdetermined in the early nineteenth century by the image of Chatterton. The sheer number of the comparisons of Keats to Chatterton by critics, friends and enemies both before and after Keats's death would suggest that the parallel cannot but have been apparent to Keats. But my point is that the very texture of the corpus of Keats is constituted in part by that other body, that other life and writing. In other words, we cannot help but read Keats through the corpus of Chatterton – a corpus visualised in commemorative handkerchiefs, in engravings such as 'The Death of Chatterton' by Edward Orme (1794), and in later paintings such as Henry Wallis's 'The Death of Chatterton' (1855–56). Chatterton's life provides an early version of the myth of neglected genius which is distilled in the life and writing of Keats: Keats's presience is, in part, the trace of another poetic life and death, another body, name and corpus.

As this might suggest, one way to talk about the inscription of Keats's death in his writing is to talk about the poet's failing body. In his review

of Milnes's *Life* in *The North British Review*, Coventry Patmore articulates
the intimate relation that the nineteenth-century critical and biographical tradition asserts between the poet's 'genius' and his sickness: 'In
almost every page of the work before us, the close connection between
the genius of Keats and his constitutional malady pronounces itself'.[33]
Patmore goes on to suggest that a true assessment of Keats's character
is made particularly difficult by 'the necessity of constantly distinguishing between signs of character and the products of a very peculiar physical temperament, always subject to the influences of a malady, which,
in its earliest stages, is frequently so subtle as to defy detection, and to
cause its identification for a long period, with the constitution that it is
destroying'.[34] In this telling passage, Patmore presents the Keatsian body
as a site of semiotic disturbance in which malady and genius, sickness
and character, or disease and the body are largely indistinguishable: to
talk about Keats's character or his genius, and thus to talk about his
poetry, is to talk about his sickness and ultimately his bodily dissolution.
In this respect, I suggest that Keats's prescience is, first of all, somatic.
'Perhaps', as Aubrey de Vere suggests in another review of Milnes's biography, 'we have had no other instance of a bodily constitution so poetical' as that of Keats – and, famously, 'His body seemed to think'.[35]

   In his review of Keats's 1820 volume, Josiah Conder argues that 'The
true cause of Mr Keats's failure' involves the 'sickliness' of 'his productions', 'his is a diseased state of feeling' (*KCH* 238). To read Keats in this
way, to read Keats through his body, and with that body figured as both
weak and sickly, would be to go against the grain of much recent criticism and biography. Such writing would protect or, rather, cure the
Keatsian body of a morbid and unhealthy nineteenth-century
figuration. The most remarkable instance of bio-critical body-building
is, no doubt, Lionel Trilling's claim that Keats 'stands as the last image
of health at the very moment when the sickness of Europe began to be
apparent';[36] but more recently, in a study of the early biographies,
William Marquess has stated that 'The notion of an all-pervasive illness
that casts a fatally Romantic pall over Keats's entire career is, of course,
simply wrong;'[37] and in her study of Keats and medicine, Hermione de
Almeida has asserted moral and physiological well-being for Keats:
'Keats points the way through sickness, sorrow, and pain – through the
medium of a poetry of life – to spiritual wholeness and imaginative
health'.[38] Without simply rejecting such pronouncements,[39] I want to
suggest that one of the most pressing aspects of Keats's engagement with
his own after-fame is his articulation of the fragility and vulnerability of

the poet's body. The poet, in his exploration of the possibility that he will live on, figures himself, his body, as *sick*.[40]

The most obvious example of this trope is Keats's sonnet 'On Seeing the Elgin Marbles', which presents the poet as a sick eagle looking longingly at the sky.

> My spirit is too weak – mortality
>   Weighs heavily on me like unwilling sleep,
>   And each imagined pinnacle and steep
> Of godlike hardship tells me I must die
> Like a sick eagle looking at the sky.
>   Yet 'tis a gentle luxury to weep
>   That I have not the cloudy winds to keep
> Fresh for the opening of the morning's eye.
> Such dim-conceived glories of the brain
>   Bring round the heart an undescribable feud;
> So do these wonders a most dizzy pain,
>   That mingles Grecian grandeur with the rude
> Wasting of old time – with a billowy main –
> A sun – a shadow of a magnitude.

This is one of the least coherent of Keats's well-known poems, a poem impelled by a sense of 'wasting' – most clearly figured in the fragmentary dissolution of the last lines. Keats's bodily response to the immortality of Grecian sculpture is a proleptic experience of death, of wasting, fragmentation and dissolution. The poet not only acknowledges that he 'must die', but enacts that wasting, sickness and death in the poem.[41] This death is not only in the future but is incorporated or embodied in the inscription – in the act of inscribing – itself. The second sentence (lines 6–8), for example, enacts or embodies, in its wasted syntax, its semantically and grammatically indeterminate acedia, a figurative wasting of the poet himself. This is the poetry of failure, poetry which *works* precisely in and through its acknowledgement and articulation of a certain deficiency. The 'glories of the brain' are 'dim-conceived', the 'feud' is 'undescribable', the 'wonders' produce a 'dizzy pain', and the magnitude is but a shadow of itself. And the poem fails, in the second sentence, by producing the 'gentle luxury' of unmeaning, the failure of communication. But if this sentence resists reading, resists the sense-making demands of reception, it does so in accordance with both the necessities of the principle of posterity, and with a poetics of what, in a different context, Leo Bersani and Ulysse Dutoit term 'impoverishment'.[42] And it is the weight of this poem, its mortal oppression by a somatic and semantic *heaviness*, that reminds us proleptically of that other Keats poem which begins in a first-person possessive pronoun ('My heart aches') and records multiple bodily failures and fadings – 'Ode to a Nightingale'. These are failures which also occur in Keats's second sonnet on the Elgin marbles, 'To Haydon with a Sonnet Written on Seeing the Elgin Marbles', where the poem's language wastes away in a wasting evacuation of sense – 'Forgive me, Haydon, that I cannot speak / Definitively on these mighty things; / Forgive me that I have not eagle's wings – / That what I want I know not where to seek' (lines 1–4). 'That what I want I know not where to seek' describes the failure of desire, the failure of not achieving one's desire and of not even knowing where to look for it. And it also articulates a failure of language, it expresses somatic failure in a devastation of semantic acuity: the line is remarkable for a flatness of diction which hardly rises from the commonplace and for an emphatic semantic and alliterative repetition – I, I; what, want, where – which allows little scope for imaginative or linguistic flight. It is difficult to find another line of Keats's poetry which achieves failure with such consummate acumen. The poet asks Haydon to forgive him that he 'cannot speak / Definitively on these mighty things', but our line – 'That what I want I know not where to seek' – is the very evacuation of the definitive, undefines, wastes language away.

It is a condition of Keats's poetic success that he fails.[43] This is evident from numerous moments of professed failure in his poems. The odes, for example, are a catalogue of inability, weakness, insufficiency, ignorance, and so on. 'Ode on a Grecian Urn' is full of unanswered questions and ends by articulating the wasting of the living – 'When old age shall this generation waste, / Thou shalt remain'; 'Ode to a Nightingale' figures the poet imagining himself drugged or drunk, disabled in consciousness, while the climactic moments of aesthetic apprehension are those of sensory failure – 'I cannot see', 'I have ears in vain' – and the poem ends with the failure of somnolent discrimination, an epistemological uncertainty which constitutes a defining moment in the development of Keatsian aesthetics – 'Do I wake or sleep?'; 'Ode on Indolence' concerns the poet's 'Benumb'd' senses, a poet who imagines 'drowsy noons', 'evenings steep'd in honied indolence' and 'an age . . . shelter'd from annoy'; and 'Ode to Psyche' is a poem which is too late properly to pay homage to the poet's goddess, 'too late for antique vows, / Too, too late for the fond believing lyre'. The poetry of failure is central to Keats's project, central to the success of his poetry.

Success for Keats, then, involves a failure of inscription, success promulgated on the possibility that this writing, now, is inadequate or insufficient. But this failure of success also involves the wasting of the poet's body, its weakness, dissolution or fainting – what I call, borrowing the word from its exemplary occurrence in 'Ode to a Nightingale', 'fading'. Most commonly in Keats, this involves sensory degradation or deprivation – forms of fading in which the world fades as a result of the fading of the senses. The Keatsian body – the poet's body, his corpus or corpse – is repeatedly inscribed in the poetry in terms of the character-ological body dissolving and disempowered, as weak, wasted or failing.[44] There is Endymion's repeated bodily failing, his swooning, for example; Saturn's deathly stillness in the opening to 'Hyperion', his scriptive right hand lying 'nerveless, listless, dead' (1.18); Porphyro's climactic melting in 'The Eve of St. Agnes'; the palely loitering knight in 'La Belle Dame sans Merci'; Lamia's dissolution and Lycius's immediate lifelessness; the poet's 'slow, heavy, deadly' pace as he mounts the steps to Moneta in 'The Fall of Hyperion' (1.128); as well as the 'Ode on a Grecian Urn' imagining a heart 'high-sorrowful and cloy'd, / A burning forehead, and a parching tongue', the 'Ode to a Nightingale' presenting a catalogue of sensory dissolution and 'fading', and 'Ode on Melancholy' producing a very thesaurus of sickness and homeopathic cure. Each of Keats's major poems, that is to say, may be read as centred around a moment of bodily failure, of mortal fading. But I also want to suggest that this wasted corpus of Keatsian writing is the very condition of the afterlife of that corpus. Keats's corpus – his body/of work – is also his failed body, his corpse. If immortality for Keats is associated with a failure of the body, a corporeal fading or dissolution, this failing body is precisely the condi-tion of Keats's success in his afterlife, the necessary correlate of his after-fame.[45] The failed or failing body in or of Keats is a condition of the poetry's permanence: without the wasted or dissolved, dispensed-with but indispensible body, Keats's poetry, his corpus, does not live. Without the disfunctional Keatsian body, the body failed or failing, there is no after-fame.[46]

The condition of Keats's renown, then, is that it comes after life. It is fame which is produced by the necessary previous dissolution of the body (of the poet). In this sense, Keats's writing involves the articulation of a relatively common figuration of 'true' fame in the early nineteenth century.[47] Keats's poetry, however, is the first fully to integrate this sense of the necessary deferral of recognition into the poetry itself, making deferral, delay, posteriority, a necessary precondition for that poetry.

Deferred response, after-fame, reading after life, becomes the topic of poetry and what it produces. If 'Ode to Psyche' laments the poet's lateness in building a 'fane' for the goddess, it also suggests the necessary delay of such worship. It is only now, in this late after-time, that the goddess can properly be represented and worshipped. The same goes by implication here, and more explicitly elsewhere, for the poetry of John Keats. Keats's deferral of reception, his sense that he will be 'among the English Poets' after his death (*LJK* 1.394), his inscription of the body of dissolution, a degraded, incomplete, fetishised or failing body, the body fading, is also, necessarily, a precondition of Keatsian reception. Indeed, it is not difficult to demonstrate that the poetry of Keats does in fact alter, once-and-for-all, in an ineluctable and absolute sense, on the poet's death. Byron's grudging acknowledgement of the importance of 'Hyperion', for example, *after* Keats's death and his appeal to John Murray to delete any negative references from his published writing is just one example (*KCH* 131); Shelley's writing of the dead Keats into the poetic tradition in *Adonais* is another. As Susan Wolfson has pointed out, dying, for Keats, 'was a good career move'.[48] Just as Shelley's heart, that imperishable, shrivelled and blackened organ, snatched from the funeral pyre, becomes the fetishised object of readerly and critical desire in the poet's after-fame, so the diseased, sickness-consumed, failing body is the central signifier of Keatsian notoriety in the years after his death.[49] It is the death of Keats, his bodily disintegration and dissolution, which is at the heart of most of the posthumous commentary published after his death in February 1821. It is his death which constitutes his renown. Almost immediately, the death-scene of Keats as reported in letters by his friend and companion Joseph Severn began to be disseminated both privately and publicly. And most of the more substantial of the fifty or so tributes, notices, obituaries and memorial verses published within a year of the poet's death commented in medico-biographical terms on Keats's physical dissolution as well as remarking on the supposed connection between that death and the reviews of Keats's poetry during his life.[50] As early as April 1821, less than two months after Keats's death, Barry Cornwall published an essay on the poet which includes a reference to his scene of dying – 'solitary and in sorrow, in a foreign land' – in which Cornwall (mis-)reports Joseph Severn's story of Keats's desire for an epitaph:

A few weeks before he died, a gentleman who was sitting by his bed-side, spoke of an inscription to his memory, but he declined this altogether, – desiring that there should be no mention of his name or country; 'or if any', said he, 'let it be – *Here lies the body of one whose name was writ in water!* – There is something in this to us most painfully affecting; indeed the whole story of his later days is well calculated to make a deep impression.

But Cornwall also inscribes into the critical reception of Keats a crucial connection between poet and poetic prescience when he appropriates the 'Ode to a Nightingale' as a prophetic commentary by the poet on his own life:

His sad and beautiful wish is at last accomplished: it was that he might drink 'of the warm south', and 'leave the world unseen', – and – (he is addressing the nightingale) –
    And with thee fade away.

Cornwall then quotes stanza three of the poem, italicising line six, 'Where youth grows pale, and spectre-thin, and dies'.[51] By dying, that is to say, and by dying in a certain way – early, of consumption, in another country, virtually alone, poor, neglected by the public, and, according to the increasingly widely disseminated myth, as a direct result of the reception of his poetry – Keats is inscribed into a tradition of dead, young, misrepresented and misunderstood poets which includes most famously Chatterton and Henry Kirke White. At its most extreme, the figure of the poet dying as a result of the reviews becomes, in an apocryphal account by Gerald Griffin, an image of the poet drinking poison: Fanny Brawne and Fanny Keats 'say they have oft found him on suddenly entering the room, with that review in his hand, reading as if he would devour it – completely absorbed absent and drinking it in like mortal poison'.[52] And the image is both established within the literary tradition and literalised in an extraordinary medicalisation of reading in the preface to Shelley's *Adonais*: 'The savage criticism on his *Endymion*, which appeared in the *Quarterly Review*, produced the most violent effect on his susceptible mind; the agitation thus originated ended in the rupture of a blood-vessel in the lungs; a rapid consumption ensued, and the succeeding acknowledgements from more candid critics, of the true greatness of his powers, were ineffectual to heal the wound thus wantonly inflicted'.[53] In his study of the Victorian reception of Keats's poetry, George Ford has remarked that in 'the reputation of no other English poet has the question of personality played such a significant role in its development':[54] this personality is most memorably one of the body in dissolution. And this is a tradition of Keats criticism which continues to the present day: the blurb for the Penguin *Collected Poems*, for example, announces in its first sentence the relation between

Keats's poetic survival and his death: 'Keats survives as the archetypal Romantic genius who suffered a tragically early death'; and a recent popularising biography, by Stephen Coote, is sold in terms of a similar rhetoric, framing Keats as 'the image of genius dying tragically young'.[55] As Wolfson comments, 'If it is bad medical pathology and a distortion of Keats to say that he was snuffed out by an article, in terms of cultural discourse it was a truth universally acknowledged'.[56] But it is not, as Wolfson implies, a truth restricted to the nineteenth-century tradition: what is remarkable about such a dissolution is the extent to which it has been inscribed as a necessary attribute of Keats's poetry itself. And it is a death, I am arguing, that is indelibly marked in Keats's poetry, inscribed in or on that corpus that we know as 'Keats'. The literal and figurative body of Keats is both present and prescient in the writing.

As I suggested at the beginning of this chapter, one of the most impor-tant and overlooked poems in the context of Keats's prescience is his sonnet on Robert Burns, 'This mortal body of a thousand days'. The opening line, in particular, raises a series of questions: What is the status of such a statement? What does it mean? How can we read 'this'? Should we take it as 'literal'? The poem repeatedly maps the living body of the speaker onto the dead body of Burns:

> This mortal body of a thousand days
>   Now fills, O Burns, a space in thine own room,
> Where thou didst dream alone on budded bays,
>   Happy and thoughtless of thy day of doom!
> My pulse is warm with thine own barley-bree,
>   My head is light with pledging a great soul,
> My eyes are wandering, and I cannot see,
>   Fancy is dead and drunken at its goal;
> Yet can I stamp my foot upon thy floor,
>   Yet can I ope thy window-sash to find
> The meadow thou hast tramped o'er and o'er, –
>   Yet can I think of thee till thought is blind,
> Yet can I gulp a bumper to thy name, –
>   O smile among the shades, for this is fame!

As in so much of Keats's writing, the poem articulates a narrative of bodily failure – the speaker's 'head is light', his 'eyes are wandering', and 'cannot see', his 'Fancy is dead and drunken', and as in 'When I have fears that I may cease to be', the poet imagines a dissolution of con-sciousness, of thought, thinking 'till thought is blind'.[57] Indeed, in a letter to J.H. Reynolds, Keats comments on writing 'some lines' in Burns's cottage, but says that 'they are so bad I cannot transcribe them', and to Benjamin Bailey he comments that 'I had determined to write a Sonnet in the Cottage. I did but lauk it was so wretched I destroyed it': the failure of the poem is such that it cannot even be transcribed.[58] Just as Keats claimed in a letter to find the 'beauties' of poetry so intense in themselves that he could write and burn every night's outpourings with no sense of loss but also felt impelled to record this impulse of writing in a letter, to make it remain as a record of compositional intensity, and just as the paradigmatic gesture of Keatsian composition may be understood to be his thrusting of the manuscript sheets of 'Ode to a Nightingale' between his books, an act which both secretes the poem and inserts it into the literary tradition, the poem on Burns's fame is both destroyed and recorded as having been destroyed.[59] In each case, the destruction of poetic work is itself crucial to the inscription of that work within a certain (Romantic) poetic tradition which returns to the Chattertonian figure, represented most memorably in Henry Wallis's 1856 depiction of the suicide framed by the poet's torn-up manuscripts. By effacing or destroying the poem, the poet guarantees its status as an intensely experienced, spontaneous but therefore flawed and even psychically dangerous text, a text which expresses the person of the poet and thereby gives too much away. Nevertheless, like 'This living hand', the uncanny deictic references of 'This mortal body' assert a certain survival for the poet. By conflating the living poet, 'Keats', 'this mortal body', with the absent, mortal but immortalised body of Burns, the poem allows for an identification of the living poet with the immortal one, an identification most clearly articulated in the ambiguous deixis of the final line – 'for this is fame!' – which leaves open the question of whether *this* is fame for Burns or for Keats (or both). The poem's multiple identifications of the living with the dead poet, Keats with Burns, the bodily replacement of one poet by another, presciently inscribe the living poet into a posthumous life, into after-fame.[60]

'In literature', declares Jean-Luc Nancy in an essay on the literary body, 'there is nothing but bodies'. But this assertion is made on condition that, at the same time 'the body is not a locus of writing':

No doubt one writes, but it is absolutely not where one writes, nor is it what one writes – it is always what writing exscribes. In all writing, a body is traced, is the tracing and the trace – is the letter, yet never the letter, a literality or rather a lettericity that is no longer legible. A body is what cannot be read in a writing.[61]

For Keats – for every poet – writing poetry takes place as a certain embodiment in which inscription both bodies forth and disembodies, makes literal and figures: the body as what Nancy calls 'the last signifier, the limit of the signifier'.[62] But from a very early stage in the life of Keats such embodiment signifies a proleptic autobiographical inscription – albeit largely illegible – of the poet's own bodily dissolution: the writing of the Keatsian body figures what, in a different context, Louis Marin has termed the 'autobiothanatographical'.[63] Keats's mortality is figured in a body which increasingly takes on the status of a signifier of dissolution. And this dissolution also affects or infects the distinction between body and writing, corpus and corpus. Gittings, by his rejection of the Keatsian body in his judgement of the pure rhetoricity of 'This mortal body of a thousand days' – repeated by Morris Dickstein in his assertion that Aileen Ward's is an 'excessively literal reading of the poem'[64] – paradoxically *literalises* the Keatsian body. By refusing to read the body in the poem, by effacing, disembodying or *figuring* the corpus of writing, Gittings guarantees a reading of the body, of 'what cannot be read in writing': he reinstates, re-embodies, like a ghostly prosopopoeia, the dying corpus, the corpse, of Keats. Gittings's articulation of the unreadability of the literal body re-figures John Keats, re-embodies the poet – a poet whose writing, according to Coventry Patmore in his review of Milnes's biography, can never, with his particular 'physical organization', be anything other than 'sensual, or literal'.[65]

The exemplary inscription of the Keatsian body is, precisely, 'This mortal body of a thousand days' – the phrase and the poem – just as the exemplary figuration of the body writing in Keats is the performing hand in that haunting and grasping poem 'This living hand', and just as the exemplary figuration of Keatsian reading is that of the only other Keats poem to begin in 'This' – 'This pleasant tale is like a little copse'. In each case, the uncanny presence of the written and writing body and its uncanny prescience, too, is indicated by the opening deictic reference – '*This* mortal body', '*This* living hand' and, less obviously, '*This* pleasant tale'.[66] But this involves a deictic opacity of language, language which goes beyond language, which points and refuses to point, deixis as a figure which refuses figuration. Inscription is *this*: *this* body, here, now, not here, not now.[67] But I have also tried to suggest that the Keatsian body has a further dimension, that posthumous existence for Keats, the reading of his work since his death, is irreducibly bound up with the dissolute body – that the death of John Keats, the dissolution of the poet's body, is an inescapable element of any reading of his work. The poetry, in this sense, is an embodiment – with its hands, throats, breath, mouths, tongues, skin, tears, hearts, blood, eyes, ears, sickness, disease – or, more accurately an *encorpsement*, of the poet 'himself'. Keats's poetry cannot be read – has not been read – apart from a certain figuration of poetic biography, a life which hinges on prescient dissolution, on the corporeal disappearance, sickness or fading of the poet, resuscitated, reinscribed, re-embodied in the illegible, disembodied figurative act that, as in this chapter, we name, again and again, in all our hubris thinking that we know what we mean, 'reading John Keats'.

CHAPTER 7

Shelley's ghosts

The future can only be for ghosts.

(Derrida, *Specters of Marx*)

It is with Percy Bysshe Shelley that the issues raised in the present book become most acute and most polarised. In addition to writing Romanticism's most famous account of the relationship between the neglect and future fame of genius in *Adonais*, and its most impassioned theoretical rendering of the nature of genius and its relationship with posterity in *A Defence of Poetry*, Shelley's poetry and prose provides pervasive, complex and often contradictory evidence for my suggestion that posterity is central to Romantic poetry and poetics. On the one hand, Shelley's desire to change the world, to effect reform if not revolution through his poetry and prose, makes his work utilitarian, polemical and direct. On the other hand, and increasingly as time goes by and Shelley finds his work neglected, abused, censored and censured, he relies increasingly on a minority readership and on the political and aesthetic after-effects of his writing. Three comments by Shelley in letters and in conversation express very clearly the kinds of issues by which he understands himself to be challenged, and the ways in which his work conceptualises the Romantic culture of posterity. In moods of despair such as that expressed in a letter to John and Maria Gisborne dated 30th June 1820, Shelley mocks his own desire for posthumous fame, as a 'shadow', the 'seeking of sympathy with the unborn and the unknown', and declares that, anyway, such sympathy is beyond his own grasp: 'What remains to me? Domestic peace and fame? You will laugh when you hear me talk of the latter; indeed it is only a shadow. The seeking of a sympathy with the unborn and the unknown is a feeble mood of allaying the love within us; and even that is beyond the grasp of so weak an aspirant as I' (*PBSL* ii.206–7). Second, in a report by Trelawny, Shelley is said to have expressed his own contemporary obscurity, and explained it in terms of being 'haunted' by his own creations, by his own imagination: 'If you ask me why I publish what few or none will care to read, it is that the spirits I have raised haunt me until they are sent to the devil of a printer. All authors are anxious to breech their bantlings' (White II.344). Finally, again in despair at his own reception, Shelley asserts the judgement of posterity not in neo-classical terms as the arbiter of poetic value but as the 'court' which will decide on the very identity of the poet himself: 'The decision of the cause whether or no *I* am a poet is removed from the present time to the hour when our posterity shall assemble: but the court is a very severe one, & I fear that the verdict will be guilty death' (*PBSL* II.310). Despite – or perhaps because of – the negativity of such comments, however, Shelley's poetry and prose includes some of the most committed accounts of the Romantic culture of posterity from the period. In this chapter, I examine the writing of Shelley in the context of his concern with audience and posterity and seek to suggest that what I term Shelley's ghosts – his sense of being haunted and his poetics and politics of haunting – might account for the complexities of this relationship.

A Defence of Poetry was written in response to Peacock's claim in *The Four Ages of Poetry*, baldly summarised in a letter to Shelley of December 1820, that 'there is no longer a poetical audience among the higher class of minds' and that 'the poetical reading public' is 'composed of the mere dregs of the intellectual community' (*PBSL* II.245).[1] Shelley's argument in *A Defence of Poetry* that 'Even in modern times, no living poet ever arrived at the fulness of his fame', together with the concomitant assertion that 'the jury which sits in judgement upon a poet . . . must be impanelled by Time from the selectest of the wise of many generations' (*SPP* 486), is a claim, responding to contemporary conditions of publication, which displaces reception from a degenerate present to an eternal future.[2] Perhaps Shelley's most well-known statement concerning posterity comes at the end of his *Defence*:

Poets are the hierophants of an unapprehended inspiration, the mirrors of the gigantic shadows which futurity casts upon the present, the words which express what they understand not; the trumpets which sing to battle, and feel not what they inspire: the influence which is moved not, but moves. Poets are the unacknowledged legislators of the World. (*SPP* 508)

To engage with the subject of poet as legislator is, above all, to elaborate questions of reading and the law of reading. 'All laws', Paul de Man suggests in *Allegories of Reading*, 'are future-oriented and prospective; their illocutionary mode is that of the promise.'[3] Shelley's inscription of the law into the discourse of poetry, not only in the sense of poets as legislators but in various ways and in many different texts, can be read in terms of a projection of poetry into or towards the future. Shelley's writing delineates a future determined by the radical absence of the poet: poetry is future-oriented and prospective because of its necessary engagement with a reception which can only occur in a time beyond the poet's own death. Shelley's biographer, Newman White, argues that Shelley hoped for 'a vitality of spirit that would long survive him in the world to which he was physically dead'. The 'slow abolition' of such a hope as a result of Shelley's 'conviction of martyrdom' was, White argues, 'the worst hell that life imposed upon him' (White II.389). Michael O'Neill, however, reinforces the Romantic culture of posterity by suggesting that 'the greatness of Shelley's later poems' may derive 'partly from his increasing weariness of ever finding an audience'.[4]

Shelley's most sustained account of the Romantic theory of posterity – whereby genius inevitably encounters obscurity followed by later recognition – occurs in the first three paragraphs of his review of Hogg's *Memoirs of Prince Alexy Haimatoff*, published in *The Critical Review* in December 1814. The review opens with a paragraph which frames the discourse of posterity:

Is the suffrage of mankind the legitimate criterion of intellectual energy? Are complaints of the aspirants to literary fame, to be considered as the honourable disappointment of neglected genius, or the sickly impatience of a dreamer miserably self-deceived? the most illustrious ornaments of the annals of the human race, have been stigmatised by the contempt and abhorrence of entire communities of man; but this injustice arose out of some temporary superstition, some partial interest, some national doctrine: a glorious redemption awaited their remembrance. There is indeed, nothing so remarkable in the contempt of the ignorant for the enlightened: the vulgar pride of folly, delights to triumph upon mind. This is an intelligible process: the infamy or ingloriousness that can be thus explained, detracts nothing from the beauty of virtue or the sublimity of genius. But what does utter obscurity express? if the public do not advert even in censure to a performance, has that performance already received its condemnation? (*SCW* VI.175)

The passage raises a series of related questions in a characteristically dizzying stream of prose. The question with which the review opens – 'Is the suffrage of mankind the legitimate criterion of intellectual energy?' – inaugurates a series of possibilities from 'miserable' self-deception in the writer, to the 'injustice' of contemporary opinion. The question which closes this passage is answered later, in the third paragraph, when Shelley explains that in addition to 'the contempt . . . of the multitude', *neglect* may also be the fate of the writer of genius: 'Circumstances the least connected with intellectual nature have contributed, for a certain period, to retain in obscurity, the most memorable specimens of human genius' (*SCW* vi.175). In particular, Shelley argues that the challenges to convention – infringements of the 'canons of criticism', breaks with formal tradition and generic decorum – which characterise works of genius, condemn any such work for 'the majority of readers' who are 'ignorant and disdaining toleration'. 'It is evidently not difficult', Shelley continues, 'to imagine an instance in which the most elevated genius shall be recompensed with neglect', since 'Mediocrity alone seems unvaryingly to escape rebuke and obloquy, it accommodates its attempts to the spirit of the age, which has produced it, and adopts with mimic effrontery the cant of the day and hour for which alone it lives' (*SCW* vi.176). This declaration, which ends the introduction to Shelley's review, suggests that the poet of genius not only risks neglect, but necessarily *is* neglected, since only mediocre talent – that which simply reproduces the conventions of the day – can escape 'obloquy'.[5]

A similar sense of the poet as unacknowledged genius traverses a series of some of the most well-known moments in Shelley's poetry. 'Alastor', for example, concerns a poet 'whose untimely tomb / No human hands with pious reverence reared' (lines 50–1): this fictionalised self-representation concerns a poet who 'lived, he died, he sung, in solitude' (line 60). In 'Stanzas Written in Dejection, Near Naples', the pathos of neglect is even more naked and direct, as the final stanza records a self who is 'one / Whom men love not': he is a man who, 'Unlike this day' which the verses record and which, once it has gone, 'Will linger though enjoyed, like joy in Memory yet' (lines 41–5), will be forgotten, erased from memory. In 'To a Skylark', however, neglect is simply a necessary prelude to recognition. The bird is famously compared to a poet in stanza 8:

> Like a Poet hidden
>   In the light of thought,
> Singing hymns unbidden,
>   Till the world is wrought
> To sympathy with hopes and fears it heeded not . . . (lines 36–40)

The poet is present but concealed by his 'thought' from the view of the public, writing poems 'unbidden' until, finally, that public – somewhat like a work of art itself – is *wrought*, made up and made over into sympathy with what it can finally heed and understand. And the poem ends with the demand that the bird will teach the poet to sing with 'Such harmonious madness' until a time when 'The world should listen then – as I am listening now' (lines 103–5). 'Letter to Maria Gisborne' also opens with an appeal to a future in which the speaker will be heard and properly appreciated. The poet is presented as weaving a 'soft cell' round his own 'decaying form', 'From the fine threads of rare and subtle thought': the poem continues:

> . . . a soft cell, where when that fades away,
> Memory may clothe in wings my living name
> And feed it with the asphodels of fame,
> Which in those hearts which must remember me
> Grow, making love an immortality.   (lines 10–14)

In this poem, reading is linked to love, immortality, and death: the asphodels, immortal flowers of the Elysian fields, grow in the hearts of those that remember the poet, a death inhabiting and growing within readers. As we shall see, for Shelley, the poet's afterlife involves a kind of haunting or, here, more specifically, a *growth*: the memory of the poet will go on, like cancerous cells in the minds and bodies of his readers. The translation of Dante which prefaces 'Epipsychidion' recalls Wordsworth's 'Essay, Supplementary to the Preface' and Milton's *Paradise Lost*:

> My song, I fear that thou wilt find but few
> Who fitly shall conceive thy reasoning,
> Of such hard matter dost thou entertain . . . (lines 1–3)[6]

The poem ends with another exhortation to the verses to declare that Love's reward is 'in the world divine / Which, if not here, it builds beyond the grave': 'So shall ye live when I am there' (lines 595–9). In each of these cases, Shelley propounds a poetics of neglect and, in 'To a Skylark', 'Letter to Maria Gisborne' and 'Epipsychidion', he imagines a posthumous life for his writing.[7]

'Nothing is clearer about his early boyhood', declares Newman White of Shelley, 'than the fact that he craved an audience' (White I.54). The problem of audience was, I suggest, and as critics such as Michael O'Neill and Stephen Behrendt have made clear, in multiple and changing ways, crucial to the writing of Shelley throughout his life.[8] The reception history of Shelley, like that of other Romantic poets, is, of course, far more complicated than his complaints in poetry and prose might suggest. Not only was Shelley not ignored – Newman White counts thirty reviews and forty 'brief incidental notices' in 1820 and 1821

(White II.302–3) – but many of the reviewers, often while abusing Shelley's politics and obscurity, noted his 'genius' and argued for the survival of his poetry over time.[9]

As Timothy Clark suggests, poetic immortality for Shelley is bound up, in the first place, with technologies of publishing. Clark quotes Trelawny quoting Shelley: 'Intelligence should be imperishable; the art of printing has made it so on this planet'.[10] The poet, it seems, is made imperishable by print technology. Reading Shelley's letters, we find that during the twelve years of his publishing career he became expert in the various technologies which constitute the art of publishing – in the knowledge related to such skills as printing, copy-editing, binding, and paper selection, and in the associated skills of advertising, distribution to reviewers, bookshops and individuals, and in the monitoring of reviews. The 'art of printing', then, was a craft which Shelley took pains to learn in order to make himself imperishable in print: 'He was', comments White, 'always eminently practical in achieving publication' (White II.527). This being the case, it is significant that the phrase 'the art of printing' itself occurs in Leigh Hunt's review of *The Revolt of Islam*. After registering the urgency of the social and political message of the poem and at the same time its obscurity and inevitable unpopularity, Hunt ends his review with a eulogy on this art:

although the art of printing is not new, yet the Press in any great and true sense of the word is a modern engine in the comparison, and the changeful times of society have never yet been accompanied with so mighty a one. *Books* did what was done before; they have now a million times the range and power . . . (*SCH* 114)

Hunt explicitly contrasts this potential power and influence of 'Books' with the inevitable neglect of Shelley's poem which, he says, 'cannot possibly become popular'. In purely pragmatic terms, then, the 'art of printing' is understood to be crucial because of its potential social and political influence. But this potential should be seen within the context of the relative unpopularity of Shelley's work: only one of Shelley's books went into an authorised second edition in his life-time, and the largest print-run of any of his books, 1489, was that of his first volume – it is thought that no more than 100 copies were sold.[11]

The technologies of mass book-production and their potential social effects, then, are contrasted, explicitly by Hunt and implicitly for Shelley throughout his career, with his failure to reach a popular audience.[12] This produces a crucial fissure of publication which reminds us, if nothing else, of the necessary prolepsis of Romantic poetic address: it reminds us that, in some sense, Romantic discourse *must* be imperishable precisely because it must perish under contemporary neglect. As we have seen, in certain configurations Romantic discourse is congruent with what comes to be called the *avant-garde*, with an appeal to a necessarily deferred reception. Shelley repeatedly articulates the Romantic ideology of poetic neglect but is ambivalent in his predictions for his own future name. As White comments, 'Shelley's letters consistently professed the indifference of a man who felt himself already sentenced to nothing but neglect or abuse' (White II.300). Writing to Byron in September 1817, he explicitly alludes to the possibility of his own politico-poetical martyrdom, declaring that he will publish *Laon and Cythna* despite obvious dangers since 'I am careless of the consequences as they regard myself'. He resents persecution only because he laments 'the depravity and mistake of those who persecute. As to me', Shelley continues, 'I can but die; I can but be torn to pieces, or devoted to infamy most undeserved' (*PBSL* 1.557). In another letter, to Thomas Love Peacock, dated July 1816, Shelley asks what has become of *Alastor*: 'I hope it has already sheltered itself in the bosom of its mother, Oblivion, from whose embraces no one could have been so barbarous as to tear it except me' (*PBSL* 1.490). He also, however, 'counsels' Byron, in September, not to 'aspire to fame' but to express his own thoughts, 'to address yourself to the sympathy of those who might think with you': 'Fame will follow those whom it is unworthy to lead'. It is by *not* striving for fame, that is to say, that Byron might gain fame and 'communicate [his] feelings . . . perhaps to the men of distant ages' (*PBSL* 1.507).[13] For himself, though, Shelley often expresses his own neglect as not only a contemporary but also a future predicament. 'You will say', he writes to Leigh Hunt in December, 'that I am morbidly sensitive to what I esteem the injustice of neglect'. In fact, he is not unjustly neglected, since 'the oblivion which overtook my little attempt of Alastor I am ready to acknowledge was sufficiently merited in *itself*' –

but then it was not accorded in the correct proportion considering the success of the most contemptible drivellings. I am undec[e]ived in the belief that I have powers deeply to interest, or substantially to improve, mankind . . . thus much I do not seek to conceal from myself, that I am an outcast from human society; my name is execrated by all who understand its entire import . . . (*PBSL* 1.517)

While Shelley continued to believe both that he could and that he should be properly appreciated by reviewers, then, he also expressed acute anxiety and ambivalence over his contemporary and future reception.[14] Writing to Ollier in November 1821, for example, he urges his publishers to send him news of his publications, especially of *Adonais*: 'I confess I should be surprised if *that* Poem were born to an immortality of oblivion' (*PBSL* II.365). Writing two months later, in January 1822, Shelley asks Hunt whether he thinks a bookseller would give him '150 or 200 pounds' for the copyright to a drama on Charles the First:

You know best how my writings sell; whether at all or not, after they failed of making the sort of impression on men that I expected, I have never until now thought it worth while to inquire. This question is now interesting to me inasmuch as the reputation depending on their sale might induce a bookseller to give me such a sum for this play (*PBSL* II.380–1).[15]

Later in the same letter, Shelley declares, even more forcefully, his interest in sales and his own reputation, declaring that 'My faculties are shaken to atoms & torpid' and that the very act of writing is bound up with popular and critical success: 'I can write nothing, & if Adonais had no success & excited no interest what incentive can I have to write?' (*PBSL* II.382). An earlier letter, written in the summer of the same year to Peacock also records the despair that Shelley feels on his own failure to reach a contemporary public. The letter talks about Byron's *Don Juan* canto five – 'every word of it is pregnant with immortality' (*PBSL* II.330) – but ends with a complex cagey denial of his own abilities and his failures:

I write nothing, and probably shall write no more. It offends me to see my name classed among those who have no name. If I cannot be something better, I had rather be nothing, and the accursed cause to the downfall of which I dedicated what powers I may have had – flourishes like a cedar and covers England with its boughs. My motive was never the infirm desire of fame; and if I should continue an author, I feel that I should desire it. This cup is justly given to one only of an age; indeed, participation would make it worthless: and unfortunate they who seek it and find it not. (*PBSL* II.331)

It is, according to this letter, the desire for what Byron has – fame – that causes Shelley to stop writing. It is what he calls in *Queen Mab* the 'thirst for fame' (v.254), that 'worst desire of fame' (vi.213), which both impels and inhibits his writing.[16] Fame is, for Shelley, as he says in a letter, a 'phantom' (PBSL I.430). In a later letter of August 1821, in the context of a discussion of the 'reputation and success' of Byron and Hunt, Shelley declares that the 'universal voice of my contemporaries forbids me either to stoop or aspire to' a 'station in modern literature' comparable to that occupied by Hunt: 'I am', he goes on, 'and I desire to be, nothing' (*PBSL* II.344). In a letter of September of the same year, he declares sarcastically that he should write a flattering ode to the reviewers, otherwise they will 'put me off with a bill on posterity, which when my ghost shall present, the answer will be – ' "no effects" ' (*PBSL* II.354). And writing to Joseph Severn with a copy of *Adonais*, Shelley identifies himself with Keats, a poet who, in spite of his 'transcendent genius' 'was never nor ever will be a popular poet': the 'astonishing remnants of his mind' lie in 'total neglect & obscurity' (*PBSL* II.366). In his essay 'On the Devil, and Devils', Shelley breaks off at one point to write a paragraph on the importance of audience and the paradox of the desire for fame: 'No poet develops the same power in the heat of his composition when he feels himself insecure of the emotions of his readers, as in those when he knows that he can command their sympathy' (*SCW* VII.101). Similarly, in a letter of May 1820, Shelley categorically declares the relation between writing and audience when he talks about the popularity which 'in a certain proportion to their merit almost every poem acquires – and if mine never acquire it . . . I shall believe that they never deserve it' (*PBSL* II.200). And later, in July, Shelley again links writing with reception when he comments that 'I wonder why I write verses, for nobody reads them' (*PBSL* II.213).[17] But, like Keats, Shelley declares to his publisher in September 1819 that 'I write less for the public than for myself' (*PBSL* II.116).[18] Instead, he will write for the future – as he puts it in 'Letter to Maria Gisborne', he writes for 'the dread Tribunal of *to come*' (line 200), a different version of fame. A similar appeal to the future occurs in a letter to William Godwin from Dublin in 1812 concerning his attempts to alter the course of political history: Shelley declares that 'I will look to events in which it will be impossible that I can share, and make myself the cause of an effect which will take place ages after *I* shall have mouldered into dust' (*PBSL* I.277). 'Posterity', Shelley comments in the parodic and ambivalent preface to 'Peter Bell the Third', 'sets all to rights' (*SPP* 324).[19] By 1822, however, writing, for Shelley, amounts to little more than a 'jingling food for the hunger of oblivion' (*PBSL* II.374).

On 26th December 1811, Shelley ended a letter to Elizabeth Hitchener from Keswick in the Lake District, with a one-sentence paragraph, 'I *will* live beyond this life' and with a signature, 'Yours yours [*sic*] most imperishably Percy S.–' (*PBSL* I.214). His next surviving letter, dated 2nd January 1812, is also to Hitchener. This letter includes a quotation of seven-and-a-half stanzas from Wordsworth's 'A Poet's Epitaph', but most of the letter is taken up with one of Shelley's many attempts to prove to Hitchener the impossibility of the existence of a creative deity. Much of the argument concerns what Shelley sees as the logical contradictions of the Bible and its conflict with modern science: 'Moses', says Shelley, 'writes the history of his own death whic[h] is almost as extraordinary a thing to do as to describe the creation of the World' (*PBSL* 1.216). The reference to Moses writing the history of his own death seems to refer to the way that the Book of Deuteronomy opens, in the King James version, with the pronouncement 'These be the words which Moses spake' and ends with the narrative of that prophet's death.

In these two letters Shelley presents early configurations of what might be termed 'posthumous writing'. His extravagant claim in the December letter that he will live beyond 'this life', imperishably, returns a week later, rather differently, in a quotation from Wordsworth's fiction of posthumous poetic address in 'A Poet's Epitaph', and in the reference to Moses. In such texts as his essays 'On a Future State' and 'On the Punishment of Death', Shelley argues against an afterlife or the possibility of our knowing in what such an afterlife might consist: his claim that he will live on after this life would seem to involve the writer living on in his writing in the minds and thoughts of readers – in posterity.[20] But Shelley's configuration of posterity in these letters already involves an unconventional formulation: the idea of Moses writing the history of his own death suggests that posterity might be constituted by the writer *writing* after his own death – posthumous writing.

In the conventional sense of an interest in the question of immortality and in the possibility of remains, of the remains which writing constitutes, Shelley's poetry and prose is almost obsessively concerned with the notion of permanence. It is, Shelley argues in a note to *Hellas*, the 'province of the poet' to conjecture 'the condition of that futurity towards which we are all impelled by an unextinguishable thirst for immortality'.[21] Similarly, Shelley's essay 'On a Future State' ends with an assertion that the desire to remain is unavoidable and accounts for hypotheses concerning the afterlife: 'This desire to be for ever as we are; the reluctance to a violent and unexperienced change, which is common to all the animated and inanimate combinations of the universe, is, indeed, the secret persuasion which has given birth to the opinions of a future state'.[22] Examples in the poetry include, in particular, *Queen Mab* II.109–243 (on the inevitable perishability of mankind and of man-made monuments – a kind of precursor to the more concise 'Ozymandias'), III.138–69 (on the desire for *lasting*, rather than ephemeral fame), V.1–21 (on the way that 'generations' survive like fallen leaves, fertilising the

land as they rot, 'Surviving still the imperishable change / That reno-
vates the world', lines 3–4), and VIII.203–11 (on the 'time-destroying
infiniteness' of thought[23]). In *Epipsychidion*, monogamous love is said to
build 'A sepulchre for its eternity' (line 173) by contrast with the ideal of
nature's 'green and golden immortality' (line 469), and writing and
reading poetry and making music are themselves figured as acts of
immortalisation: the poet has 'fitted up' a home and an island:

> I have sent books and music there, and all
> Those instruments with which high spirits call
> The future from its cradle, and the past
> Out of its grave, and make the present last
> In thoughts and joys which sleep, but cannot die,
> Folded within their own eternity.   (lines 519–24).[24]

The two letters to Hitchener, however, mark a more unusual concern in
Shelley's writing. He is here concerned not only with the possibility of
sublunary survival, but with a particular – and, I suggest, characteristically Shelleyan – version of such survival: posthumous writing, a kind of
ghost-writing. In fact, these two letters are far from isolated occurrences
of such a figure of remains. Shelley's first volume of poetry (written with
his sister Elizabeth), *Original Poetry; by Victor and Cazire*, for example,
includes on its title-page an epigraph from Scott's *Lay of the Last Minstrel*,
which refers to Nature mourning the dead poet, and his second collection of poems explicitly develops this fiction in its very title: *Posthumous
Fragments of Margaret Nicholson*. In an unfinished piece entitled 'The
Elysian Fields: A Lucianic Fragment' written a few years later, the
speaker addresses the living from beyond the grave. Towards the end of
his life, Shelley announced in the first sentence of the Advertisement to
his anonymous *Epipsychidion*, that 'The Writer of the following Lines died
at Florence' (*SPP* 373). And even more curious than this relatively conventional fiction of poet as editor of posthumous poetry, is Shelley's suggestion in a letter to his publisher Charles Ollier that 'indeed, in a certain
sense, [*Epipsychidion*] is a production of a portion of me already dead;
and in this sense the advertisement is no fiction' (*PBSL* II.262–3).
Newman White suggests that the 'unburied bones' (line 60) in the
opening to 'Lines Written Among the Euganean Hills' which remain
unlamented are those of Shelley himself, so bringing together neglect
with posthumous writing (White II.41). For Shelley, indeed, writing after
death, making history of oneself, was a good devoutly to be desired.
Thus, in a letter to Hogg of August 1815, Shelley comments on contemporary historical events by declaring that in considering such events 'I

endeavour to divest my mind of temporary sensations, to consider them as already historical' (*PBSL* 1.430). Writing to Byron in July 1821, Shelley comments on his own 'public neglect' before expressing his admiration for Byron's poetry mediated by a hope for the older poet's future work: 'You say', Shelley continues, 'that you feel indifferent to the stimuli of life. But this is a good rather than an evil augury. Long after the *man* is dead, the immortal spirit may survive, and speak like one belonging to a higher world' (*PBSL* 11.309). Once again, Shelley hints at a contemporary posterity: Byron's ennui makes possible a posthumous writing, writing which takes its authority from the poet's death.[25]

These fictions of posthumous writing, then, begin to suggest a radical displacement and disturbance of conventional notions of posterity and to construct a peculiarly Shelleyan version of the Romantic culture of posterity. If posterity is understood to be constituted by those who come after, those who live on after the poet, the audience for poetry after his death, Shelley's figuration of the poet as already dead warps this temporality, collapsing a posthumous and always anticipated or deferred reception in posterity into the present. By writing after his own death, Shelley can live his own posterity, he can live on or survive himself in a haunting and ghostly writing of the future.

The temporal convulsions articulated in such a theory of posterity are suggested most clearly in Shelley's 1819 essay *A Philosophical View of Reform*. Towards the end of this tract Shelley argues for the importance of poets and philosophers, the 'unacknowledged legislators of the world' (*SCW* vii.20), as propagandists for reform. He suggests that Godwin, Hazlitt, Bentham, and Hunt, should write 'memorials' demonstrating 'the inevitable connection' between political freedom and the economic health of the country on the one hand, and moral, scientific, and 'metaphysical' enquiry on the other. Shelley then explains the potential persuasive force of the arguments of such writers:

These appeals of solemn and emphatic argument from those who have already a predestined existence among posterity, would appal the enemies of mankind by their echoes from every corner of the world in which the majestic literature of England is cultivated; it would be like a voice from beyond the dead of those who will live in the memories of men, when they must be forgotten; it would be Eternity warning Time. (*SCW* vii.52)

The passage is immensely suggestive in what I have called its temporal convulsions:[26] Shelley is attempting to endow living writers with the authority of writing from posterity. These writers, he suggests, are *already* speaking from beyond their own lives. Although the passage appears to present a particularly unusual figuration of posterity, I would suggest that what is being invoked here is, in fact, the very possibility of the time of posterity itself. Shelley suggests that posterity is a call to the future determined by the past and received in the present. Posterity concerns the possibility that living writers are traversed by their own mortality, that mortality is necessarily inscribed in their writing: posterity is only possible on condition of the inscription in writing of the writer's death. In this way, posterity is a kind of haunting of the present by the future. As Shelley says in *A Defence of Poetry*, in one of many formulations of the idea, 'the future is contained within the present as the plant within the seed' (*SPP* 481). Shelley in posterity, his ghosts, then, involves an attempt to fold or collapse the future into the present.[27]

There are ghosts and there are ghosts. There are 'real' ghosts, that is to say, ghosts that figure in ghost stories, both 'fictional' and 'historical'. Such 'real' ghosts, however, just in so much as they are real, are not proper ghosts at all. And then there are hallucinated, imagined, dreamed ghosts, ghosts which, just in so much as they cannot be empirically guaranteed to exist, just in so much as they are *not* 'real', are proper ghosts. But this is putting it too simply, since the proper ghost may be said to haunt an unlocatable and undecidable space between hallucination and appearance: the proper ghost is, precisely, an *apparition* (that which both does and does not appear). To be a ghost, that is to say, you must inhabit that liminal and undecidable site between truth and fiction, life and death, illusion and reality. To be a ghost is not to be. Ghosts tremble on the verge of our disbelief: they deconstruct positivist notions of the verifiable or falsifiable. In this sense, we can never be rid of ghosts, they will never leave us. The ghost, to put it bluntly, is deconstruction. If a ghost was to be verified in an empirically falsifiable manner, it would no longer be a ghost since, after all, the ghost is the scandal or contradiction of empiricism. The ghost is precisely not logical and not possible: it is the site of denial of conventional logic, the site of impossibility. This, in part, is why ghost stories as such tend to be so disappointing – unless, as Todorov argues of the fantastic, they function in the uncanny space of hesitation between the 'natural' and the 'supernatural'.[28] The difficulty with ghosts is that, on the one hand, they are the very epitome of the human, they are that which defines the human, the soul or spirit, *geist*, the incorporeal part of what we think of as ourselves. But on the other hand, it is precisely by virtue of this essence, this incorporeal centre, this soulfulness, that ghosts become the scandal of the human, the soul, now the soul of the dead, turned phantom or spectre. To give a person a soul, a spirit, an incorporeal essence or presence, that is to say, is to allow for a separation of the person from the body, and consequently to allow for the dissolution of the border between life and death, to allow for ghosts. And yet a ghost, as I have suggested, is the *scandal* of the human since one of the crucial qualities of human-ness, of personality or personhood, is the quality of being alive. To be human is to be alive: nervous of the dead, we call them names – the dead, corpse, the deceased, ghost, *revenant*. What we do with dead bodies is different from what we do with live ones. The difference is strikingly expressed by Southey when he comments on the corpse of his mother: 'the whole appearance was so much that of utter death – that the first feeling was as if there could have been no world for the dead'.[29] There is, to be sure, a certain ambivalence in our relation with dead bodies – their difference from a piece of meat or wood, for example – but that very ambivalence denotes their difference. If dead spirits come back to haunt us were just human we would not need to call them ghosts. Nor would they be terrifying. What alarms us in ghosts is precisely this scandalous transgression of the borders between the human and the nonhuman, between the living and the dead. Strangely, ghosts figure hardly at all in the otherwise voluminous secondary literature on Shelley (with the exception of Derrida's tangential 'reading' of *The Triumph of Life*[30]), despite the fact that, as Richard Holmes comments, 'ghosts and hauntings were endemic to his poetry'.[31] This may be because ghosts are an academic scandal, as Derrida comments:

There has never been a scholar who really, and as scholar, deals with ghosts. A traditional scholar does not believe in ghosts – nor in all that could be called the virtual space of spectrality. There has never been a scholar who, as such, does not believe in the sharp distinction between the real and the unreal, the actual and the inactual, the living and the non-living, being and non-being ('to be or not to be', in the conventional reading), in the opposition between what is present, and what is not, for example in the form of objectivity.[32]

It is Mary Shelley, in fact, who links Percy's name with ghosts in an essay published in the *London Magazine* for March 1824, two years after the poet's death. 'On Ghosts' is an essay haunted by Percy's death. 'Yet is it true that we do not believe in ghosts?', she asks, after recounting the ravages that science has made on incredulity and superstition.[33] For her part, Mary claims, 'I never saw a ghost except once in a dream'. This assertion introduces a paragraph in which she remembers a scene of desire for a ghost, desire to see a ghost, as she recounts her mourning for

Percy 'a few months' after his death. She describes the undecidable nature of the ghostly – the only proper apparition of the ghost – as she evokes a sense of spectral presence:

The wind rising in the east rushed through the open casements, making them shake; – methought, I heard, I felt – I know not what – but I trembled. To have seen him but for a moment, I would have knelt until the stones had been worn by the impress, so I told myself, and so I knew a moment after, but then I trembled, awe-struck and fearful. Wherefore? There is something beyond us of which we are ignorant. The sun drawing up the vaporous air makes a void, and the wind rushes in to fill it, – thus beyond our soul's ken there is an empty space; and our hopes and fears, in gentle gales or terrific whirlwinds, occupy the vacuum; and if it does no more, it bestows on the feeling heart a belief that influences do exist to watch and guard us, though they be impalpable to the coarser faculties. (p. 336)

The danger in such thinking, as Mary is quick to acknowledge in the following paragraph, is that it dematerialises the ghostly to the extent that it no longer has the scandal-provoking and terrifying force of the phantom – in other words, that we are no longer talking about ghosts. The line between this sense of things existing just beyond our ken and the 'true' ghost, the one 'who lift[s] the curtains at the foot of your bed as the clock chimes one' (p. 337), is activated and put into question by Coleridge and by Percy:

I have heard that when Coleridge was asked if he believed in ghosts, – he replied that he had seen too many to put any trust in their reality; and the person of the most lively imagination that I ever knew echoed this reply. But these were not real ghosts (pardon, unbelievers, my mode of speech) that they saw; they were shadows, phantoms unreal; that while they appalled the senses, yet carried no other feeling to the mind of others than delusion, and were viewed as we might view an optical deception which we see to be true with our eyes, and know to be false with our understandings. I speak of other shapes. (p. 336–7)[34]

And yet Mary's quick rejection of such 'phantoms unreal' – 'I speak of other shapes' – belies the extent to which this passage negotiates the impossible site of the ghostly, since it is precisely that which is seen 'to be true with our eyes' and yet empirically unverifiable which is the ghost. And it is precisely within the mortal space between belief and the recognition of the delusory nature of such belief that ghosts are located. The ghost, that is to say, cannot be shared and cannot be distinguished from delusion, from seeing things. Coleridge's and Percy's paradoxical formulation of their belief or scepticism with regard to ghosts is precise: they have 'seen too many to put any trust in their reality', which is to say that they both believe and refuse to believe, that they have seen ghosts and refuse to credit their vision. It is this paradoxical, impossible logic – ghost-logic, or deconstruction – which Mary's essay brings out so well and which determines Percy's thinking of posterity. For Percy Shelley, I want to suggest, the impossible logic of posterity is the impossible logic of ghosts, of haunting.

If posterity involves the possibility of a haunting of the present by the future, writing after life, it must, more conventionally, include the possibility of a haunting of the present by the past (or, from the poet's perspective, a haunting of the future by the present). Shelley describes fame as a 'phantom' (*PBSL* 1.430) and his relationship with posterity as that of a ghost to a debtor (*PBSL*, II.354). Others noticed a certain ghostliness in Shelley's presence and his writing. 'Here is a man at Keswick', writes Southey of Shelley in a letter of January 1812, 'who acts upon me as my own ghost would do' (*SCH* 55). A later reader of Shelley has a similar sense of his haunting presence: Carlyle describes Shelley as 'a kind of ghastly object' who sounds 'shrieky' and 'frosty', 'as if a ghost were trying to sing to us'.[35] It is, I would like to suggest, Shelley's ability to act as a ghost upon his readers, as well as being acted upon by ghosts, that characterises his writing and his poetics. In fact, Shelley's very description of consciousness comes down to a sense of being haunted, at times. In a passage from his 'Speculations on Metaphysics', which seems to have unearthly echoes of the phantasmagoria of Coleridge's 'Ancient Mariner' and 'Kubla Khan', for example, Shelley provides an account of the difficulties of describing the mind: thought 'is like a river whose rapid and perpetual stream flows outwards; – like one in dread who speeds through the recesses of some haunted pile, and dares not look behind. The caverns of the mind are obscure, and shadowy; or pervaded with a lustre, beautifully bright indeed, but shining not beyond their portals' (*SCW* VII.64). What is remarkable about this sentence is the way that it drifts from a relatively conventional description of consciousness as like the stream of a river to the unexpected and, I think, unprecedented notion of thinking as being haunted, as a state of dread.[36] In his journal written in Geneva in August 1816, Shelley writes about his belief in ghosts as well as recording the ghost stories told by Matthew Lewis: 'We talk of Ghosts. Neither Lord Byron nor M.G.L. seem to believe in them; and they both agree, in the very face of reason, that none could believe in ghosts without believing in God.' But, Shelley goes on to argue, such assertions of disbelief do not hold up in the context of 'loneliness and midnight' (*SCW* VI.147).[37] Shelley's literal 'belief' in ghosts is echoed by the repeated references to ghosts and haunting which pervade his poems. In 'Alastor', for example, the speaker refers to sleeping 'In charnels and on coffins' in an attempt to force 'some lone ghost, / Thy [Nature's] messenger, to render up the tale / Of what we are' (lines 24–9). Similarly, in 'Mont Blanc', the speaker refers to his 'human mind' 'Seeking among the shadows that pass by / Ghosts of all things that are, some shade of thee, / Some phantom, some faint image' (lines 45–7). In both of these examples, nature, and its perception by the mind, is to be apprehended, finally, in the ghostly or phantasmatic. Once again, in 'Hymn to Intellectual Beauty', the speaker remembers having 'sought for ghosts' amongst caves and ruins, hoping for 'high talk with the departed dead' (lines 49–52) and tells of the 'shadow' of the 'Spirit of BEAUTY' (lines 13) falling on him of a sudden (lines 59): in dedicating his 'powers' to this spirit, he 'call[s] the phantoms of a thousand hours / Each from his voiceless grave' (lines 64–5). Rather differently, in 'The Cloud', Shelley ventriloquises the cloud, ending in a sense of the eternal gathering and dissolution of air:

> I silently laugh at my own cenotaph,
>   And out of the caverns of rain,
> Like a child from the womb, like a ghost from the tomb,
>   I arise, and unbuild it again. –   (lines 81–4)

In *Hellas*, Mahmud sees 'the ghost of [his] forgotten dream' (line 842) – a ghost of a ghost, in effect – and then sees the ghost of Mahomet the Second (lines 861ff), who predicts that 'like us' he will 'rule the ghosts of murdered life, / The phantom of the powers who rule thee now' (lines 882–3). In *The Triumph of Life*, Shelley presents himself as speaking to the ghost of Rousseau, the 'shape all light', who comments on the figure of the ghostly dead as they pass by. Shelley, then, the most apostrophic and arguably the most ventriloquistic of the canonical Romantic poets, repeatedly effects a prosopopoeial resuscitation of the dead and absent: his poetry is particularly and peculiarly concerned with the absent presence of the ghostly. Perhaps one of the most telling and compelling effects of the ghost in Shelley is the phantom-effect of political upheaval or revolution: the single long, suspended sentence which constitutes 'England in 1819' builds towards an affirmation that the social and political repressions of the current regime 'Are graves from which a glorious Phantom may / Burst' (*SPP* 311).[38]

Figurations of posterity in Romantic writing tend, necessarily, to be hidden, disguised, distorted, or displaced. In Shelley, such representations take the form of an acknowledgement of what I have elsewhere suggested is the submerged figure of Romantic posterity, the death of the reader.[39] Posterity as constituted by the death of the reader must be read but is not, by definition, susceptible to reading: this, in effect, is the ghostly logic which haunts the reading of Shelleyan posterity. If I am right in suggesting that the death of the reader is inscribed in Romantic writing, this causes a fissure or fold in Romantic texts, it is a secret or crypt, a haunting, which must remain in some sense unread and unreadable.[40] Such a haunting might be taken to be the singular force of the inscription of posterity in Shelley's writing in particular. The culture of posterity in Shelley's writing is a kind of ghostly spirit set to haunt or inhabit the minds of readers. This is most powerfully suggested in *A Defence of Poetry*, where Shelley states that poetry 'acts in a divine and unapprehended manner, beyond and above consciousness' (*SPP* 486), and that its effect is one of what he calls 'entrancement' (from the Latin *trans*, meaning 'across or beyond'): poetry is precisely that which is not perceived or apprehended and which takes the reading subject outside himself or herself. Shelley figures this entrancement in terms of reading as the creation of a 'being within our being' (*SPP* 505).[41] Such a being within our being, both inside and outside the reading subject, can never be known: 'Veil after veil may be undrawn, and the inmost naked beauty of the meaning never exposed' (*SPP* 500). Similarly, in *Alastor*, the speaker listens to the poetess in a dream, entranced by this other voice which he recognises as also his own:

> Her voice was like the voice of his own soul
> Heard in the calm of thought; its music long,
> Like woven sounds of streams and breezes, held
> His inmost sense suspended in its web
> Of many-coloured woof and shifting hues. (lines 153–7)

A similar kind of suspended animation or hauntedness of consciousness is described in 'To Constantia' as the speaker's reaction to Constantia's voice: his 'brain is wild', his breath 'comes quick' and his blood 'is listening in my frame': 'I am dissolved in these consuming extacies' (lines 5–11). Just as Roland Barthes describes the *jouissance* of reading and just as Leo Bersani describes the 'self-shattering' intensity of sexuality, Shelley's account of listening to poetic voices and reading poetry calls on a bodily dissolution of self as constitutive of the act of reading.[42] 'So much for self', Shelley remarks to Hunt in 1819, '*self*, that burr that will

stick to one. I can't get it off yet' (*PBSL* II.108–9). It is, however, the condition of aesthetic and erotic experience for Shelley, that this burr of the
self *can* be discarded or dissolved. Poetry haunts, in the sense of having
the capacity to suspend consciousness, to overcome the self, to take the
self out of the self, or to inhabit the self with another self. That poets are
'unacknowledged' should, then, be understood as part of a larger claim
in *A Defence of Poetry* and elsewhere about what cannot be presented:
Shelley suggests that reading is haunted by the unreadable, the unspeakable, or the immemorial – in short, the ghostly. Reading, or, more generally aesthetic response, is figured, at its most extreme, as a form of
bodily and mental dissolution whereby the self is haunted or ghosted.
Indeed, this very unreadability of posterity, this interdiction on reading,
might itself be said to contain the 'secret' of Romantic reading: the scandalous but unreadable secret encrypted within the Romantic text is that
of posterity, the unspeakable assertion in Romantic writing of the death
of the reader, the dissolution, that is to say, of the reading subject, his or
her inhabitation or possession by an other – an effect that we might call
the ghosting of poetry.

Although this inhabitation or haunting is unspeakable and necessarily hidden, we might begin to read it, even – or especially – in its inter-
dictions of reading, within the torsions of rhetoric throughout *A Defence
of Poetry*. One formulation occurs in Shelley's well-known description of
poetic defamiliarisation:

> Poetry lifts the veil from the hidden beauty of the world, and makes familiar
> objects be as if they were not familiar; it reproduces all that it represents, and
> the impersonations clothed in its Elysian light stand thenceforward in the minds
> of those who have once contemplated them, as memorials of that gentle and
> exalted content which extends itself over all thoughts and actions with which it
> coexists. (*SPP* 487)

The light of poetry is Elysian, that of the blessed dead, and the work of
reading is inhabited by death as a work of remembering. As Karen Mills-
Courts has pointed out in a discussion of this passage, this ghostly impersonation is neither living nor dead but both.[43] But Shelley's essay makes
it clear that there is a metonymic infection of such memorialisation, that
the haunting or cryptic structure of poetry as memorialisation is a structure which not only inhabits the 'mind' of the reader, but in fact
becomes, or impersonates, the reader. At the same time, the reader may
be understood to be an impersonation, a mask of a person, constructed
by the deadly work of reading. Readers then become incarnations of
poetry, they are translated into the flesh of language, they impersonate

language, or become embodied, actualised impersonations of language: readers, in a precise and deadly sense, are figured and figured as ghosts. Readers are given a face, are subject to an eerie prosopopeia in which, as Paul de Man suggests in his reading of Wordsworth's 'Essays upon Epitaphs', they speak from beyond the grave.[44]

This reading of posterity in Shelley has significant consequences for his poetry, a number of which might be indicated by a very brief enumeration of ways in which a few of Shelley's canonical poems present the dissolution of subjectivity in reading, the phantom-effect of reading. In 'Ozymandias' Shelley presents monumentalisation in terms of the survival of the passions of the King of Kings on the 'lifeless' stone, beyond the sculptor who is explicitly described as a *reader* of those passions. Similarly, the ending of the poem presents a scene of devastation from which all living beings, including the traveller who has read the words of Ozymandias written on the pedestal, are excluded. The human, that is to say, has been evacuated by the haunting presence of this monument of and to reading. *Alastor* narrates the Poet's journey towards death after his meeting with the 'Veilèd maid' who is 'herself a poet' (lines 151, 161): the Poet is also a reader who dies after engaging with poetry. *Adonais* again presents the poet-as-reader dying into Keats's poetry. And the poem also seeks to disrupt the distinction between life and death in order to suggest that '*We* decay', we readers, decay, 'Like corpses in a charnel . . . / And cold hopes swarm like worms within our living clay' (lines 348–51). *The Triumph of Life* presents the poet as reader, this time of Rousseau: a poet-reader who thinks and is thought by the ghost of Rousseau – 'the grim Feature, of my thought aware' (line 190) – but thinks him from the regions of the dead. Finally, in 'Ode to the West Wind', the poet spreads 'dead thoughts' (line 63), like leaves, like ghosts (line 3) over the world in an equivocal attempt to 'quicken a new birth' (line 64): if the poet's dissemination of thoughts is 'like' the West Wind's dissemination of leaves and seeds, the poet is, like that wind, a 'Destroyer and Preserver' (line 14).[45] The complex dislocations of this poem, presented most compactly in the uncertainty of the poem's closing rhetorical question, may be understood in terms of the possibility that spreading dead thoughts may not revitalise but can only preserve. 'Ode to the West Wind' presents a figuration of posthumous writing, the dissemination of dead thoughts. But this posthumous writing also involves the death of the reader, who may be understood to be figured by a burial, the disseminated seed of poetic thoughts lying like 'a corpse within its grave' (line 8). To say that Shelley presents the dissolution of the reader, his or her 'death' in reading, is another way to talk about the inhabitation of readers by poetry since once the living is inhabited by the dead other he or she cannot be distinguished from that other, from the dead. This, finally, is the ghostly logic of posterity in Shelley's writing, the culmination, in effect, of the Romantic culture of posterity. And such a gothic and melodramatic account of Shelley's work is appropriate to a poet whose career begins – as it ends perhaps, in the *Triumph of Life* – in works of gothic horror where the dead live and the living are haunted and possessed by the dead.

Few works of mankind, Shelley declares from Bologna in 1818, 'are more evanescent than paintings'. By contrast, books 'are perhaps the only productions of man coeval with the human race'. But, he goes on to argue, despite the fact that the physical works of art of Zeuxis and Apelles and others are no more, 'they survive in the mind of man, & the remembrances connected with them are transmitted from generation to generation' (*PBSL* II.53). Culture, for Shelley, haunts the future, ghosts from the past. Shelley's figuration of posterity takes to their limits certain concerns in the Romantic culture of posterity – the haunting of readers by the ghostly presence of the poet; the dissolution of subjectivity in reading, its ghosting; and the radical dislocation or temporal convulsions by which writing after life, posthumous writing or ghost writing, is effected within the strange, the dread logic of posterity.

CHAPTER 8

Byron's success

Not in the air shall those my words disperse,
Though I be ashes; a far hour shall wreak
The deep prophetic fullness of this verse,
And pile on human heads the mountain of my curse!

(Byron, *Childe Harold*, book 4)

As so often happens, the cause of [Byron's] momentary fashion is
the cause also of his lasting oblivion.

(Walter Bagehot)

In November 1816, Byron wrote to Douglas Kinnaird from Venice
explaining that his 'greatest error' had been to remain in what he terms
'your country', England, 'that is to say – my greatest error but *one* – my
ambition' (*BLJ* v.135). Byron declares that he 'would never willingly
dwell in that "tight little Island" ' and that if he could manage to arrange
his 'pecuniary concerns in England', then Kinnaird 'might consider me
as posthumous' (*BLJ* v.136). For England, then, that tight little island,
Byron is dead. Indeed, he is only to return, eight years later, in a coffin.
In this respect, his departure earlier in the year may be read as an act of
self-exile and, in terms of England, as an act of self-annihilation.

This departure was framed by a dramatic rehearsal for death, by
Byron playing dead. The day before he left England in April, Byron had
visited and lain down in the grave of the poet Charles Churchill
(1732–64) – a visit immortalised in a poem written later that year, entitled 'Churchill's Grave: A Fact Literally Rendered'. The facts literally
rendered (in Leslie Marchand's biography) of Byron's visit to Churchill's
grave, are as follows: early on the morning of 23 April, Byron left
Piccadilly Terrace in London for the continent together with Polidori
and three servants – accompanied by Hobhouse and Scrope Davies as
far as Dover, and just ahead of the bailiffs. After stopping off at
Canterbury to admire the cathedral, the troupe arrived in Dover at 8.30

p.m. The next day, finding the wind to be blowing in the wrong direction, Byron was forced to delay his departure to the continent for twenty-four hours. The group ate an evening meal at five o'clock, and then walked to the graveyard of the ruined church of St Martin-le-Grand where Churchill was buried. Hobhouse records only that 'Byron lay down on his grave and gave the man a crown to fresh turf it'. Marchand also notes that during Byron's brief sojourn in Dover, female members of the local aristocracy disguised themselves as chambermaids in order to gain a glimpse of the notorious lord in the Ship Inn, and that when he went down to the quay the next day to board the packet boat for France, Byron walked through 'a lane of spectators'.[1] Byron's departure from England, then, his assumption of a certain posthumous existence, is framed by the phenomenon of his immense notoriety and by a strange rehearsal of death.

In fact, Byron's playing dead on Churchill's grave was repeated seven years later, in August 1823 when, in Cephalonia, Byron and some companions visited some open sarcophagi. Thomas Smith records that 'Something to our surprise, Lord Byron clambered over into the deepest, and lay in the bottom at full length on his back, muttering some English lines'. The lines were tentatively identified by Smith as 'unconnected fragments of the scene in "Hamlet", where he moralises with Horatio on the skull'.[2]

What is the relationship between Romanticism and playing dead? We might remember one other occurrence of such a corpse-effect, such rehearsal of death. This time, the actor is Wordsworth and it is an incident of which Byron was probably ignorant. But it is an event which has since become well known in the reception of the Wordsworthian poet, and thus a significant item in our understanding of what has come to be known as 'Romanticism'. Dorothy Wordsworth's entry in her journal for Thursday 29 April 1802 includes the following:

We then went to Johns Grove, sate a while at first. Afterwards William lay, & I lay in the trench under the fence – he with his eyes shut & listening to the waterfalls & the Birds. There was no one waterfall above another – it was a sound of waters in the air – the voice of the air. William heard me breathing & rustling now & then but we both lay still, & unseen by one another – he thought that it would be as sweet thus to lie so in the grave, to hear the *peaceful* sounds of the earth & just to know that ones dear friends were near.[3]

Playing dead, encorpsing the body in a simulacrum of mortality, making remains of the living corpus is, like the associated practices of taking life masks and death masks, and making casts of the hands and even the feet of the dead, an exemplary Romantic practice and representation, a Romantic event, a self-dramatisation which, I suggest, is disseminated in dispersed, fragmented and displaced forms in numerous contemporary texts. Before considering Byron's engagements with questions of fame, the literary market, posterity and 'immortality', I shall discuss just one text which may be said both to record and efface Byron's placement of his body over the corpse of a dead poet: his poem recording his visit to Churchill's grave.

> I stood beside the grave of him who blazed
> The comet of a season, and I saw
> The humblest of all sepulchres, and gazed
> With not the less of sorrow and of awe
> On that neglected turf and quiet stone,
> With name no clearer than the names unknown,
> Which lay unread around it; and I ask'd
> The Gardener of that ground, why it might be
> That for this plant strangers his memory task'd
> Through the thick deaths of half a century;
> And thus he answered – 'Well, I do not know
> Why frequent travellers turn to pilgrims so;
> He died before my day of Sextonship,
> And I had not the digging of this grave'.
> And is this all? I thought, – and do we rip
> The veil of Immortality? and crave
> I know not what of honour and of light
> Through unborn ages, to endure this blight?
> So soon and so successless? As I said,
> The Architect of all on which we tread,
> For Earth is but a tombstone, did essay
> To extricate remembrance from the clay,
> Whose minglings might confuse a Newton's thought
> Were it not that all life must end in one,
> Of which we are but dreamers; – as he caught
> As 'twere the twilight of a former Sun,
> Thus spoke he, – 'I believe the man of whom
> You wot, who lies in this selected tomb,
> Was a famous writer in his day,
> And therefore travellers step from out their way
> To pay him honour, – and myself whate'er
> Your honour pleases', – then most pleased I shook
> From out my pocket's avaricious nook
> Some certain coins of silver, which as 'twere
> Perforce I gave this man, though I could spare
> So much but inconveniently; – Ye smile,

I see ye, ye profane ones! all the while,
Because my homely phrase the truth would tell.
You are the fools, not I – for I did dwell
With a deep thought, and with a soften'd eye,
On that Old Sexton's natural homily,
In which there was Obscurity and Fame,
The Glory and the Nothing of a Name. (*CW* IV.1–2)

'Churchill's Grave' deconstructs reading and posterity: it amounts to one of Byron's most carefully honed engagements with and ironisations of the Romantic culture of posterity. For this reason it is worth spending some time detailing the rhetorical strategies at work in this complex figuration of posthumous survival. While the poem constitutes a direct attack on the Romantic emphasis on the value of posthumous poetic life, it also involves shifting and shifty strategies of indirection. In particular, this meditation on the Romantic culture of posterity questions the relationship between posterity and representation, a problem which, as has become clear during the course of this book (in our discussions of Wordsworth's crisis of representation in relation to survival, Coleridge's antimimetic noise, Keats's literalisation of the posthumous body, his figuration, Shelley's representational haunting), goes to the heart of what I call 'literature after life'.

The subtitle to 'Churchill's Grave' – 'A Fact Literally Rendered' – itself raises a series of difficult questions. In the first place, we might ask which 'fact' the title is intended to invoke. There are multiple possibilities: the fact of Byron's visit to the grave; the fact of the existence of the grave; the fact of Churchill's former fame or that of his current obscurity (or the combination of these two facts); the fact that Churchill's grave is no more marked than others belonging to the unknown dead; the fact that 'frequent travellers' make pilgrimages to the grave, or the apparently contradictory fact that the poet is now 'obscure'; the fact that the sexton finds it difficult to remember who is buried in this 'select' grave; the fact that the speaker responds to the sexton's 'homily' 'with a deep thought, and with a soften'd eye'; and so on. The literalness of these facts, their multiplicity and resistance to singularity effects a disturbance of both event and representation: working against the literalist assumption of the title, its assertion of referential stability and unity, the poem effects a dissolution of the border between historical event and literary representation.[4]

The singularity of the subtitle's assertion of a *fact* is, in respect of the multiplicity of the facts 'rendered' in 'Churchill's Grave', rather curious.

Such a disturbance of referential reading becomes more, rather than less, problematic in the context of a preface to the poem which Byron wrote but never published: 'The following poem (as most that I have endeavoured to write) is founded on a fact; and this detail is an attempt at a serious imitation of the style of a great poet – its beauties and its defects: I say, the *style* for the thoughts I claim as my own' (*CW* IV.447). Once again, the 'fact' to which Byron refers is uncertain. It could be the visit, the state of the grave, the act of giving the silver coins, or any number of a series of objects and events referred to in the poem. But the preface also produces a slippage from 'a fact' to 'a serious imitation', from the *fact* represented in the poem to the *act* of writing: 'this detail is an attempt at a serious imitation' suggests that the 'fact' presented by the text is the fact of imitation, the act of writing. In this respect, Byron's poem is as much concerned with the representation of writing as with the representation which writing constitutes, as much with the representational nature of the scriptive act, as with the representation of the written, the object or referent of the text. 'Churchill's Grave', as its subtitle suggests, is about the inconceivable, unpresentable representational 'fact' which is the act of inscription.

In fact, however, the subtitle multiplies the disturbances of the literal in its use of the word 'literally'. If we assume that the fact 'literally rendered' is one of the multiplicity of facts represented or referred to in the poem – the grave, its neglect, the monetary exchange, the 'homily', and so on – then it is difficult to see how the epithet 'literally' could be justified. The opening lines, for example, immediately present a striking and unignorable *figure* of fame: Churchill as one 'who blazed / The comet of a season'. Similarly, in the 'plant' of line 9, Churchill's body is figured both metonymically as a literal 'plant' which grows on the grave and 'stands for' the poet's body,[5] and metaphorically as the name for the corpse of the poet, the body metaphorically 'planted' in the grave. The process of being immortalised in posterity is similarly figured in line 16, when it is described in terms of the 'veil of immortality' being 'ripped'. Even the apparently simple act of tipping the sexton is expressed figuratively in lines 32–4: the money is concealed in the anthropomorphic 'avaricious nook' of the speaker's pocket, and the gift is one which is represented as both forced and not forced ('as 'twere / Perforce I gave this man', where the metalinguistic marker of similitude 'as 'twere', which repeats lines 25–6 – 'as he caught / As 'twere the twilight of a former Sun' – emphasises the undecidable nature of reference in this apparently simple narrative of fact). 'Literally' in the subtitle, then, is misleading or inaccurate if it is taken to refer to the exclusion of figuration, if it is taken literally. But literally speaking Byron's use of the word 'literally' to denote 'exact fidelity of representation' (*OED*, 'literally', 2b) is itself a usage in what the *OED* discreetly refers to as a 'transferred sense'. Since the *OED* gives Byron's use of 'literally' in 'Churchill's Grave' as its sole example, we can surmise that this particular usage is at least uncommon, if not actually unique in the early nineteenth century. Byron appears to be using the word with a certain representational force implied by such a neologistic or catachrestic figure. In this respect, we might recall the more conventional sense of 'literally' as a word-for-word repetition of a previous report or representation, and that the etymological or 'literal' sense of the word pertains to the Latin *littera*, meaning 'letter of the alphabet', and is particularly associated with *written* letters, with writing. In its figurative sense, then – 'literally' as exact representation, one presumably devoid of the contaminating linguistic effects of figuration – the word is far from literal. The word suggests ways in which any reading of 'facts' is irretrievably bound up with writing, never literally literal.

It may be, though, that we are taking the word too literally, as referring to 'A Fact' rather than to 'rendered'. It may be that we should read the subtitle in terms of the 'fact' being not so much rendered in a literal way as literally (rather than metaphorically) *rendered*: it may be a question of reading 'rendered' properly, literally, to the letter. Literally, or etymologically, 'render' signifies 'give back' – (*re-* plus Latin *dare*, give). Literally, then, we are dealing with a fact which is given back, returned, delivered, handed over or surrendered, paid as a duty, as well as with the act of showing forth, repeating, representing or reproducing, performing, translating or even reading. 'Rendered' involves both gift and representation.

How can we begin to think about this poem in terms of services rendered, in terms of gifts and gifts returned? To do so would be to observe, in the first place, that the author – the one who inscribes the poem, giving it both title and subtitle as well as content and structure, and giving it to be read, rendering it in writing, apparently without demand – that such an author is already, before this rendering, in receipt of a gift. In this sense, the 'fact' that the poem records or renders, literally, is that of a gift, but a gift which is not only that which the speaker renders to the sexton (a gift anyway not freely given, not a gift in the 'proper' sense of the word, but one which is, or may have been, forced – 'as 'twere / Perforce') but also a gift received by the poet. If we were to identify the poet as the speaker, then what is given might be the information of the sexton or, more generally, the experience of visiting Churchill's grave and the knowledge or epiphany of recognition that ensues from that visit. But if we then attempt to identify the author with Byron, the lord who is making his hasty way from England, finally leaving the tight little island in which he is both famous and infamous, encumbered by debt and hounded by women, bailiffs, and a scandalised society, seeking refuge in exile, then the object for which recompense is required is less clearly definable. Rather than gifts, in fact, the visit to Churchill's grave and the record of that visit take part in a complex series of exchanges by which nothing is rendered outside of a system of valuation and exchange. This is most clearly evident in the relationship between Hobhouse's prose record of the financial exchange between Byron and the sexton, and the poetic representation of that exchange in Byron's poem. According to Hobhouse, Byron 'gave the man a crown to fresh turf' the grave. By the time Byron came to write the poem, however, both the value of the payment and its motivation had altered. In the first draft of the poem, the speaker hands over 'five and sixpence', while the published version is less precise in denoting 'some certain coins of silver'. In neither the draft nor the published version is there any mention of new turf. The marginal increase in payment in the first draft, from five shillings to five-and-sixpence, rather than the inflationary effect of memory, may be accounted for as due to the unavoidable facts of metre and rhythm. But the alteration of the payment from an exchange for a service rendered to that of a gratuitous, if enforced gift, is significant. There is, we might begin to see, a circulation of finance which reconfigures the reception of the text as an 'aesthetic' object. Such alterations disturb the very limits of debt and gift, of duty and generosity, of rendering and giving.

Payment and repayment, indeed, are fundamental to the facts represented in Byron's poem. And what the text enforces is a recognition of the relationship between poet and posterity as itself one of exchange. If the topos of the gift and of financial exchange defines the poem, it is one which is articulated onto the question of posterity and posthumous fame. First there is the inadequate compensation that the world pays in attention to the poet's grave:

> And is this all? I thought, – and do we rip
> The veil of Immortality? and crave
> I know not what of honour and of light
> Through unborn ages, to endure this blight?
> So soon and so successless?   (lines 15–19)

The questions in these lines go to the heart of the debate over posterity, articulating the possibility of the return – the 'bright reversion' (*Don Juan*, Dedication, stanza 9) – due to the poet in his afterlife. The ripping and craving that 'we', poets, perform is returned by the 'blight' of obscurity: the poet is successless, without success, because he has no succession, no future which will equal the blazing career of his life. Success, in this sense, is judged by succession. Byron's use of 'successless' in this context emphasises the ways in which success involves triumph through temporal succession. The fact that Byron's poem succeeds the poetry of Churchill – as well as that of Wordsworth[6] – is, in part at least, constituted by the way in which the later poem may be said to 'render' the 'fact' of Churchill's success as well as his failure.

But the sexton does eventually remember, and, to that extent, pay honour to the famous dead by recording the honour paid to him by travellers:

> I believe the man of whom
> You wot, who lies in this selected tomb,
> Was a famous writer of his day,
> And therefore travellers step from out their way
> To pay him honour   (lines 27–31)

The sexton neatly turns this figurative payment or repayment of the honour due to the famous dead to his own account by playing on the double sense of 'pay' – payment as recognition and payment as financial transaction. The sexton's syntax hardly falters:

> To pay him honour, – and myself whate'er
> Your honour pleases . . .   (lines 31–2)

The sexton's zeugmatic figure locates and dislocates payment in the following path: (1) travellers pay honour to Churchill; (2) Byron is a traveller who pays honour; (3) the sexton pays honour to the honourable Lord Byron by honouring him ('Your honour'); (4) the honour is returned as a (monetary) payment. Behind such transactions are the questions of Byron's payment to Churchill and, more generally, posterity's payment to dead poets. In each case, payment is rendered not so much as a gift but as due payment, the reversion of what is owed. And 'honour' itself alters from that which is paid to the epithet employed by the payee to enforce payment – 'honour' finally designates the one who pays. Rather than being paid, in this (dis-)honourable transaction, honour pays. Indeed, the payment which the speaker makes to the sexton is both forced and not forced, on both sides both honourable and dishonourable:

> ... and myself what e'er
> Your honour pleases', – then most pleased I shook
> From out my pocket's avaricious nook
> Some certain coins of silver, which as 'twere
> Perforce I gave this man, though I could spare
> So much but inconveniently ...   (lines 31–6)

The payment is unforced, honourable, in the sense that the speaker is 'most pleased' and therefore, presumably, pleased to pay, and pleased, it seems, to pay over the odds ('Some certain coins of silver'), and more than he can afford ('inconveniently'). But this payment is also undecidably forced ('as 'twere / Perforce') and dishonourable, ungracious, in that the forcing and the grudging act of giving is explicitly remarked upon, literally and metaphorically *rendered* in the metonymic anthropomorphism of the pocket's 'avaricious nook'. Rendering is itself ambiguous, indicating, as it does, both the act of giving and the repayment of what is due. In this exchange, the undecidability of the gift – of 'rendering', but also of the gift more generally – is played out in the forcing and not-forcing ('as 'twere / Perforce'), in the honour and dishonour of the payment.[7]

In return for such payment – in return, that is, both for the payment and for the rendering or the representation of this payment – the speaker is, apparently, mocked:

> Ye smile
> I see ye, ye profane ones! all the while,
> Because my homely phrase the truth would tell. (lines 36–8)

The speaker represents himself as mocked for this literal rendering, for this rendering which is literal and for this literal representation of a rendering or payment. He is mocked, it seems, *because* he gives the facts, *because* 'my homely phrase the truth would tell'. It is, in part at least, the literalness of this representation, its sincerity, directness and openness – the way that the truth of the gift, of the impossibility of giving, is represented or rendered – that is being mocked. And the speaker is mocked because, like Wordsworth before him and like the sexton with his 'natural homily' (line 41), he employs the 'humble phrase'.[8] But this turn to the figured reader also involves the possibility that reading is itself a relation of payment, that reading should be understood in terms of rendering. In the poem's fiction of reading, its rendering, readers do not render to the poem what belongs to it, they remain the 'fools', misreading the speaker's representation of due payment. Indeed, it might be argued that the poem renders reading as, necessarily, misreading. In this respect, the neglect of Churchill's grave, the fact that the poet's name is 'no clearer than the names unknown', names which 'lay unread' around Churchill's tomb, is already figured in and by this poem too, rendered to this poem. 'Churchill's Grave', like Churchill's grave, is caught up in a circulation of payment and repayment, of misrecognition and obscurity, which figures the dead and, in particular, dead poets. It is this, perhaps, which accounts for the fact that, according to Hobhouse, Byron lay on the grave, rehearsing (for) death, playing dead, and why the poem renders the poet as standing, not lying, in line 1.

Byron's attitude towards audience and more generally towards what he calls 'the vanity of authorship' which, as early as 1811 he claimed to have 'outlived' (*BLJ* II.48), is notoriously mobile. 'I know the precise worth of popular applause', declares Byron in April 1819, 'for few Scribblers have had more of it' although at the same time, he claims that he has not written for an 'English' audience or 'for their pleasure' (*BLJ* VI.106).[9] Similarly, in February 1821, Byron explains to John Murray that he never writes for the public: 'did I ever write for *popularity*? – I defy you to show a work of mine (except a tale or two) of a popular style or complexion' (*BLJ* VIII.78), and in August 1819, he tells Murray that 'I never will flatter the Million's canting' and that although he may 'lead the public opinion . . . the public opinion – never led nor ever shall lead me' (*BLJ* VI.192). Byron's dismissal of the importance of audience for writing is born out by comments on fame which give the impression that his popularity is dispensable: in a journal entry for January 1821, for example, he declares that 'The only pleasure of fame is that it paves the way to pleasure' (*BLJ* VIII.28). On the other hand, Byron's poems and their prefaces repeatedly remark on the value of audience by suggesting, for example, that in the cases of both *Childe Harold* and *Don Juan*, further cantos will be or have been written and published according to public demand.[10] And some of Byron's comments suggest a critical desire for immediate popularity: he declares, for example, that 'I shall adapt my own poesy, please God! to the fashion of the time, and, in as far as I possess the power, to the taste of my readers of the present generation; if it survives me, *tanto meglio*, if not, I shall have ceased to care about it.'[11]

Such contradictions in Byron's attitude towards publication and popularity become particularly clear in relation to the question of financial reward for writing and the notion of writing as a profession. As is well known, many of Byron's comments suggest a profound antagonism towards the idea that authorship is a profession, an aristocratic indifference to professionalisation. In September 1811, for example, Byron declares that there is nothing 'so despicable as a Scribbler', the ranks of which he admits to recently having joined since publishing *Hours of Idleness* in 1807 and *English Bards and Scotch Reviewers* in 1809 (*BLJ* 11.88). In the next year, two months after the publication of cantos 1 and 2 of *Childe Harold* and on the cusp of unprecedented fame and popularity, Byron declares that 'I do not think publishing at all creditable either to men or women' and that he 'very often feel[s] ashamed of it myself' (*BLJ* 11.175). A decade later, things have changed significantly. Writing to Thomas Moore in March 1822, Byron declares that although he has 'no exorbitant expectations of fame and profit' for a number of minor poems, nevertheless he 'wish[es] them published because they are written, which is the common feeling of all scribblers' (*BLJ* IX.118). Byron's comments on the 'profession' or 'vocation' of authorship are also ambivalent and changeable: in an earlier letter to Thomas Moore of February 1817, Byron declares that literature 'is nothing' and that 'I do not think it my vocation' (*BLJ* v.177), while writing in June 1818 he castigates Leigh Hunt for thinking Wordsworth 'at the head of his own *profession*': 'I thought that Poetry was an *art*, or an *attribute*, and not a *profession*' (*BLJ* vi.47). By contrast, in 1821, Byron writes that he had 'at least had the name and fame of a Poet – during the poetical period of life (from twenty to thirty)', but goes on to say that 'whether it will last is another matter'.[12] While he is happy to be named as Poet, the idea that such a role should amount to a profession is an anathema to Byron.

This dislike and distrust of the professionalisation of writing is made evident in Byron's remarks on writing for money. Until late 1814, Byron was in the habit of giving away the copyright to his poems and collections of poems to his cousin Robert Dallas. When, in 1814, Byron is charged by reviewers with having 'received and pocketted' large sums of money for his poems, Dallas is able to affirm that Byron had 'never received a shilling for any of his work'.[13] Later in the same year, however, Byron begins to accept money for his work, taking £700 for the copyright of *Lara* (the first money he received for his poems).[14] By September 1817, Byron is negotiating for better terms for canto 4 of *Childe Harold's Pilgrimage*. Murray offered 1,500 guineas but Byron refused anything less than 2,500. In his response, Byron calculates very precisely the value of his poems by comparing payments to other contemporary authors:

if Mr. Eustace was to have had two thousand for a poem on education – if Mr. Moore is to have three thousand for Lallah &c. – if Mr. Campbell is to have three thousand for his prose on poetry – I don't mean to disparage these gentlemen or their labours – but I ask the aforesaid price for mine. (*BLJ* v.263)

By the 1820s, Byron was habitually haggling with his publisher over copyright payments. In August 1821, Murray offered Byron 2,000 guineas for three cantos of *Don Juan*, together with *Sardanapalus* and *The Two Foscari*. The offer triggered what is, perhaps, Byron's most violent attack on the mercenary nature of booksellers in a postscript to a letter to Murray dated 23 August:

P.S. – *Can't* accept your courteous offer. –

For Orford and for Waldegrave
You give much more than me you *gave*
Which is not fairly to behave
                    My Murray!

Because if a live dog, 'tis said,
Be worth a Lion fairly sped,
A *live lord* must be worth *two* dead,
                    My Murray!

And if, as opinion goes,
Verse hath a better sale than prose –
Certes, I should have more than those
                    My Murray!

But now – this sheet is nearly crammed,
So – if *you will* – *I* shan't be shammed,
And if you *want* – *you* may be dammed,
                    My Murray!

These matters must be arranged with Mr. Douglas K. – He is my trustee – and a man of honour. – To him you can state all your mercantile reasons which you might not like to state to me personally – such as 'heavy season' [']flat public' 'don't go off' – [']Lordship writes too much – Won't take advice – declining popularity – deductions for the trade – make very little – generally lose by him – pirated editions – foreign edition – severe criticisms. &c.['] with other hints and howls for an oration – which I leave Douglas who is an orator to answer. – You can also state them more freely – to a third person – as between you and me they could only produce some smart postscripts which would not adorn our mutual archives. (*BLJ* viii.187)

Byron's fiery letter articulates payment for poetry, very properly, within the context of the commercial considerations of publishing – listing, in a parodic prophecy of Murray's excuses, the limitations on sales of his work. The comments are ironic not least because, as both Murray and Byron know, Byron has become the best-selling poet of his generation. Byron's comments on posterity at the end of the postscript, his self-reflexive reference to 'mutual archives' suggests the extent to which *posthumous* fame is also implicitly involved in such negotiations. The gesture both inscribes commercial considerations into the after-fame of the poet and refers to the way in which such considerations are best excluded in order to attain a poetic afterlife.[15]

An exchange of letters in early 1819 concerning the publication of the first cantos of *Don Juan* illustrates a number of points in Byron's articulation of publication, fame and writing for money. Writing to Hobhouse and Kinnaird on 19 January 1819, Byron rejects any cuts to *Don Juan* 1 and 2: 'I will have no "cutting & slashing" . . . Don Juan shall be an entire horse or none . . . in no case will I submit to have the poem mutilated'. At the same time, he declares that he has been 'cloyed with applause & sickened with abuse' and that he cares 'for little but the Copyright' and that '*I* care for nothing but "monies" ': 'what I get by my brains – I will spend on my b–ks – as long as I have a tester or testicle remaining' (*BLJ* VI.91–2). A week later, writing to Douglas Kinnaird, Byron complains about the fears of Hobhouse and John Hookham Frere concerning the publication of the first canto of *Don Juan*. From Byron's letter, we understand that while Hobhouse had assured Byron that he 'had, and deserved to have, by far the greatest reputation of any poet of the day', he also argued that *Don Juan*'s 'sarcasms' towards Byron's estranged wife, its 'licentiousness' and 'downright indecency', its 'flings at religion' and its 'slashings right and left at other worthy writers of the day' compromised the poem's contemporary and future reception. Hobhouse had also pointed out that Don Juan would inevitably be identified with Byron himself and credence would thereby be given to 'idle stories about your Venetian life'.[16] At this point, Byron reluctantly agreed that the poem should not be published, despite the financial loss that would entail: 'This acquiescence is some thousands of pounds out of my pocket – the very thought of which brings tears into my eyes'. The letter then goes on to connect money with the 'reversion' of posterity:

God only knows how it rends my heart – to part with the idea of the sum I should have received from a fair bargain of my recent 'poeshie' the Sequins are the great consideration – as for the applauses of posterity – I would willingly sell the Reversion at a discount – even to Mr. Southey – who seems fond of it – as if people's Grandchildren were to be wiser than their forefathers – although no doubt the simple Chances of change are in favour of the deuce-ace turning up at last – just as in the overturn of a Coach the odds are that your arse will be first out of the window. – I say – that as for fame and all that – it is for such persons as Fortune chooses – and so is money. (*BLJ* vɪ.98)

Byron carefully equates fame – both contemporary and posthumous – with the financial reward which may be forthcoming from publication, and asserts the arbitrary, contingent nature of both. The legal rhetoric of posthumous fame as a 'Reversion', which appears in the 'Dedication' to *Don Juan*, ironises and deflates the importance of the textual afterlife, making of it a transferable quality, equivalent to a 'sequin' in a financial transaction. Byron also undercuts what he sees as the fiction of posterity that 'people's Grandchildren' will be 'wiser than their forefathers'. Finally, he equates posthumous fame with a game of dice such that it is only a matter of time before the 'deuce-ace' of fame (itself a worthless value in dice) will turn up. This passage expresses in brief the complex articulations of Byron's deconstruction of the Romantic culture of posterity: for Byron, fame both is and is not, in multiple ways, valuable, just as, differently, the recognition of posterity, 'Reversion at a discount', is also bound up in complex calculations of financial and other rewards. Like other Romantics, Byron is sceptical about the value of contemporary renown but, unlike others, equally sceptical about the culture of posterity.[17]

In a letter of October 1819, Byron makes a similar reference to posterity and satirises the neglected poet's desire for posthumous fame:

Perhaps I did not make myself understood – [Murray] told me the sale had not been great – 1200 out of 1500 quarto I believe (which is nothing after selling 13000 of the Corsair in one day) but that the 'best Judges &c.' had said it was very fine and clever and particularly good English & poetry and all those con- solatory things which are not however worth a single copy to a bookseller – and as to the author – of course I am in a damned passion at the bad taste of the times – and swear there is nothing like posterity – who of course must know more of the matter than their Grandfathers. (*BLJ* vɪ.237)

Byron parodies the arguments and justifications of such contemporaries as Southey and Wordsworth in this satire of the neglected author. This is a ventriloquism of the Romantic author as an unjustly neglected poet, 'despising a popularity which he will never obtain' (*BLJ* ɪv.325), as Byron remarks of Wordsworth's 'Essay, Supplementary' in a letter of October 1815.[18] It is, in fact, just such a fictionalisation of the figure of the author which underlies *Don Juan* more generally. This ironic distancing of self from self, the ironic construction of the persona or figure of the author, is fundamental to Byron's writing life, as he himself argues in an entry to his journal of 27 November 1813:

To withdraw *myself* from *myself* (oh that cursed selfishness!) has ever been my sole, my entire, my sincere motive in scribbling at all; and publishing is also the continuance of the same object, by the action it affords to the mind, which else recoils upon itself. If I valued fame, I should flatter received opinions, which have gathered strength by time, and will yet wear longer than any living works to the contrary. But, for the soul of me, I cannot and will not give the lie to my own thoughts and doubts, come what may. If I am a fool, it is, at least, a doubting one; and I envy no one the certainty of his self-approved wisdom. (*BLJ* III.225)

Byron expresses and disturbs notions of subjectivity, of the self, of 'selfishness' and sincerity: it is Byron's 'sincere motive' to 'withdraw *myself* from *myself*', so that the sincerity of Byron's writing life is designed to articulate the impossibility or the other of sincerity. Both sincere and insincere in his proclamation of sincerity, Byron asserts the paradox of the expression of the self: as Kim Michasiw puts it, Byron is 'the popular author of scandalous reputation whose works' appeal is all but inseparable from the readers' desire to read through the text to the life implied'.[19] It is this deconstruction of the 'subjectivity' of the author, I suggest, which leads to a Byronic questioning of the culture of posterity: what remains in conventional Romantic notions of posterity is the afterlife, the remains of a certain subjective presence, inscribed in text, written into poetry, an effect of writing. But Byron's complex deformations and disfigurations of the notion of sincerity, of the 'expression' of the self of the author, also put into question the very possibility of the poetic afterlife.

Writing to Isaac D'Israeli in June 1822, Byron modestly asserts that his own status as genius will not be known until after his own death: the title of 'genius', he comments, is 'dearly enough bought by most men, to render it endurable, even when not quite clearly made out, which it never *can* be till the Posterity, whose decisions are merely dreams to ourselves has sanctioned or denied it, while it can touch us no further' (*BLJ* IX.172). Similarly, in a journal entry of November 1813, Byron declares that there is 'too much' of Southey's poetry 'for the present generation', 'posterity will probably select' (*BLJ* III.214). But in spite of what Leo Braudy refers to as the 'posterity lobe' in Byron's brain,[20] many of Byron's other comments on the fiction of posterity are far more ironic or sceptical. Samuel Rogers, for example, is, according to Byron, the 'Tithonus of poetry – immortal already', whereas Byron and Thomas Moore 'must wait for it' (*BLJ* V.210). Indeed, in *Don Juan*, the poem in Byron's oeuvre which most comprehensively explores contemporary figurations of posthumous fame, an ironical critique of the self-serving appeal to posthumous reception is central to his attack on contemporary poetics. *Don Juan* may be understood to be not only 'about' fame but also an articulation of fame, an inscription of the poet as a figure of fame in his own text. The numerous passages which consider fame and posterity in *Don Juan*, then, may be read both as ironisations of the desire for fame and as a rethinking of the concept of posterity. *Don Juan*, that is to say, is one of the most radical critiques of the culture of posterity from the Romantic period that we have; it is a poem which presents a crisis in writing articulated in terms of the problematics of fame and, in particular, of posthumous fame. Byron began *Don Juan*, Jerome McGann comments, 'as a literary and political manifesto to his age', as a poem intended 'first, to correct the degenerate literary practices of the day; and second, to expose the social corruption which supports such practices.'[21] The degeneration of contemporary poetry is intimately bound up, for Byron, with the fiction of posthumous fame.

There are five major considerations of fame and posterity in the opening cantos of *Don Juan*, together with a number of minor references scattered throughout the poem. The five major considerations are as follows: the unpublished prose preface to cantos 1 and 2, in which Southey is satirised for his self-nomination for posthumous fame; the Dedication, also not published in Byron's life-time, which satirises the desire for posthumous fame in poets such as Wordsworth and, again, Southey; the ending to canto 1, which mocks the desire for earthly immortality or survival more generally; two stanzas in canto 3 (stanzas 88–89), which consider the 'strange' way that names survive; and a longer passage in canto 4 (stanzas 99–109), which considers the paradox that, 'Though fame is smoke', people still strive for a posthumous name. It is such concerns which govern the prominent and repeated reflections on fame which punctuate *Don Juan*, a poem which represents, from its dedication onwards, a deconstruction of the Romantic figure of posterity.

In the unpublished preface to cantos 1 and 2, Byron parodically explains that the 'dedication to Mr Southey and several stanzas of the poem itself' have been 'interpolated by the English editor', which, Byron argues, in a satire on Wordsworth's prose explanation of the character of the narrator of 'The Thorn', accounts for the 'tenor' of the dedication:

It may be presumed to be the production of a present Whig, who after being bred a transubstantial Tory, apostatized in an unguarded moment, and incensed at having got nothing by the exchange, has, in utter envy of the better success of the author of *Walter Tyler* [*sic*], vented his renegade rancour on that immaculate person, for whose future immortality and present purity we have the best authority in his own repeated assurances. Or it may be supposed the work of a rival poet, obscured, if not by the present ready popularity of Mr Southey, yet by the post-obits he has granted upon posterity and usurious self-applause, in which he has anticipated with some profusion perhaps the opinion of future ages, who are always more enlightened than contemporaries, more especially in the eyes of those whose figure in their own times has been dispro-portioned to their deserts.[22]

Byron's objects of ridicule are not only Wordsworth's pedantry and Southey's arrogance, but more generally the redemptive trope by which unsuccessful poets justify their work to themselves and to their public. Characteristically, Byron demystifies posterity, revealing what he sees as the economic basis of the culture of posterity in the metaphor of 'post-obits' and figuring such 'self-applause' as 'usurious'. Byron, that is to say, is traducing the cult of posterity by which, as we have seen, contempo-rary writing is increasingly defined.

The dedication itself engages with Wordsworth and Southey in terms of the Lake poets' claims on posthumous fame. According to Byron, these poets 'deem' that 'Poesy has wreaths' for themselves alone (stanza 5). Byron's antagonism towards the two poets primarily concerns his charge of political 'apostasy': the dedication is, as McGann comments, 'as republican in its literary theory as it is in its politics'.[23] But mixed up with the charge of apostasy is a secondary consideration of the way in which the two poets, secluded in the Lake District, look to posterity for recognition. The elitism of the poets' political views, Byron suggests, is related to that of their own poetical self-presentation. Byron argues that the appeal to posterity and rejection of contemporary opinion does not necessarily result in posthumous fame, and even that those who appeal to the future may indeed be those who have little to offer:

> He that reserves his laurels for posterity
>   (Who does not often claim the bright reversion?)
> Has generally no great crop to spare it, he
>   Being only injured by his own assertion (stanza 9)[24]

Towards the end of canto 1, Byron returns to the subject of fame and being remembered, to make a less strongly political and somewhat more conventional point about the transience of human endeavour:

> What is the end of fame? 'tis but to fill
> A certain portion of uncertain paper:
> Some liken it to climbing up a hill,
> Whose summit, like all hills, is lost in vapour;
> For this men write, speak, preach, and heroes kill,
> And bards burn what they call their 'midnight taper',
> To have, when the original is dust,
> A name, a wretched picture, and worse bust. (stanza 218)[25]

The stanza is followed by one which parodically echoes Shelley's 'Ozymandias' in recording the inevitable disappearance of even the most apparently permanent monument: 'Let not a monument give you or me hopes, / Since not a pinch of dust remains of Cheops' (stanza 219). Finally, Byron ends the canto, three stanzas later, by quoting lines from Southey's 'L'Envoy' to *The Lay of the Laureate* (1816):

> 'Go, little book, from this my solitude!
> I cast thee on the waters, go thy ways!
> And if, as I believe, thy vein be good,
> The world will find thee after many days'.
> When Southey's read, and Wordsworth understood,
> I can't help putting in my claim to praise –
> The four first rhymes are Southey's every line:
> For God's sake, reader! take them not for mine. (stanza 222)

As McGann comments on Southey's lines, 'Dull and sublimely forgettable in their original context, Byron yet saves them from the oblivion they deserve . . . [he] makes poetry of Southey's trash'.[26] As McGann suggests, there is a complex intertextual irony involved in the way that these lines about the uncertainty of future reception and the chanciness of being read is spliced onto another text, rent from its context so that it will reflect in a self-ironical paradox, on its own transience. While *these* lines survive, they do so in a way which obliterates the original intention, or, rather reverses their sense. For Byron, this is the irony, the intertextual irony, of the survival of writing: the stanza acknowledges the Derridean instability and non-saturability of context,[27] the way in which any attempt to shore up meaning against the ruins of time is subject to the catachresis of others' citation, or more generally to the scandal of the unpredictability and arbitrariness of reading itself. The unpredictable fate of writing and implicitly of survival in posterity is dramatised in the grafting of Southey's lines onto the text of *Don Juan*.

In canto 3, the strangeness of textual survival becomes the topic of two stanzas. Byron articulates a central paradox in his conception of fame and posterity – the strange power of written words, their power of remaining and of influencing future generations, but, at the same time, the arbitrary or contingent and finally futile nature of such survival, the way in which it is divorced from the writing subject:

> But words are things, and a small drop of ink,
> Falling like dew, upon a thought, produces
> That which makes thousands, perhaps millions, think;
> 'Tis strange, the shortest letter which man uses
> Instead of speech, may form a lasting link
> Of ages; to what straits old Time reduces
> Frail man, when paper – even a rag like this,
> Survives himself, his tomb, and all that's his.
>
> And when his bones are dust, his grave a blank,
> His station, generation, even his nation
> Become a thing, or nothing, save to rank
> In chronological commemoration,
> Some dull MS. oblivion long has sank,
> Or graven stone found in a barrack's station
> In digging the foundation of a closet,
> May turn his name up, as a rare deposit. (canto 3, stanzas 88–9)

'Glory', however, is both arbitrary and contingent, "'Tis something, nothing, words, illusion, wind – / Depending more upon the historian's style / Than on the name a person leaves behind' (stanza 90). What survives, then, is finally neither name, status, nor the body of the writer, let alone any kind of subjectivity or self. What survives is the material of writing – letters – inscribed in ink, a 'rare deposit' which records a name. But the fantasy works in terms of the possibility of *retrieval* from oblivion rather than survival *per se*, the retrieval of a disembodied and possibly fragmentary manuscript, one which has been cut off from its human and historical context. The kind of survival posited here is a minimal survival, contingent upon the accident of rediscovery and the arbitrary interpretations of historians – a 'something, nothing, words, illusion, wind'. In order to demonstrate the contingency of fame and posterity, the ultimately reductive and necessarily futile reception of dead poets, Byron goes on to list certain trivial biographical facts concerning Milton ('whipt at college – a harsh sire – odd spouse'), Shakespeare ('stealing deer'), Burns and others (stanzas 91–2). This attenuation of subjectivity in the afterlife of the writer is, for Byron, all that will survive.

The final substantial consideration of fame and posterity in *Don Juan* occurs in canto 4, where ten stanzas discuss the futility of the desire for

fame and textual immortality, impelled by a consideration of whether
Byron's own fame 'be doom'd to cease . . . Or of some centuries to take
a lease' in stanza 99. Developing the idea of posterity as expressed in
canto 3, Byron declares that 'Life seems the smallest portion of existence' for poets from the past (stanza 100). 'Great names', Byron
declares, 'are nothing more than nominal, / And love of glory's but an
airy lust' (stanza 101). Memory, memorialisation is itself doomed to dissolution and forgetting:

> The very generations of the dead
> Are swept away, and tomb inherits tomb,
> Until the memory of an age is fled,
> And, buried, sinks beneath its offspring's doom:
> Where are the epitaphs our fathers read?
> Save a few glean'd from the sepulchral gloom
> Which once-named myriads nameless lie beneath,
> And lose their own in universal death. (stanza 102) [28]

Having declared that even Dante's tomb will disappear and the poet be
forgotten, Byron returns to the inevitable desire for fame:

> Yet there will still be bards; though fame is smoke,
> Its fumes are frankincense to human thought;
> And the unquiet feelings, which first woke
> Song in the world, will seek what then they sought . . . (stanza 106)

The passage ends with another parody of Wordsworth's argument that
the true poet is not appreciated in the present: 'What, can I prove "a
lion" then no more?' asks Byron, 'then I'll swear, as poet Wordy swore /
(Because the world won't read him, always snarling) / That taste is gone,
that fame is but a lottery, / Drawn by the blue-coat misses of a coterie'
(stanza 109).[29]

Byron's success, then, is to deconstruct Romantic posterity, which is to
say that his writing both questions and disturbs the logic of posthumous
fame and, at the same time, in various and complex ways, performatively
inscribes that logic within this very rejection. Unlike poets such as
Hemans and Landon, for whom, as we have seen, personal or domestic
affection is the true source of comfort, for Byron, posterity is the only
antidote to the tribulations of contemporary fame. While Hemans and
Landon ironise posterity for themselves and celebrate it in others (in
male poets, that is to say), Byron ironises such a redemptive force in
others while celebrating its possibility, albeit ambivalently, for himself.
Byron's 'bright reversion' both is and is not the desired end of writing, is

rejected and embraced by his poetry. Byron's writing and his writing life, his life in writing, the performative autoscription of his textual existence, constitutes a counter-discourse of Romantic posterity. But it is a discourse which may finally be seen to emphasise the significance of the Romantic reinvention of posterity since by his clamorous rejection of that discourse, Byron emphasises its centrality to the project of Romantic poetry and poetics: Byrons's deconstruction of posterity also articulates, in reverse, the cultural centrality of posterity in Romantic writing.

Afterword

Not the least of our fascinations with Romantic poetry concerns the intimation that we have of the fascination that Romantic poets have with us. Romantic poets, that is to say, want to know what we think about them and what we think about them is largely a function of what they think of our thinking. This book seeks to engage with both dimensions of this reflexive fascination. Broadly speaking, the bifurcation outlined here coincides with the division of the present book into two parts. On the one hand, in part I, I have attempted to consider the culture of posterity as a crucial, pervasive element in Romantic poetics, to suggest that one of the key motivations of the literary as it was conceived and defined in the Romantic period is the possibility of future, posthumous recognition or canonisation. I have attempted to show how that fascination with and desire for a future audience is deeply embedded – often in paradoxical or conflictive ways – within the writing, theoretical and otherwise, of the major authors of the period. On the other hand, in part II, I have attempted to elaborate the extent to which this paradoxical, conflicted concern with posterity helps to account for the enduring significance of these poets' work. By working through deeply vexed issues of posthumous survival and recognition in part II, and naming them 'trembling', 'noise', 'prescience', 'ghosts' and 'rendering' in successive chapters, I have attempted to explore the kinds of conceptual, formal and linguistic pressures which this strange account of audience – deferred, anonymous, inhuman – places on literary texts. There is something unsettling about this theory, something paradoxical, and I have tried to suggest that there is something – what we might call, for the sake of argument, 'language' – for which this theory cannot finally account. Language, the very texture of poems, may be said to be the unaccountable, uncontainable, destabilising other, the irruption of desire and unreason which plays against the containing, thetic and redemptive ambitions of posterity theory. And I have attempted to explore ways in which that theory is self-divided in fundamental and paradoxical ways. Indeed, the Romantic culture of posterity is inhab-ited, traversed, founded in and, at the same time, destabilised and ungrounded by a series of irreconcilable internal differences: the pos-sibility that survival is, finally, non-survival; the fact that posterity means both future individuals and an anonymous, abstract and inhuman futurity; the realisation that, according to the logic of this theory, recep-tion is *endlessly* deferred; the problem that by inscribing himself, his *self*, into poetry, the writer dissolves and disseminates the self; the fact that one cannot experience one's own posterity; the anxiety surrounding the way that the apparently permanent nature of the material, written word becomes, precisely through its materiality, ephemeral; the fact that becoming 'eternal' or 'immortal' in one's work means dying; the sense that the return of the abjected, feminised other of the ephemeral is unavoidable in the Romantic culture of posterity.[1] I have attempted to suggest that it is those moments at which there are uncanny surfacings of deeply embedded conflicts within the theory of Romantic posterity that allow and allow for a future fascination, obsession, even, with these poets' work.

For Leo Braudy, neglect is Romanticism's 'special turn' on posterity:[2] but I have tried to suggest that, more than this, posterity is Romanticism's special turn on poetry itself. Posterity, in this sense, turns, tropes poetry. Posterity is a force-field of reception which displaces and disturbs the very production of poetry. The final lack or absence denoted by the term 'posterity' – the absence of the author at the moment of reception and, differently, the absence of audience as a function of the endless deferral which posterity in this sense truly predicates – produces a kind of theoretical and practical dislocation, an aporia, at and as the origin of inscription. The Romantic theory of posterity engages with what, for Derrida, is the structure of writing in general – writing as allied with absence and death – and it does so in a manner which brings home the ultimately futile desire for fully responsive, undeviating and unerring reception.[3] The Romantic culture of posterity, then, is a reception aes-thetics, a theory of the audience of the future, which folds back into itself to deny the possibility of its own fulfilment. And it is, according to the logic of this argument, the finally inescapable dissolution of community, reception, subjectivity, which energises the strange dislocations of Romantic poetry, dislocations which, in turn, strangely allow – impel is perhaps not putting it too strongly – such texts to endure. It is the *difficulties* which confound such texts – trembling, noise, prescience, ghosts, rendering – their stubborn semantic, hermeneutic, representational and conceptual resistances predicated on the fiction of posthumous response, which induce our continuing fascination, and our sense that reading them will not stop with us.

My larger claim, then, is that the endurance of canonical Romanticism – of the work, in particular, of Wordsworth, Coleridge, Keats, Shelley, Byron – is ultimately bound up with the dislocative effects of its particular take on or reformulation of posterity theory, effects which come into force at a time of increasing alienation of the poet from his audience. Much of the most important work in Romantic studies published in recent years seeks to complicate our understanding of the Romantic period by engaging with the multiple and historically heterogeneous contexts of such writing. By deploying such contexts in revivifying accounts of the work of authors whom the literary critical institution has, until recently, largely forgotten, such work has had wide-ranging implications for the Romantic canon. In this light, the concerns of the present book, with its interest in five canonical writers and its marginalisation of others (including women poets), will look very traditional, even retrograde. But there is a certain inevitability in my own perhaps rather stubborn insistence on this focus. Indeed, looked at another way, it may be seen that this book attempts to account for precisely the canonisation that it appears to confirm and reinforce. What has interested me in writing this book is the apparently self-fulfilling logic of the Romantic culture of posterity, the way in which those poets who were self-consciously concerned with the nature of the future reception of literary texts have been isolated from their many contemporaries and inserted – have inserted themselves – into a tradition of high literary culture. This is not so much to do with the way that writing for the future ensures a future audience (it doesn't, of course, far from it), but with the way that an investment in that cultural imperative – the true poet writes for the future, is neglected in his lifetime – can itself produce the very disturbances and dislocations which allow such works to endure, to become, in posterity, sites of conflict and fascination, sites of desire and devotion. To put it simply, what we know as Romanticism has become a site of endless (vexed, troubling, difficult) reading by virtue of its (vexed, troubling, difficult) engagement with and investment in the Romantic culture of posterity.

Notes

INTRODUCTION

1 See Timothy Clark, *The Theory of Inspiration: Composition as a Crisis of Subjectivity in Romantic and Post-Romantic Writing* (Manchester University Press, 1997).
2 Friedrich Nietzsche, *Untimely Meditations*, trans. R.J. Hollingdale (Cambridge University Press, 1983), p. 69.
3 For Shelley's comment, see *SPP* 486; for Mill's, see his 'Thoughts on Poetry and its Varieties', in *Autobiography and Literary Essays*, ed. John M. Robson and Jack Stillinger (University of Toronto Press, 1981), p. 348.
4 Leo Bersani, *The Culture of Redemption* (Cambridge, MA: Harvard University Press, 1990).
5 Since William Blake was, more than any of the other poets studied here, neglected during his lifetime only to gain recognition long after his death, his exclusion from this book might appear to be perverse. However, the precise configuration of Blake's sense of what 'posterity' means – his unique and unconventional mysticism, his visionary and spiritual imagining of such an afterlife – together with his artisanal, hand-made technologies of production, raise very different questions from those addressed here. In fact, it is precisely his virtual invisibility during the early nineteenth century which explains his exclusion, since this book is more about the cultural production of the myth of the neglected genius than about the actual obscurity of any individual poet: while Blake is undoubtedly part of the 'culture of posterity' the poetics that I seek to trace in this book were developed in the early nineteenth century independently of his work.

I WRITING FOR THE FUTURE

1 See, for example, Nigel Llewellyn, *The Art of Death: Visual Culture in the English Death Ritual, c.1500–c.1800* (London: Reaktion Books, 1991).
2 Leo Braudy, *The Frenzy of Renown: Fame and Its History* (New York: Oxford University Press, 1986), p. 28.
3 Quoted in Mark Storey, *Robert Southey: A Life* (Oxford University Press, 1997), pp. 156–7.

4 Wallace Stevens, 'A Postcard from the Volcano', in *The Collected Poems* (New York: Knopf, 1954); for an intriguing consideration of remains in poetry, see Steven Winspur, 'The Problem of Remains', *SubStance* 60 (1989), 43–59.

5 See Andrew Bennett, *Keats, Narrative and Audience: The Posthumous Life of Writing* (Cambridge University Press, 1994), where a number of ideas addressed in the present study were first broached.

6 Louis Marin, 'Montaigne's Tomb, or Autobiographical Discourse', *Oxford Literary Review* 4 (1981), 45; see also Jacques Derrida, *The Post Card: From Socrates to Freud and Beyond*, trans. Alan Bass (University of Chicago Press, 1987), p. 333, on 'autothanatography', and p. 336, on the 'auto-bio-thanato-hetero-graphic scene of writing'.

7 Nicolai Hartmann, *Ethics*, trans. Stanton Coit, 3 vols. (London: George Allen, 1932), II.312–3; extracts from this section are reprinted as 'Love of the Remote', in Ernest Partridge (ed.), *Responsibilities to Future Generations: Environmental Ethics* (Buffalo, NY: Prometheus Books, 1981), p. 305.

8 Ernest Partridge, 'Why Care About the Future?', in Partridge (ed.), *Responsibilities*, p. 204.

9 Avner de-Shalit, *Why Posterity Matters: Environmental Policies and Future Generations* (London: Routledge, 1995), p. 34.

10 *Ibid.*, p. 37; see also pp. 38–40.

11 Zygmunt Bauman, *Mortality, Immortality and Other Life Strategies* (Cambridge: Polity, 1992), p. 15; for a more detailed consideration of such concerns in the work of especially Freud, Bauman, Blanchot and Derrida, see my essay 'On Posterity', in *The Yale Journal of Criticism* 12:1 (1999). For a critical view of what he sees as Bauman's historical naivety, see Jonathan Dollimore, *Death, Desire and Loss in Western Culture* (London: Allen Lane, 1988), pp. 121–7.

12 Quoted in Bauman, *Mortality*, p. 13.

13 Bauman, *Mortality*, p. 31.

14 Cicero, *The Speeches*, trans. N.H. Watts (London: William Heinemann, 1923), pp. 37–9; an example of this idea from the Renaissance is Izaak Walton's account of Donne's death in *The Life of John Donne* (1640), in *The Lives of Dr John Donne, Sir Henry Wotton, Mr Richard Hooker, Mr George Herbert* (1670; repr. Menston: Scolar Press, 1969), p. 74: 'It is observed, that a desire of glory or commendation is rooted in the very nature of man . . . and, we want not sacred examples to justifie the desire of having our memory to out-live our lives'.

15 Brian Vickers (ed.), *The Oxford Authors: Francis Bacon* (Oxford University Press, 1996), p. 167.

16 Otto Rank, *Art and Artist: Creative Urge and Personality Development*, trans. Charles Francis Atkinson (New York: Norton, 1989), p. 11 (further references are cited in the text).

17 An example from the classical tradition is Seneca's Epistle 79 in *Epistulae Morales*, trans. Richard M. Gummere (London: Heinemann, 1962), II.209–11; see also a comment from the 'Preface of the Author' to the 1681

edition of Cowley, on the *'Portion'* which poetry 'brings of *Fame'* as an
'Estate' which 'hardly ever comes in whilst we are *Living* to enjoy it': rather,
it is a *'fantastic kind of Reversion to our ownselves*: neither ought any man to envy
Poets this posthumous and imaginary happiness, since they finde so com-
monly so little in the present' (quoted in *CN* II.3197n); for a consideration
of fame both in and after life in the Renaissance, see Alastair Fowler, *Time's
Purpled Masquers: Stars and the Afterlife in Renaissance English Literature* (Oxford:
Clarendon, 1996).

18 Osip Mandelstam, 'About an Interlocutor', in *Selected Essays*, trans. Sidney
Monas (Austin, TX: University of Texas Press, 1977), pp. 58, 59.

19 *Ibid.*, p. 64; for a useful discussion of the futuring of audience for the liter-
ary work in Celan and Derrida, see Timothy Clark, *The Theory of
Inspiration: Composition as a Crisis of Subjectivity in Romantic and Post-Romantic
Writing* (Manchester University Press, 1997), ch.11.

20 See Robert Zaller, 'Robinson Jeffers, American Poetry, and a Thousand
Years', in Zaller (ed.), *Centennial Essays for Robinson Jeffers* (Newark, DE:
University of Delaware Press, 1991), pp. 41–2.

21 Antoine Compagnon, *The Five Paradoxes of Modernity*, trans. Franklin Philip
(New York: Columbia University Press, 1994), p. 32.

22 Compare Braudy, *Frenzy*, pp. 379–80, on the way that in eighteenth-
century 'worries over the judgment of posterity we can glimpse the seed of
the avant-garde art soon to be celebrated by Romanticism', and the idea
of an *avant-garde* as 'yet a further refinement of the idea of posterity' (see
also p. 425); see also Compagnon, *The Five Paradoxes*, pp. 33–8. On the relationship between Romanticism and the *avant-garde*, see Renato Poggioli,
The Theory of the Avant-Garde, trans. Gerald Fitzgerald (Cambridge, MA:
Harvard University Press, 1968), ch.3; see also Brian Wilkie, 'Wordsworth
and the Tradition of the Avant-Garde' *JEGP* 72 (1973), 194–222.

23 Leo Bersani, *The Culture of Redemption* (Cambridge, MA: Harvard
University Press, 1990); see also Leo Bersani and Ulysse Dutoit, *Arts of
Impoverishment: Beckett, Rothko, Resnais* (Cambridge, MA: Harvard University
Press, 1993); and see Compagnon, *Five Paradoxes*, p. 46, on the 'modern tra-
dition's attachment to salvation through art'; and Richard Bourke, *Romantic
Discourse and Political Modernity: Wordsworth, the Intellectual and Cultural Critique*
(London: Harvester Wheatsheaf, 1993). For a recent expression of the 'con-
solation' of Romantic poetry or poetry as 'curative', see Michael O'Neill,
Romanticism and the Self-Conscious Poem (Oxford: Clarendon, 1997), especially
pp. xliv, 34, 48, 55, 56; and see David Bromwich on 'the genius of recov-
ery' whereby the 'disease of consciousness' is able to 'cure itself by writing',
(*A Choice of Inheritance: Self and Community from Edward Burke to Robert Frost*
(Cambridge, MA: Harvard University Press, 1989), pp. 5–6).

24 Bersani and Dutoit, *Arts of Impoverishment*, p. 8

25 Bersani, *The Culture of Redemption*, p. 1.

26 Stephen Gill (ed.), *The Oxford Authors: William Wordsworth* (Oxford
University Press, 1984), p. 225.

27 Walter Jackson Bate, *The Burden of the Past and the English Poet* (London: Chatto and Windus, 1971); Harold Bloom, *Poetry and Repression: Revisionism from Blake to Stevens* (New Haven, CT: Yale University Press, 1976).

28 On the 'Romantic interest in literature as an expression of the self', see Annette Wheeler Cafarelli, *Prose in the Age of Poets: Romanticism and Biographical Narrative from Johnson to De Quincey* (Philadelphia, PA: University of Pennsylvania Press, 1990), p. 2 and *passim*; see also Ashton Nichols, 'The Revolutionary "I": Wordsworth and the Politics of Self-Presentation', *Bucknell Review* 36:1 (1992), 66–84, who refers to Wordsworth as an 'autographer – a self writer – whose product, in *The Prelude*, is an autography: a text that is the self it represents' (p. 66).

29 John Milton, *Areopagitica*, in *Complete Prose Works of John Milton, 1643–1648*, 8 vols., ed. Douglas Bush *et al.* (New Haven, CT: Yale University Press, 1959), II.492.

30 See Neil McKendrick, John Brewer and J.H. Plumb, *The Birth of a Consumer Society: The Commercialization of Eighteenth-Century England* (London: Europa Publications, 1982), pp. 1, 9, and *passim*; see also Colin Campbell, *The Romantic Ethic and the Spirit of Modern Consummerism* (Oxford: Basil Blackwell, 1987).

31 On the transformation of poetry and publishing, see Alvin Kernan, *Printing, Technology, Letters and Samuel Johnson* (New Jersey: Princeton University Press, 1987), p. 49 and *passim*, and Kathryn Sutherland, 'Events . . . have made us a world of readers': Reader Relations 1780–1830', in David B. Pirie (ed.), *The Romantic Period* (London: Penguin, 1994), pp. 1–48; for a contemporary view, see [Charles Knight], 'The Market of Literature' in *The Printing Machine* 1 (15 February 1834), 1–5. On copyright law, see Mark Rose, *Authors and Owners: The Invention of Copyright* (Cambridge, MA: Harvard University Press, 1993), and Richard G. Swartz, 'Wordsworth, Copyright, and the Commodities of Genius', *Modern Philology* 89 (1992), 482–509; on the history of the book, see Lucien Febvre and Henri-Jean Martin, *The Coming of the Book: The Impact of Printing, 1450–1800*, trans. David Gerard (London: New Left Books, 1976); and more generally on book-culture in the eighteenth century, see John Brewer, *The Pleasures of the Imagination: English Culture in the Eighteenth Century* (London: HarperCollins, 1997), especially chs. 3 and 4. On the role of the writer before the eighteenth century, see, for example, Edwin Haviland Miller, *The Professional Writer in Elizabethan England: A Study of Nondramatic Literature* (Cambridge, MA: Harvard University Press, 1959).

32 On the changing (but persisting) nature of literary patronage in the late eighteenth century, see Dustin Griffin, *Literary Patronage in England, 1650–1800* (Cambridge University Press, 1996); for a contemporary view, see James Raymond's 'Introduction' to his edition of Thomas Dermody's poetry, *The Harp of Erin*, 2 vols. (1807), which argues forcefully that patronage is not dead (pp. ix–xvi); see also Dermody's poem 'The Curse of Patronage' (II.145–8), for a gothicised attack on unresponsive potential patrons and his assertion that the poet's name will last longer.

33 These figures are given respectively by Jerome McGann (*CW* III.444) and Marilyn Butler, 'Why Edit Socially?', *London Review of Books* 16:20 (1994), 33. Byron himself puts the figure for one day's sale of *The Corsair* at 13,000 (*BLJ* VI.237), and in his *Life of Lord Byron* (London: John Murray, 1851), p. 319, Thomas Moore increases this to 14,000. Other figures recorded by McGann show that, for example, *The Corsair* sold 25,000 copies in just over a month; *The Bride of Abydos* (1813) sold 12,500 copies in the first six editions (1813–14); *Lara* (1814) sold almost 10,000 copies in the first four editions (1814); 6,000 copies of the first edition of *The Siege of Corinth* (1816) were printed and there were two more editions in 1816; and so on. Scott's sales included 800 copies of the first edition of *The Minstrelsy of the Scottish Border* (1802), sold in the first year; 15,000 copies of *The Lay of the Last Minstrel* (1805) are estimated to have been sold in five years; 8,000 copies of *Marmion* (1808) were sold in three months; *The Lady of the Lake* (May 1810) had sold more than 30,000 copies by the end of the year (see John Sutherland, *The Life of Walter Scott: A Critical Biography* (Oxford: Blackwell, 1995), pp. 86, 105, 126, 144). See Wordsworth's comment in 1814 that with Scott and Byron 'flourishing at the rate they do, how can an honest *Poet* hope to thrive?' (*MY* II.148).

34 Jerome Christensen, *Lord Byron's Strength: Romantic Writing and Commercial Society* (Baltimore, MD: Johns Hopkins University Press, 1993), p. 147.

35 *Ibid.*, p. 145.

36 *PBSL* II.388 ; for a summary of Wordsworth's sales, see p. 218, n.42, below; for a summary of Shelley's sales, see p. 252, n.11, below

37 Quoted in Walter Jackson Bate, *John Keats* (Cambridge, MA: Harvard University Press, 1963), p. 150.

38 Hyder Edward Rollins (ed.) *The Keats Circle: Letters and Papers, 1816–1878*, 2nd edn, 2 vols. (Cambridge, MA: Harvard University Press, 1965), I.215; see also I.52–3 and 118 for accounts of the small number of sales for *Endymion*.

39 *Ibid.*, I.118, 225.

40 Quoted in Tim Chilcott, *A Publisher and his Circle: The Life and Work of John Taylor, Keats's Publisher* (London: Routledge and Kegan Paul, 1972), pp. 48, 51; Chilcott points out that in 1828, Taylor was still advertising the first edition of the 1820 volume.

41 Quoted in Edmund Blunden (ed.), *Shelley and Keats as They Struck Their Contemporaries* (London: C.W. Beaumont, 1925), p. 82.

42 Bertrand Harris Bronson, *Facets of the Enlightenment: Studies in English Literature and its Contexts* (Berkeley, CA: University of California Press, 1968), p. 299, 302–3.

43 Jean-François Lyotard and Jean-Loup Thébaud, *Just Gaming*, trans. Wlad Godzich (Manchester University Press, 1985), p. 9. See Karl Kroeber's comment that 'we need to perceive Romantic art as a reshaping of the relationship between artwork and audience' (*British Romantic Art* (Berkeley, CA: University of California Press, 1986), p. 1). On the 'irony' of a situation where the possibilities for publishing were enormously expanded at a time when the influence of poets was often dismayingly small, see Lee Erickson,

The Economy of Literary Form: English Literature and the Industrialization of Publishing, 1800–1850 (Baltimore, MD: Johns Hopkins University Press, 1996), p. 189; see also Clark, *Inspiration*, pp. 102–10.

44 On the tradition of such a distinction, see Fowler, *Time's Purpled Masquers*, p. 122.

45 *Selected Prose of John Hamilton Reynolds*, Leonidas M. Jones (ed.) (Cambridge, MA: Harvard University Press, 1966), pp. 192–3; see also pp. 70–76, 80–81.

46 Robert Southey (ed.) *Specimens of the Later English Poets*, 3 vols. (London, 1807), I.iv; the distinction between fame and reputation is also made by Southey in *New Letters of Robert Southey*, Kenneth Curry (ed.) (New York: Columbia University Press, 1965), I.370, II.112; and, in 1842, by Wordsworth (*LY* IV.312).

47 Byron is here thinking most of all, no doubt, of Southey, an interesting case in view of his constant appeals to posterity and confidence in his own genius, the official recognition he gained as Poet Laureate, the unequalled abuse that he suffered in contemporary reviews, and his posthumous neglect. For Southey on his own survival in posterity, see, for example, *New Letters*, 1.39, 113, 370, 443; II.107, 112, 272; among Southey's poems, see 'The Holly Tree' (1798), line 18, 'My Days Among The Dead Are Past' (1818), 'Little Book, in Green and Gold' (1831), 'Proem' to 'The Poet's Pilgrimage' (1816) lines 125–6, 139–44, 'Proem' to 'Lay of the Laureate', stanzas 8–11, and 'L'Envoy' (1816) (interestingly, as Jack Simmons points out in *Southey* (London: Collins, 1945), p. 118, Southey's *The Remains of Henry Kirke White* (1807) (one of the archetypes of the figure of the neglected Romantic poet), 'came nearer to being a "best-seller" than anything else he ever produced'). For Southey's complacent satisfaction with his contemporary reception (itself a cause of irritation to reviewers), see, for example, *New Letters* 1.108, 306, 407, 471; II.113; and his comment in the Preface to vol. 1 of his 1837–38 collected poems that his poetry has 'obtained a reputation equal to my wishes' (*The Poetical Works of Robert Southey* (London: Longmans, Green and Co., 1884), p. iii); on this point, see Simmons, *Southey*, pp. 104–5, 161–2; see also Mark Storey, ' "A Hold Upon Posterity": The Strange Case of Robert Southey' (University of Birmingham, School of English, 1993).

48 Compare Byron's curt response to the essay: 'I will not go so far as Wordsworth in his postscript, who pretends that *no* great poet ever had immediate fame, which being interpreted, means that William Wordsworth is not quite so much read by his cotemporaries [*sic*] as might be desirable. – This assertion is as false as it is foolish' (Andrew Nicholson (ed.), *Lord Byron: The Complete Miscellaneous Prose* (Oxford: Clarendon, 1991), p. 108; compare *BLJ* IV.325); Byron then goes on to provide his own literary history to counter Wordsworth's (see Nicholson (ed.), *Miscellaneous Prose*, pp. 108–9); compare Peter T. Murphy, *Poetry as an Occupation and an Art in Britain, 1760–1830* (Cambridge University Press, 1993), pp. 195–6; on the significance of Wordsworth's essay, see Sutherland, 'Events . . . ', pp. 40–1.

49 Ovid, *Metamorphoses*, trans. A.D. Melville (Oxford University Press, 1986),

p. 379, *The Love Poems*, trans. A.D. Melville (Oxford University Press, 1990), p. 27 (line 15).

50 See Horace, *The Complete Odes and Epodes*, ed. W.G. Shepherd (Harmondsworth: Penguin, 1983), p. 164 (book III, ode 30): 'I have achieved a monument more lasting / than bronze, and loftier than the pyramids of kings, / which neither gnawing rain nor blustering wind / may destroy, nor innumerable series of years, / nor the passage of ages. I shall not wholly die . . . '; on the tradition of this boast (and its anti-tradition), see Richard Hillyer, 'Better Read than Dead: Waller's "Of English Verse" ', *Restoration* 14 (1990), 33–43.

51 *The Art and Thought of Heraclitus: An Edition of the Fragments with Translation and Commentary*, Charles H. Khan (ed.) (Cambridge University Press, 1979), p. 73 (fragment xcvii); on the importance of the immortality topos in the European Middles Ages, see Ernst Robert Curtius, *European Literature and the Latin Middle Ages*, trans. Willard R. Trask (London: Routledge and Kegan Paul, 1953), pp. 476–7; see also Jacob Burkhardt, *The Civilization of the Renaissance in Italy*, trans. S.G.C. Middlemore (Harmondsworth: Penguin, 1990), pp. 104–10, for a brief account of another earlier age which saw a rather different cult of eternal fame; and see Braudy, *Frenzy*, pp. 251–64 and *passim*. In *Mortals and Immortals: Collected Essays* (New Jersey: Princeton University Press, 1991), p. 58, Jean-Pierre Vernant draws a parallel between classical notions of literary immortality and modern ones.

52 Michel Foucault, *Language, Counter-Memory, Practice: Selected Essays and Interviews*, ed. Donald F. Bouchard (Oxford: Basil Blackwell, 1977), p. 53.

53 Harold Bloom, *The Western Canon: The Books and School of the Ages* (London: Macmillan, 1994), p. 19; Bloom traces the 'conceit' of textual immortality to Petrarch and to Shakespeare's sonnets and as a 'latent element' in *The Divine Comedy*.

54 Raymond Himelick (ed.), *Samuel Daniel's 'Musophilus', Containing a General Defense of all Learning* (West Lafayette: Purdue University Studies, 1965), p. 37.

55 Bloom, *The Western Canon*, p. 19; compare Hugh Kenner's comment on the question of whether there was any 'inherent scandal' in Shakespeare's not having been assimilated into the canon during his lifetime: 'In 1600 there was no canon, literary history not yet having been invented' ('The Making of the Modernist Canon', in Robert von Hallberg (ed.), *Canons* (University of Chicago Press, 1984), p. 363); see also Trevor Ross, 'The Emergence of "Literature": Making and Reading the English Canon in the Eighteenth Century', *ELH* 63 (1996), 397–422.

56 *The Poems of Robert Herrick*, ed. L.C. Martin (London: Oxford University Press, 1965), p. 265.

57 See Achsah Guibbory, *The Map of Time: Seventeenth-Century English Literature and Ideas of Pattern in History* (Urbana, IL: University of Illinois Press, 1986), ch.5.

58 *Sir William Davenant's Gondibert*, ed. David F. Gladish (Oxford: Clarendon, 1971), p. 25.

59 *Ibid.*, p. 25–6.
60 *Ibid.*, p. 26.
61 Quoted in Mary Edmond, *Rare Sir William Davenant* (Manchester University Press, 1987), p. 117.
62 Himelick (ed.), *Musophilus*, p. 31. See also Daniel's prefatory verses 'To the Reader' (1607), quoted in *ibid.*, p. 9: 'I know I shal be read, among the rest / So long as men speak english . . . '; and see Himelick's comment (quoting from *Defence of Rhyme*) that 'like most men of his time, he also had a melancholy awareness of the "slippery foundation of opinion, and the world's inconstancy"'; see also Daniel's Dedication to *The Tragedie of Cleopatra* (1623), in *The Complete Works in Verse and Prose of Samuel Daniel*, ed. Alexander B. Grosart, 5 vols. (1885; repr. New York: Russell and Russell, 1963), III.23–7: 'And now must I with that poore strength I have, / . . . arme against Oblivion and the Grave, / . . . So that if by my Penne procure I shall / But to defend me, and my name to save, / Then though I die, I cannot yet die all / But still the better part of me will live . . . ' (lines 41–9). As is conventional, however, the dedication takes as its primary task the remembrance and survival of its dedicatee. On the tradition of such appeals to posterity, see Himelick (ed.), *Musophilus*, pp. 37–41; for another consideration of such tropes, see Geoffrey Bullough (ed.), *Poems and Dramas of Fulke Greville*, 2 vols. (Edinburgh: Oliver and Boyd, 1943), pp. 62–4. As Ian Hamilton comments, the idea of posterity in the seventeenth century was 'mostly nebulous, and deeply interfused with the idea of heaven, with Temples of Fame, celestial roll-calls, good talk in the Elysian Fields' (*Keepers of the Flame: Literary Estates and the Rise of Biography* (London: Pimlico, 1992), p. 33).
63 Robert N. Watson, *The Rest is Silence: Death as Annihilation in the English Renaissance* (Berkeley, CA: University of California Press, 1994), p. 232.
64 John Milton, *Complete Shorter Poems*, ed. John Carey, 2nd edn (London: Longman, 1997), pp. 248–9 (lines 70–84).
65 Vickers (ed.), *The Oxford Authors: Francis Bacon*, p. 168.
66 John Milton, *Paradise Lost*, ed. Scott Elledge, 2nd edn (New York: Norton, 1993), p. 163 (book 7, line 31).
67 Isaac D'Israeli, *Quarrels of Authors*, 3 vols. (repr. New York: Johnson Reprint Co., 1970), II.277); compare similar comments by Coleridge in *BL* 1.36–7; but see Byron's brusque comment that 'Milton's politics kept him down', by comparison, he notes, with most major English and European writers, who were 'as popular in their lives as since' (Nicholson (ed.), *Prose*, p. 109).
68 J.W. Saunders, *The Professsion of English Letters* (London: Routledge and Kegan Paul, 1964) p. 90: as Saunders comments, 'There was no evidence that [Milton] was other than satisfied by this "fit audience, though few". General sales of his books proceeded well enough to serve as a means to the main end of addressing the intellectual *élites* of Europe'; see also Bronson, *Facets*, pp. 302–3.
69 John Lyon, 'The Test of Time: Shakespeare, Jonson, Donne', *Essays in Criticism* XLIX (1999).

70 Ian Donaldson, *Jonson's Magic Houses: Essays in Interpretation* (Oxford: Clarendon, 1997), p. 189.

71 On Jonson's quarrels with his audience, see Richard Helgerson, 'The Elizabethan Laureate: Self-Presentation and the Literary System', *ELH* 46 (1979), 193–220; Alexander Leggatt, *Ben Jonson: His Vision and His Art* (London: Methuen, 1981), pp. 233–74; George E. Rowe, Jr., 'Ben Jonson's Quarrel with Audience and its Renaissance Context' *SP* 81 (1984), 438–60; Achsah Guibbory, 'A Sense of the Future: Projected Audiences of Donne and Jonson', *John Donne Journal* 2:2 (1983), 11–21.

72 See Anne Ferry, *All in War with Time: Love Poetry of Shakespeare, Donne, Jonson, Marvell* (Cambridge, MA: Harvard University Press, 1975), p. 4, who comments that allusions to the convention of the 'immortalisation' of the beloved in verse occur 'more often in Shakespeare's than in any other group of English sonnets'.

73 On the classical and Renaissance epideictic tradition and its relation to permanent fame, see O.B. Hardison, Jr., *The Enduring Monument: A Study of the Idea of Praise in Renaissance Literary Theory and Practice* (Westport, CT: Greenwood Press, 1973), who reminds us that the celebration of others is seen by certain theorists as both the origin of poetry and its highest form. See also Stephen Murphy, *The Gift of Immortality: Myths of Power and Humanist Poetics* (Cranbury, NJ: Associated University Presses, 1997).

74 *Shakespeare's Sonnets*, ed. Stephen Booth (New Haven, CT: Yale University Press, 1977).

75 Jonathan Swift, 'Thoughts on Various Subjects', in *A Tale of a Tub With Other Early Works 1696–1707*, ed. Herbert Davis (Oxford: Basil Blackwell, 1939), p. 242. For an influential discussion of the poetic immortalising of heroes, see Ariosto's *Orlando Furioso*, xxxv.14–30; for an example of the argument nearer the time, see Pope's Imitation of Part of the Ninth Ode of the Fourth Book of Horace.

76 See Horace, *Epistles Book II and Epistle to the Pisones*, ed. Niall Rudd (Cambridge University Press, 1989), p. 44 (2.1.34–49).

77 Francesco Petrarca, *Rerum familiarium, libri I–VIII*, trans. Aldo S. Bernardo (Albany: State University of New York Press, 1975), pp. 15, 19.

78 Samuel Johnson, 'Preface to Shakespeare', in *Rasselas, Poems and Selected Prose*, ed. Bertrand H. Bronson, 3rd edn (New York: Holt, Rinehart and Winston, 1971), p. 262; compare Trevor Ross, 'The Emergence of "Literature"', pp. 409, 411. For a recent defence of such a view, see Anthony Savile, *The Test of Time: An Essay in Philosophical Aesthetics* (Oxford: Clarendon, 1982), who lists as 'proponents of the practice' of the test a predominantly eighteenth-century cast: Johnson, Longinus, Horace, Kames, Hume, Burke, Pope, Joseph Warton, Hurd, Edward Young, J. Moir (*Gleanings*, 1785), as well as Wordsworth and a small number of twentieth-century writers (p. 301n).

79 Johnson, *Selected Prose*, pp. 262–3.

80 Johnson, *Selected Prose*, p. 629; but see Fowler, *Time's Purpled Masquers,*

pp. 125–6, on the Enlightenment's 'belittling' of 'aspirations to immortality' (quoting Johnson's *Rasselas*).

81 David Hume, *Essays Moral, Political, and Literary*, 2 vols., ed. T.H. Green and T.H. Grose (London: Longmans, Green and Co., 1875), 1.271; compare the opening to Joseph Warton's *An Essay on the Genius and Writings of Pope* (1756), quoted in Scott Elledge (ed.), *Eighteenth-Century Critical Essays*, 2 vols. (Ithaca, NY: Cornell University Press, 1961), 11.720.

82 Quoted in Elledge (ed.), *Eighteenth-Century Critical Essays*, 11.978.

83 Johnson, *Selected Prose*, p. 261.

84 Edward Young, *Conjectures on Original Composition* (Leeds: The Scholar Press, 1966), pp. 110–11. Young's significant phrase 'the age of authors' may be an allusion Johnson's phrase in the *Adventurer* 115 (11 December 1753): 'The present age, if we consider chiefly the state of our own country, may be stiled, with great propriety The Age of Authors' (*The Idler and The Adventurer*, ed. W.J. Bate, John M. Bullitt and L.F. Powell (New Haven, CT: Yale University Press, 1963), p. 457.

85 Edward Young, *Love of Fame, The Universal Passion*, 5th edn (London, 1752), p. 70.

86 William Godwin, *The Enquirer: Reflections on Education, Manners and Literature in a Series of Essays* (repr. New York: Augustus M. Kelley, 1965), p. 283.

87 *Ibid.*, p. 287.

88 Coleridge, *Shorter Works and Fragments*, ed. H.J. Jackson and J.R. de J. Jackson (London: Routledge, 1995), 1.22.

89 *Ibid.*, 1.23; Cicero considers the problem that 'after death I shall be insensible' to the 'undying memory' that he has 'sown' throughout the world: 'Be that as it may, now at any rate I find satisfaction in the thought and in the hope' (*The Speeches*, p. 39). See pp. 56–61, for Coleridge's later, rather different, assessment of the significance of posthumous fame.

90 G.S. Rousseau, 'Pope and the Tradition in Modern Humanistic Education: " . . . in the pale of Words till death" ', in G.S. Rousseau and Pat Rogers (eds.), *The Enduring Legacy: Alexander Pope Tercentenary Essays* (Cambridge University Press, 1988), p. 199; see also Hamilton, *Keepers of the Flame*, pp. 48–9.

91 *The Poems of Alexander Pope*, ed. John Butt (London: Methuen, 1963): in both cases, Pope seems to be echoing Shakespeare's sonnet 81 ('You still shall live – such virtue hath my pen – / Where breath most breathes, ev'n in the mouths of men'), as does Coleridge in his comment on 'fly[ing] through the mouths of men'.

92 Quoted in Donald Fraser, 'Pope and the Idea of Fame', in Peter Dixon (ed.), *Alexander Pope* (London: G. Bell, 1972), p. 296.

93 *Ibid.*, p. 302.

94 See, for example, *The Correspondence of Alexander Pope*, 5 vols., ed. George Sherburn (Oxford: Clarendon, 1956), 111.366, 1v.27–8; see also 11.480, 481; 1v.362.

95 See *Le Pour et le contre, ou Lettres sur la postérité*, in Denis Diderot, *Oeuvres com-*

plètes, ed. Emita Hill *et al.*, vol.xv (Paris: Hermann, 1986). On the impor-
tance of this exchange for an understanding of Diderot's work, see Arthur
M. Wilson, *Diderot* (New York: Oxford University Press, 1972), pp. 508, 714.
See also Jeffrey Mehlman, *Cataract: A Study in Diderot* (Middletown, CT:
Wesleyan University Press, 1979), pp. 76–87; James Creech, 'Diderot and
the Pleasure of the Other: Friends, Readers, and Posterity', *Eighteenth
Century Studies* 11 (1977–78), 439–56.

96 *Pour et Contre*, p. 88 (my translation).

97 Quoted in P.N. Furbank, *Diderot: A Critical Biography* (London: Secker and
Warburg, 1992), p. 305: Furbank's translation.

98 *Ibid.*, pp. 304–5.

99 *Ibid.*, pp. 305–6.

100 Diderot, *Pour et Contre*, p. 51.

101 Quoted in Wilson, *Diderot*, p. 715; compare Diderot's article entitled
'Encyclopédie' from his *Encyclopaedia*, quoted in Geoffrey Bennington,
'Towards A Criticism of the Future', in *Writing for the Future*, ed. David
Wood (London: Routledge, 1990), p. 23–4.

102 *The Oxford Authors: Alexander Pope*, ed. Pat Rogers (Oxford University Press,
1993), p. 375.

103 Elledge (ed.), *Eighteenth-Century Critical Essays*, 1.281.

104 Johnson, *Selected Prose*, p. 289.

105 Johnson, in fact, frequently addressed issues of fame, popularity and posterity in his essays, most often with a wary scepticism towards the benefits
of fame (especially literary fame), and towards the possibility of achieving
it (in life or after): see, for example, *The Rambler* nos. 2, 106, 146, 203; *The
Idler* no. 65; on the rewards of posterity, in particular, see *The Rambler* no.
49, in which Johnson argues for a balanced, proportionate perspective on
its possibilities, linking it to 'virtue'.

106 *The Oxford Authors: Ben Jonson*, ed. Ian Donaldson (Oxford University Press,
1985), p. 454 (lines 17, 43).

107 Wordsworth, *The Prelude 1799, 1805, 1850*, ed. Jonathan Wordsworth, M.H.
Abrams and Stephen Gill (New York: Norton, 1979), p. 482; *The Oxford
Authors: William Wordsworth*, p. 351.

2 THE ROMANTIC CULTURE OF POSTERITY

1 On the reconceptualisation or even 'invention' of literature during the
period, see, for example, David Bromwich, 'The Invention of Literature',
in *A Choice of Inheritance: Self and Community from Edmund Burke to Robert Frost*
(Cambridge, MA: Harvard University Press, 1989), pp. 1–19; M.H.
Abrams, 'Art-as-Such: The Sociology of Modern Aesthetics', in *Doing
Things With Texts: Essays in Criticism and Critical Theory* (New York: Norton,
1989), pp. 135–58; Trevor Ross, 'The Emergence of "Literature": Making
and Reading the English Canon in the Eighteenth Century', *ELH* 63
(1996), 397–422; John Guillory, *Cultural Capital: The Problem of Literary Canon*

Formation (University of Chicago Press, 1993), ch.5; Clifford Siskin, *The Work of Writing: Literature and Social Change in Britain, 1700–1830* (Baltimore, MD: Johns Hopkins University Press, 1998); and see Michel Foucault, *The Order of Things: An Archeology of the Human Sciences* (London: Tavistock, 1970), pp. 299–301, and *Language, Counter-Memory, Practice: Selected Essays and Interviews*, trans. Donald F. Bouchard (Oxford: Basil Blackwell, 1977), pp. 59–68. On the 'consumer revolution' of the eighteenth century, see Neil McKendrick, John Brewer and J.H. Plumb, *The Birth of a Consumer Society: The Commercialization of Eighteenth-Century England* (London: Europa Press, 1982), and Colin Campbell, *The Romantic Ethic and the Spirit of Modern Consumerism* (Oxford: Blackwell, 1987); on the changing nature of the book-reading public, see James Raven, *Judging New Wealth: Popular Publishing and Responses to Commerce in England, 1750–1800* (Oxford: Clarendon, 1992), pp. 13–14 and *passim*; on changes in poets' relations with their audience during the period, see Ian Jack, *The Poet and His Audience* (Cambridge University Press, 1984), chs.3 and 4. For a consideration of corresponding developments in Germany, see Martha Woodmansee, *The Author, Art, and the Market: Rereading the History of Aesthetics* (New York: Columbia University Press, 1994).

2 Raymond Williams, *Culture and Society 1780–1950* (Harmondsworth: Penguin, 1963), p. 53; see also Williams's discussion of different theorisations of the 'institution' of the artist in *Culture* (Glasgow: Fontana, 1981), pp. 33–56; and see *The Long Revolution* (London: Chatto and Windus, 1961).

3 Williams, *Culture and Society*, p. 57.

4 On the 'birth' of the author, see Michel Foucault, 'What is an Author?' in *Language, Counter-Memory, Practice*, pp. 113–18; Woodmansee, *Author*, pp. 36ff.; Siskin, *The Work of Writing*, ch.6; and see Frank Donoghue, *The Fame Machine: Book Reviewing and Eighteenth-Century Literary Careers* (Stanford University Press, 1996). For a critical discussion of the idea of the 'invention' of the author, see David Saunders and Ian Hunter, 'Lessons from the "Literatory": How to Historicise Authorship' *CI* 17 (1991), 479–509.

5 Mark Rose, *Authors and Owners: The Invention of Copyright* (Cambridge, MA: Harvard University Press, 1993), p. 6

6 *Ibid.*, p. 49; but compare John Feather, *Publishing, Piracy and Politics: An Historical Study of Copyright in Britain* (London: Mansell, 1994), p. 5, who argues that despite its importance the 1710 Copyright Act 'says nothing and implies little about the rights of authors'.

7 See Rose, *Authors and Owners*, p. 91.

8 See Feather, *Publishing*, p. 124

9 See Rose, *Authors and Owners*, pp. 111–12

10 Robert Southey, 'Inquiry into the Copyright Act', *Quarterly Review* 21 (1819), 211; see also Rose, *Authors and Owners*, pp. 104–5. On the new eighteenth-century sense of the literary as a form of property, see also Margreta de Grazia *Shakespeare Verbatim: The Reproduction of Authenticity and the 1790 Apparatus* (Oxford: Clarendon, 1991), ch.5.

11 See ch.8, below, for a brief review of Byron's concern with the financial aspects of poetry publishing; on Keats's ambivalence, see my *Keats, Narrative and Audience: The Posthumous Life of Writing* (Cambridge University Press, 1994), ch.2; compare Wordsworth's distrust of 'trading Authors of any description, Verse men or Prose men' (*LY* II.518).

12 Wordsworth, 'To the Editor of the Kendal Mercury' (*Prose* III.310).

13 Wordsworth, 'Petition to the Select Committee of the House of Commons' (*Prose* III.319).

14 *MY* II.535; compare *MY* I.266; and compare Isaac D'Israeli, 'The Case of Authors Stated', in *Calamities of Authors* (London, 1812), I.24–43; see Rose, *Authors and Owners*, p. 110. For Wordsworth's interventions in the copyright debate see *LY* II.225, 265, 306; III.21–2, 407, 536, 574, 602; IV.17–18, 42–3, 93, 293–4; and see also Woodmansee, *Artist*, pp. 145–7; Richard G. Swartz, 'Wordsworth, Copyright and the Commodities of Genius', *MP* 89 (1992), 482–509; Susan Eilenberg, 'Mortal Pages: Wordsworth and the Reform of Copyright', in *Strange Power of Speech: Wordsworth, Coleridge and Literary Possesssion* (New York: Oxford University Press, 1992), pp. 192–212. On the structure of deferral as definitive of what he calls 'modern hedonism' and the way in which such deferral is bound up with both the ideology of Romanticism *and* that of modern consumerism, see Campbell, *The Romantic Ethic*, pp. 86–7.

15 *Prose* III.318; for a discussion of Wordsworth's essay in this context, see my *Keats, Narrative and Audience*, pp. 31–5; see also Woodmansee, *Artist*, pp. 117–18; Swartz, 'Wordsworth', 490–93; Annette Wheeler Cafarelli, *Prose in the Age of Poets: Romanticism and Biographical Narrative from Johnson to De Quincey* (Philadelphia, PA: University of Pennsylvania Press, 1990), pp. 95–101; and the 'Introduction' to Martha Woodmansee and Peter Jaszi (eds.), *The Construction of Authorship: Textual Appropriation in Law and Literature* (Durham, NC: Duke University Press, 1994), p. 4.

16 Martha Woodmansee 'On the Author Effect: Recovering Collectivity', in Jaszi and Woodmansee (eds.), *The Construction of Authorship*, p. 16.

17 See Feather, *Publishing*, p. 125.

18 Southey, 'An Inquiry', 212–13.

19 Compare David G. Riede, *Oracles and Hierophants: Constructions of Romantic Authority* (Ithaca, NY: Cornell University Press, 1991), pp. 3–4, and *passim*.

20 Roger Chartier, *The Order of Books: Readers, Authors, and Libraries in Europe between the Fourteenth and Eighteenth Centuries*, trans. Lydia G. Cochrane (Cambridge: Polity, 1994), p. 37.

21 Terry Eagleton, *The Ideology of the Aesthetic* (Oxford: Basil Blackwell, 1990), pp. 64–5; compare Rose, *Authors and Owners*, p. 120.

22 Howard Erskine-Hill and Richard A. McCabe, 'Introduction' in Erskine-Hill and McCabe (eds.), *Presenting Poetry: Composition, Publication, Reception* (Cambridge University Press, 1995), p. 5.

23 Rose, *Authors and Owners*, p. 128.

24 On the Genius as considered in the late eighteenth century as 'the highest

human type', see Penelope Murray (ed.), *Genius: The History of an Idea* (Oxford: Basil Blackwell, 1989), p. 2.

25 Guillory, *Cultural Capital*, p. 329.

26 See Lucy Newlyn, 'Coleridge and the Anxiety of Reception', *Romanticism* 1:2 (1995), 206–38; and my *Keats, Narrative and Audience*, p. 5; see also Jon P. Klancher, *The Making of English Reading Audiences, 1790–1832* (Madison, WI: University of Wisconsin Press, 1987); William G. Rowland, Jr., *Literature and the Marketplace: Romantic Writers and Their Audiences in Great Britain and the United States* (Lincoln, NE: University of Nebraska Press, 1996); Bertrand Harris Bronson, *Facets of the Enlightenment: Studies in English Literature and Its Contexts* (Berkeley, CA: University of California Press, 1968), ch.14; Alvin Kernan, *Printing, Technology, Letters and Samuel Johnson* (New Jersey: Princeton University Press, 1987); Alan Richardson, *Literature, Education and Romanticism: Reading as a Social Practice, 1780–1832* (Cambridge University Press, 1994), pp. 267–8; Raven *Judging New Wealth*, p. 21.

27 Compare Woodmansee, *Artist*, p. 89, on the growth of readerships and the so-called 'reading epidemic' in late eighteenth-century Germany; for Coleridge on the degradation of the 'feeble Frenchified Public', see *CL* III.281–2; and see Wordsworth's comments on 'the rage for low priced Books' (*LY* III.599), on the 'moral monster' of the public (*MY* 1.264), and on the 'transient or corrupt taste of the day' (*LY* IV.18). For a polemical account of the way in which such views develop into an association of aesthetics with fascism in certain modernist writers, see John Carey, *The Intellectuals and the Masses: Pride and Prejudice among the Literary Intelligentsia, 1880–1939* (London: Faber and Faber, 1992).

28 Coleridge, *Lay Sermons*, ed. R.J. White (London: Routledge and Kegan Paul, 1972), pp. 36–8; see Newlyn, 'Anxiety of Reception'; and see Annette Wheeler Cafarelli, 'The Common Reader: Social Class in Romantic Poetics', *JEGP* 96:2 (1997), 222–46.

29 Arthur H. Hallam, 'Essay on the Philosophical Writings of Cicero', in *Remains in Verse and Prose of Arthur Henry Hallam* (London: John Murray, 1863), p. 164; Martha Woodmansee, *Author*, p. 72, quotes Schiller's *On the Aesthetic Education of Man* to similar effect; see also Swartz, 'Wordsworth', p. 502.

30 Riede, *Oracles and Hierophants*, p. 27.

31 Quoted in William Wordsworth, *The Prelude, 1799, 1805, 1850*, ed. Jonathan Wordsworth, M.H. Abrams and Stephen Gill, (New York: Norton, 1979), pp. 537–8.

32 Compare comments by Wordsworth in *MY* 1.146–50; and see Alan G. Hill's comment that Wordsworth 'never wavered in his sense of his own greatness' (*LY* 1.xxviii); see also Patrick Cruttwell, 'Wordsworth, The Public, and The People', *Sewanee Review* 64 (1956), 71–80.

33 *Henry Crabb Robinson on Books and Their Writers*, ed. Edith J. Morley (London: Dent, 1938), 1.188.

34 Harold Bloom, *The Western Canon: The Books and School of the Ages* (London: Macmillan, 1994), p. 250.

35 Compare Wordsworth's comment to Edward Moxon in December 1826 on youths who are 'addicted' to the 'Composition of verse' (*LY* 1.497); Mrs Davy records of Wordsworth in 1849 that 'in a way very earnest, and to me very impressive and remarkable, [Wordsworth] disclaimed all value for, all concern about, posthumous fame' (Alexander B. Grosart (ed.), *The Prose Works of William Wordsworth* (London: Edward Moxon, 1876), III.458); and see Aubrey de Vere's similar record of a comment by the elderly Wordsworth: 'As for myself, it seems now of little moment how long I may be remembered' (*ibid.*, III.493). Hazlitt makes a similar point in his essay 'On Sitting for One's Picture' (1823), on the 'poor compensation' of 'surviving ourselves in our pictures' (*Works* XII.116); and see Byron, *Childe Harold* III.1045: 'Fame is the thirst of youth . . .'.

36 See Stephen Gill, *William Wordsworth: A Life* (Oxford: Clarendon, 1989), pp. 164, 172–3, 185, 261–2, 267–9, 271, 289–91, 295, 300, 304, 311 for comments on Wordsworth's concern for the reputation and sales of his poetry; and compare Peter T. Murphy, *Poetry as an Occupation and an Art in Britain, 1760–1830* (Cambridge University Press, 1993), pp. 182–3, on Wordsworth's ambivalence towards popularity.

37 For Wordsworth's sense of the originality of the *Lyrical Ballads*, see *EY* 310.

38 *EY* 267; see also pp. 267–8; and see Dorothy's letter to Wordsworth in March 1808, urging her brother to ignore the 'outcry' against his 1807 volume: 'without money what *can* we do?' she asks: 'New House! new furniture! such a large family! two servants and little Sally! we *cannot* go on so for another half-year . . . Do, dearest William! do pluck up your Courage – overcome your disgust to publishing – It is but a *little trouble*, and all will be over, and we shall be wealthy, and at our ease for one year, at least' (*MY* 1.207). By contrast, in 1849, Mrs Davy records Wordsworth commenting that he had 'never written a line with a view to profit' (Grosart (ed.), *Prose* III.457). On Wordsworth's sense of his own inevitable unpopularity, see also *MY* II.211, *LY* II.634; on his shunning popular regard, see also *MY* II.273.

39 See also Wordsworth's comments in a letter of March 1808 on the 'wretched and stupid Public', his distaste for the 'criticasters', and his desire to write 'for the sake of the People' (*Supplement*, p. 11); the distinction betweeen the 'Public' and the 'People, philosophically characterised' is, of course, developed at the end of the 'Essay, Supplementary' (see *Prose* III.84). For similar comments towards the end of his life, see *LY* IV.307, 390; on the importance or lack of importance of sales, see also *MY* II.165, 181, 286–7, 213; on the private versus the public man, see also *EY* 401; *MY* 1.383; and see *LY* IV.312 for Wordsworth's indifference to reputation or fame.

40 Thomas De Quincey, *Recollections of the Lakes and the Lake Poets*, ed. David Wright (Harmondsworth: Penguin, 1970), p. 117. See also *MY* 1.370; II.3, 144: see Mary Moorman's comment on the period 1806–20 as years of 'unrelenting disfavour from most of the critics, but at the same time

steadily increasing fame' (*MY* I.vi). Aubrey de Vere comments that 'general
fame did not come to him till about fifteen years before his death' (Grosart
(ed.), *Prose* III.493). But, as Thomas M. Raysor points out, the *Lyrical Ballads*
were relatively well received critically and sold reasonably well ('The
Establishment of Wordsworth's Reputation', *JEGP* 54 (1955), 71).

41 See Gill, *Wordsworth*, pp. 335, 347–8, 366, 373, 382–3, 396, and *Wordsworth
and the Victorians* (Oxford: Clarendon, 1998), ch.1, on Wordsworth's growing
reputation; see also Peter J. Manning, 'Wordsworth in the *Keepsake*, 1829',
in John O. Jordan and Robert L. Patten (eds.), *Literature in the Marketplace:
Nineteenth-Century British Publishing and Reading Practices* (Cambridge
University Press, 1995), pp. 44–73, on Wordsworth's attempt to exploit his
'name' after 1820.

42 *LY* II.641–2; see also 656; Wordsworth acknowledges the 'interference' of
the 'Paris Edition', a cheap pirated edition of his poems as, in part,
accountable for the figures; on the lack of sales of poetry generally in the
1830s, see also 599, 669. For other comments by Wordsworth on his book
sales and publishing deals in the 1830s and 1840s, see *LY* III.62, 230, 239,
371, 384, 505, 515–16; IV.286, 815. Sales figures for Wordsworth's volumes
are as follows (print runs are 500 unless otherwise noted): *Lyrical Ballads*
(1798): 500 or 750 copies printed, sold out by 1800; *Lyrical Ballads* (1800,
1802, 1805): total sales figures of 1750 (vol. 1) and 2,000 (vol. 2); *Poems in Two
Volumes* (1807): 1,000 printed, in 1814 Longman still had 230 copies; *The
Excursion* (1814): 36 copies left in 1834; *Poems* (1815): 352 copies sold by the
end of 1817, sold out by 1820; *The White Doe of Ryleston* (1815): 750 copies
printed, a copy was still available in 1831; *Thanksgiving Ode* (1816): 220 copies
remaindered in 1834; *Peter Bell* (1819): 1,000 copies printed in first and
second editions, 139 remaindered in 1833; *The Waggoner* (1819): 49 copies
remaindered in 1833; *The River Duddon* (1820): 30 copies remaindered in
1834; *Miscellaneous Poems* (1820) sold out within nine months; *Memorials of a
Tour of the Continent* (1822): 124 copies remaindered in 1833; *Ecclesiastical
Sketches* (1827): 203 copies remaindered in 1833; *Poetical Works* (1827): 750
printed, sold out by 1832; *Poetical Works* (1832): 2,000 printed, sold out;
Yarrow Revisited (1835): 1,500 printed, sold out within nine months; *Poetical
Works* (1836): 3,000 printed, more than 2,000 copies sold by the end of the
year; *Poems, Chiefly of Early and Late Years* (1842): Wordsworth requested
Moxon print between 2,000 and 3,000 copies. See W.J.B. Owen, 'Costs,
Sales, and Profits of Longman's Editions of Wordsworth', *The Library*, 5th
series, XII (1957), 93–107; Raysor, 'Wordsworth's Reputation', 61–71; Gill,
Wordsworth; Lee Erickson, *The Economy of Literary Form: English Literature and
the Industrialization of Publishing, 1800–1850* (Baltimore, MD: The Johns
Hopkins University Press, 1996), ch.2.

43 On Wordsworth's growing sense of his own popularity, see also *LY* III.293,
336, 337, 143.

44 *MY* I.96; for Wordsworth's indifference and even disdain of contemporary
criticism, see also *MY* I.383–4, *Supplement*, pp. 145, 153, *LY* II.200, IV.645; see,

however, his concern for the damage done to the sale of his work by negative contemporary reviews in *MY* 1.155, 174, and Grosart (ed.), *Prose* III.437.
45 On Wordsworth's trust in gradual and eventual posthumous recognition,
see also *MY* 1.383–4, II.184, 275, *LY* 1.401, II.24, III.44, 533.
46 It is possible, though, that Wordsworth is remembering Robert Southey's
comment that Milton's *Paradise Lost* was 'of too high a character to become
popular, till the people were instructed to admire it', in *Specimens of the
Later English Poets*, 3 vols. (London, 1807), I.xxvii. Ironically perhaps,
Wordsworth, Coleridge and Southey are echoed by Marx's analysis of economic production *per se* in the *Grundrisse*: 'Production thus creates the consumer . . . The need which consumption fuels for the object is created by
the perception of it. The object of art – like every other product – creates
a public which is sensitive to art and enjoys beauty' (quoted in Guillory,
Cultural Capital, p. 320); compare Campbell, *The Romantic Ethic*.
47 See John Milton, *The Reason of Church Government*, in *Complete Prose Works of
John Milton, 1643–1648*, 8 vols., eds. Douglas Bush *et al.* (New Haven, CT:
Yale University Press, 1959), 1.810, on the desire to 'leave something so
written to aftertimes, as they should not willingly let it die'.
48 For other comments on posterity, see *MY* II.301, *Supplement*, pp. 163, 177, *LY*
IV.315; on Wordsworth's sense of the 'trash which hourly issuing from the
Press in England, tends to make the very name of writing and books dis-
gusting', see *LY* 1.124; see also *LY* 1.44, III.275–6.
49 *BLJ* VI.84. Byron commented that he had read D'Israeli's work 'oftener
than perhaps those of any English author whatever, except such as treat of
Turkey' (quoted by James Ogden, *Isaac D'Israeli* (Oxford: Clarendon, 1969),
p. 109); among other things, Byron was no doubt returning D'Israeli's compliment in the preface to the second edition of *The Literary Character*
(London, 1818), where he alludes to Byron as 'the great poetical genius of
our times' (p.iv).
50 *An Essay on the Manners and Genius of the Literary Character* (London, 1795), pp.
xv, xix.
51 Ibid., pp. xv. For evidence of such an increase in the production of books,
see, for example, [Charles Knight] 'The Market of Literature', *The Printing
Machine* 1 (February 1834), 4, who estimates the average number of new
books annually between 1792 and 1802 to be 372, and between 1800 and
1827 to be 588 (see J.W. Saunders, *The Professsion of English Letters* (London:
Routledge and Kegan Paul, 1964), p. 160, for similar figures); see also Nigel
Cross, *The Common Writer: Life in Nineteenth-Century Grub Street* (Cambridge
University Press, 1985), pp. 11–12, who compares the number of new books
published before 1756 (less than 100) with the number produced annually
by 1792 (370); Raven, *Judging New Wealth*, p. 31, estimates that, in terms of
fiction, a 'handful' of works were published in London in 1700, rising to
'over forty' by 1750 and to 90 each year by 1800 (see also pp. 31–41). For the
growth in readership in the early nineteenth century, see Richard D. Altick,
The English Common Reader: A Social History of the Mass Reading Public,

1800–1900 (University of Chicago Press, 1957), pp. 67–77; Morag Shiach, *Discourse on Popular Culture: Class, Gender and History in Cultural Analysis, 1730 to the Present* (Cambridge: Polity, 1989), pp. 71–100; Raymond Williams, *The Long Revolution*, pp. 125–213; Campbell, *The Romantic Ethic*, pp. 26–8.

52 *Calamities of Authors*, 1.46. D'Israeli also argues that the sixteenth and seventeenth centuries saw the 'first ages of *Patronage*' which developed in the eighteenth century into 'the age of *Subscriptions*' (1.63).

53 *Ibid.*, 1.25.

54 *Ibid.*, 11.273.

55 See, for example, *ibid.*, 11.276–7; *Calamities of Authors*, in fact, was originally written in support of the recently established Royal Literary Fund (established 1790): for an account of the fund and the social and economic circumstances of the professional writer which led to its establishment, see Cross, *The Common Writer*, ch. 1.

56 D'Israeli, *An Essay*, pp. vii-viii.

57 Isaac D'Israeli, *The Literary Character* (London: John Murrray, 1818), p. 186.

58 William Godwin, *The Enquirer: Reflections on Education, Manners and Literature in a Series of Essays* (1795; New York: Augustus M. Kelley, 1965), pp. 283, 289.

59 Leo Braudy, *The Frenzy of Renown: Fame and Its History* (New York: Oxford University Press, 1986), p. 425; see also p. 378 on the later eighteenth century as characterised by a 'twin obsession' with posterity and death.

60 Lord Byron, *The Complete Miscellaneous Prose*, ed. Andrew Nicholson (Oxford: Clarendon, 1991), p. 17.

61 W.H. Ireland, *Neglected Genius, A Poem, Illustrating the Untimely and Unfortunate Fate of Many British Poets; from the Period of Henry the Eighth to the Æra of the Unfortunate Chatterton* (London, 1812), p. xix (further references are cited in the text).

62 *Selected Prose of John Hamilton Reynolds*, ed. Leonidas M. Jones (Cambridge, MA: Harvard University Press, 1966), p. 193.

63 'P.G.J.', 'On the Neglect of Genius', *The Imperial Magazine*, 111 (October 1821), column 938.

64 'M.M.', 'On the Neglect of Genius', *The Imperial Magazine* 111 (December 1821), column 1076: M.M. goes on to quote (without acknowledgement) Bryan Waller Procter's obituary of John Keats in the *London Magazine* (April 1821), which established Keats as a neglected poet of genius (see *KCH* 241–2, for the text of Procter's review).

65 Hallam, *Remains*, p. 298.

66 *Ibid.*, pp. 303, 304.

67 *The Works of John Ruskin*, ed. E.T. Cook and Alexander Wedderburn, 39 vols. (London: George Allen, 1903–12), v111.233; see also xv1.62–4, on the 'great reciprocal duties . . . constantly to be exchanged between the living and the dead' (p. 63).

68 Brownson lists as examples, Homer, Shakespeare and Milton.

69 For Coleridge's comments on posterity, his own and others', see, for example, *CL* 1.135, 313, 563, 584, 630; 11.96, 987, 1017, 1034; 111.87, 89, 335,

361, 391; IV.591, 601, 701, 892–3, 948; V.33, 364, 510; VI.875, 1009; *CN* 432, 2727, 3302; *BL* 1.33, 35–6, 58, 60, 62, 64, 86n, 163n.

70 See Kathleen Coburn's note to *CN* 3291, which dates the distinction earlier, from 1805 'and especially from c. 1807'; but as Coburn comments, 'In the Spring of 1808 Coleridge was particularly concerned with this question'. This distinction is, of course, by no means limited to the writing of Coleridge: in her note to *CN* 3197, Coburn points out that in 1808 Coleridge may have been reading Wordsworth's 1681 edition of Cowley, in which the 'Preface of the Author' includes much the same point (Coburn calls it a 'Coleridgean *cliché*'); see pp. 21–2, above, for similar distinctions by Coleridge's contemporaries.

71 Compare *The Friend*, ed. Barbara E. Rooke (London: Routledge and Kegan Paul, 1969), II.138 (also in I.210–11; this passage is quoted in *BL* 1.41n), on the early nineteenth century as 'this AGE OF PERSONALITY, this age of literary and political GOSSIPING'.

72 A contemporary entry in his notebooks, however, expresses Coleridge's sense of the undesirability of contemporary 'reputation', when he argues that 'the praise of a Contemporary is painful to him who deserves it', since such praise 'confounds' true fame with 'vulgar' reputation (*CN* 3291).

73 See, for example, *CL* III.87, 110, 118–9.

74 See a similar etymological disquisition in *CN* 3671: 'I have assigned the true cause for the final victory of Fame (το φαμενον σοφοις και αγθοις – *fatum* a *fari*, ut FAMA a φημι) over reputation, = the opinion of those who *re*-suppose the *supposition* of others . . . ': Coburn translates the Greek phrase as 'what is said by the wise and good', and the Latin as '*fatum* [what has been said, or ordained, fate] from *fari* [to say], as FAMA [reputation] from φημι [I say]'.

75 Coleridge also seems to equate this etymon with that of 'suppose' which is, in fact, from Latin *supponere*, meaning 'to put under', 'to put next to' or 'to put in the place of', with its derivation from the prefix *sub-* and the French *poser*, meaning 'to place', from Latin *pausa*, meaning 'pause'.

76 For other references, see *CL* III.518, 523; IV.637, 647, 677, 706, 754, 967; V.28, 510; VI.541; *CN* 3197, 3321, 3325, 417, 4321; *Essays on His Times*, ed. David V. Erdman (London: Routledge and Kegan Paul, 1978), II.390, 439; *Shorter Works and Fragments*, ed. H.J. Jackson and J.R. de Jackson (London: Routledge and Kegan Paul, 1995), pp. 215–16; *BL* 1.33, II.36, 158, 260; see also *CL* III.396 on 'outward Reputation'.

77 But see *CL* VI.567, where, in a letter from February 1826, Coleridge declares that 'A Poet is one thing: the Poets of the Age, we live in, are or may be another thing – on the one our judgement must be positive, on the other relative & comparative'.

78 Braudy, *Frenzy*, p. 434; see also p. 436; see pp. 35–6, above, for Hazlitt on Shakespeare and posterity, and pp. 70–2, above, for Hazlitt on gender and posterity.

79 See Braudy, *Frenzy*, p. 392.

80 This is also Hazlitt's own fantasy, since he records it with reference to himself elsewhere: see *Works* XI.229; and his comments on Pope in *Works* XX.128.
81 For other comments on posterity, see *Works* XI.207, 216, 229, 248, 252, 258–60, 275, 309; XX.128, 242; XVII.208–9.
82 *The Poetical Works of Robert Southey* (London: Longmans, Green and Co, 1884), p. 143.

3 ENGENDERING POSTERITY

1 Sandra M. Gilbert and Susan Gubar, *The Madwoman in the Attic: The Woman Writer and the Nineteenth-Century Literary Imagination* (New Haven, CT: Yale University Press, 1979), p. 6; see also pp. 46–7.
2 Marlon B. Ross, *The Contours of Masculine Desire: Romanticism and the Rise of Women's Poetry* (New York: Oxford University Press, 1989), p. 119.
3 'Romantic Quest and Conquest: Troping Masculine Power in the Crisis of Poetic Identity', in Anne K. Mellor (ed.), *Romanticism and Feminism* (Bloomington, IN: Indiana University Press, 1988), p. 28.
4 Anne K. Mellor, *Romanticism and Gender* (New York: Routledge, 1993), p. 209.
5 Susan Wolfson, 'Individual in Community: Dorothy Wordsworth in Conversation with William' in Mellor (ed.), *Romanticism and Feminism*, p. 157; see also Margaret Homans, *Women Writers and Poetic Identity: Dorothy Wordsworth, Emily Brontë, and Emily Dickinson* (New Jersey: Princeton University Press, 1980), p. 73: 'Dorothy's tendency to omit a central or prominent self in her journals becomes much more apparent when compared to William's habitual concentration on the self'.
6 See Greg Kucich, ' "This Horrid Theatre of Human Sufferings": Gendering the Stages of History in Catharine Macaulay and Percy Bysshe Shelley', in Thomas Pfau and Robert F. Gleckner (eds.), *Lessons of Romanticism: A Critical Companion* (Durham, NC: Duke University Press, 1998), pp. 448–65, on the 'instability' and the 'porous' nature of masculine and feminine Romanticism, and on masculine romanticism as 'a fluid, many-sided phenomenon driven by its own instabilities, contradictions, and self-interrogations' (p. 463).
7 Mellor, *Romanticism and Gender*, pp. 2–3; see also pp. 209–10, for another useful summary of her argument; and see Mellor's 'Why Women Didn't Like Romanticism: The Views of Jane Austen and Mary Shelley', in Gene W. Ruoff (ed.), *The Romantics and Us: Essays on Literature and Culture* (New Brunswick, NJ: Rutgers University Press, 1990), pp. 274–87, and 'A Criticism of Their Own: Romantic Women Literary Critics', in John Beer (ed.), *Questioning Romanticism* (Baltimore, MD: Johns Hopkins University Press, 1995), pp. 29–48.
8 For a consideration of the gendering of domesticity as part of what he terms the professional middle-class cultural revolution, see Gary Kelly,

Revolutionary Feminism: The Mind and Career of Mary Wollstonecraft (London: Macmillan, 1992), especially ch.1; see also Kurt Heinzelman, 'The Cult of Domesticity: Dorothy and William Wordsworth at Grasmere', in Mellor (ed.), *Romanticism and Feminism*, pp. 52–78. Compare Jennifer Breen's comment on the 'naturalistic' and 'domestic' tendencies of Romantic women's writing in *Women Romantic Poets, 1785–1832: An Anthology* (London: Dent, 1992), p. xxvi.

9 Sonia Hofkosh, 'The Writer's Ravishment: Women and the Romantic Author – The Example of Byron', in Mellor (ed.), *Romanticism and Feminism*, p. 94. A number of critics have commented on the way that the *contemporary* audience was, by the early nineteenth century, implicitly feminised. See, for example, John Tinnon Taylor, *Early Opposition to the English Novel: The Popular Reaction from 1760 to 1830* (1943; repr. New York: King's Crown Press, 1970), ch.3. On the representation and policing of female reading practices, see Peter de Bolla, *The Discourse of the Sublime: Readings in History, Aesthetics and the Subject* (Oxford: Basil Blackwell, 1989), pp. 266–78; and see Marlon Ross on Byron's discomfort with a female readership (*Contours*, pp. 28–9; see also p. 51 on the growth of the female reading public during the period).

10 Mary Robinson, Preface to *Sappho and Phaon*, reprinted in The Folger Collective on Early Women Critics (eds.), *Women Critics 1660–1820: An Anthology* (Bloomington, IN: Indiana University Press, 1995), p. 271. For an alternative reading of this preface, see Jerome McGann, *The Poetics of Sensibility: A Revolution in Literary Style* (Oxford: Clarendon, 1996), p. 102.

11 Robinson, 'Preface', p. 272.

12 Isabella Lickbarrow, *Poetical Effusions* (1814; repr. Oxford: Woodstock Books, 1994), pp. 22–3 (italics added).

13 Reprinted in Andrew Ashfield (ed.), *Romantic Women Poets, 1770–1838: An Anthology* (Manchester University Press, 1995), p. 19. For similarly self-conscious *domestications* of 'classical' or 'male' traditions, see, for example, Elizabeth Moody's 'The Housewife's Prayer, On the Morning Preceding a Fete' (1798), and 'Sappho Burns her Books and Cultivates the Culinary Arts' (1798), both reprinted in Lonsdale (ed.), *Eighteenth Century Women Poets: An Oxford Anthology* (Oxford University Press, 1989), pp. 405–7.

14 Mellor, *Romanticism and Gender*, p. 11; compare Lucinda Cole, '(Anti)Feminist Sympathies: The Politics of Relationship in Smith, Wollstonecraft, and More', *ELH* 58 (1991), 107–40.

15 Stuart Curran, 'Romantic Poetry: The I Altered', in Mellor (ed.), *Romanticism and Feminism* p. 190; on the gender of Romantic genres and topics, see Gary Kelly, *Women, Writing, and Revolution, 1790–1827* (Oxford: Clarendon, 1993), pp. 177–9.

16 Indeed, characteristic of such 'domestic' verse – exemplified in, for example, Joanna Baillie's 'A Winter's Day' (1790) and 'A Summer's Day' (1790), Mary Robinson's 'London's Summer Morning' (1800) – is an unproblematic deictic *presencing* of sight, sound, event and object, and the

224 Notes to pages 69–72

use of the present tense to stress a crucial immediacy of reference; compare Mellor, *Romanticism and Gender*, p. 11.

17 On the influence and popularity of women's writing, in particular poetry, see, for example, Mellor, *Romanticism and Gender*, p. 7, and Stuart Curran, 'Romantic Poetry', p. 187; Roger Lonsdale comments on the fact that while in the first decade of the eighteenth century only two women published collections of poetry, by the 1790s more than thirty women did so (*Eighteenth-Century Women Poets*, p. xxi).

18 Both poems are reprinted in Jerome J. McGann (ed.), *The New Oxford Book of Romantic Period Verse* (Oxford University Press, 1994), pp. 257, 293.

19 Ross, *Contours*, p. 307; see the epigraph to Landon's 'The Laurel' (1838): 'Fling down the Laurel from her golden hair; / A woman's brow! What doth the Laurel there?' (*The Poetical Works of Letitia Elizabeth Landon, 'L.E.L., A Facsimile Reproduction of the 1873 Edition*, ed. F.J. Sypher (New York: Scholars' Facsimiles & Reprints, 1990), p. 574.)

20 For a brief reading of this essay in a similar context, see Ross, *Contours*, pp. 258–9; see also James Chandler, *England in 1819: The Politics of Literary Culture and the Case of Romantic Historicism* (University of Chicago Press, 1998), pp. 112–14, on Hazlitt's gendering of the canon in this lecture; and see Laura L. Runge, *Gender and Language in British Literary Criticism, 1660–1790* (Cambridge University Press, 1997), for an account of the way that gender is a 'constitutive element of eighteenth-century literary criticism' (p. 3).

21 Compare Hazlitt's essay on Campbell and Crabbe in *The Spirit of the Age*: 'Mr. Rogers, as a writer, is too effeminate' (*Works* XI.159).

22 See Hazlitt's comment in *The Spirit of the Age* that Thomas Moore's poems 'pander to the artificial taste of the age; and his productions . . . are in consequence somewhat meretricious and effeminate' (*Works* XI.170).

23 For a similar coding, see Hazlitt's comment on Horne Tooke in *The Spirit of the Age* as 'the reverse of effeminate – hard, unbending, concrete, physical, half-savage' (*Works* XI.54).

24 See Norma Clarke, *Ambitious Heights: Writing, Friendship, Love – The Jewsbury Sisters, Felicia Hemans, and Jane Welsh Carlyle* (London: Routledge, 1990), p. 56, on the idea that the genius 'has no sex, that was agreed'.

25 Reprinted in Ashfield, *Romantic Women Poets*, p. 28; see Hofkosh, 'The Writer's Ravishment', pp. 95–9, on women writers' resistance to fame; and see also Gilbert and Gubar, *The Madwoman in the Attic*, pp. 61–4, and Norma Clarke, *Ambitious Heights*, pp. 21–2, on the dangers of fame for women. Cheryl Walker comments on this convention in nineteenth-century America in *The Nightingale's Burden: Women Poets and American Culture Before 1900* (Bloomington, IN: Indiana University Press, 1982), pp. 34–6, when she quotes Park Benjamin's poem 'To One Beloved', which ends with the declaration that 'nothing lives but fame / To speak unto the coming age my race and name', and comments that 'This kind of poem could not have been written by a nineteenth-century woman' (p. 35). Feminist critics have recently documented the ways in which the very act of publication was

problematic for the 'proper lady': see Mary Poovey, *The Proper Lady and the Woman Writer: Ideology as Style in the Works of Mary Wollstonecraft, Mary Shelley, and Jane Austen* (University of Chicago Press, 1984), especially pp. 38–40; Homans, *Women Writers*; and Kelly, *Women, Writing, and Revolution*, pp. 10–11. As Mellor remarks, however, the 'sheer bulk' of women's publications would seem to argue against such an anxiety (*Romanticism and Gender*, p. 8).

26 Reprinted in Lonsdale (ed.), *Eighteenth-Century Women Poets*, p. 503.

27 Reprinted in Ashfield (ed.), *Romantic Women Poets*, p. 68.

28 *Ibid.*, p. 73

29 Reprinted in *ibid.*, p. 155.

30 Quoted in Lonsdale (ed.), *Eighteenth-Century Women Poets*, p. xlii. Compare Maria Jane Jewsbury's comment in a letter to Dora Wordsworth of 1829: 'I cannot conceive how, unless a necessity be laid upon her, any woman of acute sensibility, and refined imagination can brook the fever and strife of authorship' (quoted in Clarke, *Ambitious Heights*, p. 68). Women writers' resistance to the role of poet has been well documented in recent feminist criticism – most famously by Gilbert and Gubar's discussion of the female poet's 'anxiety of authorship' in *The Madwoman in the Attic*: see pp. 48–9 and *passim*.

31 Felicia Hemans, *Records of Woman* (1828; repr. Oxford: Woodstock Books, 1991), p. 110.

32 L.E.L., 'On the Character of Mrs. Hemans's Writing', *The New Monthly Magazine* 44 (August 1835), 425.

33 *Ibid.*, 432; on Hemans, her fame and its vicissitudes, see Clarke, *Ambitious Heights*, pp. 50–51; see also Susan Wolfson ' "Domestic Affections" and "the spear of Minerva": Felicia Hemans and the Dilemma of Gender', in Carol Shiner Wilson and Joel Haefner (eds.), *Re-Visioning Romanticism: British Women Writers, 1776–1837* (Philadelphia, PA: University of Pennsylvania Press, 1994), pp. 128–67.

34 A striking example of such a note is Mary Wollstonecraft's letter to Imlay of c.10 October 1795, reprinted in Janet Todd and Marilyn Butler (eds.), *The Works of Mary Wollstonecraft*, vol.6 (London: William Pickering, 1989), p. 431; see also Janet Todd, *Gender, Art and Death* (Cambridge: Polity, 1993), p. 103. For a fictionalised account of a woman's suicide as a result of the necessarily repressed emotions of women in early nineteenth-century society, see 'The Lonely Grave' by Maria Jane Jewsbury, in *Phantasmagoria; or Sketches of Life and Literature*, 2 vols. (London, 1825), II.177–88. For a critique of the association of women poets with suicide, see Germaine Greer's Epilogue to her *Slip-Shod Sibyls: Recognition, Rejection and the Woman Poet* (London: Viking, 1995).

35 But see Kenneth Johnston's comment on Wordsworth: 'The genre of the suicide note is a constant leitmotif in his movement toward becoming the master Poet of life and natural affirmation' (*The Hidden Wordsworth: Poet, Lover, Rebel, Spy* (New York: Norton, 1998), p. 778). Johnston's example, however, the 1802 manuscript poem 'These Chairs they have no words to

utter' is, like Keats's 'Ode to a Nightingale', more properly a paean to the quiescence of death than a suicide note as such (there is a crucial difference between the desire to be free of the vicissitudes of life and the desire to kill yourself).

36 Hemans, *Records*, pp. 49–50 (further references are cited in the text).

37 Compare Hemans's 'Woman and Fame', quoted in Clarke, *Ambitious Heights*, pp. 34–5; for a reading of *Properzia Rossi*, see pp. 77–8; and see Susan Wolfson, 'Gendering the Soul', in Paula R. Feldman and Theresa M. Kelley (eds.), *Romantic Women Writers: Voices and Countervoices* (Hanover, NE: University Press of New England, 1995), pp. 63–5.

38 See Ross, *Contours*, p. 290, on the personalised *affective* nature of the response desired by and presupposed in Heman's poetry generally; and pp. 297–8 on Hemans's ambivalence towards fame.

39 Reprinted in Ashfield (ed.), *Romantic Women Poets*, pp. 222–4; for a complex response, which attempts to negotiate Landon's somewhat shifty question 'Do you think of me, as I think of you?', see Elizabeth Barrett's 'L.E.L.'s Last Question' (1839); for a similar question, see Hemans's 'A Parting Song', from *Records of Woman*, pp. 321–3, with its opening and repeated question: 'When will ye think of me, my friends?'.

40 Reprinted in McGann (ed.), *Romantic Period Verse*, p. 720. For an alternative reading of the poem, see Anthony John Harding, 'Felicia Hemans and the Effacement of Woman', in Feldman and Kelley (eds.), *Romantic Women Writers*, pp. 142–5.

41 For other poetic considerations of the death of Sappho, see, for example, Landon's 'Sappho's Song', and 'Sappho', in *Poetical Works*, pp. 4, 566–8.

42 Reprinted in Ashfield (ed.), *Romantic Women's Poetry*, p. 193.

43 See the extract from canto five in Ashfield (ed.), *Romantic Women Poets*, pp. 167–8. Compare Ross's comment on Tighe's poetry as verse 'written not to be remembered . . . written to "linger" . . . in the heart, rather than to assert an immortal existence, to establish a self-perpetuating line' (*Contours*, p. 158; see also p. 164).

44 Wolfson, 'Individual in Community', p. 146; see Hemans, *Women Writers*, p. 83, for a reading of the island as 'a latent figure for the dissolving self'.

45 *The Letters of Mary Wollstonecraft Shelley*, ed. Betty T. Bennett (Baltimore, MD: Johns Hopkins University Press, 1983), ii.72.

46 Clarke, *Ambitious Heights*, p. 32; see also pp. 34–5; for other examples of the identification of femininity and the feminine identity of the poet with domesticity, see, for example, Mary Browne's 'The Poetess' (1828), and Maria Abdy's 'The Dream of the Poetess' (1836). For other examples of the equation of femininity, fame and danger, see Maria Jane Jewsbury's 'The Glory of the Heights' (1829) and 'A Summer Eve's Vision' (1829). But see Clarke, *Ambitious Heights*, p. 10, on Jewsbury's ambition and pp. 27–8 on her fame in the 1820s (see also pp. 51–68, 70–74). Indeed, in her 'The History of an Enthusiast' from *The Three Histories: The History of an Enthusiast, The History of a Nonchalant, The History of a Realist* (London, 1830), p. 25, Jewsbury

makes posterity function as a redemption for a specifically female life: 'And what good would fame do you, – a woman?' asks Mortimer. 'It would make amends for being a woman – I should not pass away and perish', replies the enthusiast, Julia.

47 Reprinted in Ashfield (ed.), *Romantic Women's Poetry*, pp. 220–1; see Ross, *Contours*, pp. 299–300; see also Landon's 'Stanzas on the Death of Mrs Hemans': 'Didst thou not tremble at thy fame, / And loathe its bitter prize, / While what to others triumph seemed, / To thee was sacrifice?' (*Poetical Works*, p. 410).

48 Reprinted in Duncan Wu (ed.), *Romanticism: An Anthology* (Oxford: Basil Blackwell, 1994), pp. 1097–8.

49 Reprinted in McGann (ed.), *Romantic Period Verse*, pp. 715–16.

50 This is not to suggest that the male Romantic poets produced no poetry of such unabashed sentimentality, but that such effects have tended to be repressed, disguised or censored out of their canonical poems or out of their canon. Despite the fact that, as Stuart Curran comments, 'the poetry of sensibility . . . is the foundation on which Romanticism was reared' ('Romantic Poetry', p. 197) sensibility is, of course, a gender-coded literary movement (of women or the feminised male) – and, as such, specifically figured as ephemeral: see, for example, Ross, *Contours*, pp. 291–2; and see Clarke, *Ambitious Heights*, on sentimentality as 'achieving definitive status as the quintessential feminine form of feeling' (p. 87); see also Claudia L. Johnson, *Equivocal Beings: Politics, Gender, and Sentimentality in the 1790s: Wollstonecraft, Radcliffe, Burney, Austen* (University of Chicago Press, 1995), and McGann, *Poetics of Sensibility*.

51 Reprinted in McGann (ed.), *Romantic Period Verse*, pp. 734–6.

52 Glennis Stephenson, *Letitia Landon: The Woman Behind L.E.L.* (Manchester University Press, 1995), p. 18.

53 See also the ending to Landon's 'The Laurel', which asserts that on the speaker's 'silent lute there is no song', and which, like 'Lines of a Life', particularises and sentimentalises the reception of posterity by confounding it with effects of personalised guilt and mourning (*Poetical Works*, p. 575)

54 Isabella Lickbarrow, *Poetical Effusions*, pp. 59–60.

55 Jewsbury, *Phantasmagoria*, II.305, 306 (further references are cited in the text).

56 Jewsbury, *The Three Histories*, pp. 134–5: this passage is quoted and discussed by Wolfson in ' "Domestic Affections" ', p. 136.

57 Jewsbury, *The Three Histories*, p. 131.

58 Ross, *Contours*, p. 3.

59 On the question of women's exclusion from the Romantic canon, see, for example, Ross on Hemans: 'How is it that a poet like Hemans, so respected in the nineteenth century, can be obliterated so entirely from literary history, covered over by romantic ideology?' (*Contours*, p. 13; see also p. 233); Ross's answer is that our exclusion of Hemans from the canon is a function of the set of values that we have inherited from (male) Romanticism

itself; see also Greg Kucich, 'Gendering the Canons of Romanticism: Past and Present', *The Wordsworth Circle* 27 (1996), 95–102; Feldman and Kelley, 'Introduction' to *Romantic Women Writers*, pp. 2–7; Ashfield, (ed.), *Romantic Women Poets*, 'Introduction'. For a contemporary attempt to explain the exclusion of women from the (French) literary canon, see Stéphanie-Félicité Ducrest, 'Preliminary Reflections' to *The Influence of Women on French Literature* (1811), in the Folger Collective (eds.), *Women Critics*, pp. 208–11.

60 Ross, *Contours*, p. 54.

61 Mellor, *Romanticism and Gender*, p. 11; Harriet Kramer Linkin takes an even more reductive view of the 'innate value' of women's poetry and the discovery of 'an aesthetic value that speaks to us' in their writing ('Taking Stock of the British Romantic Marketplace: Teaching New Canons Through New Editions?', *Nineteenth-Century Contexts* 19 (1995), 113; see also 119).

62 Ross, *Contours*, p. 316.

63 Compare McGann's discussion of Hemans's 'postmodern superficiality' in *The Poetics of Sensibility*, ch.16. McGann makes a related point about the canon and reading Romantic poetry (see pp. 184–94), and compares Wordsworth and Coleridge, who have 'embarked on a quest for permanence', with the Della Cruscans, who create only 'splendid and wonderful *im*permanences' (p. 79).

64 Barbara Herrnstein Smith, *Contingencies of Value: Alternative Perspectives for Critical Theory* (Cambridge, MA: Harvard University Press, 1988), p. 28; for a useful exploration of the phenomenon of textual survival, see pp. 47–53. For a rigorous critique of Smith's book and an account which reminds us both of the *necessity* of value judgements and their involvement with issues of economic value, see John Guillory, *Cultural Capital: The Problem of Literary Canon Formation* (University of Chicago Press, 1993), ch.5.

65 Such questions are implicit, I think, in McGann's *The Poetics of Sensibility*, a book which suggests that the acknowledgement of the aesthetics of the ephemeral would amount to a 'revolution' not only in 'literary style' but in the institutional reception of such poets.

66 Paul de Man, *The Rhetoric of Romanticism* (New York: Columbia University Press, 1984), p. 121.

67 Mary Wollstonecraft and William Godwin, *A Short Residence in Sweden and Memoirs of the Author of 'The Rights of Woman'*, ed. Richard Holmes (Harmondsworth: Penguin, 1987), p. 109. Wollstonecraft's comments might, in fact, be seen as part of a tradition of scepticism with regard to posthumous survival: see, for example, Sir Thomas Browne, *Hydriotaphia*, in *Selected Writings*, ed. Geoffrey Keynes (London: Faber and Faber, 1968), p. 149: 'But to subsist in bones, and be but Pyramidally extant, is a fallacy in duration. Vain ashes, which in the oblivion of names, persons, times, and sexes, have found unto themselves, a fruitlesse continuation, and only arise unto late posterity, as Emblemes of mortall vanities.' A considerably more obscure example, from the early nineteenth century, is an anonymous

article (signed 'A Father') on 'Death – Posthumous Memorials – Children', in the *London Magazine* 3 (March 1821), 250–5, which, like Shelley's 'Ozymandias', mocks 'all our posthumous vanity, and monumental earth-clinging': 'Ingenuity has been exhausted', comments the writer, 'in varying contrivances to defraud oblivion'; even poets, who have 'a much more substantial existence after death' since 'their minds actually survive' as their readers 'participate in a species of communion between the living and the dead', even they decay as their language becomes obsolete (pp. 251–2).

68 See Jacques Derrida, *The Gift of Death*, trans. David Wills (University of Chicago Press, 1995), p. 41: 'Death is . . . that which nobody else can undergo or confront in my place. My irreplaceability is therefore conferred, delivered, "given", one can say, by death.'

4 WORDSWORTH'S SURVIVAL

1 See Richard G. Swartz, 'Wordsworth, Copyright, and the Commodities of Genius', *MP* 89 (1992), p. 488, on Wordsworth's sense of the genius as involving what he sees as 'paternal obligations to "his" children' (see also pp. 505–9).

2 Susan Eilenberg, 'One Bit of Rock or Moor', *London Review of Books* 20:17 (1998), 8.

3 Jared Curtis (ed.), *The Fenwick Notes of William Wordsworth* (London: Bristol Classical Press, 1993), p. 61; Wordsworth also claimed that at the time of writing 'Intimations of Immortality', 'I could not believe that I should lie down quietly in the grave, and that my body would moulder into dust' (quoted in Christopher Wordsworth, *Memoirs of William Wordsworth*, 2 vols. (London: Edward Moxon, 1851), II.476). For Wordsworth and contemporary ideas of death, see Alan Bewell, *Wordsworth and the Enlightenment: Nature, Man, and Society in the Experimental Poetry* (New Haven, CT: Yale University Press, 1989), ch.5.

4 On immortality and pre-existence in the Immortality Ode and more generally in Wordsworth, see Charles Sherry, *Wordsworth's Poetry of Imagination* (Oxford: Clarendon, 1980).

5 *The Prelude, 1799, 1805, 1850*, ed. Jonathan Wordsworth, M.H. Abrams, and Stephen Gill (New York: Norton, 1979), book 6, lines 67–9 (further references are cited in the text).

6 Laurence Goldstein, *Ruins and Empire: The Evolution of a Theme in Augustan and Romantic Literature* (University of Pittsburgh Press, 1977), p. 120; see also J. Hillis Miller, *The Linguistic Moment: From Wordsworth to Stevens* (New Jersey: Princeton University Press, 1985), p. 75, on the 'memorializing of the dead by the poet or his personae' as 'so ubiquitous a theme in Wordsworth's poetry'.

7 William Wordsworth, *The Poems*, 2 vols., ed. John O. Hayden (Harmondsworth: Penguin, 1977), II.38 (line 41).

8 *The Works of Samuel Johnson, LL.D*, 9 vols. (Oxford, 1825), v.259.

9 As Johnson comments, 'The most ancient structures in the world, the pyramids, are supposed to be sepulchral monuments' (*ibid.*). See, for example, comments by Philippe Ariès, *The Hour of Our Death*, trans. Helen Weaver (London: Allen Lane, 1981), p. 475; and Zygmunt Bauman, *Mortality, Immortality and Other Life Strategies* (Cambridge: Polity, 1992), p. 51.

10 See Bauman, *Mortality, Immortality*, p. 52. As Thomas Lynch comments, 'we remember because we want to be remembered' (*The Undertaking: Life Studies from the Dismal Trade* (London: Jonathan Cape, 1997), p. 134).

11 John A. Hodgson, *Wordsworth's Philosophical Poetry, 1797–1814* (Lincoln, NE: University of Nebraska Press, 1980), p. 69; see also pp. 49, 62, 64, 69, 73, 75, 161, and ch.3 *passim*, on Wordsworth's 'memorialising' impulse and his 'postponement of oblivion'.

12 Frances Ferguson, *Wordsworth: Language as Counter-Spirit* (New Haven, CT: Yale Univesity Press, 1977), p. 155. See Douglas J. Kneale's comment in *Monumental Writing: Aspects of Rhetoric in Wordsworth's Poetry* (Lincoln, NE: University of Nebraska Press, 1988), p. xvi, that the epitaph for Wordsworth is an 'arch-genre'; Kneale also points out that Wordsworth himself refers to epitaphic inscriptions as 'epitomized biography'. Recent work on Wordsworth and the epitaphic is extensive and includes, most notably, Ernest Bernhardt-Kabisch, 'Wordsworth: The Monumental Poet', *Philosophical Quarterly* 44 (1965), 503–18; Karen Mills-Courts, *Poetry as Epitaph: Representation and Poetic Language* (Baton Rouge, LA: Louisiana State University Press, 1990), pp. 178–202; Paul H. Fry, *A Defense of Poetry: Reflections on the Occasion of Writing* (Stanford University Press, 1995), ch.8; Geoffrey H. Hartman, *The Unremarkable Wordsworth* (London: Methuen, 1987), ch.3; Miller, *The Linguistic Moment*, pp. 105–13.

13 Mills-Courts, *Poetry as Epitaph*, p. 178.

14 Hodgson, *Wordsworth's Philosophical Poetry*, p. 149.

15 For a similar reading of book 5, especially of the dream of the Arab, see Miller, *The Linguistic Moment*, pp. 104–13, on the 'linguistic moment' in Wordsworth as the 'transfer of the poet himself into language' (p. 112).

16 Trembling is explored by Jacques Derrida in a number of texts: in 'Deconstruction and the Other', he speaks of literature in terms of 'certain movements which have worked around the limits of our logical concepts, certain texts which make the limits of our language tremble, exposing them as divisible and questionable' (Richard Kearney, *Dialogues with Contemporary Continental Thinkers: The Phenomenological Heritage* (Manchester University Press, 1984), p. 112); on fear and trembling, on the *mysterium tremendum*, and on trembling and dread, see *The Gift of Death*, trans. David Wills (University of Chicago Press, 1995), especially pp. 53–6.

17 Mary Jacobus, *Romanticism, Writing and Sexual Difference: Essays on 'The Prelude'* (Oxford: Clarendon, 1989), p. 104.

18 For a discussion of this point, see Ernest Becker, *The Denial of Death* (New York: The Free Press, 1973), p. 172.

19 Paul D. Sheats, *The Making of Wordsworth's Poetry 1785–1798* (Cambridge, MA: Harvard University Press, 1973), p. 232.

20 *Poetry and Repression: Revisionism from Blake to Stevens* (New Haven, CT: Yale University Press, 1976), p. 70. Bloom enlarges on Wordsworth's 'dread of mortality' by commenting that it 'impresses us because more than any poet's, at least since the Milton of *Lycidas*, it seems to turn upon the magnificent, primal poetic urge for *divination*, in the complex sense best defined by Vico, the poet's apotropaic concern for his own immortality. Milton and Wordsworth alike feared premature death, "premature" meaning before their great epics had been written' (p. 80). For an example of such a fear, see Wordsworth's comment in a letter of April 1804: 'I pray to God to give me life to finish the works which I trust will live and do good' (*EY* 470). Perhaps such prematurity is most explicitly and concisely defined, however, in a poem by Keats, 'When I have fears that I may cease to be' (on Keats's prescient sense of his own mortality and immortality, see ch.6).

21 Hodgson, *Wordsworth's Philosophical Poetry*, p. 38, calls the ending 'proleptically self-elegiac'; compare Bloom, *Poetry and Repression*, p. 78; and Sherry, *Wordsworth's Poetry of Imagination*, p. 100.

22 Compare Frances Ferguson's comment on the importance of reading for Wordsworth as a 'doubling of consciousness' and on the way in which Wordsworth is 'able to imagine his own writing as something to be read, by himself as well as by his audience' (*Language as Counter-Spirit*, pp. xiv–xv).

23 Compare Carol Jacobs, *Telling Time: Lévi-Strauss, Ford, Lessing, Benjamin, de Man, Wordsworth, Rilke* (Baltimore, MD: Johns Hopkins University Press, 1993), p. 177, for a similar point.

24 Compare Jacobs, *Telling Time*, p. 175, and Hodgson, *Wordsworth's Philosophical Poetry*, p. 38.

25 Isobel Armstrong, '"Tintern Abbey": From Augustan to Romantic', in J.C. Hilson, M.M.B. Jones and J.R. Watson (eds.), *Augustan Worlds* (Leicester University Press, 1978), p. 272.

26 'A Father', 'Death – Posthumous Memorials – Children', *London Magazine* 3 (March 1821), 252–3.

27 Plato, *Symposium*, trans. Robin Waterfield (Oxford University Press, 1994), p. 48; for Shelley's translation of the section, see *SCW* VII.200–205. Compare Aeschylus, *The Libation Bearers*, lines 503–9 (quoted in Hodgson, *Wordsworth's Philosophical Poetry*, p. 187).

28 Plato, *Symposium*, p. 49.

29 *Ibid.*, p. 50.

30 Nicolai Hartmann, *Ethics*, trans. Stanton Coit, 3 vols. (London: George Allen, 1932), ii.314; compare Henry Staten's comment on Diotima's speech that 'eros is the *origin of idealism*' and that her ideas of 'mortal and transcendent eros' are 'consistent with the system of Platonism as a whole' (*Eros in Mourning* (Baltimore, MD: Johns Hopkins University Press, 1995), p. 2).

31 Plato, *Laws*, trans. R.G. Bury (London: Heinemann, 1967), I.311–13. See Coleridge's note from October 1812, which makes a similar point (*CN* 4168).

32 David Heyd, *Genethics: Moral Issues in the Creation of People* (Berkeley, CA: University of California Press, 1992), p. 214; and see ch.8, *passim*.

33 Plato, *Symposium*, pp. 51–2.

34 Curtis (ed.), *Notes*, p. 17.

35 Jacques Derrida, *The Post Card: From Socrates to Freud and Beyond*, trans. Alan Bass (University of Chicago Press, 1987), p. 199

36 *Ibid.*, pp. 199, 241, 305, 333. *Usteron* (or *hysteron*) *proteron* is an hysterical reversal of the womb, a 'preceding falsehood' on which a fallacious argument in based. The Greek adjective 'hysteros' (υστερ–ος) signifies, before 'womb', 'later' or 'logically posterior'. In classical rhetoric, as Richard Rand points out, the 'hysteron proteron' refers to 'a figure of speech, a trope, in which two terms are reversed according to the sequence, the order, temporal, spatial, causal, in which you ordinarily find them' ('Hysteron Proteron, or "Woman First"', *OLR* 8 (1986), 51); see also Freud, *The Standard Edition of the Complete Psychological Works of Sigmund Freud*, trans. James Strachey *et al.* (London: Hogarth, 1966), I.352–6. On the *hysteron proteron* as preposterous, see Patricia Parker, *Literary Fat Ladies: Rhetoric, Gender, Property* (London: Methuen, 1987), pp. 67–9; and see Linda Charnes, *Notorious Identity: Materializing the Subject in Shakespeare* (Cambridge, MA: Harvard University Press, 1993), pp. 38–9, 182.

37 This sense of the scandal of a young person's, in particular a child's, death, is recorded in two letters, one by Dorothy Wordsworth and one by Freud. Writing in 1806, years before the deaths of Catharine and Thomas, Dorothy writes to Lady Beaumont that 'death when it comes to a young person, is a *shock* for the survivors' (*MY* I.72); Freud's reaction to his daughter Sophie's death in 1920 is also telling: while commenting 'La séance continue', he also writes that 'Quite deep down I can trace the feeling of a deep narcissistic hurt that is not to be healed' (Ernest Jones, *Sigmund Freud: The Life and Work*, (London: Hogarth, 1957), III.20, 21. For a rather different sense of the death of children for the early nineteenth century, see an unsigned article on 'Deaths of Little Children' in *The Indicator* xxvi (5 April 1820), 201–4, in which such deaths are seen as 'natural' and even healthy for our sense of childhood. But see 'A Father', 'Death – Posthumous Memorials – Children', which ends with a contemplation of the death of children as an 'excruciating disruption' (p. 254). Despite the pain expressed in such articles (the latter is by a recently bereaved father who cannot write, let alone speak the name of his dead daughter), and despite their contrasting perspectives, they also mark an increasing sentimentalisation of the death of children in the nineteenth century. On the 'intensification of grief in the eighteenth century' in response to the loss of a child, and for the argument that 'the sufferings of parents at the death of a child revealed an extreme intensity' during the Romantic period, see Lawrence Stone, *The Family, Sex and Marriage in England 1500–1800* (London: Weidenfeld and Nicolson, 1977), pp. 246–53.

38 See Mary Jacobus's more general comments on the Wordsworthian quality of anxiousness: a 'combination of anxiety about the future (shall I be saved?) and solicitude about one's offspring (are my children/books safe?)

seems especially relevant' to Wordsworth (*Romanticism, Writing and Sexual Difference*, p. 104); for a contrasting view, see Michael Baron's comment on Wordsworth's 'almost complete absence of interest in lineage' (*Language and Relationship in Wordsworth's Writing* (London: Longman, 1995), p. 150).

39 Stephen Gill, *Wordsworth: A Life* (Oxford: Clarendon, 1989), p. 294.

40 *Ibid.*, quoting Alexander B. Grosart, *The Prose Works of William Wordsworth*, 3 vols., (London: Edward Moxon, 1876), III.489; de Vere goes on to comment, however, that he had heard that at the time of the illness of at least one of the children, 'it was impossible to rouse [Wordsworth's] attention to the danger. He chanced to be then under the immediate spell of one of those fits of poetic inspiration which descended on him like a cloud' (p. 489–90).

41 Mary Moorman, 'Wordsworth and his Children', in Jonathan Wordsworth (ed.), *Bicentenary Wordsworth Studies* (Ithaca, NY: Cornell University Press, 1970), p. 117.

42 Crabb Robinson compared Wordsworth's self-control to De Quincey's outpouring of grief (see Gill, *Wordsworth*, p. 294; and see note 48, below, on De Quincey's reaction to Catharine's death); see also Wordsworth's comment in a letter of June 1812 (*Supplement*, p. 131): 'I have not yet felt my own sorrow, only I know well that it is to come . . . I do not mean to yield to the emotions of my heart on this sad and unexpected privation'; and see also the Fenwick note to 'Maternal Grief', which is said to be 'faithfully set forth from my Wife's feelings & habits after the loss of our two children within half a year of each other' (Curtis, (ed.), *Notes*, pp. 67–8). Compare Coleridge's comment after the death of his first son on 'this strange, strange, strange Scene-shifter, Death! that giddies one with insecurity, & so unsubstantiates the living Things that one has grasped and handled!' (*CL* 1.479).

43 See Moorman's comment that the death of Catharine and Thomas made Wordsworth 'cling with an almost morbid concern and deeply anxious affection to his three remaining children' ('Wordsworth and his Children', p. 131).

44 *Supplement*, p. 141. Compare Dorothy Wordsworth's comments on Catharine's death: 'the more I think about it the more do I feel that it is a sorrow in which a comfort is found' (*MY* II.45).

45 Compare Dorothy's comment on Thomas, after his death, as a 'perpetual presence' (*MY* II.76), and Wordsworth's comment on the deaths of both children that 'they are perpetually present to my eyes' (*MY* II.361).

46 Carl H. Ketcham (ed.), *The Cornell Wordsworth: Shorter Poems, 1807–1820* (Ithaca, NY: Cornell University Press, 1989), p. 522. The phrase 'surprized by joy' is, strangely enough, an echo of a phrase in a letter from Dorothy to Catherine Clarkson of 23 June 1812, which Wordsworth is unlikely to have seen: Dorothy comments that although Dora is 'much afflicted' by the news of Catharine's death, she, Dorothy, was later 'surprized at her joyfulness' (*MY* II.33).

47 See also John Powell Ward, 'Wordsworth's Children', *The Coleridge Bulletin* new series 8 (1996), 46–64, who points out that both William and Dorothy used the epithet 'heavenly' to describe Thomas, a word which 'at the close of the sonnet "Surprized by Joy" . . . is transferred to Catharine' (p. 61); see also pp. 63–4, for comments on Wordsworth as the Darwinian 'poet of non-parentage', a point which in some ways relates to my own conclusion concerning the sonnet.

48 An alternative shadow-reading would involve the extraordinary mourning of Thomas De Quincey for Catharine and, in particular, his claim to have lain on her grave every night for two months: see Thomas De Quincey, *Recollections of the Lakes and the Lake Poets*, ed. David Wright (Harmondsworth: Penguin, 1970), p. 372: 'Never, perhaps, from the foundations of those mighty hills, was there so fierce a convulsion of grief as mastered my faculties on receiving that heart-shattering news . . . I returned hastily to Grasmere; stretched myself every night, for more than two months running, upon her grave; in fact, often passed the night upon her grave'; see also John E. Jordan, *De Quincey to Wordsworth: A Biography of a Relationship, with the Letters of Thomas De Quincey to the Wordsworth Family* (Berkeley, CA: University of California Press, 1962), pp. 263–7; and E. Michael Thron, 'The Significance of Catherine [*sic*] Wordsworth's Death to Thomas De Quincey and William Wordsworth', *SEL* 28 (1988), 559–67. For a recent psychoanalytical reading of De Quincey's mourning, see Charles J. Rzepka, *Sacramental Commmodities: Gift, Text, and the Sublime in De Quincey* (Amherst, MA: University of Massachusetts Press, 1995), pp. 204–11. Wordsworth's other poem about Catharine suffers from a similar and equally strange ambiguity of dating: in the Fenwick note, Wordsworth claims that 'Characteristics of a Child Three Years Old' was 'Written at Allan Bank, Grasmere 1811', and that it is a 'Picture of my Daughter Catharine, who died the year after': according to John O. Hayden, however, it is more likely that the poem was composed *after* the death of both Catharine and Thomas, between 3 January 1813 and late May 1814 (*Poems* 1.1044); see also De Quincey's comment in *Recollections of the Lake Poets*, that the poem is 'dated at the foot 1811, which must be an oversight, for she was not so old until the following year' (*Recollections*, p. 371).

49 See Thomas McFarland, *William Wordsworth: Intensity and Achievement* (Oxford: Clarendon, 1992), p. 90. As Michael Baron comments, the poem 'is so unspecific about formal relations that it might have been written about a person of either sex and almost any age' (*Language and Relationship*, p. 150). See Mary Moorman's more general comment that 'It is the fact, though not easy to explain, that Wordsworth wrote poems about his two daughters, but not about any of his three sons' – except, as Moorman notes, the epitaph 'Six months to six years added', a poem which apparently 'took him years to produce' ('Wordsworth and his Children', p. 117).

50 The text is the 1834 version: in view of the concerns of the present chapter, it is significant that apart from 'deep' in line 3 (previously 'long') and

various changes in punctuation, the sole alteration made by Wordsworth in the different versions of the poem published in his lifetime was to the second word in line two ('turn'): when it was first published, in the 1815 *Poems*, the word was 'wished'; in the 1820 *Miscellaneous Poems* the word was altered to 'turned'; and in 1834 it was changed again to 'turn' (see Ketcham (ed.), *Shorter Poems*, pp. 112–13).

51 Compare Paul Jay, *Being in the Text: Self-Representation from Wordsworth to Roland Barthes* (Ithaca, NY: Cornell University Press, 1984), on the 'crucial preparatory role of *forgetting*' in *The Prelude* (p. 83).

52 See Wordsworth's letter to Southey just after the death of his brother John in February 1805 for another use of the word 'pang' (*EY* 542); see also De Quincey's letter to Dorothy of 12 June 1812 (in response to a letter of Dorothy Wordsworth, *MY* II.23–4): 'what a bitter pang that we might not see her blessed face again' (quoted in Jordan, *De Quincey to Wordsworth* p. 263). Dorothy uses the word in a letter of 24 April 1814 on Thomas's death – 'the pangs which the recollection of that heavenly child causes me it is hard to stifle' (*MY* II.141) – where both 'pang' and 'heavenly child' seem to echo, or to be echoed by, 'Surprized by Joy'.

53 For a brief discussion of the poem along similar lines, see Paul Hamilton, *Wordsworth* (Brighton: Harvester, 1986), pp. 21–2. For other readings of the poem, see David B. Pirie, *William Wordsworth: The Poetry of Grandeur and of Tenderness* (London: Methuen, 1982), pp. 284 7; Geoffrey Durant, *Wordsworth* (Cambridge University Press, 1969), pp. 150–1. Compare Wordsworth's comment on 'the art of forgetting' in *MY* I.154; and see his later comment that 'the sorrows of this life weaken the memory so much' (*MY* II.122).

54 See *LY* I.475, where Wordsworth comments on Southey's loss of one of his daughters in 1826: 'One is fled – and with her no more than half the attraction, and I fear all the security that in the parents' minds hung about the other.'

55 Bearing in mind Derrida's instruction of the impossibility of constructing 'a noncontradictory or coherent concept of narcissism' in *On the Name*, trans. Thomas Dutoit (Stanford University Press, 1995), p. 13, and in 'Passions: An Oblique Offering', in David Wood (ed.), *Derrida: A Critical Reader* (Oxford: Blackwell, 1992), p. 12.

56 See Fiona J. Stafford, *The Last of the Race: The Growth of a Myth from Milton to Darwin* (Oxford: Clarendon, 1994), pp. 134–59. Perhaps it is significant in this context, that after the death of Dora in 1847, Wordsworth, as Moorman comments, 'never again wrote a poem' ('Wordsworth and his Children', p. 139).

57 Compare Heyd, *Genethics*, p. 221: the possibility of the end of human life 'would cast a grave shadow on the ability of the last generation to invest its life with meaning': 'Taking part in the transgenerational story', Heyd continues, 'is not a duty . . . but an essential part of what we conceive of as *our own* story' (pp. 221–2).

5 COLERIDGE'S CONVERSATION

1 See *Talker*, pp. 13, 17, and Tim Fulford, *Coleridge's Figurative Language* (London: Macmillan, 1991), p. 6. For a consideration of Coleridge and audience, see Kelvin Everest, *Coleridge's Secret Ministry: The Context of the Conversation Poems 1795–1798* (Sussex: Harvester, 1979), pp. 10–11, who argues that 'The problem of audience is central' in Coleridge (p. 10), and that Coleridge expresses an 'extreme anxiety' about audience (p. 8); see also p. 15, and ch.4, *passim*.

2 All quotations from Coleridge's poetry are from Samuel Taylor Coleridge, *The Complete Poems*, ed. William Keach (London: Penguin, 1997).

3 For Coleridge's comments on the relationship between writing and talking, see *CL* I.158, 176; II.736, 872, 962; III.8, 429; IV.571, 728; V.312, 510 – most of which, after the first two instances, complain about the restrictions of writing as compared to the expressive possibilities of speech. See also *BL* II.239, where Coleridge argues that the 'chief' reason for the negative reception of 'Christabel' is the difference between recitation and print as modes of dissemination. For Coleridge on his own talk, see *CL* II.789, 878, 913; III.232–3: 'The stimulus of Conversation suspends the terror that haunts my mind', he remarks in 1816 (*CL* IV.630).

4 For other comments on Coleridge and posterity, see *TT* II.333, 369, 384, 452.

5 On Coleridge as a talker, see Norbert H. Platz, 'The "Witchery of Sound" in S.T. Coleridge's Soundscape: A Second Approach to *Coleridge the Talker*', in Michael Gassenmeier and Norbert H. Platz (eds.), *Beyond the Suburbs of the Mind: Exploring English Romanticism* (Essen: Blaue Eule, 1987), 137–50, and Denise Degrois, 'Coleridge on Human Communication', in Tim Fulford and Morton D. Paley (eds.), *Coleridge's Visionary Languages* (Cambridge: D.S. Brewer, 1993); on the 'art' or discourse of conversation in the later nineteenth century, see E.A.W. St George, *Browning and Conversation* (London: Macmillan, 1993), ch.1.

6 See also *Recollections of the Lakes and the Lake Poets*, where De Quincey remembers Coleridge talking for three hours (*DQW* II.60).

7 See also, from *Talker*, Methuen, p. 305; Procter, p. 317; Talfourd, pp. 351, 353.

8 For similar comments on Coleridge's monologues rather than dialogues, see *TT* I.559 (Fenimore Cooper); II.401 (John Sterling), 409 (Carlyle), 450 (Robert Willmott); *CCH* II.30 (John Merivale); *Talker*, p. 112 (Carlyle), 130 (Philarète Chasles), 290 (Lockhart), 326 (H.C. Robinson). Coleridge himself commented on this as early as 1796: see *CL* I.260.

9 Compare Hazlitt's remark in 'On the Conversation of Authors' that Coleridge talks 'only for admiration and to be listened to, and accordingly the least interruption puts him out' (*Works* XII.35), and see Henry Holland, *Talker*, p. 263. Charles Lamb famously – and presumably apocryphally – records having to cut off his own button which Coleridge had got hold of as he spoke, eyes closed, in order to extricate himself from a conversation;

returning five hours later, Lamb claims to have found Coleridge still holding forth, not having noticed that Lamb had been away (*Talker*, pp. 279–80). See Thomas Methuen's comment that ' "the art of stopping" must have been to him singularly difficult' (*Talker*, p. 305).

10 Gillman, in *Talker*, p. 20. Coleridge himself, however, attributes the remark to a neighbour; see *BL* 1.189.

11 Fulford comments on Coleridge's apparently remarkable, even 'magical' ability to hold his listener's attention: he quotes a letter by Coleridge himself where he refers to his 'turbid Stream of wild Eloquence' (*CL* 11.1000–1; quoted in *Figurative Language*, p. 3). Coleridge also refers to his own 'Logorrhoea', a word which reminds one of his comment on a friend's talk as 'diarrhoea' in a dream-like literalisation of the metaphor: 'Tuffin – Diarrhoea of Talk – gave him a piece of paper to wipe his mouth' (*CN* 1096).

12 Compare H.C. Robinson on Coleridge's 'dreamy monologues' (*Talker*, p. 334); and see Sarah Flower Adams, in *Talker*, p. 101.

13 Compare *TT* 11.438, on the slowness of Coleridge's delivery; on Coleridge's accent, see *TT* 1.xlix, n.

14 For other comments on Coleridge's voice, see *TT* 1.lii, 564; *CCH* 11.49; *Talker*, p. 281. Compare Coleridge's comment on the 'Animal Magnetism' produced in poetic recital (*BL* 11.239); and see Nigel Leask, 'Shelley's "Magnetic Ladies": Romantic Mesmerism and the Politics of the Body', in Stephen Copley and John Whale (eds.), *Beyond Romanticism: New Approaches to Texts and Contexts, 1780–1832* (London: Routledge, 1992), pp. 60–63.

15 Compare Dorothy Wordsworth's comments in a letter to Mary Hutchinson, June 1797, *EY* 188–9.

16 Compare Charles Cowden Clarke's comments in *Talker*, p. 134.

17 David Appelbaum, *Voice* (State University of New York Press, 1990), p. 50.

18 Coleridge, *Lectures 1808–1819 on Literature*, ed. R.A. Foakes (London: Routledge and Kegan Paul, 1987), 11.217.

19 Michael Macovski, *Dialogue and Literature: Apostrophe, Auditors, and the Collapse of Romantic Discourse* (New York: Oxford University Press, 1994), p. 32; see also Garrett Stewart, *Reading Voices: Literature and the Phonotext* (Berkeley, CA: University of California Press, 1990), p. 188, on the 'foundational myth' of Romanticism, 'its glorification of the personalized and prophetic voice of lyric utterance': 'Romantic textual vocalization operates at the very core of the lyric motive itself: a text's impulse to represent the voice of its own representations'.

20 On Coleridge's attempt to write the speaking voice in his poetry, see Max F. Schulz, *The Poetic Voices of Coleridge: A Study of His Desire for Spontaneity and Passion for Order* (Detroit, MI: Wayne State University Press, 1963).

21 See Armour and Howes, 'Introduction', in *Talker*, pp. 47–8: 'the poet was in large part Coleridge the talker . . . the bulk of Coleridge's verse reflects not a separate gift for poetry but his fundamental genius for talk'. Compare Coleridge's comment on reading '*mouthis[h]ly*' in *CL* 1.357.

22 Fulford, *Figurative Language*, p. 2. But see Nicholas Hudson, *Writing and European Thought* (Cambridge University Press, 1994), ch.7, on Coleridge's sense of the 'linguistic and social benefits of writing and literacy' (p. 145) as expressed in his critique of Wordsworth in the *Biographia Literaria*. See also Macovski, *Dialogue and Literature*, on the importance of dialogue (even if with a mute interlocutor) for Romantic poetics generally: Macovski argues that the Romantics seek to 'instantiate dialogue by explicitly inscribing a listener's position into the text' (p. 23). On the other hand, however, Macovski comments that what is most characteristic about Romantic auditors is that they offer a *resistance* to the speaker/poet: 'Generally speaking', he comments, 'while dialogue persists during these literary encounters, communicative exchange does not' (p. 24). While primarily focused on the nineteenth-century novel, Garrett Stewart, in *Dear Reader: The Conscripted Audience in Nineteenth-Century British Fiction* (Baltimore, MD: Johns Hopkins University Press, 1996), similarly locates what he calls the 'conscripted' or 'interpolated' reader as a fundamental aspect of Romantic discourse.

23 See Fulford, *Figurative Language*, p. 47; Jan Plug, 'The Rhetoric of Secrecy: Figures of the Self in "Frost at Midnight" ', in Fulford and Paley (eds.), *Coleridge's Visionary Languages*, p. 35.

24 See Plug, 'The Rhetoric of Secrecy', p. 35; and see Tilottama Rajan's comments on the letter-form of 'Dejection: An Ode': 'In using the form of the verse-letter rather than the conversation, Coleridge concedes the absence of his auditor and gives up the subterfuge of an indirect auditor in order to admit the estrangement of text from voice' (*Dark Interpreter: The Discourse of Romanticism* (Ithaca, NY: Cornell University Press, 1980), p. 232).

25 Compare Macovski, *Dialogue and Literature*, p. 39, who argues that while 'the gap between Wordsworth's speaker and listener is a dissonance, that between Coleridge's interlocutors is an *aporia* – an unapproachable disjunction that denies all attempts at didacticism or rapport'.

26 Christopher Wordsworth, *Memorials of William Wordsworth*, ed. Henry Reed, 2 vols., 1851 (repr. New York: AMS Press, 1966), II.308; quoted in A. Elizabeth McKim, ' "An Epicure in Sound": Coleridge on the Scansion of Verse', *English Studies in Canada* 18 (1992), 287.

27 See Appelbaum, *Voice*, for a fascinating and eccentric study of voice which 'does not write over its authentically disturbing note' (p. xiv); and see also Paul H. Fry's argument for the 'ostensive function' of literature, and the idea that 'It is not *music* that poetry hears . . . that is, the melody, the rhythm, the architectonics, in short the semiosis of music – but rather *sound*, with its emphasis on resonance, pitch, and timbre, and an implication even of monotony' (*A Defense of Poetry: Reflections on the Occasion of Writing* (Stanford University Press, 1995), p. 45; see also ch.3). For an account which pays some attention to the noise that poems make, see William Hazlitt's review of *Biographia Literaria* in the *Edinburgh Review*, August 1817, where, in a paragraph on poetry as 'the music of language' he argues that 'Whenever articulation passes naturally into intonation, this is the beginning of poetry'

(*CCH* 1.320). For other considerations of voice and poetry, see Francis
Berry, *Poetry and the Physical Voice* (London: Routledge and Kegan Paul,
1962), who, however, overlooks Coleridge; F.W. Bateson, *Wordsworth: A Re-
Interpretation*, 2nd edn. (London: Longmans, Green and Co., 1956), pp.
187–97, who comments on the essentially aural or auditory nature of
Wordsworth's poetry; and Tilottama Rajan, who comments on the
'attempted absorption of text into voice' and the inevitable deferrals that
'conversation' entails in the conversation poems in *Dark Interpreter*, ch.5
(especially p. 220). More generally, see Raymond Chapman, *The Treatment
of Sounds in Language and Literature* (Oxford: Basil Blackwell, 1984), ch.14; and
Garrett Stewart, *Reading Voices* (see pp. 150–7 and 189–91 on Coleridge).
Eric Griffiths's, *The Printed Voice of Victorian Poetry* (Oxford: Clarendon,
1989), analyses the difficulties of hearing poetic voices but is finally concerned with the productive 'ambiguities' of the predicament, its *meanings*
rather than its *noise*, in the tradition of William Empson's assertion that
'there is no value in verbal expression apart from semantic value' (quoted
in Fry, *Defense*, p. 65; see Empson's *Seven Types of Ambiguity*, 2nd edn.
(Harmondsworth: Penguin, 1965), pp. 8–16); see Adam Piette, *Remembering
and the Sound of Words: Mallarmé, Proust, Joyce, Beckett* (Oxford: Clarendon,
1996), for an argument concerning the affective, mnemonic nature of literary sound. Finally, see Roland Barthes's eulogy for the 'grain of the
voice' at the end of *The Pleasure of the Text*, trans. Richard Miller (New York:
Farrar, Straus and Giroux, 1975), pp. 66–7.
28 See Platz, ' "Witchery" ', p. 142: 'Coleridge may have aimed at a particular "auditory experience" even when he communicated in print'.
Generally, Platz's somewhat informal and provisional essay seeks to
account for a certain 'phonocentricity' (p. 142) in Coleridge's writing and
in particular his appeal to auditors.
29 Jacques Derrida, *Of Grammatology*, trans. Gayatri Chakravorty Spivak
(Baltimore, MD: John Hopkins University Press, 1976), p. 39: ' . . . that particular model which is phonetic writing *does not exist* . . . '; see also Griffiths,
Printed Voice, pp. 18–20; Appelbaum, *Voice*, pp. 47–9.
30 As early as September 1800, Coleridge declared in a letter to James Tobin
that 'I abandon Poetry altogether', leaving the task to Wordsworth (for the
'higher & deeper Kinds') and limiting himself to 'the honourable attempt
to make others feel and understand' the writings of poets (*CL* 1.623).
Similarly, in December, he declares to John Thelwall that 'As to Poetry, I
have altogether abandoned it, being convinced that I never had the essen-
tials of poetic Genius, & that I mistook a strong desire for original power'
(*CL* 1.656). Similar comments are legion: see, for example, *CL* 1.628–9, 658;
II.714, 715, 831, 903–4; III.469–70, 893; v.li–lii; later this becomes a rejection of the designation of 'author' for himself: see *CL* III.78; v.423, 454; and
see *BL* 1.87, for Coleridge's autobiographical account, and 223–4 for
Coleridge's advice to 'youthful literati' ('NEVER PURSUE LITERATURE AS
A TRADE'). But see *CL* II.814, 1053–4; IV.565, for counter-claims by

Coleridge on his own poetry. On Coleridge's dislike of writing in general, see Mark L. Waldo, 'Why Coleridge Hated to Write: An Ambivalence of Theory and Practice', *TWC* 1 (1985), 25–32. See also L.D. Berkoben, *Coleridge's Decline as a Poet* (The Hague: Mouton, 1975), for an alternative religio-philosophical account. From relatively early on in the history of Coleridge's reception, he was thought to have wasted his poetic talents: see, for example, the opening to the review of *Aids to Reflection* in the *British Review*, August 1825: 'We can recollect no instance, in modern times, of literary talent so entirely wasted' (*CCH* 1.485). For a sceptical view of Coleridge's claims to have given up poetry, see Thomas Barnes, 'Mr. Coleridge', *Champion* 26 March 1814 (*CCH* 1.189–91).

31 On the 'symbolic relationship between sound and silence that prevails throughout the conversation poems', see Jill Rubenstein, 'Sound and Silence in Coleridge's Conversation Poems', *English* 21 (1972), 54–60; see also K.M. Wheeler, *The Creative Mind in Coleridge's Poetry* (London: Heinemann, 1981), pp. 74–7, who argues that 'The meanings of the words are flooded into oblivion by the power of their music' (p. 74).

32 Coleridge uses the phrase 'articulate sounds' in an essay on 'Ghosts and Apparitions', from *The Friend* (1818): 'Even when we are broad awake, if we are in anxious expectation, how often will not the most confused sounds of nature be heard by us as articulate sounds?' (*The Friend*, ed. Barbara E. Rooke (London: Routledge and Kegan Paul, 1969), 1.146).

33 Plug, 'The Rhetoric of Secrecy', p. 35, puts it slightly differently: 'As Coleridge addresses his son, he suggests that the child's breathing is itself a form of articulate voice that speaks to him'.

34 See Jacques Derrida, *Limited Inc*, ed. Gerald Graff (Evanston, IL: Northwestern University Press, 1988), p. 14: 'consciousness, the conscious presence of the intention of the speaking subject in the totality of his speech act'.

35 Christopher Ricks, 'John Milton: Sound and Sense in *Paradise Lost*', in *The Force of Poetry* (Oxford: Clarendon, 1984), p. 68: it is precisely the insistence on the *sense* of poetic sounds in Ricks's essays (developed in greater detail in Griffiths's *Printed Voice*) that I seek to question here (see Ricks's rejection of T.S. Eliot's comments on the 'noise' of Milton's rhymes, p. 70 and *passim*). In insisting on the meaningfulness of sounds, that is to say, critics such as Ricks and Griffiths foreclose an alternative experiential dimension of reading discussed by Fry as the 'ostensive function' of literature in *A Defense of Poetry*.

36 See Fulford, *Figurative Language*, p. 44, on the poem's origins in conversation; see also pp. 43–61 on the conversation poems and talk, and Everest, *Secret Ministry*, *passim*. Both Fulford and Everest, however, argue for talk as a redemptive empowering of the sense of community for Coleridge, rather than, as I would suggest, itself a form of crisis, of rupture, lack or disturbance: see, for example, Fulford, *Figurative Language*, p. 161; Everest, *Secret Ministry*, p. 290. Such claims are implicitly countered by Susan Eilenberg

in *Strange Power of Speech: Wordsworth, Coleridge, and Literary Possession* (New York: Oxford University Press, 1992), p. 22, on the conversation poems as 'based on the thwarted desire for response' and as such 'not conversations at all'.

37 As Richard Payne points out, 'The archaisms of the *Ancient Mariner* were almost universally condemned by contemporary critics of *Lyrical Ballads*' (' "The Style and Spirit of the Elder Poets": The *Ancient Mariner* and English Literary Tradition', *MP* 75 (1978), 368); and see Wordsworth's notorious response to these critics in June 1799 in *EY* 264.

38 See Arden Reed's comment on Coleridge's poem as seeming to 'swim against the current of Romantic literature, since it is the recurring pattern of that literature to privilege speech . . . over the dead letter of a written text, or the life-in-death of rime' ('The Mariner Rimed', in Reed (ed.), *Romanticism and Language* (London: Methuen, 1984), p. 201). On silence and muteness in the poem, see Raimonda Modiano, 'Words and "Languageless" Meanings: Limits of Expression in *The Rime of the Ancient Mariner*', *MLQ* 38 (1977), 42–3.

39 Compare Wendy Wall, 'Interpreting Poetic Shadows: The Gloss of "The Rime of the Ancient Mariner" ', *Criticism* 29 (1987), 182.

40 In each one of the three substantially different versions of the poem published in Coleridge's lifetime the last of these lines was altered: from 'Like noises of a swound' of 1798 to 'A wild and ceaseless sound' of 1800, to 'Like noises in a swound' from 1817 on.

41 The noises of a swound are re-emphasised by a notebook entry from 1801 made by Coleridge as he practises the sounds of poetry and poetic metre, which includes the following lines:

> Earthly Hearings hear unearthly sound,
> Hearts heroic faint & sink aswound (*CN* 2224, folio 81)

42 On the intellectual context for the phrase 'A light in sound, a sound-like power in light' from 'The Eolian Harp', see M.H. Abrams, 'Coleridge's "A Light in Sound": Science, Metascience, and Poetic Imagination', *Proceedings of the American Philosophical Society* 116 (1972), 458–76; see also Stewart, *Reading Voices*, pp. 152–3.

43 Susan Eilenberg's reading of the poem concerns precisely the inhumanity and uncanniness of the poem's 'voice': Eilenberg argues that the poem 'comes to speech through the medium of an alien voice – archaic, inhuman, uncanny' (*Strange Power of Speech*, p. 31); the poem is 'thoroughly haunted, possessed, dispossessed, and characterless, and thereby most deeply and characteristically Coleridgean' (p. 59).

44 This identification is also suggested by A.M. Buchan in 'The Sad Wisdom of the Mariner', *Studies in Philology* 61 (1964), 669–88, who comments that 'in the single word ['stunned'], the experience of the Mariner becomes that of the common man who is made to share it' (p. 676).

45 See Degrois, 'Coleridge on Human Communication', p. 105. Compare

Eilenberg's comments on the Mariner as 'almost . . . an aphasic' (*Strange Power of Speech*, p. 32; see also pp. 34–5).

46 For another example of Coleridge's use of 'jargoning', see *CN* 2812; see also Degrois, 'Coleridge on Human Communication', p. 102.

47 Coleridge does talk about hearing in a nightmare, but he considers nightmares to be special cases of dreams, akin to reveries or stupors; see Jennifer Ford, *Coleridge on Dreaming: Romanticism, Dreams and the Medical Imagination* (Cambridge University Press, 1998), pp. 108–29.

48 Compare Coleridge's comments in a note on the desire to 'have a continued Dream, representing visually & audibly all Milton's Paradise Lost' (*CN* 658).

49 Compare Freud, *The Interpretation of Dreams*, PFL iv.83–91.

50 *The Standard Edition of the Complete Psychological Works of Sigmund Freud*, trans. James Strachey *et al.* (London: Hogarth, 1966), 1.248. But see *The Interpretation of Dreams*, where Freud is careful to insist on the aurality of dreams on a number of occasions (see *PFL* iv.94, 114, 650–1), while noting the predominance of the visual. In Finnish, at least, you *see* dreams: 'minä näin unta', one says, 'I saw a dream'; while in Russian you see *in* a dream: 'videt v snye'. For a brief consideration of sounds-poems-dreams in Wordsworth, see Geoffrey Hartman, *The Unremarkable Wordsworth* (London: Methuen, 1987), pp. 100–101.

51 See another dream recorded a little later in a notebook entry in which 'a noise of one of the Doors, strongly associated with Mrs. Coleridge's coming in to awake me, awaked me' (*CN* 1649); and see *CN* 2470: 'Those Whispers just as you have fallen or are falling asleep – what are they and whence?'.

52 Quoted in I.A. Richards, *Interpretation in Teaching*, 2nd edn. (London: Routledge and Kegan Paul, 1973), p. 12.

53 The impossibility of representing Coleridge's talk in writing is repeatedly referred to in contemporary accounts: see, for example, *TT* i.cv, cix, cxv, 14; ii.7, 12–13, 32, 445; *CCH* ii.32; Hazlitt, *Works* xvii.114; Coleridge himself commented on the difficulty of capturing others' talk in writing: see *CL* 1.392–4.

6 KEATS'S PRESCIENCE

1 Jacques Derrida, *Signéponge/Signsponge*, trans. Richard Rand (New York: Columbia University Press, 1984), p. 116. The sense that we read Keats too quickly might be contrasted with the frequent repetition of the idea that we have already read Keats, that we have finished with him. F.R. Leavis, for example, begins his essay on Keats in *Revaluation: Tradition and Development in English Poetry* (London: Chatto and Windus, 1936) by declaring that 'The excuse for writing at the present day on Keats must lie not in anything new to be said about him, but in a certain timely obviousness' (p. 241); Ernest de Sélincourt, 'The Warton Lecture on Keats', in *The John*

Keats Memorial Volume (London: John Lane, 1921), p. 3, comments that 'In a sense there is no more to be said' on Keats; and John Bailey, 'The Poet of Stillness', in *ibid.*, p. 30, declares that 'There is nothing very new to say about Keats'.

2 On the congruence of 'renown' and 'renaming' (both *renommée* in French, from which 'renown' derives), see Derrida, *Signéponge*, pp. 2/3.

3 See, for example, *KCH* 71, 73, 115, 204, 205, 213, 227.

4 For example, *KCH* 21, 22, 24.

5 *Blackwood's Edinburgh Magazine* xiv (July 1823), 67.

6 *KCH* 98, 110; 100, 109; 102; see J.R. MacGillivray's comment in *Keats: A Bibliographical and Reference Guide with an Essay on Keats' Reputation* (University of Toronto Press, 1949), p. xxii, that 'whenever the name "Johnny" is given to the poet . . . the writer is not merely being jocular or contemptuous; he is making it plain . . . that he shares Lockhart's opinion'.

7 On the origins of the name Keats, see Robert Gittings, *John Keats* (Harmondsworth: Penguin, 1971), p. 23.

8 Grant F. Scott, *The Sculpted Word: Keats, Ekphrasis, and the Visual Arts* (Hanover, NH: University Press of New England, 1994), p. xi.

9 Nicholas Roe (ed.), *Keats and History* (Cambridge University Press, 1995); the authors are as follows: Roe, p. 5; Daniel P. Watkins, p. 93; Kelvin Everest, pp. 111, 125; Theresa M. Kelly, p. 212; Nicola Trott, p. 272; John Kerrigan, p. 304. My *Keats, Narrative and Audience: The Posthumous Life of Writing* (Cambridge University Press, 1994) also wantonly employs such locutions (*passim*). Compare Daniel Watkins on the question of Keats's name in 'History, Self, and Gender in "Ode to Psyche"', in Roe (ed.), *Keats and History*, p. 88.

10 Derrida, *Signéponge*, p. 24.

11 Aileen Ward, *John Keats: The Making of a Poet* (London: Secker and Warburg, 1963), p. 200; Gittings, *John Keats*, p. 333; compare Andrew Motion's mediating comments on the line's 'uncanny premonition': it 'may have been intended as a purely rhetorical phrase; we cannot read it without realising that Keats died almost exactly a thousand days after writing it' (*Keats* (London: Faber and Faber, 1997), p. 283). The fullest treatment of this neglected poem that I am aware of is John Glendening's 'Keats's Tour of Scotland: Burns and the Anxiety of Hero Worship', *Keats–Shelley Journal* 41 (1992), 76–99, especially 92–5; Glendening, however, refrains from commenting on the first line.

12 *LJK* ii.67. On Keats's life as allegory, see especially Marjorie Levinson, *Keats's Life of Allegory: The Origins of a Style* (Oxford: Basil Blackwell, 1988).

13 Richard Monckton Milnes (ed.), *Life, Letters, and Literary Remains, of John Keats*, 2 vols. (London: Edward Moxon, 1848), i.i.

14 Milnes, *Life*, i.i–2. More recent biographers concur: see Ward, *John Keats*, p. 39: 'Keats's poems in general have a more direct relation to his life than the work of most poets'; and Gittings, *John Keats*, p. 628: 'With no other poet are the life and the works so closely linked'. For a sense that the life of

Keats is itself somehow uncannily prescient, see Walter Jackson Bate, *John Keats* (Cambridge, MA: Harvard University Press, 1963), p. 2: 'the life of Keats – even at first reading – has always seemed haunted by a feeling of familiarity. It reads like something we have read before, and are eager to hear again'. The idea that the life or character throws a light on the writing is expressed in Coventry Patmore's review of Milnes's biography in the *North British Review*: 'the shortest way of establishing the general prevalence of a quality in a man's writings is to shew it to have been constantly present in his personal character' (*KCH* 331). By contrast, writing in an 1818 review of *Endymion*, J.H. Reynolds makes the distinction between the poem as a representation of the poet and the poem as a dissolution of subjectivity, a mark of the difference between other modern poets and Keats: 'The secret of the success of our modern poets, is their universal presence in their poems – they give to every thing the colouring of their own feeling' whereas Keats 'goes out of himself into a world of abstractions' (*KCH* 89).

15 Sidney Colvin, *John Keats: His Life and Poetry, His Friends, Critics, and After-Fame*, 3rd edn. (London: Macmillan, 1920).

16 Milnes, *Life*, 1.2.

17 *Ibid.*

18 Hazlitt, for example, complains that Keats's poetry suffers from 'a deficiency in masculine energy of style' and that 'all he wanted was manly strength and fortitude' (*KCH* 248), while Leigh Hunt, by contrast, argues that Keats 'was a very manly, as well as delicate spirit' (*KCH* 249). On the gendering of the corpus of Keats in the nineteenth century, see George H. Ford, *Keats and the Victorians: A Study of His Influence and Rise to Fame, 1821–1895* (1944; repr. Hamden: Archon Books, 1962), p. 68; and Susan J. Wolfson, 'Feminizing Keats', in Hermione de Almeida (ed.), *Critical Essays on John Keats* (Boston: G.K. Hall, 1990), pp. 317–56.

19 For Keats's prophetic sense of his own death, see his letter to Shelley of August 1820, where he refers to his own death as 'a circumstance I have very much at heart to prophesy' (*LJK* II.322); see Ward, *John Keats*, p. 185: 'For some reason or other, Keats became convinced that he had only three more years to live . . . Though he made no explicit mention of his foreboding, he let slip half a dozen references to the possibility of his early death in his letters during the next two months' (Ward, p. 427, n.4, lists *LJK* I.281, 293, 325, 343, 387, of which a letter to Benjamin Bailey of July 1818, just after writing 'This mortal body of a thousand days' is the most pertinent: 'I intend to pass a whole year with George if I live to the completion of the next three', *LJK* I.343); see also Susan J. Wolfson, 'Keats Enters History: Autopsy, *Adonais* and the Fame of Keats', in Roe (ed.), *Keats and History*, p. 18. For contemporary comparisons between Keats, Kirke White and Chatterton, see, for example, *KCH* 117, 132, 134, 135, 147, 294, 298, 301, 302–3, 320, 349; see also Lewis M. Schwartz (ed.), *Keats Reviewed by his Contemporaries: A Collection of Notices for the Years 1816–1821* (Metuchen, NJ: The Scarecrow Press, 1973), pp. 317–18, 320; on a number of occasions, Richard

Woodhouse compared Keats to Chatterton and Kirke White while he was still alive: see *LJK* 1.382 (to Keats) and 384; see also Wolfson, 'Keats Enters History', pp. 20–21. In the context of a discussion of poetic immortality Isaac D'Israeli, *The Literary Character* (London, 1818), pp. 209–10, comments that 'men of genius anticipate their contemporaries and know they are creators, long before the tardy consent of the Public', and quotes Edward Smedley's poem *Prescience, or the Secrets of Divination: A Poem in Two Parts* (London, 1816): 'They see the laurel which entwines their bust, / They mark the pomp which consecrates their dust, / Shake off the dimness which obscures them now, / And feel the future glory bind their brow'.

20 It should be noted, however, that Milnes is far from the first to remark on such prescience: see, for example, L.E.L.'s 'Lines on Seeing a Portrait of Keats' (apparently writtten in 1822), in *Critical Writings by Letitia Elizabeth Landon*, ed. F.J. Sypher (New York: Scholars' Facsimiles, 1996), pp. 183–4: 'the seeds of death / Are sown within thy bosom, and there is / Upon thee consciousness of fate' (lines 10–12).

21 Milnes, *Life*, 1.12.

22 Wolfson, 'Keats Enters History', p. 18

23 See E.H.W. Meyerstein, *A Life of Thomas Chatterton* (London: Ingpen and Grant, 1930), pp. 509–12; Claude Lee Finney, *The Evolution of Keats's Poetry* (Cambridge, MA: Harvard University Press, 1936), II.708 9; Robert Gittings, 'Keats and Chatterton', *KSJ* 4 (1955), 47–54; Nai-tung Ting, 'The Influence of Chatterton on Keats', *KSJ* 5 (1956), 103–8, and 'Chatterton and Keats: A Re-examination', *KSJ* 30 (1981), 100–17; Linda Kelly, *The Marvellous Boy: The Life and Myth of Thomas Chatterton* (London: Weidenfeld and Nicolson, 1971), pp. 94–103.

24 See Paul Baines, 'The Macaroni Parson and the Marvellous Boy: Literature and Forgery in the Eighteenth Century', *Angelaki* 1:2 (1993/94), 95–112, especially pp. 107–9, on the development of the Chatterton myth from the debate concerning forgery and authenticity to the notion of the neglected genius; on Chatterton's *success* in getting into print, see Michael F. Suarez, S.J., 'What Thomas Knew: Chatterton and the Business of Getting into Print', *Angelaki* 1:2 (1993/94), 83–94.

25 Compare John Goodridge's argument on the importance of the Chatterton myth on Clare, in 'Identity, Authenticity, Class: John Clare and the Mask of Chatterton', *Angelaki* 1:2 (1993/94), 133.

26 Thomas Dermody, *The Harp of Erin*, 2 vols. (London, 1807), II.131.

27 Quotations from Keats's poems are from *The Poems of John Keats*, ed. Jack Stillinger (London: Heinemann, 1978).

28 See Hyder Edward Rollins (ed.), *The Keats Circle: Letters and Papers 1816–1878*, 2nd edn, 2 vols. (Cambridge, MA: Harvard University Press, 1965), II.276n; Gittings, 'Keats and Chatterton', 48.

29 *The Works of Thomas Chatterton, Containing His Life, By G. Gregory, D.D. and Miscellaneous Poems* (London, 1803), p. lxxx (further references are cited in the text).

30 Gittings, 'Keats and Chatterton', 50.
31 Compare the penultimate stanza of Mary Robinson's 'Monody to the Memory of Chatterton': 'If sorrow claims the kind embalming tear, / Or worth oppress'd excites a pang sincere; / Some kindred soul shall pour the song sublime, / And with the Cypress bough the Laurel twine, / Whose weeping leaves the wint'ry blast shall wave / In mournful murmurs o'er thy unbless'd grave (*Ibid.*, p. xcix).
32 References include Keats's sonnet on Chatterton, his dedication to *Endymion*, and his comment on associating Chatterton with autumn and his being 'the purest writer in the English Language' (*LJK* ii.167; see also ii.212).
33 *The North British Review*, 10 (1848), 70.
34 *Ibid.*, 72.
35 *KCH* 343; compare David Masson's comments in an 1860 article in *Macmillan's Magazine* on the overriding importance of the Keatsian body in his writing (*KCH* 375–7, 379). For a consideration of Keats's body and last sickness, see Jennifer Davis Michael, 'Pectoriloquy: The Narrative of Consumption in the Letters of Keats', *European Romantic Review* 6 (1995), 38–56.
36 Lionel Trilling, *The Opposing Self: Nine Essays in Criticism* (London: Secker and Warburg, 1955), p. 49.
37 William Henry Marquess, *Lives of the Poet: The First Century of Keats Biography* (University Park, PA: Pennsylvania State University Press, 1985), p. 41.
38 Hermione de Almeida, *Romantic Medicine and John Keats* (New York: Oxford University Press, 1991), pp. 12–13.
39 Although we might question what is involved in, for example, 'spiritual wholeness and imaginative health': such an assertion sounds unhealthily close to what Leo Bersani analyses in *The Culture of Redemption* (Cambridge, MA: Harvard University Press, 1990), as the repressive modernist ideologies of 'art's beneficently reconstructive function in culture' which 'depend on a devaluation of historical experience and of art' (p. 1).
40 On the tradition of reading Keats as weak and sickly, see Marquess, *Lives of the Poet*, pp. 40, 63–4, 66; Ford, *Keats and the Victorians*, p. 68, comments that 'For over sixty years after Keats's death, the lingering conception of his character was that he had been a puny weakling'; John Gibson Lockhart's famous attack on Keats in *Blackwood's* uses the rhetoric of sickness evocatively (*KCH* 98; for other references, see 183, 238). The trope is not restricted to the body of Keats, of course. Isaac D'Israeli, for example, argues that sickness is intrinsic to genius: 'The imagination of genius is the breath of its life, which breeds its own disease ... It is now an intermittent fever, now a silent delirium, an hysterical affection, and now a horrid hypochondriasm' (*The Literary Character*, p. 219).
41 See Scott, *The Sculpted Word*, pp. 55–6, on the way that Keats is 'paralyzed by the marbles and oppressed by their spirit', and on the poem's 'structural weakness'; see also Marjorie Levinson, *Keats's Life of Allegory*, p. 248, on the way that Keats 'attenuates himself'.

42 Leo Bersani and Ulysse Dutoit, *Arts of Impoverishment: Beckett, Rothko, Resnais* (Cambridge, MA: Harvard University Press, 1993). Such failure, indeed, may be understood to be related to the Romantic culture of posterity more generally: see, for example, comments by Leigh Hunt (*KCH* 255) and Arthur Henry Hallam (*KCH* 268). On Keats's actual neglect between 1821 and 1848, see Ford, *Keats and the Victorians*, p. 2: 'The work of no other major English poet had received such neglect as Keats's'; see also MacGillivray, *Keats*, pp. xlvii–lxviii; and see p. 20, above, for an account of the poor sales of Keats's poems.

43 For a similar comment, on Keats and his poetry as *wanting*, see Levinson, *Keats's Life of Allegory*, p. 6.

44 Compare W.M. Rossetti's rather crude remarks on the way in which characterological weakness has been read as the 'namby-pamby' poet's own fragility: 'It has often been pointed out that Keats's lovers have a habit of "swooning", and the fact has sometimes been remarked upon as evidencing a certain want of virility in himself' (*The Life of John Keats* (London: Walter Scott, 1887), p. 209).

45 Critics have often noted the fetishised corpulent particularity of Keats's writing – for example, the way that, as Christopher Ricks shows, blushing generally or engorged *foreheads* more particularly carry such an extraordinary weight of Keatsian pathos and intellectual and sensuous intentionality, or the way that, as Susan Wolfson has recently suggested, the dismembered hand is a crucial Keatsian inscriptor, or finally the way that the masturbating body calls for the assertion of an onanistic poetics for Keats elaborated by Byron and more recently by Marjorie Levinson. See Christopher Ricks, *Keats and Embarrassment* (Oxford University Press, 1974), Susan J. Wolfson, 'The Magic Hand of Chance: Keats's Poetry in Facsimile', *Review* 14 (1992), 213–17; Levinson, *Keats's Life of Allegory*; Byron's comments are conveniently collected, although in expurgated form, in *KCH* 128–32.

46 In this respect, it is significant that there was a considerable focus on Keatsian physiognomy in the reviews and obituaries of the poet's work after his death, a sense even that his face was more poetic than his poetry and that the poet's death was inscribed on his face or hand: see an article in *The Olio* in January 1828, possibly by Barry Cornwall: 'John Keats was handsome, indeed his face might be termed intellectually beautiful; it expressed more of poetry than even his poetry does . . . It was such a face as I never saw before nor since . . . There was a lustre in his look which gave you the idea of a mind of exquisite refinement, and high imagination; yet, to an observing eye, the seeds of early death were sown there; it was impossible to look at him, and think him long-lived' (*KCH* 256). Coleridge's observing hand also notices signs of death in Keats when in *Table Talk* he records meeting Keats and shaking his hand: 'There is death in his hand I said to Green . . . Yet this was before the consumption showed itself' (*TT* 1.325).

47 Ironically, perhaps, many of the reviewers writing in Keats's lifetime who

praised his poetry referred to his potential 'immortality': see, for example, *KCH* 46, 54, 83, 86, 119–20, 146. See also B.R. Haydon's letter to Keats of March 1817 in which he predicts immortality for both himself and his friend (*LJK* 1.124–5), and Keats's reply (*LJK* 1.140–41); see also Richard Woodhouse's comments on Keats's 'rank' before and after death (*LJK* 1.384). A number of hostile reviewers, however, also frame Keats in terms of the future, but as a poet who will *not* be remembered: see *KCH* 72–3, 236, 237. For *posthumous* comments on Keats's immortality, see *KCH* 250, 255. See also Joseph C. Grigely, *Keats and Fame* (unpublished doctoral thesis: Oxford, 1984), p. 39: 'one of the first things we recognise in [Keats's] poetry and letters is this commitment to posterity'; and Aileen Ward, ' "That Last Infirmity of Noble Mind": Keats and the Idea of Fame', in Donald H. Reiman, *et al.*, *The Evidence of the Imagination: Studies in the Interaction Between Life and Art in English Romantic Literature* (New York University Press, 1978), pp. 312–33.

48 Wolfson, 'Keats Enters History', p. 22

49 For an illuminating discussion of the bio-poetic mythography of the post-humous heart of Shelley, see Timothy Webb, 'Religion of the Heart: Leigh Hunt's Unpublished Tribute to Shelley', *Keats–Shelley Review* 7 (1992), 1–61.

50 See G.M. Matthews, *KCH* 1. 16–17. For the figure of fifty articles, see Schwartz (ed.), *Keats Reviewed*, p. 312 (for examples, see pp. 317–19, 328–9); and see Hyder Edward Rollins, *Keats' Reputation in America to 1848* (Cambridge, MA: Harvard University Press, 1946), pp. 7–8; for the after-life of this myth in America, see pp. 11, 13–14; see also Colvin, *John Keats*, pp. 519–22. As late as 1883, in his entry for Keats in the *Encyclopedia Britannica*, A.C. Swinburne deems it necessary to argue strongly against the assumption that Keats was effectively killed by the reviewers (the article is reprinted in *The Complete Works of Algernon Charles Swinburne*, ed. Edmund Gosse and Thomas James Wise (London: Heinemann, 1926), XIV. 302). As Wolfson comments, 'the cultural processing of "the death of John Keats" was one of the main routes by which the "romance" of "Romanticism" emerged in the nineteenth century' ('Keats Enters History', p. 19). As will be clear, my discussion of the processing of Keats in the nineteenth century is indebted to Wolfson's important essay, but while Wolfson explores this 'cultural processing' of Keats, I am interested in the ways in which Keats's work itself engages with such a posthumous process, the way in which, if you like, not only is Keats processed by the later nineteenth century but the later nineteenth century – and the twentieth century, for that matter – is processed by Keats.

51 *KCH* 242; for Severn's account of Keats's death, see *LJK* II.361–3, 367–70, 371–3, 375–6, 377–9, and Charles Armitage Brown, *The Life of John Keats*, ed. Dorothy Hyde Bodurtha and Willard Bissell Pope (London: Oxford University Press, 1937), pp. 83–5, 88–9. Cornwall's reproduction of Severn's account is repeated in a later review in the *New Monthly Magazine* (see *KCH* 243) and was disseminated widely, often without acknowledge-

ment, in the next few years: one interesting example, in this context, is a
letter to *The Imperial Magazine*, vol.3 (December 1821), column 1076–80, by
'M.M.', entitled 'On the Neglect of Genius', which quotes verbatim from
Cornwall's article, but without acknowledgement.

52 Brown, *Life*, p. 27; see Matthews, 'Introduction', in *KCH* 17 on this story;
    George Gilfillan summarises Griffin's comments in even more melodra-
    matic terms, as Keats 'hanging over the fatal review in the *Quarterly* as if fas-
    cinated, reading it again and again, sucking out every drop of poison' (*KCH*
    307).

53 *SPP* 391. On Shelley's 'fabrication' of the 'strange story' of Keats's death
    by negative reviews, and on this story as 'slander', see James A.W.
    Heffernan, '*Adonais*: Shelley's Consumption of Keats', *SiR* 23 (1984),
    295–315; Heffernan's assertion (p. 296) that Shelley 'created' this version of
    Keats's death is odd in the context of the wide dissemination of the narra-
    tive before the publication of *Adonais*: in the first volume of his *Table Talk*,
    for example, published in January 1821, *before* Keats's death, Hazlitt
    remarks that the epithet 'cockney' 'proved too much for one of the writers
    in question, and struck like a barbed arrow in his heart. Poor Keats! What
    was sport to the town, was death to him . . . unable to endure the miscreant
    cry and idiot laugh, [Keats] withdrew to sigh his last breath in foreign
    climes' (Schwartz, (ed.), *Keats Reviewed*, pp. 307–8); for another early version
    of this death, see Charles Cowden Clarke's letter to the *Morning Chronicle* of
    27 July 1821 (*ibid.*, pp. 328–9). As Schwartz comments, 'The theme of
    neglected genius, popularised by the early deaths of Chatterton, White
    and, now, Keats created a popular sentiment in which the idea of martyr-
    dom took root, even before Shelley published *Adonais* in July 1821' (*ibid.*, pp.
    312–13). Compare D'Israeli's *The Literary Character*, pp. 217–18, on geniuses
    who have 'died of criticism' (D'Israeli includes the Abbé Cassagne
    (1636–79), John Scott of Amwell (1730–83), Racine, Montesquieu, and
    John Hawkesworth (c. 1715–73)). A similar point is made in an anonymous
    review of *Adonais* in *The Literary Chronical and Weekly Review* (1 December
    1821), when the reviewer lists Hawkesworth, Tasso and Newton as writers
    who may be said to have died of criticism (*SCH* 296).

54 Ford, *Keats and the Victorians*, p. 68.

55 John Barnard, (ed.), *John Keats: Collected Poems*, 2nd edn. (Harmondsworth:
    Penguin, 1977, back cover); Stephen Coote, *John Keats: A Life* (London:
    Hodder and Stoughton, 1995, dust jacket).

56 'Keats Enters History', p. 27.

57 See Glendening, 'Keats's Tour of Scotland', pp. 84–5, on the poem's
    diction as that of sickness and death.

58 *LJK* 1.324, 343; see also 332. See Aileen Ward's explanation of this desire
    to destroy the poem in terms of psychic repression: the thought that 'he
    meant never to express', that he had only three years to live, 'slipped out,
    and as soon as he regained his balance he tried to expunge it. This is the
    only way of accounting for his extraordinary act of destroying his own

poem' (*John Keats*, p. 200). But Brown, *Life*, p. 51, comments that the con-
version of the cottage into a 'whiskey-shop, together with its drunken land-
lord, went far towards the annihilation of [Keats's] poetic power'.

59 See Keats's comment in *LJK* 1.388, that 'I feel assured I should write from
the mere yearning and fondness I have for the Beautiful even if my night's
labours should be burnt every morning and no eye ever shine upon them';
but the next sentence is telling, too: 'But even now I am perhaps not speaking from myself; but from some character in whose soul I now live' (and see
Hyder Edward Rollins's comment that 'One wishes it were possible to
prove that Keats knew Daniel's *Musophilus*, lines 567–78' (*ibid.*)). For an
account of the composition of 'Ode to a Nightingale', see Brown, *Life of
Keats*, pp. 53–4; for a brief reading of this gesture of poetic effacement, see
my *Keats, Narrative and Audience*, pp. 172–3. In fact, both the 'Ode to a
Nightingale' and the poem on Burns are 'saved' by Charles Brown.

60 As John Glendening comments, 'Keats's reduction of himself to a body
and his province to a space suggests the constrained inertness of a corpse
in its coffin' ('Keats's Tour of Scotland', 93); on Keats's identification with
Burns, see p. 80. As I have suggested, one of the more intriguing aspects of
'This mortal body of a thousand days' is its almost complete effacement in
the criticism of Keats – even Glendening's reading is somewhat perfunc-
tory, by contrast with his fuller treatment of Keats's earlier sonnet 'On
Visiting the Tomb of Burns'. There is really no place, I suggest, for this
poem: it both saturates Keats's reception, his afterlife and, in literalising
that afterlife, must be effaced by it.

61 Jean-Luc Nancy, 'Corpus', in *The Birth to Presence*, trans. Brian Holmes, *et
al.* (Stanford University Press, 1993), pp. 193, 198; it is Nancy's argument
that the body is 'both sense and the sign of its own sense . . . *Sign of itself*
and *being-itself of the sign*' (p. 194).

62 *Ibid.*, p. 195.

63 Louis Marin, 'Montaigne's Tomb, or Autobiographical Discourse', *OLR* 4
(1981), 45.

64 Morris Dickstein, *Keats and his Poetry: A Study in Development* (University of
Chicago Press, 1971), pp. 175–6.

65 *KCH* 331; see also Patmore's comment on Keats's characteristic faults as
'extreme literalness of expression' (*KCH* 337).

66 'This pleasant tale' does, in fact, articulate a corporeal intensity of reading
such that, by the end of the poem, the opening deixis marks both the
inscription of the speaker's (/reader's) body into the act of reading and the
uncanny heart-stopping mortality of that act: the reader 'full hearted stops;
/ And oftentimes he feels the dewy drops / Come cool and suddenly
against his face'.

67 On the instability of the referent of 'this', see G.W.F. Hegel, *Phenomenology
of Spirit*, trans. A.V. Miller (Oxford: Clarendon, 1977), pp. 58–66; for readings of this passage, see Andrej Warminski, 'Dreadful Reading: Blanchot
on Hegel', *Yale French Studies* 69 (1985), 267–75, and Timothy Clark, *Derrida,*

Heidegger, Blanchot: Sources of Derrida's Notion and Practice of Literature (Cambridge University Press, 1992), pp. 70–72; see also Jacques Derrida, 'At this very moment in this work here I am', in Robert Bernasconi and Simon Critchley (eds.), *Re-Reading Levinas* (London: Athlone, 1991), pp. 11–48; and see Derrida's questions from an interview in 1976: 'What is it that writing de-clings of a here-now? And how could a here-now pass through writing unscathed?' (*Points . . . : Interviews, 1974–1994*, ed. Elisabeth Weber (Stanford University Press, 1995), p. 11).

7 SHELLEY'S GHOSTS

1 See also Peacock's comment that 'poetical reputation is not only not to be desired, but most earnestly to be deprecated' (*PBSL* II.245).

2 For considerations of *A Defence of Poetry* in terms of audience and posterity, see White II.275, and Michael O'Neill, *Percy Bysshe Shelley: A Literary Life* (London: Macmillan, 1989), pp. 143–5.

3 Paul de Man, *Allegories of Reading: Figural Language in Rousseau, Nietzsche, Rilke, and Proust* (New Haven, CT: Yale University Press, 1979), p. 273.

4 O'Neill, *Shelley*, p. 5; see also p. 125, on 'Adonais'.

5 On Shelley's sense of his own neglect and his contemporary reception, see White II.216, 235; see also Miriam Allott, 'Attitudes to Shelley: The Vagaries of a Critical Reputation', in Miriam Allott (ed.), *Essays on Shelley* (Liverpool University Press, 1982), pp. 2–5.

6 See *Prose* III.70 and *Paradise Lost* VII.31. Shelley is no doubt responding to and pre-empting charges of 'obscurity' with which contemporary and later reviewers and other readers assessed his writing: see, for example, *SCH* 116, 152, 217, 226–7, 254ff, 272–3, 282, 311, 329, 404. In a significant number of such comments, Shelley's semantic or hermeneutic 'obscurity' is linked to his public obscurity, his lack of fame and permanent lack of popularity with the reading public (see, for example, *SCH* 272–3, 311, 329). Michael O'Neill links such double 'obscurity', in part, to the social and political conditions of the time: 'the fear of repression led writers such as Peacock and Shelley to write in an oblique, indirect, coded way – thus cutting themselves off from the wider audience on which their political hopes depended' (*Shelley*, p. 50). Timothy Webb also traces a movement away from 'didacticism' towards a 'richer and wiser distillation of experience' in Shelley's work (*Shelley: A Voice Not Understood* (Manchester University Press, 1977), p. 85; see also pp. 87–8).

7 For more specifically political posthumous effects, see the ending to *The Revolt of Islam*, lines 3667–720; see also Webb, *Shelley*, pp. 114–15.

8 See O'Neill, *Shelley*, on Shelley's 'search for and increasing despair of finding an appropriate audience' (p. 4), and Stephen C. Behrendt, *Shelley and His Audiences* (Lincoln, NE: University of Nebraska Press, 1989).

9 See, for example, *SCH* 104, 113–14, 152, 160, 200, 206, 241–2, 243; see also White II.301; O'Neill, *Shelley*, p. 92. On Shelley's neglect by his contemporaries, see Barcus, *SCH* 1–2, 33.

10 Timothy Clark, *Embodying Revolution: The Figure of the Poet in Shelley* (Oxford University Press, 1989), p. 222.

11 The print runs and sales figures for Shelley's volumes of poetry published during his lifetime are as follows: *Original Poetry* (1810): print run, 1489; known sales, c.100 (then withdrawn and destroyed). *Posthumous Fragments* (1810): print run and sales unknown. *Queen Mab* (1813): first edition print run, 250 (but not published); said to be 'selling by the thousands' in a pirated edition by 1821, subsequently goes into fourteen editions, official and unofficial, within twenty years (White II.304). *Alastor* (1816): print run, 250; copies remaining in 1820. *Laon and Cythna* (1817): 750 printed but edition cancelled; altered and republished as *The Revolt of Islam* (1818); copies still being advertised for sale in 1829 (Walter Edwin Peck, *Shelley: His Life and Work* (London: Ernest Benn, 1927), II.43). *Rosalind and Helen* (1819): print run and sales unknown. *The Cenci* (1820): print run, 250; 'written for the multitude, and ought to sell well', according to Shelley (*PBSL* II.174; see also 263); goes into second edition in 1821. *Prometheus Unbound* (1820): print run unknown; written 'for the elect', for '5 or 6 persons', and Shelley expects sales of 20 (*PBSL* II.200, 388, 174; see also 263). *Oedipus Tyranus* (1820): print run unknown; sales 7 but immediately suppressed. *Epipsychidion* (1821): print run c. 200; written, Shelley comments, 'for the esoteric few' (*PBSL* II.263); after his death, Ollier tells Mary Shelley that Percy had wished the remaining 160 copies of the book to be suppressed (*SPP* 371). *Adonais* (1821): 'little adapted for popularity', according to Shelley (*PBSL* II.299); print run and sales unknown. *Hellas* (1822); print run and sales unknown. When the Olliers went out of business in 1823, they sold the remaining copies of Shelley's work to John and Henry Hunt: these included *Epipsychidion, Hellas, Rosalind and Helen, Prometheus Unbound, The Cenci, The Revolt of Islam* and *Adonais*. See Peck, *Life*; White I.191, 291, 548; II.127, 225, 255, 269, 304, 325–6; *SCH* 3–4; J.L. Bradley, *A Shelley Chronology* (London: Macmillan, 1993); Charles E. Robinson, 'Percy Bysshe Shelley, Charles Ollier, and William Blackwood: The Contexts Of Early Nineteenth-Century Publishing', in Kelvin Everest (ed.), *Shelley Revalued: Essays from the Gregynog Conference* (Leicester University Press, 1983), pp. 183–216; David Palmer, *Shelley: His Reputation and Influence* (Doncaster: no publisher, no date (reprinted MA thesis, Sheffield University, 1978)), ch.1.

12 A number of critics have recently commented on the importance of posterity in Shelley's writing towards the end of his life: I suggest, however, both that this recognition should be extended back even to Shelley's first publications, and that critics have yet to register the strange torsions which posterity exerts on his writing: see P.M.S. Dawson, *The Unacknowledged Legislator: Shelley and Politics* (Oxford University Press, 1980), pp. 252–4; Behrendt, *Shelley and His Audiences*, pp. 233–4; Clark, *Embodying Revolution*, pp. 212–13. For an essay which complements or supplements the present chapter, see Christine Berthin, 'Shelley's Prospective Reader', in James

Hogg, (ed.), *Shelley, 1792–1992* (Salzburg: Institut für Anglistik und Amerikanistik, 1993), pp. 137–47.

13 Compare *PBSL* II.339: 'So on this plan I would be *alone* & would devote either to oblivion or to future generations the overflowings of a mind which, timely withdrawn from the contagion, should be kept fit for no baser object'.

14 Such ambivalence is suggested by Angela Leighton's reading of the ending to *Adonais*: 'what we have in the last verses of the poem is a terrible and haunting suspicion that the poem's triumphant statement of creative power is, in fact, a celebration of despair' ('Deconstruction Criticism and Shelley's *Adonais*', in Everest (ed.), *Shelley Revalued*, p. 163). On Shelley's ambivalence towards questions of audience, fame and posterity, see Webb, *Shelley*, pp. 109–11.

15 See also a letter to Thomas Hookham of December 1812, concerning 'a Volume of Minor Poems' that Shelley is preparing: 'A very obvious question would be. – Will they sell or not?' (*PBSL* 1.340; see also 571).

16 See also *PBSL* II.379: 'The reviewers & journals . . . continue to attack me, but I value neither the fame they can give, nor the fame they can take away'.

17 See also *PBSL* II.245; 262 ('nothing is so difficult and unwelcome as to write without a confidence of finding readers'); 289 ('I am, perhaps, morbidly indifferent to this sort of praise or blame; and this, perhaps, deprives me of an incitement to do what now I never shall do, i.e., write anything worth calling a poem'); 309.

18 For similar comments by Keats, see, for example, *LJK* 1.267.

19 See also *PBSL* 1.317: 'Honor & the opinion either of contemporaries, or (more frequently) of posterity is set so much above virtue, as according to the last words of Brutus to make it nothing but an empty name'.

20 See John Freeman, 'Shelley's Early Letters', in Everest (ed.), *Shelley Revalued*, p. 126, on Shelley's 'desire to believe in a future state, in spite of his own scepticism' as one of his 'most abiding impulses.'

21 Quoted in Webb, *Shelley*, p. 231–2.

22 *SCW* VI.209; see also p. 208, and 'The Coliseum', in *SCW* VI.304, on the desire to live on; see Webb, *Shelley*, 231–4.

23 Compare *Hellas*, lines 795–806.

24 For Shelley on immortality, including his own, see, for example, *PBSL* 1.193, 220, 226, 237; on Shelley's prose considerations of the question of immortality, see Webb, *Shelley*, pp. 182–5.

25 See Kelvin Everest, 'Shelley's Doubles: An Approach to "Julian and Maddalo" ', in Everest (ed.), *Shelley Revalued*, p. 75, on Shelley's 'preoccupation . . . with the death of the Shelleyan poet'.

26 'Convulsion' is itself a heavily loaded Shelleyan word and experience, including as it does both the possibility of political disturbance or even revolution (see White 1.517, for such a usage by Shelley himself), and a mode of bodily being, since not only was Shelley the object of repeated physical

seizures, hysteria, fits and starts, and convulsions generally (see, for example, White 1.500), but convulsions are also a familiar characterological predicament in his poetry (see, for example, *Queen Mab* vi.9, ix.233; *Alastor* lines 296, 349; *Epipsychidion* line 370; *Hellas* line 807). In this sense, convulsions may themselves be read as forms of haunting, whereby the inanimate, inhuman bodily machine overcomes the *animus* of the living being, a form of posthumous life while a person still (officially) lives. On a darker note, it might be recalled that Mary and Percy's first, premature, baby died of 'convulsions' in March 1815 (see *The Letters of Mary Wollstonecraft Shelley*, ed. Betty T. Bennett (Baltimore, MD: Johns Hopkins University Press, 1980), 1.11). See also Nigel Leask, 'Shelley's "Magnetic Ladies": Romantic Mesmerism and the Politics of the Body', in Stephen Copley and John Whale (eds.), *Beyond Romanticism: New Approaches to Texts and Contexts, 1780–1832* (London: Routledge, 1992), pp. 53–78. Compare Jerome Christensen, *Lord Byron's Strength: Romantic Writing and Commercial Society* (Baltimore, MD: Johns Hopkins University Press, 1993), pp. 23–4 on Byronic convulsions.

27 For Shelley on the future, see his comment in a letter of March 1820: 'I have a motto on a ring in Italian – "Il buon tempo verra". – There is a tide both in public & in private affairs, which awaits both men & nations' (*PBSL* 11.177). More strangely, perhaps, and more forcefully, on one or two occasions, Shelley articulates the possibility of prophecy: in a letter of May he writes of 'a theory I once imagined, that in everything any man ever wrote, spoke, acted, or imagined, is contained, as it were, an allegorical idea of his own future life, as the acorn contains the oak' (*PBSL* 11.192); see also his remark on his *'pure anticipated cognition'* of Jane Williams (11.438). It would be impossible to resist, at this point, what we know must only be considered as insignificant in Shelley's life and writing, his repeated references to and enactments of drowning and shipwreck before 8 July 1822. See, for example, White 1.510; 11.156, 189, 156, 343, 368; *PBSL* 11.128; 'Lines Written Among the Euganean Hills', lines 10–65. See Orestes Brownson's comments on Shelley's 'passion for water' (despite the fact that he never learnt to swim – a suicidal passion, one might think) in the *Boston Quarterly Review*, October 1841 (*SCH* 385). I draw no conclusion from this, but the reader may like to consider it within the context of Keats's prescience and/or Byron's playing dead (see chapters 6 and 8, respectively).

28 Tzvetan Todorov, *The Fantastic: A Structural Approach to a Literary Genre*, trans. Richard Howard (Ithaca, NY: Cornell University Press, 1975). On ghosts and the spectral in the Romantic period, see Terry Castle, *The Female Thermometer: Eighteenth-Century Culture and the Invention of the Uncanny* (New York: Oxford University Press, 1995), especially ch.10.

29 Quoted in Mark Storey, *Robert Southey: A Life* (Oxford University Press, 1997), p. 154. The 'inanimate corpus', writes one doctor, who has seen more than his share of them, is 'the least of all the things that makes us human' (Sherwin B. Newland, *How We Die* (London: Vintage, 1997), p. 63).

30 Jacques Derrida, 'Living On: Border Lines', in Harold Bloom *et al.*, *Deconstruction and Criticism* (New York: Seabury Press, 1979), pp. 79–176.
31 Richard Holmes, *Shelley: The Pursuit* (London: Quartet, 1976), p. 114.
32 Jacques Derrida, *Specters of Marx: The State of the Debt, the Work of Mourning, and the New International*, trans. Peggy Kamuf (New York: Routledge, 1994), p. 11.
33 *The Mary Shelley Reader*, ed. Betty T. Bennett and Charles E. Robinson (New York: Oxford University Press, 1990), p. 335 (further references are cited in the text).
34 Mary Shelley may be mixing up a memory of speech with one of writing, since the comment by Coleridge appears in an essay on 'Ghosts and Apparitions' from *The Friend*, ed. Barbara E. Rooke (London: Routledge and Kegan Paul, 1969), 1.146, and 11.118). A kind of mirror image of Coleridge's very properly paradoxical and decisively undecidable comment on ghosts comes in Derrida's response to the question of whether he believes in ghosts in the film *Ghost Dance*: 'That's a hard question', he replies, 'because, you see, I *am* a ghost' (quoted by Maud Ellmann, 'The Ghosts of *Ulysses*', in R.M. Bollettieri Bosinelli, C. Marengo Vaglio and Chr. van Boheemen (eds.), *The Languages of Joyce* (Philadelphia, PA: John Benjamins, 1992), p. 103).
35 Quoted in Allott, 'Attitudes to Shelley', p. 21.
36 Shelley breaks off the next section – and the 'Speculations' as a whole – two pages later, on the point of recounting a dream. Mary Shelley records Percy's remark that '*Here I was obliged to leave off, overcome by thrilling horror*', and comments on his susceptibility to such horror: 'I remember well his coming to me from writing it, pale and agitated, to seek refuge in conversation from the fearful emotions it excited. No man, as these fragments prove, had such keen sensations as Shelley. His nervous temperament was wound up by the delicacy of his health to an intense degree of sensibility, and while his active mind pondered for ever upon, and drew conclusions from his sensations, his reveries increased their vivacity, till they mingled with, and made one with thought, and both became absorbing and tumultuous, even to physical pain' (*SCW* vii.67). Compare Tilottama Rajan's comment on *A Defence of Poetry* and the sense of poetry as 'a ghostly rather than spiritual force' (*The Supplement of Reading: Figures of Understanding in Romantic Theory and Practice* (Ithaca, NY: Cornell University Press, 1990), p. 282.
37 For Shelley's collection of ghost stories, see *SCW* vi.147–50, 303–4. Compare Shelley's comment on ghosts and the haunting of the past in *PBSL* ii.114 and see White 1.461; ii.104, 368–9, 378. Ghost stories are, of course, central to one of the most famous holidays in literary history, the *ménage* on Lake Geneva of Percy, Mary, Byron, Polidori and Claire in the Summer of 1816 when they read together Coleridge's 'Christabel' and a collection of stories in French, *Fantasmagoriana, ou Recueil d'histoires d'apparitions de spectres, revenants, fantômes, etc.* (see Holmes, *The Pursuit*, pp. 328–31);

and see Everest, 'Shelley's Doubles', pp. 64–7, on the ghost-effect of the *doppelgänger* and the uncanny: in Freud's reading of the uncanny, the *doppelgänger* is a figure for personal immortality – as well as, therefore, a 'harbinger of death' (*PFL* xiv.356–7).

38 See James Chandler, *England in 1819: The Politics of Literary Culture and the Case of Romantic Historicism* (University of Chicago Press, 1998), pp. 25–6, on the way that this phrase echoes one about a 'glorious Phantom' in Shelley's 1817 pamphlet, *An Address to the People on the Death of Princess Charlotte*.

39 See my *Keats, Narrative and Audience: The Posthumous Life of Writing* (Cambridge University Press, 1994), pp. 11–14.

40 This vocabulary of 'crypts' and 'haunting' is taken from the psychoanalysis of Nicolas Abraham and Maria Torok: see *The Wolf Man's Magic Word: A Cryptonymy*, trans. Nicholas Rand (Minneapolis, MN: University of Minnesota Press, 1986). See also Esther Rashkin, *Family Secrets and the Psychoanalysis of Narrative* (New Jersey: Princeton University Press, 1992).

41 Compare 'Epipsychidion', line 455 on love as 'a soul within the soul'.

42 See Roland Barthes, *The Pleasure of the Text*, trans. Richard Miller (Oxford: Basil Blackwell, 1990), and Leo Bersani, *The Freudian Body: Psychoanalysis and Art* (New York: Columbia University Press, 1986). See also the preface to 'Julian and Maddalo' on Maddalo's talk: 'His more serious conversation is a sort of intoxication; men are held by it as by a spell' (*SPP* 113); and compare my discussion of the effects of Coleridge's talk in chapter 5.

43 Karen Mills-Courts, *Poetry as Epitaph: Representation and Poetic Language* (Baton Rouge, LA: Louisiana State University Press, 1990), p. 37; see pp. 36–9, 45–6, 54, 60, on Shelley's conception of poetic language as 'haunting' (see also p. 177 on Wordsworth's sense of the imagination as a 'ghostlike power'): while Mills-Court focuses on the haunting nature of language for Shelley, I would want to emphasise the way in which Shelley's poetry haunts and is haunted by its future audience.

44 Paul de Man, *The Rhetoric of Romanticism* (New York: Columbia University Press, 1984), p. 78.

45 We might remember Hazlitt's comment on the 'poet's cemetery' as 'the human mind, in which he sows the seeds of never-ending thought' (*Works* xi.78). See White's comment on the poem as Shelley's 'personal prayer that as a poet he might have his share in producing one of the great human revolutions it was the function of poetry to produce' and his 'deep dejection as he became convinced that his voice was failing to find an audience' (White ii.280–1).

8 BYRON'S SUCCESS

1 Leslie A. Marchand, *Byron: A Biography* 3 vols. (London: John Murray, 1957), ii.608.

2 Marchand, *Byron* iii.1111; I am indebted to Richard Lansdown, *Byron's Historical Dramas* (Oxford: Clarendon, 1992), p. 64, for this reference as well

as for his reading of 'Churchill's Grave' which alerted me to the interest and significance of this poem.

3 Dorothy Wordsworth, *The Grasmere Journals*, ed. Pamela Woof (Oxford: Clarendon, 1991), p. 92.

4 An intriguing comment in his journal for November 1813 suggests the problematic nature of Byron's notion of poetic 'facts': 'I began a comedy and burnt it because the scene ran into *reality*; – a novel, for the same reason. In rhyme, I can keep more away from the facts' (*BLJ* III.209). See also Byron's various comments in *Don Juan* on the fiction that his poem 'records only facts' (for example: v.258, vi.677–80, vii.641–4, viii.681–8). Compare Zachary Leader's comments on Byron's 'fetish for literal accuracy', in *Revision and Romantic Authorship* (Oxford: Clarendon Press, 1996), p. 101.

5 See Churchill's *The Candidate*, lines 145–54, where the poet asks that 'one poor sprig of Bay' might be 'planted on my grave' (quoted in *CW* iv.448).

6 See *CW* iv.447.

7 My reading of the gift in this section is indebted, not least, to Jacques Derrida, *Given Time: 1. Counterfeit Money*, trans. Peggy Kamuf (University of Chicago Press, 1992); on Byron and the gift, see Jerome Christensen, *Lord Byron's Strength: Romantic Writing and Commercial Society* (Baltimore, MD: Johns Hopkins University Press, 1993), pp. 19–20.

8 Indeed, there is an important identification, here paronomastically marked, of the speaker with the sexton, of the '*homely* phrase' with the 'natural *homily*'.

9 A number of Byron's miscellaneous comments on audience and posterity are usefully collected in Bruce Wallis (ed.), *Byron: The Critical Voice*, 2 vols. (Salzburg: Institut für Englische Sprache und Literatur, 1973), pp. 72–5, 163. For Byron's appeals to posterity, see for example, *BLJ* v.352; vi.25, 37, 121, 155–6. Byron's repeated use of 'scribbler(s)' and 'scribbling' is itself indicative of a sense of the importance of maintaining an *amateur*, even *dilettante* relationship to writing. Marlon B. Ross has commented on the use of the word 'scribblers' by early eighteenth-century writers, who use the word to 'indicate the intrinsically wayward nature of producing script': see his 'Authority and Authenticity: Scribbling Authors and the Genius of Print in Eighteenth-Century England', in Martha Woodmansee and Peter Jaszi (eds.), *The Construction of Authorship: Textual Appropriation in Law and Literature* (Durham, NC: Duke University Press, 1994), pp. 231–58.

10 See, for example, the first paragraph of the Preface to *Childe Harold* cantos 1 and 2; *Don Juan* v.1270–71.

11 Quoted in Ian Jack, *The Poet and His Audience* (Cambridge University Press, 1984), p. 88.

12 Quoted in *ibid.*, p. 88. Jerome Christensen's summary of Byron's relationship with his publisher John Murray in four periods is useful here: '*first*, the highly mediated period of aristocratic amusement in 1811 and 1812 when Byron's dealings with Murray were left with conspicuous negligence to the

management of Charles Dallas . . . ; *second*, a period in 1813–16 of direct if desultory correspondence between Byron and Murray . . . a period during which Byron vacillated in his response to Murray's offers of substantial sums of money . . . ; *third*, the earnest and businesslike negotiations with Murry over payment for Byron's poetry . . . ; *fourth*, the break with Murray and the formation in 1822 of an alternative publishing connection with John Hunt' ('Byron's Career: The Speculative Stage', *ELH* 52 (1985), 64–5). On Byron writing for money, see Peter J. Manning, 'Childe Harold in the Marketplace: From Romaunt to Handbook', *MLQ* 52 (1991), 180–1. As Manning comments, 'The wavering between the protocols of gift exchange and the business of buying and selling copyrights in this dialogue between Murray and Byron, the businessman and aristocrat, manifests the as yet not fully articulated arrangements of the conditions of publication' (p. 181). For an account of Byron's relationship to his own fame, see Sonia Hofkosh, 'The Writer's Ravishment: Women and the Romantic Author – The Example of Byron', in Anne K. Mellor (ed.), *Romanticism and Feminism* (Bloomington, IN: Indiana University Press, 1988), pp. 93–9; on Byron and his public generally, see Philip W. Martin, *Byron: A Poet Before His Public* (Cambridge University Press, 1982).

13 Marchand, *Byron*, 1.435.

14 Marchand, *Byron*, 1.467. But see 11.556, on Byron refusing 1000 guineas from Murray in 1815; see also 1.424.

15 See Byron's allusion to Samuel Johnson's dictum that 'No man but a block-head ever wrote, except for money' (James Boswell, *Life of Johnson* (London: Oxford University Press, 1953), p. 731): 'I know only *one* motive for publishing *any thing* with a sensible man – and I think Johnson has already quoted that' (*BLJ* IX.68). But compare Byron's scathing comments on the notion of writing as a *profession* (quoted in Jerome J. McGann, *Don Juan in Context* (London: John Murray, 1976), p. 57).

16 Marchand, *Byron* 11.764–5.

17 See, for example, *BLJ* IX.161.

18 Compare Andrew Nicholson (ed.), *Lord Byron: The Complete Miscellaneous Prose* (Oxford: Clarendon, 1991), p. 108.

19 Kim Ian Michasiw, 'The Social Other: *Don Juan* and the Genesis of the Self', *Mosaic* 22:2 (1989), 29–30. On the question of the relationship between the authorial, narratorial and biographical 'self' in Byron, see Peter J. Manning, '*Don Juan* and the Revisionary Self', in Robert Brinkley and Keith Hanley (eds.), *Romantic Revisions* (Cambridge University Press, 1992), pp. 210–26; Jean Hall, 'The Evolution of the Surface Self: Byron's Poetic Career', *KSJ* 36 (1987), 134–57; Frederick Garber, *Self, Text, and Romantic Irony: The Example of Byron* (New Jersey: Princeton University Press, 1988); and Christensen, *Lord Byron's Strength*. While all these critics tend to assume that the Byronic self may be said to be a social product, a construct of social forces, I want to suggest that the Byronic 'self', in all its multiplicity and undecidability, is, in addition, a function of writing – and therefore,

of course, of reading, a function of the future. See also Leader's argument for the fluidity and multiplicity of the 'constructed' Byron as itself an expression of a coherent and consistent identity (*Revision*, ch.2); and see Andrew Elfenbein, *Byron and the Victorians* (Cambridge University Press, 1995), ch.2, on the importance of Byron's subjectivity for his nineteenth-century reception.

20 Leo Braudy, *The Frenzy of Renown: Fame and its History* (New York: Oxford University Press, 1986), p. 407.

21 McGann, *Don Juan in Context*, pp. 57, 65. The principle point of such a manifesto, according to McGann, was to challenge the orthodoxy of the value of contemporary obscurity (in the sense of hermeneutic difficulty): 'According to Byron's quite trenchant analysis, this obscurity has developed from the increasing emphasis upon privacy and individual talent in Romantic verse. Wordsworth's "imagination", Byron says, involves him in his private "reveries", which ultimately prevent an engagement with the audience' (p. 78; on Byron's critique of contemporary poetics, see also pp. 107–8). See also McGann's comment in 'Byron and "The Truth in Masquerade"', in Brinkley and Hanley (eds.), *Romantic Revisions*, p. 195, on the 'frequent charge' in criticism of Byron, that 'his work lacks authenticity because he was too preoccupied with his audiences and their reactions. His poetry aims, it is judged, for cheap and factitious effects by pandering to the (presumably debased) expectations of his reading publics' (see also Manning, '*Don Juan* and the Revisionary Self', 215–16). In particular, I suggest, Byron's poem is concerned to challenge the increasingly prevalent view that poetry can only be understood in the future. Byron's is, to use McGann's word, a 'functional' poetics (*Don Juan in Context*, p. 79), one in which poetry has specific effects on readers, in which there is a connection between work and audience. And unlike some of the other poems studied in the present book, *Don Juan* is exemplary in its explicit attention to audience, to the extent of being self-professedly *directed* by its audiences: as Manning comments, 'Byron never forgets or lets us forget, that *Don Juan* is a text shaped by the literary market . . . making visible the conditions which shaped the particular form of his writing and the self represented in it' (p. 221).

22 Byron, *Don Juan*, ed. T.G. Steffan, E. Steffan and W.W. Pratt (Harmondsworth: Penguin, 1973), pp. 39–40.

23 McGann, *Byron in Context*, p. 110.

24 Byron's 'bright reversion' may contain an echo of Wordsworth's 'bright reversion' in his poem addressed to Haydon, 'High is our calling, Friend', first published in *The Champion* in 1816.

25 For a detailed reading of *Don Juan* 1, stanzas 217–22, see Paul Elledge, 'Parting Shots: Byron Ending *Don Juan* 1', *SiR* 27 (1988), 570–75. In September 1811, Byron records a similar scepticism towards the notion of immortality more generally in a letter to Francis Hodgson: 'I will have nothing to do with your immortality; we are miserable enough in this life,

without the absurdity of speculating upon another. If men are to live, why die at all? and if they die, why disturb the sweet and sound sleep that "knows no waking"? "Post mortem nihil est, ipsaque Mors nihil . . . quaeris quo jaceas post obitum loco? Quo *non* Nata jacent" ' (*BLJ* 11.88–9). See also Byron's journal for 25 January 1821: 'It has been said that the immortality of the soul is a "grand peut-être" – but still it is a *grand* one. Every body clings to it – the stupidest, and dullest, and wickedest of human bipeds is still persuaded that he is immortal' (*BLJ* vIII.35).

26 McGann, *Don Juan in Context*, p. 78; Southey's lines, in fact, are themselves a recirculation of the opening to Edward Spenser's 'To His Booke' which prefaces *The Shepheardes Calender*, an opening which in turn reproduces Chaucer's 'Go, litel bok' of *Troilus and Criseyde* v.1786.

27 See, for example, Jacques Derrida, *Limited Inc*, ed. Gerald Graff (Evanston, IL: Northwestern University Press, 1988), pp. 136–8.

28 The name, in fact, and its correspondence with fame, posterity and aristocracy is central to Byron's writing. And Byron's name – somewhat unusually for a man – is unstable, changing twice within his lifetime – born George Gordon Byron, he became Lord Byron when only 10 years old, and in 1822, after the death of his wife's parents, he became Noel Byron: see Marchand, *Byron* III.970–71.

29 But see canto 7, stanza 33, where fame really *is* a lottery: 'Renown's all hit or miss; / There's Fortune even in fame, we must allow'. For Byron's scepticism concerning the judgement of posterity, see also canto 12, stanzas 18–19; on fame, see canto 13, stanza 51 and canto 15, stanza 19.

AFTERWORD

1 For a discussion of the way that some of these difficulties are addressed in the work of, especially, Blanchot and Derrida, see my essay 'On Posterity' in the *Yale Journal of Criticism* 12:1 (1999).

2 Leo Braudy, *The Frenzy of Renown: Fame and Its History* (New York: Oxford University Press, 1986), p. 425.

3 See, for example, Jacques Derrida, *Margins of Philosophy*, trans. Alan Bass (Brighton: Harvester, 1982), 315–18.

Index

CAMBRIDGE STUDIES IN ROMANTICISM

General editors
MARILYN BUTLER, *University of Oxford*
JAMES CHANDLER, *University of Chicago*